RELIGION, SECULARISM & POLITICAL BELONGING

EDITED BY LEEROM MEDOVOI
AND ELIZABETH BENTLEY

RELIGION, SECULARISM & POLITICAL BELONGING

Duke University Press · *Durham and London* · 2021

© 2021 Duke University Press. All rights reserved

Designed by Courtney Leigh Richardson
Typeset in Portrait and Fira Sans Regular by Westchester Publishing Services
Library of Congress Cataloging-in-Publication Data

Names: Medovoi, Leerom, [date] editor. | Bentley, Elizabeth, [date] editor.
Title: Religion, secularism, and political belonging / edited by Leerom Medovoi, Elizabeth Bentley.
Description: Durham : Duke University Press, 2021. | Includes bibliographical references and index.
Identifiers: LCCN 2020030821 (print) | LCCN 2020030822 (ebook) | ISBN 9781478010395 (hardcover) | ISBN 9781478010784 (paperback) | ISBN 9781478012986 (ebook)
Subjects: LCSH: Religion and politics. | Secularism. | Globalization—Religious aspects.
Classification: LCC BL65.P7 R4528 2021 (print) | LCC BL65.P7 (ebook) | DDC 306.6—dc23
LC record available at https://lccn.loc.gov/2020030821
LC ebook record available at https://lccn.loc.gov/2020030822

Cover art: *Big Thumper*, 2017. Oil pastel and watercolor on paper, 84 × 72 inches. © Rusty Shackleford. Courtesy of the artist and Cindy Rucker Gallery, New York.

This book is dedicated to Srinivas Aravamudan

Contents

Acknowledgments · xi

Introduction: Translated Secularisms, Global Humanities · 1
Leerom Medovoi and Elizabeth Bentley

PART I: SECULARISM

Keyword: Neutrality · 35
Elizabeth Bentley

Keyword: Science · 43
John Vignaux Smyth

1. Strict Neutrality Reconsidered: Religion and Political Belonging in the Netherlands · 49
Pooyan Tamimi Arab

2. Confucian Secularism in Theoretical
and Historical Perspective · 69
Albert Welter

3. From Exclusive to Inclusive Secularity: Religion, State,
and the Public Space in Tunisia after the Revolution · 85
Mohanad Mustafa

4. Neoliberal Political Theology · 107
Marcia Klotz and Leerom Medovoi

5. "Christian Atheism" on Twitter: Dutch Populism
and/as Culturalized Religion · 125
Ernst van den Hemel

PART II: RELIGION

Keyword: Nationalism · 139
Ernst van den Hemel and Markus Balkenhol

Keyword: Fundamentalism · 147
Leerom Medovoi

---

6. Religion, Politics, and Nationalism, a Case Study:
The Palestinian Islamic Jihad Movement · 155
Raef Zreik and Mohanad Mustafa

7. Trains on Time: Faith, Political Belonging,
and Governability in Israel · 175
Ori Goldberg

8. Making Sense by Comprehending Sensibility:
A View of Chinese Religions · 191
Mu-chou Poo

9. Evangelical Christianity, Big Business, and the
Resurgence of American Conservatism during the 1970s · 207
David N. Gibbs

10. Among New Believers: Religion, Gender,
and National Identity in the Netherlands · 223
Eva Midden

PART III: POLITICAL BELONGING

Keyword: Faith · 239
Ori Goldberg

Keyword: Civil Religion · 243
Mu-chou Poo

11. Muslim Migration, Citizenship,
and Belonging in U.S. Politics of Secularism · 251
Kambiz GhaneaBassiri

12. Commemorating the African Ancestors: Entanglements of
Citizenship, Colonialism, and Religion in the Netherlands · 265
Markus Balkenhol

13. Transsecular Incarnations: Destabilizing the
(Cis)Gender Politics of Secularism · 283
Zeynep Kurtuluş Korkman

14. Christianity and the Political Religion of China · 305
Francis Ching-Wah Yip

15. Critical Israel: Toward a Contemporary
Political Theology of the Particular · 325
Shaul Setter

Contributors · 343

Index · 347

Acknowledgments

This volume grows from a joint effort across institutions, fields, and continents. It began through the inspired effort of the Consortium of Humanities Centers and Institutes (CHCI) to scale up humanities research to the global level through its Integrating the Humanities Across National Boundaries pilot grant from the Andrew W. Mellon Foundation. The Religion, Secularism, and Political Belonging (or RelSec) project was a key early part of that program. We wish to thank collectively the three consecutive presidents of the CHCI, the late Srinivas Aravamudan, Ian Baucom, and Sara Guyer, for their generous guidance of our project throughout, as well as for the brilliant practical support of Sylvia Miller, the CHCI's project manager. We especially thank the Andrew W. Mellon Foundation for its ambitious promotion of the global humanities and for the exciting opportunity to conduct the three-year investigation that led to this book.

Ann Pellegrini provided truly sagacious advice about how to globalize the design of this project at its earliest stage. We also owe thanks to individuals at each of the five participating institutions who fashioned this project. At the

University of Arizona (UA), we could not be more grateful to the late Peter Foley, former director of the Institute for Religion and Society. His abiding curiosity and warm, open spirit made him an inspiring collaborator whom we miss terribly. Thanks also go to Karen Seat, director of the Religious Studies Program. Both Peter and Karen guided the launching of the RelSec project at UA when help was most needed. Thanks as well to Javier Duran, director of the Confluencenter, and Mary Wildner-Bassett, former dean of humanities, for their critical support. Pete Figler and Chris Sloman provided the finest research assistance and good humor one could hope for.

Rosi Braidotti, former director of the Centre for Humanities at Utrecht University, was an ingenious collaborator on the original proposal and offered outstanding leadership for the Dutch leg of the project. We owe special gratitude to Raef Zreik, then codirector of the Minerva Humanities Center, for his brilliant and invaluable collaboration in the earliest formulations of this project, and for his intellectual comradeship. Adi Ophir and Shaul Setter also provided big-hearted help with the Israel/Palestine piece of this project. At the Chinese University of Hong Kong, we warmly thank Mu-chou Poo as well as Hsiung Ping-chen, director of the Humanities Research Institute, for their collaborative work and their leadership of the Chinese portion of this project. Finally, kudos to the inestimable Michael Clark, former director of the Portland Center for Public Humanities.

We are grateful to all the contributors to this volume, not just for their fine chapters but for the spirit of "working together" that we shared. Kenneth Wissoker at Duke University Press provided thoughtful support in shepherding this book all the way to publication, and Nina Foster has provided wonderful editorial assistance. Special thanks to Marcia Klotz for her patient help with numerous drafts of the introduction to this volume. Two anonymous readers also provided engaging commentary and criticism that have made this a far stronger book.

Finally, we want to express our warmest thanks to someone we have recently lost. Srinivas Aravamudan was president of the CHCI when the RelSec project was first proposed. Without his intellectual generosity, critical acumen, and cosmopolitan passion for the global humanities, this project would never have been born. This book is dedicated to his memory.

INTRODUCTION
Translated Secularisms, Global Humanities
LEEROM MEDOVOI AND ELIZABETH BENTLEY

Provincializing Secularisms

This collection reckons with the growing certainty that nearly everywhere today, whether in Trump's America, the unraveling Europe Union, the post–Arab Spring Middle East, or rising China, we are being ushered into tumultuous new political worlds whose markedly altered religious and secular vectors demand our critical attention. This book, however, does not seek a singular secular point of reference (the secular state, the immanent frame, a disenchanted world, or even a unified scholarly language) from whose perspective we might claim to measure or compare those changing vectors. Instead, it presumes that the secular vantage points of its international contributors are nonidentical. Secularism in its most general sense is worldliness (a claim we will elaborate), but different worlds beget different forms of worldliness. The hard work of translation across political worlds—with their distinctive historical situations, critical languages, and social agents—therefore guides this book's basic approach to the fluctuating global conditions of religion, secularism, and politics.

In their landmark 2008 collection, *Secularisms,* Janet Jakobsen and Ann Pellegrini were among the first to urge scholars to discard a monolithic conception of secularism in favor of an approach that engages its many global forms. Jakobsen and Pellegrini still referred to a single "dominant narrative of universal secularism" that had developed in Europe in the aftermath of the Protestant reformation, but they reframed that narrative as one whose claims to universality amounted to a form of self-misrecognition. In their account, post-Protestant Western secularism has propagated a "secularization narrative" through which the West views itself as a champion of enlightened reason marching inexorably forward to emancipate the world from magical thinking, superstitious beliefs, and religion's improper interference in political life. For Jakobsen and Pellegrini, however, secularism had not so much spread alongside capitalism and European empire as it had multiplied and mutated. Everywhere that secularism arrived around the globe, it took on new local forms, whether in relation to America's competing Protestantisms, Islam and Hinduism's cohabitation in India, syncretic traditions in Latin America, or Buddhism in China. Today, argued Jakobsen and Pellegrini, we live in a world of many secularisms just as surely as we live in a world of many religions.[1]

Jakobsen and Pellegrini's account is ultimately ambiguous when it comes to the task of provincializing Western secularism. On the one hand, it calls upon us to always specify the secularisms that we seek to study. But on the other hand, their account also maintains that the world's various secularisms, even while constituted by local conditions, are always also "articulated in relation to the dominating discourse of universal secularism, which is tied to the Protestant secularism of the market."[2] This claim, contrary to the general thrust of their argument, seems to make Western secularism different from all others; its false universalism paradoxically becomes genuine insofar as every other secularism must always be defined in relation to it.

This collection heeds the first rather than the second of Jakobsen and Pellegrini's calls. It engages the plurality of secularisms, asking what it would mean for scholars of religion, secularism, and politics to take seriously the diversity and differences among the world's secular formations when they collaborate with interlocutors from other parts of the world. *Religion, Secularism, and Political Belonging* grows out of coordinated research conducted by four teams of scholars who have worked together to investigate the rapidly changing political environments of the early twenty-first-century Netherlands, United States, Israel/Palestine, and China as well as the historical conditions and contexts within which those changes occur.[3] In the various chapters of this book, our authors approach the politics of religion and secularism in light of such recent historical events as the aftermath of the Arab Spring, Chinese economic ascendancy, neoliberalism's global resilience, burgeoning right-wing populisms, and the international migrant crisis.

Our book relinquishes the assumption that there is a general type of "Western secularism" with which every part of the world (and every local secularism) must contend. Years ago, Dipesh Chakrabarty suggested that postcolonial historical criticism could only move forward by "provincializing Europe," by which he meant learning to treat Europe as one place among many others rather than as the sociological standard for modernity against which all other histories needed to be measured (and found wanting).[4] This volume approaches the world politics of religion and secularism in much the same spirit, emphasizing the particularity and provinciality of every region's (re)configurations of the secularism/religion binary.

This approach admittedly risks inviting criticism from scholars who have come to fear that the rejection of secularism's unitary significance undermines what they see as its necessary role in grounding the activist scholar's critical responsibilities. For critics such as Stathis Gourgouris, Bruce Robbins, and Aamir Mufti, the world may be home to multiple secularisms, but what makes them all "secular" is nonetheless the intrinsic sharing of an indispensable virtue: their common commitment to questioning established dogmas or theologies, especially those of their own culture.[5] "Critique and interrogation—as autonomous self-altering practices—are the persistent conditions of the secular," writes Gourgouris.[6] This perspective draws actively on Edward Said's notion of "secular criticism" both for intellectual inspiration as well as the conviction that the secular outlook constitutes a necessary precondition for intellectuals to effect critically grounded political change.[7] As Robbins puts it: "Said was also embodying secularism in the terms he most consistently used about it: as self-scrutiny, hence also as openness to further thought, further effort, and further change. These are virtues of scholarly writing but also of political action in the public sphere."[8] For Robbins, it was Said's resolute willingness to question and indeed indict the "pieties of the tribe" that made him secular. To be secular, from this perspective, is to be a universalist precisely in the sense that one is axiomatically irreligious and philosophically iconoclastic in relation to any particular faith (and once again especially one's own). The secular critic names someone with the intellectual courage to shatter the idols of orthodoxy that would keep us enthralled to the political status quo. Without the secular, no critique. Without critique, no new way of thinking. And without a new way of thinking, no undogmatic vision of how to make the world a better place.

We share this incisive commitment to the principle of secular criticism but approach it with a somewhat different lineage and valence of the secular that can also be gleaned from Said's work. Was "self-scrutiny" what Said actually meant by the "secular" when he advocated for secular criticism? A nuanced attention to his use of the word in his classic essay "Secular Criticism" suggests otherwise. And in fact, we propose that an alternative reading of what Said intended by this freighted word offers a useful and productive framework for this book's diverse forms of engagement with the global vicissitudes of secularism, religion, and political belonging.

Secularism as Worldly Practice

When Said brought the words "secular" and "criticism" together, he did so primarily to rebuke literary critics of his moment (the 1970s and 1980s) for disengaging critically and politically from the social worldliness of literary works in order to pursue instead their textual ambiguity: "In having given up on the world for the aporias and unthinkable paradoxes of a text, contemporary criticism has retreated from its constituency, the citizens of modern society, who have been left to the hands of 'free' market forces, multinational corporations, the manipulation of consumer appetites."[9] It is these striking images of critics "giving up on the world" or of their criticism "retreating from its constituency" that captures the meaning of the secular that most interested Said. Academic literary critics, he argued, have come to inhabit the academy's ivory tower as if it were a monastery, a place where one retreats to reflect on works of literature as though they were the word of God. Said's "secular critic" is thus not literally an atheist but someone who rejects confinement to the ivory tower; her thoughts and actions are enough "in the world" to trouble the "quasi-religious authority of being comfortably at home among one's people."[10]

"Religion" functions here as a kind of metaphor for quietism that requires further consideration. Why would Said call "religious" (or more cautiously, "quasi-religious") that which renders someone comfortable with their failure to trouble the world? Throughout his essay, Said repeatedly figures this religiosity by way of various spatial images of places—the cloister, the monastery, the labyrinth—whose chief characteristic is their insularity. To inhabit these "religious" spaces is to escape into another world altogether. In that relatively untroubled and secluded world there seems to be no contact with the world events and societies, which modern intellectuals, critics, and societies have in fact built."[11] This peculiar manner of pitting the secular against the religious becomes legible once we recognize it as an allusion to perhaps the earliest usage of the word "secular," the first one appearing in the *Oxford English Dictionary*, where it is defined as "living 'in the world' and not in monastic seclusion, as distinguished from 'regular' and 'religious.'"[12] In the Middle Ages, the term "secular" served originally to distinguish between two kinds of clergy. While religious or regular clergy took vows to carry out their ministry within the spiritual confines of a monastic or religious order, thus cloistering themselves from the world of ordinary people, the secular priests worked in the parish, supervising the worldly activities of what Michel Foucault has called pastoral power, the oversight of the church's flock.[13]

This specifically worldly form of religious activity was called "secular" because it involved living within the *saeculum*, which in Latin simply named a lengthy unit of time, approximating one hundred years (thus the words *siècle* in French or *siglo* in Spanish that designate a century).[14] Living inside the temporality of human history, the secular clergy cared for the souls of their parishioners by tending to their temporal (their practical or historical) needs or difficulties. To use the terminology of the Fourth Lateran Council of 1215, secular priests were the *medicis advocent animarum*, or "physicians of the soul," healing the world's malevolent effects on spiritual well-being, or the inward aspect of what would later be called the "commonweal" of their flock.[15]

This account of secularism leads to a substantially different way of thinking about its historical meanings and aims. Consider, for example, how much it diverges from Charles Taylor's highly influential argument that we live in a secular age primarily in the sense that we have come to inhabit an immanent frame that renders optional (and perhaps even difficult) any "belief" in a transcendent power beyond our world. For Taylor, "religion" is the name for the transcendental perspective of a "beyond," while the secular names the condition within which the transcendent has retreated to become a dispensable elective position.[16] Today, argues Taylor, even believers must live in accordance with a secular imaginary that renders religious belief as one choice among many, quite different from a believer's situation five hundred years ago. As a key illustration of this argument, Taylor suggests that once upon a time, "we" (i.e., presecular Europeans) believed a "fulfilled life" to require something more than "ordinary human flourishing," namely a faithful love and worshipfulness toward God. According to Taylor, the secular age is marked above all by the disappearance of anything beyond "ordinary human flourishing" as the necessary purpose of life.[17]

Notice how disruptive the figure of the secular priest becomes for Taylor's underlying argument. The secular priest was necessarily concerned with human flourishing, for how could the pastor not care, first and foremost, for the well-being of the flock? And yet, as the physician of the soul, the secular work of the pastor served a notion of well-being that transcended that of the everyday. Secularism, in other words, did not begin in the way Taylor conceives, as a retreat from the transcendental. Instead, it represented a way of bringing a concern with everyday human flourishing into alignment with something higher, more abstract, or indeed transcendent. These grander objectives of secularisms, along with their sublime ideological objects, have certainly changed over time and in different places: they began as the redemption of souls or the love of God but later they would take up loyalty to the state, the glory of the nation, the purity of the race, the *pax imperium*, the imperatives of economic growth, national security, human rights, or even the "greatest good for the greatest number." Regardless of its particular aim, we can think of secularism as the umbrella term for the many projects that have concerned the administration of lives, the conduct of conduct, on behalf of those many ends we might call a "higher purpose." Secularism, so conceived, does not presume an immanent frame at all. It is simply that the transcendent good it pursues remains always inextricable from (and only achievable through) the historically and socially specific world that it administers and seeks to better. From this vantage point, secularism should not be seen as a successor to religion, even in the quite sophisticated way that Taylor intends. It rather emerges within what will later be called religion, spins off as a project that sometimes wins autonomy from religion (but need not do so), and continues throughout to develop alongside religion, often in close relation to it.

It is more in keeping with this alternative understanding of the "secular" that Said criticized the literary critics of his day for secluding themselves from their "constituency," abandoning the "citizens of modern society" to the sway of markets, corporations, and consumer manipulations. Said never called on literary critics to become secular by foregoing their (religious) calling. On the contrary, he urged critics to become secular precisely in the sense of zealously attending to people's worldly needs.[18]

If the account of secularism we have offered here (as worldliness or pastoral care) does not sound very much like what Said called for, we would have to agree. Secularism in itself is not sufficient for the kind of political engagement that he wanted from scholars. But, and this is our point, Said never just called on us to become secular. He urged us to become secular *critics* because the critical stance is the one that impels us to interrogate the ideological basis of secular assumptions about what any world needs. Without a critical dimension, secularism lapses into the more ambiguous notion of governmentality or political regulation that is consistent with the way we have characterized it.

We cannot emphasize too strongly here the nonidentity of "secularism" and "criticism." Secularism concerns values or missions that demand our worldly attention. It orients us (like a secular priest) toward a responsibility to minister on behalf of what people need. Criticism is a different value, equally important to Said's project and ours because through it we discover that what people actually need may well diverge from what our "religious orthodoxies" tell us. Criticism can be conceived as an openness to the heretical insight. Even a secular priest should be prepared to question church orthodoxy upon discerning that the well-being of the parishioners depends on it.

To live up to Said's fullest aspirations, therefore, we must become both secular *and* critical. Secularism without criticism means being immersed in the world without making the effort to consider what might be wrong or misguided about the norms of one's culture. But criticism without secularism is merely cloistered activity, a discriminatory attentiveness to language or meaning that never circles back to help people in what Said called their "local and worldly situations."[19] Once we distinguish the "secular" from the "critical," we can discern that secular critics need not be antireligious at all. In fact, they might paradoxically be deemed highly religious in precisely the medieval sense of the secular: as people who, like the parish priest, bring their zealous concern for the souls of the flock into the world through the worldly practice of their criticism.

The question at hand is this: What if the secular is not religion's opposite at all but the politically ambiguous project of ministering to populations that was at first intrinsic to religion, and only gradually gained some independence from it? How does this change our view of the scholar's critical responsibilities? Perhaps the right way to understand "secularism" is that it always involved a kind of protopolitics, having originated in the worldly or temporal dimension of religious practice. If the secular originally named the sacred mission to conduct a population's temporal life in support of its spiritual salvation, then what Foucault called "governmentality" in fact grew precisely out of the secular responsibilities of religion. To govern well is to take the world and its temporal affairs carefully into account, to adopt an uncloistered concern for the population as one administers to its deepest needs. Little wonder that even as the notion of the "secular" came also to be applied to princes, emperors, and kings, who also were expected to care for the temporal needs of their subjects, it nevertheless remained historically bound, for better or worse, to religion and its political sense of belonging.

Secularism, so viewed, cannot be indicted in any general way as a synonym for pernicious imperialist or capitalist political reason, even if certain versions of secular activity surely have been that. Neither is secularism always and everywhere the guarantor of critical thinking and enlightened change even if it is indeed true that secular criticism (or heresy) intercedes in what we would now call the "political." This genealogy helps us to set aside the impasse of the so-called postsecularism debates. Secularism is more like power itself, a broader and open-ended analytic term for worldly interventions within which we discover (and can enjoin) the history of political struggles and critical interventions over what kind of care a population actually needs and to what ultimate purpose. Worldly critics must by definition *intervene* in the secular. But the secular in itself neither guarantees such critical interventions nor precludes them.

This genealogy of secularism as worldly pastoral care might initially appear hard to reconcile with a more conventional understanding of secularism as rule by the religiously neutral state or disenchanted reason, but in fact they are closely linked. If we trace the genealogies of secularisms in their historic mutations and diffusions, we can see that state power and enlightened reason are important themes along the way. This is true even if we remain focused on the work of secularism within the Western Church. In the immediate aftermath of the Protestant Reformation, for example, the reshaping of religion's worldly activity is illuminated by the itinerary of the "minister." One key innovation of reformed Protestant Churches was that, unlike the ordained priesthoods of Roman Catholicism, they preached a doctrine of universal priesthood (every Christian a priest), advancing a form of Church governance by lay "elders" that dispensed with any fixed distinction between clergy and laypeople.[20] Secular care of the congregation thus became self-administered, conducted by "ministers" who were selected from among the members of the congregation to preach and care for their fellow congregants.

This quasi-democratic conception of the congregation converted it into a miniature model of a governmental society, a prototype for early social contract theory, and a site for fierce debates about the legitimate basis for what John Milton would call "church government."[21] Radicals such as Milton or even the more moderate John Locke contended that church government could only draw its religious authority through the consent of the governed (those in the congregation whom it ministered), offering arguments running parallel to those emerging around the same time in relation to "civil government." Secularism, in this context of the new Protestant churches, was hardly a project outside, above, or beyond religion but was a project of democratizing worldly care that would have broader ramifications.

On the side of the state, we might examine Thomas Hobbes's foundational treatise of modern political philosophy, *Leviathan*, which is normally remembered as a reasoned defense of the absolute sovereignty of the state. If one looks closely at the famous frontispiece of Hobbes's book, however, it may be noticed that the king is equipped not only with the sword of the law but also with the crosier, the staff of the shepherd. Because he considered the sovereign to be he who acts as "judge of what opinions and doctrines are averse, and what conducting to peace," Hobbes held him responsible for "the well-governing of opinions consisteth [in] the well-governing of men's actions."[22] In this sense, the sovereign was charged with ensuring the civil religiosity of the population.

In part III of *Leviathan*, subtitled "Of a Christian Commonwealth," Hobbes zeroes in on the question of how this general responsibility over civil religiosity manifests for a Christian sovereign. His answer is that a Christian king or ruler necessarily becomes the "supreme pastor, to whose charge the whole flock of his subjects is committed."[23] Both the clergy of the Church and the civil magistrates of the state are "but his ministers," those to whom the sovereign delegates the shepherdly duty of conducting the public good in both its temporal and spiritual aspects. Put another way, Hobbes saw the state becoming secular, not when it left religion behind but on the contrary by embracing its worldly duty to oversee religion. Put even more bluntly, the Hobbesian state becomes secular by becoming *more* religious, not less. For Hobbes, this duty explicitly takes the form of an established Church under the authority of the sovereign. But it is not hard to see how this authority might lead in a different direction, in a compromise with the Lockean option, for example, so that the duty of the state over the "well-governing of opinion" becomes the maintenance of a neutral playing field among all those religions that are judged as "conducting the peace." In either formulation, all religions become civil religions insofar as they serve the people under the state's authority by augmenting the cohesiveness of the social bond. They come to serve the end of political belonging broadly construed.

It is not just that the state assumes pastoral responsibility over religion, however, but that the state becomes pastoralized in the far deeper sense of absorbing broad secular responsibilities for the population. Following the English Civil War, one sees the rise of "ministerial" government along lines that parallel the uses of ministry in Church government. The post of prime minister literally emerges in England for the first time during the early eighteenth century, under the government of Horace Walpole. But equally important, subordinate governmental ministries also emerged, each of which tends to some temporal aspect of the incipient national population's commonweal (in its relation to treasure, foreign power, military capacity, labor power, health, education, and so forth).[24] What makes these kinds of ministries secular is not some intrinsic exclusion of religion but the reverse: the persistence and deepening of the state's pastoral responsibilities for national well-being. And among these responsibilities, as Hobbes indicated, one may find the management of religion itself.

The globalization of secularisms that accompanied the various colonial and capitalist expansions of European power cannot be adequately reviewed here, but we can briefly say that the new political worlds of colonies and markets were sites for the exercise of power that required intensive pastoral strategies for secular governance. At the same time, secular formations themselves were transformed in relation to the radically different worlds in which they were now being practiced. Can one separate European rule over the colonized from the so-called government of souls? We know that conversion of the heathen was one important colonial strategy of power. But as we look beyond missionary activity, we can see new worldly practices at work: colonial anthropology, Orientalism, and even the study of comparative religion developed as new forms of imperial knowledge/power that are inextricable from governmental activity that reshapes the worlds they study. David Chidester has referred to the comparative study of African religions in late nineteenth- and early twentieth-century Britain as a project that sought to "classify and conquer."[25] Anuradha Dingwaney Needham and Rajeswari Sunder Rajan have similarly suggested that the best place to begin accounting for secularism in India is with the techniques used by British colonial bureaucracy (laws, the census, electoral constituencies, and the like) to create "religious and caste identities as political categories, with far-reaching consequences." When the British invented the category of Hinduism, they delineated a religion that also had the effect of producing a population ("Hindus") analytically separable from (and soon politically pitted against) Muslims of the Raj.[26] Such cases can be read as histories of secular scientific knowledge about religion. But they are just as self-evidently the histories of a certain strategy of secular knowledge-power, practices of pastoral government in which a way of knowing a population also operated as a mechanism of political administration. The secular politics of anticolonial nationalisms are also part of this history, and the postcolonial critique of colonial secularisms surely needs to also account for the ways that the politics of bettering the worldly affairs of the colonized through independence constituted a series of Third World countersecularisms.

Similar observations are necessary concerning capitalism's royal science: the study of political economy. Karl Marx pointed out long ago that the classic political economists mistook the historically specific characteristics of capitalism for unchanging natural laws.[27] In this straightforward sense, they were ideological. But the scientific knowledge of political economy also had a governmental dimension: it worked to reshape social relations at large in the image of market relations. The expansion of capital (as Marx also stresses) required a range of important governmental actions upon the laboring population: stripping them of their common access to land, socially and legally normalizing the treatment labor as a commodity (the wage form), and disciplining workers in the factory, among many others. Political economy must be understood as the science of how to manage human conduct so it might serve the maximization of wealth. It is tied directly to policy (*polizeiwissenschaft*), so that by the twentieth century, what we mean by economics would come to include the problem of manipulating a population's aggregate demand, managing the velocity of its currency flows, or even caring for what John Maynard Keynes would call its "animal spirits."[28] In his famous lecture on governmentality, Foucault observed that, almost from its start, the objectives of "government" cleaved to political economy as the chief form of knowledge/power that ministers to the wealth/population/territory triad.[29] Economic science was secular, not because it embodied disenchanted reason but because it brought knowledge concerning the production and circulation of wealth to bear upon what it construed as the worldly betterment of populations.

Consider, as one final example, the historical figure who is widely acknowledged to have coined the word "secularism": George Jacob Holyoake.[30] Author of the manifesto *The Principles of Secularism*, Holyoake was actually a nineteenth-century British Owenite Socialist who preached "secularism" as a kind of creed that applied science to the practice of pastoral government. In that book, Holyoake defined secularism as "the study of promoting human welfare by material means; measuring human welfare by the utilitarian rule, and making the service of others a duty of life."[31] Secularism is nothing for Holyoake if not a ministerial enterprise, albeit one that no longer requires a church because science proves a more powerful and effective means of achieving what were always the secular aims of religion.

Holyoake apparently named his project "secularism" in part to distance it from the hostility toward religion signaled by "atheism": he did not mean to oppose religion's capacity to promote human betterment. But he also chose the word "secularism" because it connoted his own ministerial mission. "The Secular," he asserted, "is sacred in its influence on life, for by purity of material conditions the loftiest natures are best sustained and the lower the most surely elevated."[32] Secularism, in short, meant the "sacred" pursuit of human betterment by the full employment of our knowledge of the material world, including, but not limited to, scientific knowledge. For Holyoake, secularism was closely related to socialism, but its relationship to various political projects or religious denominations was flexible, so long as its engagement with the improvement of temporal affairs remained front and center.

If secularisms need not be understood as finding their antithesis in religion, as this genealogical journey has suggested, then how else should we characterize their relation? Because there is no singular answer to this question, we must circle back to where we began: with the plurality of world secularisms and the need always to provincialize. In certain times and places, secular formations have constituted religion as something that itself needs to be ministered by the state (by way of a state religion, a separation of church and state, or an avowed state neutrality toward religion). As we have stressed, however, religions have long served as sites for secular responsibilities, caring for the worldly affairs of people in forms that can range from classical notions of charity (the principles of *zakat* in Islam or *tzedaka* in Judaism) on the one hand to fully statist projects of explicitly religious government on the other. Indeed, in the new forms of religious politics we see today (the Christian right, political Islam, Hindutva electoral politics), we seem to be witnessing a striking *resecularization* of religion as it increasingly assumes direct pastoral political responsibility for its communities. Some of our contributors might wish to call these postsecular conditions, but could they not more accurately be interpreted as the reactivation of some rather early inflections of the secular?

What view should we take concerning such resecularizations of religion? Our point is that we cannot know in advance of a careful and critical consideration. And why would a true secular critic expect otherwise? Without question, the politicization of religion today is a phenomenon that often proves damaging to just and inclusive projects of political belonging. In a context like U.S. Christian evangelism, for instance, the politicization of religion has undoubtedly served to reconcile subjects to their own immiseration by neoliberal market forces. In Europe today, the politicization of "Judeo-Christian values" has provided right-wing European populisms with a weapon that strikes against already precarious refugee populations. Hindutva party politics provides both a basis for the honeycombing of Indian citizenship and an ideology with which to justify acts of violence against Muslim and other South Asian religious minorities. These are all examples of pervasive reactionary mobilizations of religion in contemporary political life. At the same time, we do not consider the entry of religion into the political or public sphere to be necessarily pernicious. Context is critical. We share, for example, our colleague Mohanad Mustafa's view (found in this book) that the incorporation of Islamic values in post–Arab Spring Tunisia has actually expanded political inclusivity. It is no more helpful to subscribe a priori to the narrative that religion is everywhere the passive victim of secularism than it is to assume that only secularism allows us to transcend our provincialisms and dogmatic particularities.

Toward a New Secular Criticism: Particular, Global, Translational

It has now been nearly a quarter century since Edward Said originally published his urgent plea for critics to uphold their secular responsibilities. At that historical moment, Said too was responding to the changing vectors of a particular world, namely a shift in American political circumstances that he pithily described as the "ascendancy of Reaganism, or for that matter [with] a new cold war, increased militarism and defense spending, and a massive turn to the right on matters touching the economy, social services, and organized labor."[33] Throughout his career as a secular critic, Said interrogated and challenged a Western imaginary that legitimated its acts of violence (whether against the American poor or the villagers of Central America) as the self-defense of liberal freedom. Said's writings frequently return to the question of how and why defending the secular principle of Western freedom had come to justify both a cold war against the "oriental" communist states of the East (the Soviet Union but also Vietnam and China) as well as a domestic war against the "totalitarian bureaucracy" of the Keynesian welfare state. Said's magnum opus, *Orientalism*, can be usefully approached as a study of the nineteenth-century imperial ideologies that postwar American anticommunism had inherited and reinvigorated. By the time Said had published *Covering Islam* in 1981 (in the wake of the Iranian Revolution), he was further observing how Orientalized images of Islam as the exemplary enemy of Western freedom were folding into a fruitful strategy for advancing Reaganite neoliberalism at home and American power abroad in the name of fighting terrorism. Said, in other words, was not so naive as to think that the championing of "secularism" could not itself be an ideological maneuver that secular criticism needed to analyze and indict.

Circumstances have changed considerably since Said's time, although the political uses of anti-Islamism have only grown. The age of three worlds associated with the cold war has given way to a far more unstable geopolitical situation with multiple centers of power (a weakened United States; a more independent Europe, China, and India in ascendancy) and a stunning proliferation of governing ideologies and strategies of power. The twentieth century's principal governmental strategies—the state secular models associated with Western liberalism, communism, and even postcolonial nationalism—are today either greatly diminished or changed. In their place, we sometimes find political religions stepping into governmental roles, while in other places we see the growing appeal of populist nationalisms that claim to defend the people against various figurations of foreign and/or religious enemies.

What then might we most urgently want and expect from our secular critics in such a world? Given the distinct political trajectories at work across different countries and regions, perhaps first and foremost we need forms of secular criticism that are resolutely particular in their engagement with local conditions and strategies of governance. How does a secular formation minister to the "freedom" of the neoliberal marketplace in the United States, the minoritization of immigrant communities in the "pillarized" society of the Netherlands, the Jewishness of the "Jewish state" of Israel, or the management of religious minorities in Communist China? Said, of course, characterized secular critics as people who are not "at home" in the world about which they write, who call into question the self-justifying strategies of power that govern that world. The open question, of course, is what our criticism of local conditions can also tell us about the global turbulence that is characteristic of this new century.

Like good Saidian secular critics, the scholars from the four RelSec teams whose work appears in this book critically engage the political forces that they see reshaping the particular worlds they inhabit. We can offer some generalizations about the distinctive set of concerns that animates the work of each team. The American scholars, for instance, are primarily interested in interpreting the conditions that have enabled the emergence of a complex coalition in the post-9/11 United States among neoliberal market advocates seeking a "deregulated" capitalism, a Christian right bent on fighting a culture war against liberal secular humanism, and a xenophobic politics that leans ideologically upon Islamophobic discourses of civilizational war against terrorism.[34] The Dutch team, meanwhile, examines the complex implications across the European Union's ideological spectrum as political reactions to new African and Middle Eastern immigrant and refugee populations drive many Europeans away from a strict Enlightenment framework for the European public sphere and toward a range of postsecular arguments proffered both by the multicultural left and the populist right.

The central concern for our scholars from Israel/Palestine consists in debating what is being lost and what might potentially be gained from the steady erosion of secular nationalisms in the Middle East in favor of expanding political religiosities, whether those are the rise of religious Zionist movements in Israel (once upon a time a political contradiction) or various forms of political Islamism found in occupied Palestine as well as in the rest of the Arab world.

By contrast, our Chinese scholars are primarily concerned with the uneven adaptations of Western discourses of secularism and religion in the new context of Chinese wealth and power, particularly as they concern the Chinese state's simultaneous efforts to regulate religion on the one hand and to reframe Confucianism in light of secular Western notions of "civil religion" on the other.

If the governmental problems raised by the secularism/religion dyad are so distinctive in these four parts of the world, what then is the value in bringing these particularities together under one cover? We would reply that, across all these regions, the increasingly explosive relationship between religion and secularism on one side, and political life on the other, seems to have become one of the "wicked problems" of our times. Here we find the universal moment in our analysis. A "wicked problem," as the policy and science disciplines understand, is an especially vexing and insoluble problem that is characteristically multivalent, too complex to formulate exactly, lacking any ideal solution, and likely symptomatic of other problems.[35] So it is here. Whether one begins with the rise of Islamophobia in the West, the virulent political theologies of the populist right, the steep decline of secular Zionism and Arab nationalism in the Middle East, or the communist Chinese state's growing adaptation of Confucian principles for civil order, one sees simultaneous transformations in worldly governmental practice that we could easily call "global climate change," were that phrase not already claimed by natural scientists to describe a different wicked problem. In a very general way, of course, we can trace these transformations back to certain traveling forces—the decline of American power, the neoliberalization of capital, indeed a warming Earth (Syrian refugees are climate refugees in both senses)—all of which are disrupting the comparatively stable arrangements that obtained in the latter half of the twentieth century. Like the planetary climate crisis to which it is certainly connected, however, the global picture one might draw of the crisis in the religion/secularism/politics triad looks quite different wherever one happens to look. In both cases, the climate is changing but the weather is local.

It is in the face of such a global picture of crisis that the temptation to universalize is surely the strongest. Étienne Balibar, in asserting that the prospect of planetary catastrophe will require us to invent a worldwide discourse of political solidarity, calls the new language that we need today "secularism secularized" because, in his view, global solidarity will necessarily take the form of a civic articulation, a citizenship language (*articulation citoyenne*), that has undergone so ruthless a critique of any residual particularity or partiality that it can emerge as genuinely universal: "The question of a secularism for the global age does not really differ from that of the development of universalism or the very meaning of the category of universality in the current conjuncture. What language do we have with which to convince ourselves that there exists risks and interests 'common to all humankind'?"[36] We will have to invent and share such a common language, Balibar suggests, even while we continue as native speakers of our particular languages. To use a Gramscian idiom, he aspires to a planetary common sense that can subsequently become "translatable into a multitude of discourses and language spoken by a multitude of groups and social conditions."[37] Balibar's call marks a powerful Hegelian return to the secular as a universal by which we overcome our particularities—our local forms of worldly loyalty and embeddedness—through a critical process that leads at last to genuine cosmopolitical solidarity. The difficulty, as he sees it, is how to get there. The process will surely involve translation across difference, but translation understood as an act of translingual communication that moves us toward commonality. He also appears to suggest that this translational process will purge us of the "religious" along the way because "when it is possible to translate one religious universe into another, the reason is *precisely that it is not purely religious*."[38] What actually translates is always the secular dimension, that which is waiting to be dialectically elevated toward the universal language of solidarity.

Taken as a whole, our book suggests a different path. This is not a collection that hopes to move us toward a cosmopolitical Esperanto, even as a vanishing mediator, nor do we imagine that what global crisis calls for today is an effort to be pried dialectically out of our local worlds into a shared planetary perspective. We cannot run the biblical story of the Tower of Babel in reverse. In this book, translation is also important, not because it produces communication that can lead to a higher commonality but because it makes us better secular critics of our own world, and perhaps better neighbors too, when we are confronted with the foreignness of some other world's secular criticism.

Our inspiration comes from the great German Jewish critic and thinker Walter Benjamin, who, in his essay "The Task of the Translator," argued that the value of translation is not that it converts the content of another language into our own but that it makes our own words strange to us when we hear the echoes of a different language in the translated text.[39] In his famous yet simple example, Benjamin explains that the German word *Brot* and the French word *pain* do not have the same "intention" but in fact exclude each other's meaning, because bread means something different in German than it does in French.[40] It is not only that bread itself is lived and used differently but also that the words carry different cultural connotations and values that make them noninterchangeable and indeed opposed, agonistic. Citing his contemporary Rudolph Pannwitz, Benjamin writes: "Our translations, even the best ones, proceed from a wrong premise. They want to turn Hindi, Greek, English into German instead of turning German into Hindi, Greek, English. Our translators have a far greater reverence for the usage of their own language than for the spirit of the foreign works."[41] The translator's task should not be to change the language of the other into our own, nor for that matter into an Esperanto that transcends both languages. Instead, the task is to render *our own language foreign*. Judith Butler has eloquently characterized this approach to translation as seeking the "condition of a transformative encounter, a way of establishing alterity at the core of transmission."[42] And yet this establishment of alterity by way of transmission is in fact very difficult to achieve, not least because of our own psychic investments in the languages that we already use for our critical work.

Consider, to offer just one example, a Dutch scholar bent on the question of how to widen European secularism's promise of toleration so as to encompass new migrant refugee communities. Upon encountering (and seeking to translate into a critical secular European idiom) a Palestinian or Israeli scholar's effort to activate certain religious frameworks for political cohabitation, it might be difficult for Dutch researchers to read it as anything other than a dangerous regression from what they understand as secularism's promise of universal inclusion. We are here trying to translate across the critical secularisms of two political worlds. What will it actually take for that Dutch scholar to rearticulate his own scholarly language into one that can effectively absorb the Israeli scholar's sense that a return to religion might offer more critical insight and worldly political promise than a "secular" Zionism that has steadily made it impossible to imagine an Israel that is both Jewish and democratic? Or to engage the reasons why an Islamist framework might seem critical to achieving a fully inclusive Palestinian political project or perhaps even an eventual one-state solution to the conflict? How must the very idiom of Dutch secular criticism change, what kind of transference must occur, for such alterity to enter the act of transmission? And how will that effort to reorient the Dutch situation ramify back upon the critical outlook and interventions of the Palestinian and Israeli scholars?

What such transferential and transformational moments of translation offer is a difficult but more genuine pathway to a global solidarity whose methodological foundation and political aim is not progress toward universalism but an openness to being changed by the foreign, and perhaps then to a kind of agonistic identification with that foreignness, that strange particularity. The particular could at least momentarily seek its opposite not in the universal but, quite literally, in the translated, that which names the reverberations sounding when two or more particulars, by colliding with one another, are both transformed.

Does such an approach to secularism leave us with any overarching conception of the global at all? We should be clear that we are not proposing that the universal be rejected in the name of the particular. A one-sided embrace of particularism can lead to the relativistic valorization of "local values" that only undermines our capacity to take a critical stand against the authoritarian tendencies of our times. We therefore do not think it is wise to "back" the particular any more than the universal. There is no choosing sides between them. What we are arguing, instead, is that no access to the universal is possible except *by passing through the particular*. The particular is not that which we ought to leave behind (or shed) as we dialectically purify ourselves and our thought process of its contaminants. We can never become purely universal (secular) subjects. We can, however, catch a glimpse of the universals that connect particulars and that ground our impulses to critique when we attend to the moments of estrangement that occur when we translate back and forth between those particulars. When we refer to our project as a kind of "global humanities," we are honoring the importance of the universal. It is just that we do not think you can do global humanities without working through the local, and that you do not find the universal by rejecting the particular.

Benjamin's term for the universal in "The Task of the Translator" aligns with what we have in mind. According to his essay, when we let our own language fall under the spell of another, and let it be thereby changed, opened up, recast in the other language's modality or *intentio*, we approach something that he calls "pure language." Perhaps the most vexing and controversial of his concepts, "pure language" evokes a seeming impossibility. It is certainly not Balibar's universal language of "secularized secularism," a language we imagine (or want) everyone to speak. Rather, it corresponds to no actually existing tongue, nor any tongue that ever could be. It articulates a place in which, by hearing the echoes of one language through a translation rendered in another, we catch whispers of some third language that is entirely free of content and particularity. By way of a metaphor, Benjamin imagines a broken vessel whose fragments, when glued together, "must match one another in the smallest details, although they need not be like one another. In the same way, a translation, instead of resembling the meaning of the original, must lovingly and in detail incorporate the original's mode of signification, thus making the original and the translation recognizable as fragments of a greater language, just as fragments are part of a vessel."[43] This well-known religious metaphor, which is known in Jewish Kabbalistic literatures as *shevirat hakelim*, tells the story of the shattering of primordial vessels that gave rise to the diversity of creation. In its religious register, pure language does indeed reverse Babel: it references a self-complete Adamic language that existed before the linguistic fragmentation of humanity. But there is no putting the vessel back together out of its fragments. In Benjamin's secular idiom, in its worldly purpose, the concept of "pure language" theorizes the work of translation by reconceiving the relation of the particular and the universal. The *part* is that which we can see, hear, and speak, while the *totality* (as is also the case for Fredric Jameson) is that concrete universal that can never be grasped on its own terms, and so must always be approached through the relationships that emerge among the particulars it contains, through their mutual translations.[44]

For the kind of secular criticism that is this book's aim, "pure language" expresses the impossible asymptotic (and thus never-ending) project of the global humanities. The global will never resolve itself into a singular universal language that transparently apprehends and thoroughly criticizes the secular forces of every part of the world in the name of a higher secularism. We will not solve our wicked political problems by speaking from the viewpoint of such a universal. Nevertheless, the global points toward a pure language we can never reach directly. To use Benjamin's image, the "global" is best grasped as the shattered vessel of global secular criticism itself, a project that emerges into view only through comparative studies that might reveal how one fragment of local knowledge fits perfectly with that of another locale yet does not thereby need to resemble it.

Itinerary of This Book

This book is organized with a translational glimpse of the global in mind. It does not provide separate, self-contained dossiers for each region. Instead, its work is divided into three sections—on religion, secularism, and political belonging, respectively—that serve to juxtapose the secular criticisms of different if related political worlds. Each section begins with two keyword entries, composed by RelSec scholars, that frame a critical intervention into the particular political context that generated it. But "Brot" is quickly followed by "pain." The subsequent chapters talk back to the informing contexts and the assumed interventional value of the keywords. In the process, each section repeatedly reframes the significance of the section's opening acts of criticism within other worlds.

Part I, which revolves around the plurality of secularisms, launches with two keyword entries, on "neutrality" and "science," each of which challenges the worldly claims of their respective (and quite different) secular practices. The keyword entry on "neutrality" is politico-juridical in focus, tracing neutrality's rise as a new legal norm in the United States (in place of "separation") that has increasingly provided evangelical movements with access to governmental powers. "Science," meanwhile, in tracking three different levels at which the secular claims of science are deemed (in)compatible with religion, concludes that it is precisely when science tries to offer an account of the power of religious faith or the sacred that it most clearly fails to meet the standards of its own truth protocols.

In the first chapter of part I, Pooyan Tamimi Arab strategically reverses the critique of the neutrality keyword by arguing that, in Western Europe at least, a strict neutrality paradigm is both traditional and remains indispensable as a secular framework for the political governance of religion. Disputing the American philosopher Martha Nussbaum's argument that neutrality should be supplanted by contextually sensitive political accommodations of religious difference, Tamimi Arab suggests that Nussbaum's dilution of the neutrality framework's importance is itself contextually insensitive. It misses the challenges arising in the Dutch context, where a growing aversion to Islamic presence in the public sphere has led to attempted legal restrictions on the visibility of Muslim life. If, as this introduction has argued, secularism intervenes in a population's everyday life in the name of their pastoral needs, Tamimi Arab shows that, absent a robust principle of neutrality, the Dutch state's secular management of religion may well acquiesce to the banning of Muslim sartorial practices, mosques, and Islamic calls to prayer, and that it may lead to erosion in the political claims of Muslim citizens.

Despite a proliferation of research into secularisms across the globe, Chinese modes of secularism remain understudied, perhaps because many conventional Western assumptions (that secularism must be about separation of church and state or represent a modern break with traditional religious beliefs) seem not to apply. Albert Welter's chapter proceeds in two steps. First, he shows how European concepts of religion and secularism did find translation into Chinese, albeit through native words that reorganized their meaning in local ways. Second, he suggests that these concepts had to operate in a social framework vastly different from the public/private-sphere distinction that was so important in European theory and practice. Welter brings these questions back to the possible understanding of Confucianism as a species of secularism insofar as it played a role in the administration of religion in China—specifically Buddhism. However, it did so by way of what he calls a "sphere of proximity"—a continuous terrain where public and private, secular and sacred aims converged. As such, Confucian secularism is characterized not through a Westernized separation of church and state but through a framework wherein the state strategically sanctions religious institutions and activities that support governmental policy.

In the next chapter, Mohanad Mustafa considers the unique context for the practice of postsecular politics in post–Arab Spring Tunisia, exploring the significant political accommodations of Islam that have occurred in the public sphere. Prior to this first (and arguably only successful) iteration of the Arab Spring revolutions, Tunisia was one of the most emphatically antireligious secular states in the Arab world; its government in the postcolonial period combined a rigidly authoritarian regime with a radical secularization project that attempted to both exclude religion from the public space and suppress political Islam. The 2010 popular revolution led to the collapse of the authoritarian regime, the beginning of processes of democratization, and a resurfaced questioning of the relationship between religion and politics in Tunisian public discourse. Mustafa argues that two concurrent, differential forces—the rise of political Islam and the attempted break with the deposed regime's radical secularist legacy—have produced an inclusive mode of secularity that compromises on the status of "religion." This inclusive secularity, in which a mutually beneficial separation of church and state paradoxically complements the injection of religion in the public sphere, offers in his view a very rare model for envisioning postsecular democratization in the Arab world.

In the penultimate contribution of part I, Marcia Klotz and Leerom Medovoi critique the sacralization of markets by way of considering why neoliberalism, which appears in many parts of the world as a "secular" force, nonetheless is so often closely allied with religious traditionalism. Tracing the genealogies of political economy that would enable such relationships, Klotz and Medovoi outline a long-standing theological foundation to liberal economic thought that, even in its contemporary permutations, has proven attractive to certain forms of organized religion in the United States. The durability of America's neoliberal regime of power, which has survived severe economic crises, financial meltdowns, and waves of strong political opposition, according to the authors, owes a great deal to its religious form of self-legitimation and its unique form of theological subjection through investing in acts of faith through uncertain times.

In the final chapter of part I, and in a reading of the Dutch context that diverges strikingly from that of Tamimi Arab, Ernst van de Hemel considers the uses of religion in the sharp turn to the political right occurring today not only in the Netherlands but throughout Western Europe. Whereas Tamimi

Arab makes a case for the viability of a "strict neutrality" conception of political secularism, van den Hemel instead emphasizes the ways in which populists are "deneutralizing" European political secularism by directly asserting its cultural equivalence with Judeo-Christian religious traditions. European populists assert the basis of Western secularism in Christianity, not (like Talal Asad, for one) in order to critique its provincial particularity but as a means of forging a populist national selfhood that legitimates the xenophobia of such parties and movements as the Dutch Partij voor de Vrijheid (PVV, Freedom Party). Van den Hemel explores these developments through a close reading of the PVV's Twitter feeds, where one finds a remarkably high number of references to religion, albeit as a concept that becomes retroactively interchangeable with progressive Dutch "heritage" or "culture" even while justifying the exclusion of Muslim immigrants.

Part II of the book turns from a general concern with the secular toward the belonging claims of religion, launching with lexical entries on "nationalism" and "fundamentalism," each of which map out a different framework for political belonging that has in its own way mobilized the secularism/religion binary. The "nationalism" keyword calls into question nationalism's alleged status as the paradigm for secular political belonging to the state par excellence by showing how it is repeatedly shadowed by religious belonging. The entry also calls attention to the growing capacity for envisioning nonnational states, citing important contemporary examples such as the European Union or the Islamic state, where state formations appear to be finding alternatives to nationalistic strategies (civil and religious, respectively) for grounding their project of secular governance. Meanwhile, the "fundamentalism" keyword entry traces the discursive delineation of "bad religion" by considering the development of "fundamentalism" as a political discourse that has always worked to produce regressive enemy figures. Beginning with evangelicals in the early twentieth century but making an international jump in the late 1970s to political Islamism, the fundamentalist stands as a category for the religious abnormal, a dogmatic fanaticism whose resistance to modernity itself serves to threaten civil society.

Working in tension with one or both of these keywords, the chapters that follow challenge these readings of "nationalism" and "fundamentalism" in a number of contexts where the "religious" has found its political mobilizations. In their chapter, Raef Zreik and Mohanad Mustafa, for example, explore the vital role that religion has played in the revolutionary and anticolonial political thought of the Palestinian nationalist movement through a close consideration of Dr. Fathi Shaqaqi, founder of the Islamic Jihadist movement. Through a close reading of Shaqaqi's work, they show not only how Islam could be conceived as always having represented the anticolonial heart of Palestinian nationalist activism but more generally how religion and nationalism at times operated (at least in movements like Islamic Jihad) as inextricable twin elements in a sacral politics of liberation that neither of the keyword entries on nationalism or fundamentalism are in a position to entertain.

A quite different interweaving of religious and national forms of belonging has also emerged in recent years on the Israeli side of the conflict, a subject that Ori Goldberg explores in his chapter on the evolution of Israeli "national religious" party politics. Goldberg focuses on the party once known as the National Religious Party (Mafdal) and re-formed as Habayit Hayehudi (the Jewish Home), examining the constitutive interaction between the party's religious vision and its social and economic positions. The mainstay of Israeli national religious politics has traditionally been support for a "greater" Israel through the settlement of occupied Palestinian territory. While this religious vision is still in focus, Habayit Hayehudi's economic position has shifted significantly from moderate fiscal and social conservatism to a radically capitalist, free-market approach. Goldberg employs critical theological theory to examine these shifting nodes of interaction, highlighting the ominous political theology underlining radical transformations of this nature.

In his chapter on aspects of Chinese religion, Mu-chou Poo takes a deep dive into the dense history of the management of religion in the Chinese context, which, as he observes, raises methodological problems because the range of social phenomena that might be considered religious in China differs so dramatically from dominantly Abrahamic regions of the world. For Poo, the question of what has counted as religion, or how it should be regulated in Chinese history, needs to be considered in light of three principal contexts: the historically continuous expectation of the strong state's "celestial authority" in China, the historical tension between Chinese intellectuals and the commoners regarding such popular activities as deity worship and divination, and, most recently, the influence of Western intellectual traditions in religious studies. Poo suggests ultimately that the secular/religious divide cannot be sustained in the Chinese context even as there is room for rich analysis of the uses of the sacred for the reproduction of civil relations and Chinese political belonging.

David N. Gibbs returns to a theme that runs through many of the American contributions, namely the historical convergences between market economics, Christianity, and political belonging in the U.S. political sphere. In this case, the investigation concerns the way that so-called fundamentalism has in fact been critical in the hegemonic shaping of recent American nationalism.

Gibbs's chapter, in an interesting parallel to Goldberg's reflections on the Jewish Homeland Party in Israel, considers how the rise of evangelical Protestantism influenced a decisively conservative political shift in the U.S. Republican Party of the 1970s. Gibbs argues that this conservative shift was led by business elites, who sought free-market economic policies and military expansion but pursued those objectives by establishing common cause with evangelical Christians. This emerging power bloc, which proceeded by condemning Democratic "secularists" and claiming to support the renewal of "traditional values," led to a lasting business-Christian alliance whose combination of money, votes, and religious fervor remains a distinctive feature of contemporary U.S. politics today.

Although, as the "fundamentalism" keyword rightly suggests, Islamic subjects have been repeatedly and adversely mapped as "fundamentalist" in many contemporary secular political contexts, Eva Midden focuses her attention on a complex situation within this framework in the Netherlands: the gendered tensions that ensue when European women of Christian origin adopt traditional Islamic religious practices. Midden's chapter, "Among New Believers," focuses on the controversial position that these women hold in Dutch society, where they are often confronted with questions of national identity (are they still "Dutch"?) and of emancipation (did they make a conscious choice, and how does it influence women's emancipation?). Midden grounds her analysis in a reading of the Dutch television show *Van Hagelslag naar Halal* (*From Dutch Chocolate Sprinkles to Halal*), wherein a group of Dutch female converts travel to Jordan with their mothers in hopes of developing mutual understanding within the context of their newly defined relationships. Midden analyzes the show's staged dialogue not as a realistic depiction of these relationships but as symptomatic of the gendered tensions between religion and national identity that circulate in Dutch popular media. Midden argues that these converts' religious choices are interpreted as a direct challenge to—and incompatible with—the secular values that presumably define Dutch identity.

Part III bridges the two preceding sections in a consideration of when and how the secular and the religious can come together to create complex and sometimes politically positive forms of belonging. This section begins with two keywords, which evoke contrapuntal approaches to negotiating religion, secularism, and political belonging: "civil religion," an entry composed by Muchou Poo of the Chinese team, emphasizes the secular worldly purposes that religion can be asked to serve, while "faith," contributed by Israeli scholar Ori Goldberg, gestures toward the religious intentions, the higher purpose, that is potentially offered by the nominally secular forms of citizenship and political belonging.

In chapter 11, Kambiz GhaneaBassiri challenges the positive inflection of civil religion espoused in the keyword entry by taking stock of the intensely Islamophobic challenges that Muslim citizens of the United States have faced when it comes to participating in the civil vision of the American polity since the 9/11 attacks. GhaneaBassiri proceeds by analyzing the virulent backlash to American Muslim leader Feisal Abdul Rauf's activism and writings by anti-Shariʿa activists. Although the concept of civil belonging in a republican framework does operate under certain conditions in American society, GhaneaBassiri observes how the question of who belongs in America inevitably pivots back to identity markers, particularly given the challenges to civil acceptance posed both by transnational notions of Muslim religious community and by the political anxiety that organizes around Shariʿa. GhaneaBassiri demonstrates that the discourses surrounding Muslim belonging reveal a struggle in contemporary American politics between liberal conceptualizations of citizenship—wherein the exercise of civic duties works to renew the social contract between the state and communities—and an illiberal, nativist, and isolationist understanding of citizenship as an act of will on the part of those whose race, religion, and gender represent the embodiment of America in a popular imaginary.

Similarly interested in the redefinition of citizenship by (and against) minoritarian subjects, but more hopeful about the possible outcome, is Markus Balkenhol, who explores how the claims to citizenship articulated by the Netherlands' Afro-Surinamese community route through their religious practice. Beginning with the paradigmatic shift to integration in the early 1990s, Surinamese Dutch of African descent have mobilized the colonial past—particularly Dutch involvement in the transatlantic slave trade—to formulate claims to citizenship. For the self-identified "descendants of the enslaved," full citizenship constitutes a form of emancipation—the realization of the promise held by the abolition of slavery. Notably, however, these claims to citizenship are not prefaced upon dominant understandings of emancipation-as-secularization. Rather, these claims are put forth with an understanding of emancipation that encapsulates both formal, legal citizenship and *cultural* emancipation: the revaluation of cultural forms and practices that have been suppressed or disavowed under colonialism. Drawing upon ethnographic research from Winti ceremonies in the Dutch public sphere, Balkenhol demonstrates how "descendants of the enslaved" articulate a critical position in which participation in secular political life in the Netherlands and religious practice are not delineated as separate practices that must stay on their respective sides of a public/private divide.

In chapter 13, Zeynep Kurtuluş Korkman consciously attends to a peripheral social actor in contemporary Turkey whose confounding of secular and religious forms of piety reveals the wounds that both Kemalist secularism and Recep Tayyip Erdoğan's Islamist politics have left on Turkish body politics. Korkman investigates Vedia Bülent Önsü Çorak, the controversial leader of an eclectic Turkish religious group that combines deep devotion to the Kemalist celebration of the Turkish state with New Age and Islamic beliefs ranging from UFOism to Sufism. Drawing upon ethnographic research and the media discourse surrounding Çorak, Korkman reads Çorak's unique brand of secularist religious authority through the epistemological interventions of transgender studies. Her aim is to explore what she calls a "transsecular" form of Turkish belonging, performed by Çorak, that cuts across the sharp divisions between the radical secular norms inherited from Atatürk on one side and the Islamic public piety that has grown dominant today on the other.

Francis Ching-Wah Yip's chapter observes the political challenges that arise when Chinese state authority itself becomes enshrined as "political religion" (a quasi-totalitarian concept that he contrasts directly with the more benevolent concept of "civil religion," employed by Poo). Chinese political religion, argues Yip, precisely due to its own theological claims, ends up seeking to govern the theological and political impact of such minority faiths as Protestant Christianity. Yet this attempted governance does not fully succeed, as Yip shows by examining the popular responses to the theological discourse of the state-sanctioned Protestant Church in the People's Republic of China. Looking at official Church periodicals, Yip traces the complex interactions—involving adaptation, negotiation, and competition—that have unfolded between Protestant Christianity and a conception of Chinese state authority that is itself cast in a theological frame. Yip shows how the official theological discourse is not embraced by the majority of Chinese Christians, less because it encourages the uncritical acceptance of the premises of political religion than because it deviates too much from the conservative theological tradition of Chinese Protestantism. Religion here operates in parallel, one official and in alignment with state expectations, the other unofficial, popular, and committed to theological principles that are not opposed to the state but also do not embrace it. The account of contemporary Chinese religion and state authority we are left with is both complex and politically unsettled.

In the final chapter, Shaul Setter offers a rich, culminating treatment of one of this book's most central themes, namely the critical potentialities of theorizing from the perspective of the particular over and against the universal. Setter engages this question in the unique context of Israel/Palestine, proposing a situated yet globally informed politico-theological project that he terms "critical Israel." Critical Israel suggests the rethinking of the political content and form of Jewish particularity, and its great challenge lies in forming various relations to what might seem to be its opposite—the Palestinian, the Muslim, the Arab—but that can perhaps join it to coarticulate the politics and theology of the particular. Setter positions this turn within the genealogy of critical theory in Israel, showing the ways it diverts from the universalist tendency structuring the first generation of Israeli critical research. The dramatic change in Israeli political discourse of the last decade required the retooling of an intellectual stance that could critically address its basic presuppositions: contemporary mainstream neonationalist particularist political theology is challenged here in the development of a nonnationalist theology of the particular. This critical move delves into historical, social, textual, and linguistic potentialities that reside at the heart of the translation of "humanities"—figured here as both a discipline of inquiry and a mode of activity. Setter presents the writings of scholar and poet Haviva Pedaya as a central critical-creative project that opens up the possibility of a Jewish particularism against both universalist humanism and nationalist chauvinism, taking its theological position as a mode of radical critique for the present.

Remaining Thoughts

A new global condition can perhaps be discerned in certain questions that recur across the chapters of this book. Why is the rhetoric of civilizational clashes increasingly cast as wars of religion? Why have public expressions of Islamophobia and antisemitism become increasingly normalized in the West? Why have political religion and economic neoliberalism become such predictable political bedfellows? To knit these locally inflected questions together into a large one, this book might be said to ask: What do we make of the fact that the defining characteristic of our many political worlds today is that they are simultaneously marked by politically active religions and by aggressively antireligious politics?

These shared questions are undoubtedly shaped by the fact that the regions represented in this volume—Western Europe, North America, the Middle East, and East Asia—share encounters with globally interrelated forces: an interstate system that presupposes a secular (if tacitly theological) notion of political sovereignty, capital flows within the world market, and the circulation of such geopolitical discourses as the "war on terror" or the "clash of civilizations." Our political worlds flow into one another. And yet, despite this, circumstances could not be more starkly different in Europe, where religiosity is largely associated with migrant populations; the United States, where a secular state coexists with intensive religiosity in civil society; a Middle East caught in a brutal post–Arab Spring civil war that articulates itself through the political status of religion; and China, where the meaning of the secular/religion binary gets routed through questions of the state power over civil society at a moment of rapid economic growth.

What are the relationships between these various, often baleful circumstances? They are all surely different ways of responding to forces of globalization, defending against the ravages of the market, reacting to competition for geopolitical hegemony, and refracting the impact of climate change on access to basic human needs: water, food, and adequate shelter. In short, these are circumstances that surely require a global analytic. And yet the analysis we need cannot simply take up a universalist perspective, what Donna Haraway once called the "god trick" or the crypto-omniscient view from nowhere that is the temptation of academic knowledge.[45] The terms of our study—religion, secularism, politics—are themselves constitutive of the very problems that this book, its methods, and its form seek to address. The only vision of the global— and the only projection of a universal value—that we ultimately offer in this book is the Benjaminian asymptote of "pure language." It is a language we can never speak as such but one that we hope our readers can nonetheless hear murmuring throughout this book.

NOTES

1. Janet Jakobsen and Ann Pellegrini, "Introduction: Times Like These," in *Secularisms* (Durham, NC: Duke University Press, 2008), 13–14.
2. Jakobsen and Pellegrini, "Introduction," 13.
3. The RelSec project was funded as part of an Andrew Mellon Foundation grant to the Consortium of Humanities Centers and Institutes titled "Integrating the Humanities Across National Boundaries." For further information, see the CHCI website, accessed July 16, 2020, https://chcinetwork.org/programs/integrating-humanities-across-national-boundaries.
4. Dipesh Chakrabarty, *Provincializing Europe: Postcolonial Thought and Historical Difference* (Princeton, NJ: Princeton University Press, 2000).
5. Stathis Gourgouris, "Detranscendentalizing the Secular," *Public Culture* 20 (2008): 437–45; Bruce Robbins, "Is the Postcolonial Also Postsecular?," *Boundary 2* 40 (2013): 245–62; Aamir R. Mufti, "Why I Am Not a Postsecularist: Part One," *Boundary 2* 40 (2013): 7–19. These scholars have collectively written against the work of Talal Asad and Saba Mahmood, whom they criticize as anti-Enlightenment "postsecularists." Although we are not aware of any place where Asad or Mahmood

overtly identify with this moniker, the argument proceeds more or less as follows: Asad and Mahmood have thrown the baby out with the proverbial bathwater because, in criticizing secularism as a ruse of Western power, they attack the questioning outlook that provides the philosophical basis for the project of critique. While, as we have suggested, we endorse the project of secular criticism, we also do not find this reading of Asad and Mahmood's work to be terribly generous. These are critics whose arguments about the afterlife of Western political secularism in the postcolonial world strike us as quite nuanced. To our knowledge, neither scholar argues that secularism is everywhere and always a tool of imperial domination. Rather, their work tends to explore how the tacit privileging of the Christian subject that carried over into Western European secularism has held costly political implications for the rest of the world. Consider, just for an example, the specificity of Mahmood's argument in *Religious Difference in a Secular Age: A Minority Report* (Princeton: Princeton University Press, 2015), where she analyzes the reasons why the Egyptian state's legal adaptation of the modern category of the religious minority, which it borrowed from Western secular state theory while under colonial British rule, has incited rather than discouraged systemic violence against Coptic Christians.

6   Gourgouris, "Detranscendentalizing the Secular," 443. If it does not meet these conditions, suggests Gourgouris, then by definition a way of thought cannot yet be considered secular. In order to become genuinely secular, any way of thinking that dogmatically refuses to question its own presuppositions must first be "de-transcendentalized," by which Gourgouris means it must discard whatever transcendental, a priori commitments it retains as dogma.

7   The primary reference here is to Edward Said's "Introduction: Secular Criticism," in *The World, the Text, and the Critic* (Cambridge, MA: Harvard University Press, 1983), 1–30.

8   Robbins, "Is the Postcolonial Also Postsecular?," 252.

9   Said, "Introduction," 4.

10 Said, "Introduction," 16.

11 Said, "Introduction," 25.

12 *Oxford English Dictionary*, s.v. "secularism, n.," accessed July 15, 2018, http://www.oed.com. The editors of the collection *Rethinking Secularism* observe this early usage as well, though they do not derive from it any major reconsideration of what and how secularism signifies. Craig Calhoun, Mark Juergensmeyer, and Jonathan Antwerpen, "Introduction," in *Rethinking Secularism* (New York: Oxford University Press, 2011), 13.

13 Michel Foucault, *Security, Territory, Population: Lectures at the College de France 1977–1978*, trans. Graham Burchwell (New York: Palgrave Macmillan, 2007), 115–226. See also Michel Foucault, "Omnes et singulatim: Vers une critique de la raison politique," *Le Débat* 41, no. 4 (1986): 5–36.

14 Craig Calhoun, "Rethinking Secularism," *Hedgehog Review* 12, no. 3 (Fall 2010): 35–48.

15 Norman P. Tanner, S.J., ed., *Decrees of the Ecumenical Councils*, vol. 1, *Nicaea I–Lateran V* (Washington, DC: Georgetown University Press, 1990), 244–45.

16 Charles Taylor, *A Secular Age* (Cambridge, MA: Belknap Press of Harvard University Press, 2009), 12–13, 38.
17 Taylor, *Secular Age*, 16–17.
18 This is not to say that "religion" did not often become Said's preferred metaphor for uncritical inquiry. Said sometimes used *religion* as a code word for dogmatism. But when it comes to the word *secular*, Said clearly meant to engage the concept of worldly activity that itself emerged out of various religious traditions. We see this as the more thoughtful and indeed critical (undogmatic) side of Said's thinking.
19 Said, "Introduction," 26.
20 Elsie Anne McKee, *Elders and the Plural Ministry: The Role of Exegetical History in Illuminating John Calvin's Theology* (Geneva: Librarie Doz, 1988), 17.
21 John Milton, "The Reason of Church-Government Urg'd against Prelaty," in *Prose: Major Writings on Liberty, Politics, Religion and Education*, ed. David Loewenstein (New York: Wiley-Blackwell, 2013), 61–91.
22 Thomas Hobbes, *Leviathan* (New York: Hackett, 1994), 113.
23 Hobbes, *Leviathan*, 367.
24 See A. H. Dodd, *The Growth of Responsible Government: From James the First to Victoria* (London: Routledge, 1956). Dodd traces the development of ministerial government that is "responsible" for the well-being of civil society and thus grounded in a notion of "civil service" that we would argue is modeled on the service of the pastoral minister. See his discussion of Walpole's emergence as a prime minister among governmental ministers as well. Dodd, *Growth of Responsible Government*, 105.
25 David Chidester, *Empire of Religion: Imperialism and Comparative Religion* (Chicago: University of Chicago Press, 2014), 59–90.
26 Anduradha Dingwaney Needham and Rajeswari Sunder Rajan, "Introduction," in *The Crisis of Secularism in India*, ed. Rajeswari Sunder Rajan and Anduradha Dingwaney Needham (Durham, NC: Duke University Press, 2007), 12–13. See also William T. Cavenaugh, *The Myth of Religious Violence: Secular Ideology and the Roots of Modern Conflict* (New York: Oxford University Press, 2009), 87–92.
27 "Economists express the relations of bourgeois production, the division of labour, credit, money, etc. as fixed immutable, eternal categories. . . . Economists explain how production takes place in the above mentioned relations, but what they do not explain is how these relations themselves are produced, that is the historical movement that gave them birth . . . these categories are as little eternal as the relations they express. They are historical and transitory products." Karl Marx, *The Poverty of Philosophy* (Hartford, CT: Martino Fine Books, 2014), 114–15.
28 John M. Keynes, The General Theory of Employment, Interest and Money (London: Macmillan, 1936), 161–62.
29 Foucault, *Security, Territory, Population*, 108–14.
30 See, for example, the work of Phil Zuckerman and John Shook, who claim that it was Holyoake who "brought 'secularism' into wide usage in 1851. The word had appeared in print before then, but Holyoake connected it to an affirmative ethical and civic agenda." Phil Zuckerman and John R. Shook, "Introduction: The Usage of

Secularism," in *The Oxford Handbook of Secularism*, ed. Phil Zuckerman and John R. Shook (New York: Oxford University Press, 2017), 2.
31 George Jacob Holyoake, *The Principles of Secularism* (n.p.: CreateSpace, 2016).
32 Holyoake, *Principles of Secularism*, 9.
33 Said, "Introduction," 4.
34 This emergent political hegemony, which as Kevin Kruse has shown finds its earliest roots in a postwar reaction to the New Deal politics of the thirties, has been many decades in the making but has taken a new form through its steady incorporation of Islamophobic and xenophobic politics since the September 11 attacks in 2001. Kevin Kruse, *One Nation under God: How Corporate America Invented Christian America* (New York: Basic Books, 2015).
35 The classic formulation may be found in H. W. J. Rittel and M. M. Webber, "Wicked Problems," *Man-Made Futures* 26, no. 1 (1974): 272–80.
36 Étienne Balibar, "Secularism Secularized: The Vanishing Mediator," in *Secularism and Cosmopolitanism: Critical Hypotheses on Religion and Politics* (New York: Columbia University Press, 2018), 48.
37 Balibar, "Secularism Secularized," 49.
38 Balibar, "Secularism Secularized," 52.
39 Walter Benjamin, "The Task of the Translator," in *Illuminations: Essays and Reflections* ed. Hannah Arendt (New York: Schocken Books, 1969).
40 Benjamin, "Task of the Translator," 261.
41 Benjamin, "Task of the Translator," 80.
42 Judith Butler, *Parting Ways: Jewishness and the Critique of Zionism* (New York: Columbia University Press, 2014), 17.
43 Benjamin, "Task of the Translator," 78.
44 Jameson's classic formulation of totality's unrepresentability can be found in *The Political Unconscious: Narrative as a Socially Symbolic Act* (New York: Routledge, 2013), 55.
45 Donna Haraway, "Situated Knowledges: The Science Question in Feminism and the Privilege of Partial Perspective," *Feminist Studies* 14, no. 3 (1988): 581.

PART I.
SECULARISM

Keyword: Neutrality
ELIZABETH BENTLEY

Neutrality has become a prominent albeit controversial and highly unstable norm in recent legal debates on the parameters of religion-state relations across Europe and North America.[1] Although a "constitutionally-prescribed posture of the state towards religion" that suggests impartially or distance, neutrality's primary significance also derives from the realm of warfare and conflict.[2] The *Oxford English Dictionary* (OED) defines neutrality as "a neutral policy or attitude between contending parties or states; abstention from taking any part in a war between other states," and also as "an intermediate state or condition, a middle ground."[3] Variances across these definitions reflect a fundamental tension: neutrality can refer to an active mediation, or even intermixing, of clashing entities or opinions, but it can also refer to an intentional abstention from the terms of conflict altogether.

Borrowed originally from Latin and French, the earliest appearances of "neutrality" in the fifteenth and sixteenth centuries often reflected the political power of religious institutions; in what is now an obsolete use of the term, the archbishop of Canterbury was configured quite literally as "the neutrality" itself, the central member of a mediatory party that "persuaded the king to come to a treaty with the lords."[4] According to the popular origin myth of the United States, it was the political corruption and religious persecution born of the improper conjoining of ecclesiastical and worldly political powers within the established Church of England that provided the impetus for the U.S. Constitution's First Amendment, with its dual injunctions that "Congress shall make no law respecting an establishment of religion, or prohibiting the free exercise thereof."[5] If in the aforementioned paradigm, the Church of England figured as neutrality itself, as an active albeit presumably disinterested mediator of political conflict, the First Amendment positions religious establishment as an inherently partisan entity whose very presence must be mediated.[6] But while a degree of distance, even tension, is implied, the parameters of the relationship between religion and state are ambiguous—particularly for the interests of this entry, the extent of nonestablishment. This ambiguity created space for "neutrality" to eventually emerge as a generative and extraordinarily mutable paradigm in juridical battles over religion-state relations in the United States.

In both popular political and legal scholarly treatment of the religion clauses, "separation" is arguably the most pervasive overarching interpretive paradigm for the church-state relation, so much so that some scholars claim it has obscured the language of the First Amendment itself. The debates and tensions surrounding the uses of "separation" as a framework for managing church-state relations gradually gave rise to the reemergence of "neutrality," at first as a legal supplement to separation but eventually as an independent and competing legal paradigm.

To be sure, the general notion of a separation between church and state has an expansive legacy that points to intellectual exchange and political ferment across Europe and North America. Protestant theologians of the Reformation era, most prominently Martin Luther, proposed a doctrine of "two governments," eventually renamed the "two kingdoms" doctrine; U.S. founding father James Madison later pointed to Luther as a leader and visionary in forging distinction between "what is due to Caesar and what is due to God."[7] In the realm of modern political thought, John Locke is often credited with expanding and more thoroughly articulating the notion of separate spheres, especially in his "Letter Concerning Toleration," informed by the European wars on religion, and his social contract theory, with its emphasis on individual liberty of conscience and distinct religious and governmental realms.[8] Locke's writings, too, proved influential in U.S. legal discourse; the First Amendment framework has rightly been characterized as an intermingling of "Protestant and Enlightenment philosophy."[9]

However, separation's terminological significance in U.S. law and government is most closely linked to Thomas Jefferson's invocation of "a wall of separation between church and state" in his 1802 letter to the Danbury Baptist Association.[10] The metaphor of a separation wall suggests a rigid and impermeable barrier that provides protection against intrusion. But if separation walls are rarely (if ever) constructed with both party's best interests equally considered, who or what is the priority for protection?[11] The majority of those who have rallied around Jefferson's invocation of the phrase are primarily concerned with the risks of the religious establishment's intrusion on state affairs.[12] While Jefferson's language was first introduced to the courts in 1879, the wall metaphor rose to prominence and developed newfound significance for proponents of "strong" or "strict" separationism in the landmark 1947 *Everson v. Board of Education* case, which ruled that it was unconstitutional for the State of New Jersey to reimburse transportation funds to the parents of children attending private Catholic school.[13] *Everson* also applied the Establishment Clause to state law and effectively marked the beginning of no aid, strict separationism's legal heyday. As evidenced by court language in *Everson*, constitutionally mandated state neutrality toward religion and partisanship hinged upon the "rigid" enforcement of "complete separation between the state and religion."[14] But despite strong language about impermeable barriers, the court decision suggests that separation is a far shakier entity; church schools could benefit from government services "so separate and so indisputably marked off from the religious function" such as police, fire safety, and public transportation. As Justice Hugo Black concedes, for a "state to be neutral . . . state power is no more to be used so as to handicap religions than it is to favor them."[15]

It was during this period, which spanned until the late 1980s, that the notion of separation between church and state was increasingly intertwined with "legal secularism"—a point that is crucial to the analysis that follows.[16] As Noah Feldman observes in *Divided by God*, legal secularism was positioned as distinct from the "strong secularism" that first surfaced in U.S. political and public discourse; it was strategically framed as a legal position rather than a "general antireligious stance," one that presumably protected the rights of religious minorities by ensuring that religion was decoupled from the supposedly secular spheres of government and politics.[17] In *Everson* but also more pronouncedly in the 1963 *Abington* case and the 1971 *Lemon* case, the notion of secular purpose emerged as a "requirement of constitutionality" to ensure nonestablishment.[18] While secularism itself was not framed as inherently neutral, an overarching secular purpose was understood as vital for ensuring state neutrality toward religion.

However, these legal conditions began to shift in the late 1980s as a so-called new neutrality rose to newfound legal prominence, when the term was increasingly invoked in religion clause cases to justify the distribution of government funds to religious groups and institutions in a manner that would have been inconceivable during the no-aid, strict separation position's heyday. While neutrality was not the only interpretive principle with heightened significance in the so-called postseparationist era, and while some have resisted dichotomizing the neutrality and separationist principles, neutrality and separationism were overwhelmingly framed as competing perspectives, with neutrality cast as separationism's main successor in a slew of legal scholarship that emerged during the 1990s and the following decade.[19]

Of course, neutrality's ascent and strict separationism's decline did not occur in a vacuum. These legal trends abetted and aligned with broader cultural, political, and economic shifts in U.S. society, including the rise of Christian evangelism, increased religious plurality, and the privatization of public sector social services.[20] This period of seismic shifts in U.S. public and political life, famously termed the "culture wars" by James Davidson Hunter, was marked by a series of heated debates over issues including church-state relations, abortion, and gay rights. Hunter frames it as a war between "Progressive" and "Orthodox" voices; Feldman argues that the warring parties, as they coalesced in legislative contexts, are best characterized as the aforementioned "legal secularists" (who bemoaned the "lingering death of separationism") and "values evangelicals"(who increasingly benefited from and strategically wielded the so-called new neutrality to breathe new life into religious entities and institutions).[21] Without isolating or overdetermining neutrality's legal impact, or imposing a coherence upon a term that defies it, we must ask: How did neutrality become so conducive to advancing the agendas of "values evangelicals"?[22] Simply put, neutrality was increasingly framed as an antidiscriminatory principle that ensured "fairness" or "equality" between religious and secular entities and individuals.

In efforts to clarify neutrality's numerous and often contradictory meanings, constitutional law and religious liberty scholars have categorized neutrality into definitional subsets. I will not rehearse all these proposed subcategories here, but a few basic distinctions and fundamental tensions are worth noting. In addition to the "negative" and "positive" senses of neutrality touched upon here, another central distinction is whether state neutrality toward religion should be oriented around treatment or impact.[23] The former type—variously referred to as "formal," "strict," or "facial" neutrality—prohibits government use of religion "as a standard for action or inaction" as well as its use of religious classifications; Philip Kurland famously introduced this definition of strict neutrality in 1961.[24] In contrast, the latter approach—variously framed as "substantive," "positive," and "accommodationist" neutrality—is more overtly concerned with the outcomes or "consequences of state action upon religion."[25] This is a decidedly messier and more protean subset, as it allows for the accommodation or "special treatment" of religion to ensure that the government minimizes "the extent to which it either encourages or discourages" religious beliefs, practices, observances, or any lack thereof.[26] As this form of neutrality rose in prominence, neutrality and equality were increasingly framed as intertwined concepts, to the extent that some legal scholars began to treat them as functionally interchangeable.[27]

The standardization of Justice Sandra Day O'Connor's endorsement test, with its concomitant reframing of the Establishment Clause, was crucial toward popularizing this conception of neutrality. Examining her language also helps attenuate the friction between the secular and the new, positive neutrality. The test was introduced in O'Connor's concurrence to the 1984 *Lynch v. Donnelly* case as a reformulation of the three-pronged Lemon test, which emerged in 1971 during strict separation's heyday as a means of determining the constitutionality of government involvement in and funding for religious entities. According to O'Connor, the Lemon test's so-called purpose prong—"The statute must have a secular legislative purpose"—should be revised to consider "whether the government intends to convey a message of endorsement or disapproval of religion," which O'Connor argued stood at the heart of the Establishment Clause. As she explained: "Endorsement sends a message to nonadherents that they are outsiders, not full members of the political community, and an accompanying message to adherents that they are insiders, favored members of the political community."[28] So while the endorsement test was not inherently pro-religion, it helped shift the terms of debate in a manner that proved enormously fruitful for religious conservatives by reformulating "legal secularism's doctrine of government neutrality toward religion in terms of individual equality."[29] As Feldman observes, "The reason that governments should not get involved in the endorsement or disapproval of religion was that doing so would make some people less equal than others. The goal of government in its engagement with religion should not be secularism, it should be equality."[30] In large part due to the test's influence, positive neutrality increasingly came to replace the "secular" as a guideline for religion clause constitutionality.[31]

To return to the competing senses of neutrality introduced by the OED, for values evangelicals and liberal legal scholars found sympathetic to their claims, neutrality emerged as a mechanism for ameliorating conflict between secular and religious worldviews.[32] Religious values and personhood were perceived as under assault by secularism's unjust hegemony in the public and political arenas. If Jefferson's invocation of the "wall of separation" metaphor served as a rallying cry for those in the secularist camp, politically conservative historical revisionists critical of strict separationism pointed to the metaphor's earliest use by Roger Williams, 150 years prior to Jefferson's adaptation.[33] Williams, the so-called great dissenter and colonial founder of Rhode Island, called for a "hedge or wall of separation between the garden of the church and the wilderness of the world."[34] The emphasis here is upon the religious realm, which requires careful cultivation and protection. To this end, the nonestablishment clause can be understood as allowing for the nonpreferential government support that enables religious life to flourish.[35] In contrast, the warring parties associated with legal secularism—who in the decades since *Everson* have largely moved away from historically driven arguments—condemned the new neutrality as facilitating an unconstitutional intrusion of religion into the public sphere.[36]

This ongoing legal debate reveals that neutrality is itself not neutral, that it stands right at the heart of contemporary juridico-political struggles over the church-state relation. Because of neutrality's persistent connotation of impartiality, its legal definition and persuasiveness can act as a barometer of the dominant cultural norms and political forces that mediate religion-state relations at a given historical moment. Recent high-profile Supreme Court cases such as *Masterpiece Cakeshop v. Colorado Civil Rights Commission* (2018) and *Espinoza v. Montana Department of Revenue* (2020) demonstrate the new neutrality's ongoing success as a juridical paradigm.[37] The religious right continues to argue that the new neutrality ensures that the state is an impartial mediator in a culture war between secularism and religion. But to its critics, the new neutrality's strategic juridical wielding allows the state to be repositioned as a tacit ally of evangelical Christian political movements that are gaining unprecedented access to government power. Rather than a medium for mediation, neutrality has become a weapon of war.

NOTES

1. Rafael Palomino, "Religion and Neutrality: Myth, Principle, and Meaning," *Brigham Young University Law Review* 2011, no. 3 (2011): 657–68.
2. Claudia E. Haupt, *Religion-State Relations in the United States and Germany: The Quest for Neutrality* (New York: Cambridge University Press, 2012), 70.

3. *Oxford English Dictionary*, s.v. "neutrality, n.," accessed September 17, 2018, http://www.oed.com.
4. *OED*, s.v. "neutrality, n."
5. U.S. Constitution, Amend. 1.
6. Ruti Teitel, "A Critique of Religion as Politics in the Public Sphere," *Cornell Law Review* 78, no. 5 (1993): 759.
7. James Madison, *Letters and Other Writings of James Madison* (Philadelphia: J. B. Lippincott, 1865), 242.
8. John Locke, *The Second Treatise of Civil Government and A Letter Concerning Toleration* (Oxford: Blackwell, 1948).
9. Teitel, "Critique of Religion," 759.
10. Thomas Jefferson, "Jefferson's Letter to the Danbury Baptists: The Final Letter, as Sent," *Library of Congress Information Bulletin*, June 1998, accessed August 18, 2020, https://www.loc.gov/loc/lcib/9806/danpre.html.
11. The term *segregation* was also frequently invoked in early discussions of church-state relations, which of course went on to develop deeply troubling and oppressive implications in U.S. racial politics. See Teitel, "Critique of Religion," 756.
12. See, for example, Martha Nussbaum, *Liberty of Conscience: In Defense of America's Tradition of Religious Equality* (New York: Basic Books, 2010); Teitel, "Critique of Religion."
13. Haupt, *Religion-State Relations*, 153.
14. *Everson v. Board of Ed. of Ewing*, 330 U. S. 1 (1947).
15. *Everson v. Board of Ed. of Ewing*, 330 U. S. 1 (1947).
16. Noah Feldman, *Divided by God: America's Church-State Problem—and What We Should Do about It* (New York: Farrar, Straus and Giroux, 2005), 182.
17. Feldman, *Divided by God*, 165.
18. Feldman, *Divided by God*, 181.
19. Ira C. Lupu, "Lingering Death of Separationism," *George Washington Law Review* 62 (1994): 230-279; Stephen V. Monsma, *Church-State Relations in Crisis: Debating Neutrality* (Lanham, MD: Rowman and Littlefield, 2002). To be sure, the scholarly emphasis on neutrality did not entirely subside in the decades that followed, as evidenced by publications such as Andrew Koppelman's *Defending American Religious Neutrality* (Cambridge, MA: Harvard University Press, 2013).
20. Monsma, *Church-State Relations in Crisis*, 5; Feldman, *Divided by God*; Teitel, "Critique of Religion."
21. James Davison Hunter, *Culture War: The Struggle to Define America* (New York: Basic Books, 1991) 43–45; Feldman, *Divided by God*, 185; Lupu, "Lingering Death of Separationism."
22. Feldman, *Divided by God*, 182.
23. Palomino, "Religion and Neutrality," 663; Douglas Laycock, "Formal, Substantive, and Disaggregated Neutrality toward Religion," *DePaul Law Review* 39, no. 4 (1990): 998. See also Rex Ahdar, "Is Secularism Neutral?," *Ratio Juris* 26, no. 3 (September 2013): 404–29.
24. Philip B. Kurland, "Of Church and State and the Supreme Court," *University of Chicago Law Review* 29 (1961): 1.

25 Ahdar, "Is Secularism Neutral?" 414.
26 Laycock, "Formal, Substantive, and Disaggregated Neutrality," 1003; see also Nussbaum, *Liberty of Conscience*, 20.
27 Monsma, *Church-State Relations in Crisis*.
28 *Lynch v. Donnelly*, 465 U.S. 668 (1984).
29 Feldman, *Divided by God*, 203.
30 Feldman, *Divided by God*, 203–4.
31 Feldman, *Divided by God*, 205.
32 Nussbaum, *Liberty of Conscience*, 20.
33 There has been an "upsurge" in politically conservative historical revisionism since the mid-1980s. See Steven K. Green, "Bad History: The Lure of History in Establishment Clause Adjudication," *Notre Dame Law Review* 81 (2006): 1718.
34 Roger Williams, *The Complete Writings of Roger Williams* (New York: Russell and Russell, 1963), 392.
35 To be sure, some scholars have subsumed these interpretations under the common rubric of separationism. See Teitel, "Critique of Religion."
36 For a helpful overview and critique of the use of historical analysis in juridical decision-making, see Green, "Bad History."
37 *Masterpiece Cakeshop, Ltd. v. Colorado Civil Rights Comm'n*, 584 U. S. ___ (2018); *Espinoza v. Montana Dept. of Revenue*, 591 U. S. ___ (2020).

Keyword: Science
JOHN VIGNAUX SMYTH

The complex relations between religion(s) and science(s) may be conveniently divided into three categories of contemporary interest, especially in the so-called West.

Contemporary Religious Perspectives on the Sciences

Religious beliefs sometimes conflict with scientific theories: Christian, Muslim, and Jewish "creationists," for example, question Darwinian evolution. As counterpoint to Richard Dawkins's *The God Delusion*, "fundamentalists" of this sort may be said to propose an often (if not always) unconvincing kind of epistemological *tu quoque*: "the Fundamentalist Science Delusion" (or science as a false idol).

On the other side of the contemporary epistemological fence are what Barbara Herrnstein Smith calls "a set of efforts, primarily by scientifically knowledgeable theologians but also by some theologically inclined scientists, to reveal a cognitively satisfying consonance between the accounts of nature given in the natural sciences and traditional Christian belief."[1]

Such an attempted reconciliation between science and religion comes perhaps even more naturally to religions that are not theistic. Though the current Dalai Lama, for example, still defends Buddhist ideas of reincarnation on what he calls logical grounds, he also writes: "The reality of the world today is that grounding ethics in religion is no longer adequate. This is why I am increasingly convinced that the time has come to find a way of thinking about spirituality and ethics beyond religion altogether."[2]

This attitude may be compared and contrasted to that of Hindu claims, associated politically with the resurgence of Indian nationalism in the early twentieth century, as to the scientific or rational character of certain foundational Hindu texts. Instead of the tu quoque defense (you also are a fundamentalist believer), this might be called the *ego quoque* one (I am as scientific as you).

In addition to the mainly English-speaking "new natural theologians" treated in Smith's *Natural Reflections*, we may cite a number of European thinkers—in philosophy, the social sciences, and the relatively new field of "science studies"—who also see no necessary contradiction between science and religion. Some of these are atheists or agnostics, but others are more or less overtly religious, such as the French Catholics—diverse both in theoretical method and religious orientation—Bruno Latour and René Girard. When philosopher Michel Serres calls Girard "the Darwin of the human sciences," for instance, he means that Girard's sacrificial and in principle evolutionary theory of religion is no less scientific in aim than Darwin, and by no means necessarily claims to be "deeper than Darwin" (to cite the title of one of Smith's Anglican "new natural theologians").[3]

Latour, very different from Serres or Girard, inventor of Actor Network Theory and one of the pioneers of "science studies," is also worth mentioning as a church-going Catholic—seemingly a rather eccentric one—whose studies in the history, sociology, and epistemology of science might seem radically secular were it not for his disarmingly confessional religiosity. He is the sort of Christian who does not insist on using the term "god" (if the word is deemed no longer useful), and the sort of well-informed student of science who proposes a complex kind of epistemological symmetry between scientific "facts" and religious "fetishes." This is of course not to say that Western science is a mere fetish (a rationalist/colonialist myth) but to insist on the epistemic dignity of so-called fetishes (related etymologically to [arti]facts, or *faits*) themselves. The realm of science, in these cases, is expanded rather than limited to "make room" for religion.

The Supposed Incompatibility between Scientific Reason and Religious Faith

We have cited Dawkins as a conspicuous proponent of what anthropologist Stanley Jeyaraja Tambiah calls "the alleged incompatibility between science and religion in the West."[4] Along similar evolutionary and purportedly iconoclastic lines, as their titles suggest, are Daniel Dennett's *Breaking the Spell* and Pascal Boyer's *Religion Explained*. Yet if religious belief and ritual are thoroughly "natural" because grounded in once useful cognitive and adaptive mechanisms, as such authors more or less plausibly argue, this of course does not decide the question of whether religious belief and/or activity is now generally pernicious (as Dawkins and Dennett assert) or still perhaps evolutionarily useful (as argued, for example, by Scott Atran's *In Gods We Trust: The Evolutionary Landscape of Religion*).[5] Dawkins asserts that feeling pity for someone who cannot reciprocate and is not part of the group, or sexual desire for someone who cannot reproduce, are both "[evolutionary] misfirings, Darwinian mistakes: *blessed*, precious mistakes."[6] The fact that "God" is condemned, by contrast, as a generally malign delusion depends in part on the extent to which feeling pity and desire can be regarded as hygienically detached from (or alternatively reconciled with) epistemology, since Dawkins presumably means that these "mistakes" are not merely delusions, however deluded their conscious justification (religious or not), but "blessed" feelings ultimately compatible with justifiable (scientific) beliefs.

Smith sensibly sums up the contemporary Anglo-American (or, as Tambiah generalizes it, "Western") impasse between science and religious belief as follows: "precisely to the extent that scholars studying religion reject the absolutist, exclusivist, self-privileging conceptions of truth shared by theologians like [John] Haught" (who argues incorrectly that evolutionary accounts of religion are necessarily self-refuting because scientific beliefs must, on this account, also be a "mere" product of evolution) and "scientists like Dawkins" (who dubiously seems to deny "gods" any epistemic value other than falsity, delusion), "the more likely they are to register both the pragmatic, aesthetic, and/or epistemic value of various religious ideas and practices and also the forms of human ingenuity, artistry, and imagination involved in their past and ongoing elaboration."[7]

The Scientific Study of Religions (and of Sciences)

The weakness of many evolutionary accounts of religion lies not in being logically self-refuting but in sometimes conspicuous lack of self-reflexivity—which indeed "makes them vulnerable to the theologian's taunt of '*tu quoque*'" and sometimes also results, ironically enough (given the traditional opposition between natural science and supernatural religion), in claims that "given our evolved cognitive dispositions, religious beliefs are 'natural' for humans while scientific ideas are 'unnatural.'"[8] There is also a tendency in the "new naturalism" (Smith's phrase naming an intellectual tradition linked by her to sociobiologist E. O. Wilson's *Consilience: The Unity of Knowledge*) to discount the claims to scientificity or rationality found in accounts of religion in the social sciences and humanities in favor of a theory of science or rationality generally modeled rather narrowly on contemporary evolutionary biology and cognitive neuroscience.[9] The contemporary science-religion debate thus often provides a particular instance of the so-called two cultures divide (which has little necessarily to do with religion), so that Dawkins finds time in *The God Delusion* to attack the French sociologist/philosopher Michel Foucault, for example, not of course for being a defender of God (indeed none of Foucault's highly critical views of religion or anything else are cited) but for being an "icon of haute francophonyism"—valuing widely respected (if perhaps often incorrect) French philosophers being, for Dawkins, presumably a bit like believing in gods.[10] The debate also reflects, more generally, the thorny "fact/value" distinction that gained prominence in the twentieth century as a way of distinguishing science from (mere) philosophy.

However, at least since Émile Durkheim's *The Elementary Forms of Religious Life*, a foundational or at least important text in the sociology and anthropology of religion, it has been commonplace to point out that the study of "religion" is much larger than the study of belief in gods (which comprise a later historical phase) since it also entails "the sacred" more generally, especially sacrificial ritual and other forms of more or less worldwide practice (whatever the specific beliefs attached to them).[11] Tambiah, for example, argues that "from a general anthropological standpoint the distinctive feature of religion as a generic concept lies not in the domain of belief and its 'rational accounting' of the workings of the universe, but in a special awareness of the transcendent, and the acts of symbolic communication that attempt to realize that awareness and live by its promptings."[12]

There is no space here to survey the vast field of supposedly scientific studies of the sacred. We may conclude, however, by emphasizing that some of the most interesting contemporary perspectives—both theist and atheist—are concerned to demystify the notion that modern so-called secular behavior and theory have somehow hygienically transcended what Jean-Pierre Dupuy calls "the mark of the sacred." (Dupuy includes in his *Mark of the Sacred*, for example, the forms of pseudo-transcendence—conveniently imaged by Adam

Smith's "invisible hand"—characteristic of classical and neoclassical economics, among other modes of secular reasoning).[13] Others, such as the anthropologist Michael Taussig, following Max Horkheimer and Theodor Adorno's *Dialectic of Enlightenment*, have also argued that the Enlightenment demystification of the sacred, including "magic," is itself productive of new forms of mystification.[14] Indeed, Taussig provocatively claims that "magic and technique, as in scientific technique, flow into one another, magic, we might say, being the highest form of science."[15]

A perhaps less provocative way of putting this would be to say that if the social sciences were scientific in the sense usually ascribed to the natural ones, they would be able to predict (including, of course, influence) human behavior to a significant degree, as both ancient magic and modern hypnotism try more or less successfully to do. One of the key frontiers of modern medicine, for example, lies in its attempt to understand the so-called placebo/nocebo effect—a scientifically quantified phenomenon of enormous importance that evidently depends on both belief and ritual (including the therapeutic and research techniques and role-playings associated with medicine itself). Thus while some scientists and philosophers have been tempted to dismiss religion as a mere placebo—"the opium of the people"—it may be responded that in scientific medicine as well as unscientific religion "the word" sometimes really is "made flesh." In any case, current research has demonstrated beyond any doubt that as long as we fail to take the spectacular efficacies and dizzying complexities of placebo/nocebo effects (often more powerful than any opiates or even surgeries) in epistemological earnest, we will fail to have a plausible science not only of religion but also of science.[16]

Perhaps it is in this general spirit that the formally atheist Chinese government has recently remarkably funded no fewer than eighteen centers for the study of the theist, or at least deist, logician Alfred North Whitehead, author of *Process and Reality*.[17]

NOTES

1. Barbara Herrnstein Smith, *Natural Reflections: Human Cognition at the Nexus of Science and Religion*, Terry Lectures (New Haven, CT: Yale University Press, 2009), 95.
2. Dalai Lama, Facebook post, September 10, 2012, https://www.facebook.com/DalaiLama/.
3. See John Haught, *Deeper than Darwin: The Prospect for Religion in the Age of Evolution* (Boulder, CO: Westview, 2003); and René Girard, *Violence and the Sacred*, trans. Patrick Gregory (Baltimore: Johns Hopkins University Press, 1977). Michel Serres's description of Girard—"Je vous nomme désormais, 'le nouveau Darwin des sciences

humaines'"—can be found in René Girard and Michel Serres, *Le Tragique et la pitié: Discours de réception de René Girard à l'Académie française et réponse de Michel Serres* (Paris: Le Pommier, 2007), 63. Girard's hypothesis, in brief, is that the evolution of animal into human mimesis (imitation) gave rise to scapegoating mechanisms that were ritualized in sacrifice (etymologically "to make sacred") and in turn became the origin of the sacred in general. Though far from Richard Dawkins in many respects, Girard's evolutionary perspective is similar in emphasizing how "memes" and mimetic behavior supplement or even supplant genetic copying in evolution.

4   Stanley Jeyaraja Tambiah, *Magic, Science, Religion and the Scope of Rationality* (Cambridge: Cambridge University Press, 1990), 152.
5   See Daniel C. Dennett, *Breaking the Spell: Religion as a Natural Phenomenon* (New York: Viking, 2006); Pascal Boyer, *Religion Explained: The Evolutionary Origin of Religious Thought* (New York: Basic Books, 2001); and Scott Atran, *In Gods We Trust: The Evolutionary Landscape of Religion* (Oxford: Oxford University Press, 2002).
6   Richard Dawkins, *The God Delusion* (New York: Mariner Books, 2008), 326, emphasis added.
7   Smith, *Natural Reflections*, 115.
8   Smith, *Natural Reflections*, xxx.
9   Smith, *Natural Reflections*, 31–32. See also Edward O. Wilson, *Consilience: The Unity of Knowledge* (New York: Knopf, 1998).
10 Dawkins, *God Delusion*, 514.
11 Émile Durkheim, *The Elementary Forms of Religious Life*, trans. Karen E. Fields (New York: Free Press, 1995).
12 Tambiah, *Magic, Science*, 6. I cite this passage to illustrate views of religion that emphasize symbolic practice and communication over doctrinal or metaphysical claims, not to endorse its specific (rather unclear) appeal to "special awareness of the transcendent."
13 Jean-Pierre Dupuy, *The Mark of the Sacred* (Stanford: Stanford University Press, 2013). For his discussion of economics and the "invisible hand," see 5. The problem of how to distinguish between rationality and ritual is also discussed in "Rationality and Ritual: The Babylon Lottery," in Dupuy, *Mark of the Sacred*, 125–29.
14 Theodor Adorno and Max Horkheimer, *Dialectic of Enlightenment: Philosophical Fragments*, ed. Gunzelin Schmid Noerr and trans. Edmund Jephcott (Stanford, CA: Stanford University Press, 2002).
15 Michael Taussig, "Viscerality, Faith, and Skepticism," in *Magic and Modernity: Interfaces of Revelation and Concealment*, ed. Birgit Meyer and Peter Pels (Stanford, CA: Stanford University Press, 2003), 306.
16 See, for example, Arthur D. and Elaine Shapiro, *The Powerful Placebo: From Ancient Priest to Modern Physician* (Baltimore: Johns Hopkins University Press, 1997). I am suggesting not that religious effects or insights can be equated with placebo/nocebo phenomena but that even if they could, such phenomena are both efficacious and (so far) mysterious.
17 Alfred North Whitehead, *Process and Reality: An Essay in Cosmology* (New York: Macmillan, 1929).

1. STRICT NEUTRALITY RECONSIDERED
Religion and Political Belonging in the Netherlands
POOYAN TAMIMI ARAB

All persons in the Netherlands shall be treated equally in equal circumstances. Discrimination on the grounds of religion, belief, political opinion, race or sex or on any other grounds whatsoever shall not be permitted.—Constitution of the Kingdom of the Netherlands, Article 1

In the face of majority hostility toward Muslim citizens in Europe today, some political philosophers and social scientists have begun to question whether the promise of equal rights of religious freedom, as for example guaranteed in Article 1 of the Dutch Constitution, is an adequate way to protect religious minorities. At best, they argue, the neutrality enshrined in many European treaties and constitutions fails to deliver the grand promise of universal equality. At worst, it may actually enable bigotry and polarization or even facilitate persecution. This argument, which has been applied to other troubled regions of the world, is now being brought to bear on affluent European countries such as the Netherlands as well.[1] To counter majority bias against Muslim citizens, argue several prominent scholars of political secularism, European countries should relinquish the ideal of strict neutrality in favor of the superior conception of accommodation. This is less a rejection of European political secularism per se than it is an argument that political secularism should be sensitized to context. By attending to local situations and needs, contextual political secularism can go beyond merely treating all citizens equally and allow exemptions to general laws, or even actively support (or be hostile to) a religious practice as part of an affirmative action policy.[2]

My own understanding of political secularism is heavily indebted to these critiques and recommendations. I subscribe to the idea that Europe should, ideally speaking, cultivate greater sensitivity to citizens' divergent religious and spiritual aspirations, given its diverse peoples and unequal distributions of power. Treating everyone equally, after all, is not identical to ensuring that all religious citizens are being treated as equals. However, such critiques do not unmask the strict neutrality provision once and for all as *schijnneutraliteit*, as it is put in Dutch, as a mere appearance of neutrality without significant substance. While a measure of accommodation may help equalize religious liberty, there are important reasons it should not de facto, de jure, and therefore conceptually supersede the strict neutrality paradigm.

I present my argument in three steps. First, using Martha Nussbaum's *Liberty of Conscience* (2008) and *The New Religious Intolerance* (2012), I criticize the transition from strict neutrality to accommodation with the Dutch situation in mind. Working as she does in the Anglo-American context, Nussbaum underestimates the particular challenges that need to be considered in the context of Dutch or European political secularism. Second, in reflecting on Islam and belonging in the Netherlands, I propose that political belonging should be separated from a host of cultural forms—local, urban, national, transnational, civilizational. I do so in response to the Dutch public debate in which belonging is frequently seen in a rather "comprehensive," culturally thick sense, which can be diagnosed to be infected with Romantic notions of attachment to specific cultural street- and soundscapes.[3] My defense of strict neutrality can therefore be best understood by assessing the exercised right to Islamic "sensational forms" in the public domain, such as sartorial practices, purpose-built mosques, and amplified calls to prayer.[4] These sensational forms prompt intense feelings and are perceived as matters of belonging and the politics of home.[5] Third, I argue that strict neutrality is decisive in conceptualizing the civic right to the specific sensational form in practice and therefore secures political belonging. Prima facie, some cases are more convincing than others: amplified calls to prayer are legally protected by the 1980s Public Manifestations

Act, while Islamic face veiling is in the process of being banned by the Dutch government.[6] Nevertheless, the rigorous implementation of equal rights remains a primary condition for treating Muslims as equal citizens in place.

From Neutrality to Accommodation

In her defense of accommodation, Nussbaum begins by identifying strict neutrality with John Locke's political liberalism. Although her focus is on the development of Lockean neutrality in the United States, the liberal tradition is highly relevant to Dutch history as well. Locke wrote and published *Epistola de Tolerantia* in Holland in 1685, in exile, and was adamant about equal civil rights to both beliefs and what he termed public worship (*sacra publica*), even as this equality did not extend as far as we think it should today, to Catholics and atheists as well. The equal rights of religious commitment and practice were immediately propagated in the English and Dutch translations of the letter concerning toleration but also in the French language, which was highly relevant given the international European refugee crisis ensuing Louis XIV's dissolution of official toleration of Protestant Huguenots. Hundreds of thousands of people fled religious persecution; many landed in Holland, England, and as far as South Africa and Suriname. According to *Merriam-Webster*, the French *réfugié* was used for the first time in the English language in that same year. Refugees, in other words, were part of the transnational conceptualization context of a civil right to be tolerated, understood as more than mere informal toleration, to secure "equal justice," in the wording of Locke.[7]

Today, the idea that all should be treated equally regardless of their religion, including refugees who are granted citizenship rights, remains central to the principal understanding of the "separation of church and state" (*scheiding van kerk en staat*). Many Dutch citizens resist the populist notion that "Judeo-Christian" practices should be privileged above those of other religions, especially Islam.[8] As Dutch essayist Rob Wijnberg put it in a discussion of the so-called burqa ban: "Equal monks, equal hoods. Whether that hood is an Islamic dress code or not."[9] The sixteenth-century proverb *gelijke monniken gelijke kappen* (equal monks, equal hoods), first written down by a follower of Erasmus and a colloquial way of expressing the value of strict neutrality, is extended by Wijnberg to Islam as well. The basic idea is that bans of sartorial practices violate Article 1 of the Constitution, the prohibition of discrimination—for example, when the ban explicitly targets the face veil for being Islamic.[10] Scholars such as Nussbaum, however, go further than Wijnberg by disagreeing with the rigid view that a lawgiver can or should be indifferent toward the spiritual commitments of religious citizens, especially of minority religions. The state should instead care about citizens' deeply held beliefs or cherished practices and avoid the risk of benefiting majority religious practices and assumptions about what counts as religion to begin with. In the Netherlands, once conceived as a Protestant Fatherland, such worries about bias are warranted by a long history of persecution, or milder forms of suppression, of religious dissenters, Catholics, Jews, but also enslavement of Afro-Caribbeans.[11] Given this historical background, in which extravagant ritualism especially of Catholics was rejected in favor of an idealized, Protestant sobriety, systemic declarations of religion and color-blindness toward uncommon religious garbs such as the black Islamic face veil should be Argus-eyed. As it happened, in the nineteenth century, Protestants were willing to forego their own right to wear religious garbs in public so that Catholics could not enjoy the same privilege, a precedent that shows how "gelijke moniken," "gelijke kappen" can be accepted in name while harboring discriminating intentions.

It is moreover questionable to what extent refugees today are protected against racism and the fear of religious others by strict notions of treating all the same.[12] In the footsteps of the Huguenots from Calais to Dover, Eritreans, for example, make up the largest group to seek refuge in the United Kingdom in 2015, and the second-largest group to reach the Netherlands. Will their inclusion be part and parcel of what equality is about or seen as a pressure on "our" cherished value of equality that "they" threaten to destabilize, as in the words of the leader of the currently ruling Christian Democratic Appeal?[13]

To counter the persistent threat of white, nativist, secularist, or Protestant bias, Nussbaum writes that there is another still relevant tradition of conceptualizing equality, which she views as distinctly American in origin and which she traces back to Roger Williams's advocacy of religious freedom in the seventeenth century. Transcending strict neutrality, the tradition of accommodation allows "exceptions to general laws for conscience's sake, up to the point where the person's conduct would threaten peace and public safety."[14] Nussbaum's position is nuanced, insisting that judges may legitimately differ over an interpretive preference for either strict neutrality or a softer openness to accommodation. Her own informed opinion is that the latter position is "superior" because "it reaches subtle forms of discrimination that are ubiquitous in majoritarian democratic life."[15] This view perhaps has deeper historical roots in pluralist American traditions than in European nation-states formed by the exclusivist dictum *cuius regio eius religio*—uniting monarch, territory, and people under one dominant faith—but the practice of accommodation is not alien to Dutch governance in more recent times.

For instance, in 2006 a law was passed that requires all citizens to take out health insurance, by contracting one of the insurance policies offered by various companies. Several thousand orthodox Calvinists demanded an exemption from this general rule on the basis of liberty of conscience. Their position was summed up in the *Reformed Daily* newspaper as follows: "A conscientious objector [*een gemoedsbezwaarde*] is of the opinion that taking out insurances contradicts God's providence. The Lord governs all things and nothing in this life happens by coincidence. Prosperity and misfortune come from God's Fatherly hand. Christians may not attempt to escape God's governance with insurances."[16] In response, the government chose to accommodate the conscientious objection to insurance and offered the possibility of officially recognizing their special status. Note that accommodation in this scheme differs from Dutch policies of tolerating misconduct (*gedoogbeleid*) because the lawgiver recognizes the right of the conscientious objector and does not pragmatically turn a blind eye to his persona and actions.[17] This is realized while the average Dutch citizen—millions of whom do not identify as sincere Protestant believers—simply sees these deep spiritual commitments to providence as something out of another time.[18] To protect such religious minorities against secularist majority bias, Nussbaum believes that their practices should be limited only by serious concerns about public order and health or a compelling state interest rather than a dogmatic concern for treating all citizens in exactly the same manner. The complexity of a society such as the Netherlands, which has undergone both rapid dechurching (*ontkerkelijking*) and religious diversification in the twentieth century, calls for a nuanced approach and sensitivity to individuals' deeply felt spiritual convictions, such as orthodox Protestant *beliefs* in providence, and to relatively new *practices* of lighting a fire inside a Hindu temple, which may go against general fire safety laws. Muslim claims to accommodation in Nussbaum's sense, however, are clearly frowned upon, as in a recent case involving the Rotterdam police, which chose to ignore the 2017 advice of the Netherlands Institute for Human Rights to respect a Muslim policewoman's request to wear the hijab on duty.[19]

To adjudicate between strict neutrality or accommodation in response to these practical situations, Nussbaum launches a broader criticism of justice as a purely mathematical function or a mechanical operation, which receives input on a given case and produces an output based on an automated process. Her argument echoes that of Aristotle, who explains that an overly mathematical conception of justice flattens the tension between particular cases and general principles.[20] In *Nichomachean Ethics*, the great philosopher contrasts his own view with (an interpretation of) the Pythagoreans: "There are some who even think that what is just is simple reciprocity, as the Pythagoreans maintained, because they defined justice simply as having done to one what one has done to another."[21] Put simply, justice cannot be reduced to equal treatment. By introducing relative proportionality, the Aristotelian perspective instead requires general laws to be *interpreted* with specific cases in mind. This interpretive rather than mechanical process requires a living, thinking, and feeling person, someone whose capacity to judge is based on a never-ending process of interaction between rational speech and attentive listening to peers as well as to those without the same powers of speech, who do deserve to be heard. It is important to note, however, that Aristotle does not dispense with universal principles but brings these into dialogue with specific situations. Similarly, political secularism's ideals of strict neutrality and universality remain decisive, without going so far as to resurrect a general concept of secularism as a "scientific doctrine" in the hubristic spirit of Auguste Comte's universal history.[22] The postsecularist understanding that there are multiple, contingently formed, political secularisms, which do not follow a teleological historical trajectory, should, in line with this view, be combined with an appreciation of twentieth-century legal convergence and homogenization processes, resulting in the international standard of religious freedom as a basic human right.[23] Nussbaum's view conforms to this globally shared view, as she does not suggest that sensitivity to particular religious demands entails a departure from liberty and equality as general, overarching, guiding principles. Her view can be better grasped by the distinction she makes between a thin and cold Pythagorean or Lockean "equality" versus a rich "substantive equality" in accordance with organic complexity pulsating with life.[24]

No doubt, the step from neutrality toward accommodation, or from equality to substantive equality, is an elegant one. Yet it can be easily misunderstood as one perspective being subsumed in and expanded by another. Such a picture detracts from the value Nussbaum does attribute to the stricter perspective of neutrality in the European context.

Belonging in an Age of Enduring Civilizational Incarceration

In her analysis of neutrality, Nussbaum's main concern is to separate political belonging from thick, exclusionary notions of cultural belonging. To her, the admixture of the two in considerations of religious liberty is something rather foreign and regressive: "Europeans are still inclined to think of nationhood as a matter of blood, soil, and religious heritage."[25] A dozen years ago, the British

American philosopher Simon Critchley described the predicaments of Europe in similar terms worth citing at length. Our reality, he wrote, reveals

> violent injustice here and around the world; it shows growing social and economic inequalities here and around the world; it shows that the difference between what goes on here and around the world is increasingly fatuous. It shows the populations of the well-fed West governed by fear of outsiders, whose current names are "terrorist," "immigrant," "refugee" or "asylum seeker." It shows populations turning inward towards some reactionary and xenophobic conception of their purported identity, something which is happening in a particularly frightening manner all across Europe at present.[26]

A decade later, Critchley's pessimistic worldview allows him to see the regressive possibility of Brexit as enabled by "the majority of the people of England (but not of Scotland or Northern Ireland) [who] voted against immigration because, to put it brutally, they simply don't like foreigners and very many of them seem to be simply racist."[27] Simultaneously, between 2011 and 2017, the Syrian conflict alone pushed one million people to seek refuge, rights, and sustenance in Europe, being accommodated disproportionally by Sweden and Germany.[28] In the Netherlands, politician Geert Wilders promised to "make the Netherlands great again," in the spirit of then president-elect Donald Trump, by closing national borders for these refugees. Not coincidentally, in 2016 Wilders was convicted by a Dutch court for violating the first article of the Netherlands Constitution—the prohibition of discrimination—for hate speech against citizens of Moroccan descent. Nevertheless, his party program's relevance has not waned, including the unconstitutional proposal to stop further mosque construction. Meanwhile, leaders of other political parties, including the Socialist Party, the Labor Party, and the Liberal Party, all subscribe to lighter versions of European xenophobia. They make public demands such as "participation contracts" from refugees, immigrants, and their children; and defend "progressive patriotism" but also wish to protect "Dutch workers" and "Dutch values" first. Frans Timmermans, former minister of foreign affairs and the current first vice president of the European Commission, orated in 2014 that "the nationalism of today is not militarist, not by definition reactionary, not by definition right-wing, and not by definition xenophobic."[29] The then minister of health, Edith Schippers, added in 2016 that "our culture is much better than all others."[30] In her Freedom Lecture (Vrijheidslezing), she defended the Netherlands as standing for liberty, as opposed to Muslim refugees, who should adopt the Dutch ways.[31] Whoever cannot accept these freedoms "does not belong here." Strikingly, the word "culture" (*cultuur*) was used ten times in the lecture, in contrast with the words for "citizen" or "citizenship" (*burger, burgerschap*), which were not named once. When speaking of refugees, she ventilated that they come to the Netherlands because "our culture is so much better for all these people, that they risk their lives to get here. For the freedoms, security and economic opportunities that our culture offers them." It is hard to miss the function of the word "culture" here, creating a sharp difference between the Dutch and the non-Western rest. The possibility of belonging is culturalized in this vision of freedom and self-congratulatory, superior, Western cultures versus the inferior cultures of Muslim refugees, but the value of political rights independent of cultural identifications is purposefully ignored. There are other views, fortunately, such as former minister of justice Ernst Hirsch-Ballin's erudite analysis of refugees' right to be citizens, but these receive less publicity in comparison with public intellectuals who defend the "liberating" potential of national borders.[32]

The contemporary nationalist landscape not only hinders Europe's promise of multicultural belonging for citizens of South American, African, and Asian backgrounds.[33] It also shows the utmost importance of citizenship as political belonging, disentangled from cultural belonging and guaranteeing a minimal set of equal rights applied strictly and equally in the face of backlash from local groups with "not in my backyard" mentalities and the populist politicians and intellectuals who support them.

The construction of mosques by citizens with a Turkish migration background, the largest Muslim constituents in the Netherlands and in Germany, is well suited to clarify the idea of disentangling political and cultural or religious belonging. The recently opened Western Mosque in Amsterdam, for instance, reveals multilayered, sometimes clashing, sometimes overlapping, forms of belonging. Before the building's opening in April 2016, I gave a public presentation on amplified calls to prayer in the Netherlands, explaining that the Constitution protects such practices.[34] One of the Western Mosque's young and active board members, Ismail, responded by showing me a promotion video in which a muezzin climbs the stairs of the Amsterdam mosque and recites the *adhan* (call to prayer) for all to hear.[35] After the opening, the mosque did not actually broadcast the call as other mosques do in the Netherlands but announced the wish to do so in the near future. Since there is no permit requirement, the government's only recommended action is to make an announcement before amplification. For Ismail, the call would "complete" the new building, making it a true pendant of the seventeenth-century Western Church's daily chimes in the city center. The mosque, in other words, attaches him to the city of Amsterdam. It is named after an important church and built with red bricks that are said (by journalists, mosque representatives, and local residents) to remind one of the surrounding Amsterdam School architecture of the early twentieth century. The Islamic house of worship is thus publicized and imagined as expanding a Dutch tradition, functioning as a symbol of both "multiculturalism" and "integration" into the Netherlands, or what could be called "multicultural nationalism."[36] Some of its supporters went so far as describing it as "the most beautiful mosque of Western Europe."[37]

Next to a cultural and religious manifestation of Turkish Muslim belonging to a European nation's capital, for Ismail, the mosque also plays a role in shaping a sense of political belonging as an equal Dutch citizen. Mosque representatives like himself sometimes stress their equal rights as citizens, and at other times they demand equality on the basis of cultural belonging to the city and to the Netherlands as a nation. The same mosque chairman will speak, for instance, of "equal rights" (*gelijke rechten*) and "equal citizenship" (*gelijke burgerschap*) but—since nativist discourse is ever-present—make appeals beyond formal rights too: "We have been here for fifty years and it is *therefore* our right to publicly practice our religion."[38]

The Western Mosque is at the same time built in a neo-Ottoman style and experienced by Ismail as "a bit of Istanbul in Amsterdam."[39] The call to prayer likewise serves to maintain and renew a specifically Turkish identity in the Netherlands. For elders, it can arouse nostalgia for a youth spent in Anatolia, but the adhan is also part of contemporary politics in the Republic of Turkey, where in the twenty-first century, especially since the protests of 2013, the secular and religious divide has deepened once again. Such oppositions between the secular and the religious, and between Dutch citizens of Christian Armenian and Muslim Turkish ethnic origins, are strongly felt in the Netherlands as well.[40] The Western Mosque's different name in Turkish points to these divides: Ayasofya Camii, after the great Hagia Sophia in Istanbul, a site of regular secular-religious and Christian-Muslim contestation. No surprise, then, that just three months after hearing the first call to prayer inside the mosque in Amsterdam, Ismail rejoiced as the adhan was, for the first time in almost a century, heard inside the magnificent namesake in Istanbul itself. Turned into a museum by order of Mustafa Kemal Atatürk in 1935, the call inside the tourist attraction angered Turkish secularists but also the Greek Ministry of Foreign Affairs, which prefers it to be a heritage site rather than a mosque.[41] Enamored by the vision of a glorious Ottoman past, Ismail, then in Amsterdam, expressed his joy on Facebook: "After 85 years the call to prayer has been heard once again in the Ayasofya Mosque in Istanbul, praise be to Allah. May He grant us all the possibility of praying there." Such enthusiasm is part of a collective effervescence and surging Ottomania—an idealized, kitsch revaluation of former Ottoman glory.[42] European exclusion along cultural, religious, and racial lines thus meets well-organized transnational Turkish nationalism, marked by an ominous political preference for the authority figure of President Recep Tayyip Erdoğan.[43]

A strong sense of "us" and "them" between Turkish Europeans and others is doubly reinforced across small towns and cities in Western Europe, when notions of identity and belonging acquire additional civilizational status divided along religious lines—European and Christian, or Ottoman and Islamic.[44] These are violent illusions, we have been warned for years, that are "incarcerating people within the enclosure of a singular identity."[45] But the power of illusions endures, entrapping the senses of belonging on multiple levels. For a young Turkish Dutch man, there is no contradiction between striving for greater cultural and political belonging in the Netherlands while cultivating Ottoman civilizational pride or investing in Turkish nationalist sentiments.

In these highly specific, contingent situations, the notion of political belonging is very helpful as it allows one to unapologetically defend all minority citizens' basic rights, without adopting an uncritical stance toward any group's exclusivist orientations. Nothing hurts liberal democracy's ideal standard of reasonable public debate more than constantly questioning a minority's basic rights, such as the rights to construct houses of worship or to sound religion. Theoretical evaluations of political secularism's possibilities and deficiencies, between either strict neutrality or accommodation, should therefore avoid taking reified, exclusivist conceptions of cultural belonging for granted, nor base the limits of acceptable religious sensational forms on assumptions about the national "spirit." The normative aim of political secularism today should not be to foster (multi)cultural integration, nor to hinder deeply felt emotions of transnational belonging. Likewise, the principle of strict neutrality is not an instrument of cultural integration or social cohesion but first and foremost tasked with securing political belonging and the realization of equal civic rights for all. Strict neutrality put this way is a morally minimalist principle but with substantial effects on public Islamic presence in European Union member states with significant Muslim minority populations.

Equal Rights Contested

Is the strict neutrality I speak of really practiced broadly? Martha Nussbaum thinks not, or not sufficiently, if we consider Europe as a whole. Her view of the continent as nationalist and retrograde, as exemplified by the Romanticist and exclusivist German use of the terms *Abendland* (Occident, Evening Land) and *Heimat* (homeland) versus a cosmopolitan ideal type of American political secularism, can easily prompt a defensive response from my side of the Atlantic. She looks to Europe and finds, among others, a 2009 Swiss minaret ban, and a 2010 French ban targeting the Islamic face veil. These are instances, Nussbaum writes, of Europeans neglecting "even the demands of the weaker Lockean position," that is, of basic equal rights.[46] In the French case, an idea of neutrality is upheld in name, since the law is not phrased explicitly as against a certain kind of Islamic dress but of concealing one's face in public space (*la dissimulation du visage dans l'espace public*). In Switzerland, however, the law bluntly states that "the construction of minarets is forbidden" (*Der Bau von Minaretten ist verboten*).[47] In the Netherlands too, the minimalist Lockean position of strict neutrality is constantly contested and under negotiation, if not outright rejected. The issue at stake is in a great many cases nothing more, or less, than the equal application of equal rights rather than an extra demanding accommodation of religious difference. Muslims know this and demand "neutrality" and "equality" far more often than requesting exemptions.[48]

Purpose-built mosques are among the most significant Islamic forms enabled by the firmness of the neutrality principle. In an age of enduring civilizational incarceration, mosque construction in the Netherlands is invariably met with municipal objections, neighborhood protests, and court cases. It is important to note, however, that over the past twenty years, many new, visible mosques opened their doors across the nation and in major cities such as Amsterdam, Rotterdam, Utrecht, and Leiden.[49] This would be impossible without the equal right to construct a house of worship, guaranteed by the Constitution, a "silent giant" (*stille reus*) in the background of municipal interactions and court cases, which disciplines all and sundry when local processes of deliberation threaten to transgress the law.[50]

The amplified adhan, in Arabic, is seen as going yet another step further, crossing a red line of what can be tolerated by citizens living near the loudspeakers, and is thus a better test of the limits of applying strict neutrality. Mosques that wish to use loudspeakers are often supported by city aldermen or in Dutch *wethouders* (upholders of the law), who must strike a balance between resident complaints of noise pollution (*geluidsoverlast*) and mosque representatives' invocation of a legally codified equal right to public, aural presence. Indeed, Article 10 of the 1988 Public Manifestations Act was devised to ensure amplified Islamic calls to prayer, equating this right explicitly to that of church bell ringing: "The sounding of church bells for religious or philosophical ceremonies and funeral ceremonies, including calls to practice religion or philosophy of life, are permitted." The article further states that the municipal council is authorized to regulate the duration and volume, but—and this is important in actual governance—*never in a way that totally silences the practice.*[51] In most cases, the result for a mosque that insists on this right is either a single adhan for the busy Friday prayers in the afternoons or a daily call, also in the afternoons.[52]

The recent deliberations in the city of Enschede are noteworthy because of the fierce resistance against the adhan in 2015 and 2016, prior to the building's construction, coinciding dismally with violent protests by the extreme right against refugee asylum centers.[53] Not only did people gather for several sound tests on the future mosque site, but the municipality facilitated, among others, two grueling public hearings that each lasted more than four hours. During this time, Joost Nijhuis, a municipal councilor on behalf of the Liberal Party, contacted me to ask for my opinion as a researcher of such thorny disputes. In our written conversation, I suggested that the law allows for daily Islamic calls to prayer, and that this was already locally agreed on and practiced in nearby cities such as Deventer. Since the councilor belonged to the Liberal Party, I mentioned John Locke, provoking a response by referring to liberalism's founding father, who defended the right to organized, public worship and even included the "Mahometan" in his letter concerning toleration. The councilor replied that he represented citizens who were not looking forward to a daily call to prayer, even though they might not object to the mosque itself; he rejected the Lockean tradition in favor of a long-standing "Netherlands tradition" of religious tolerance. Arguing that the Islamic call to prayer is more than a neutral sound, and that it is "for many in the Netherlands . . . an unpleasant sound with unpleasant associations," he defended the—indeed widely prevalent—notion that faith is a private matter and thus belongs "behind the front door." In that way, atheists, humanists, and religious others would be spared, and their right to be left alone in the public domain honored. In a published column, Nijhuis explained, "In discussions over religious freedom, an appeal is often made to the thoughts and vision of philosopher John Locke, who believed that every community of faith should have the right to publicly profess his faith. The concept of tolerance that Locke employs is a beautiful abstract ideal image that, however, is far removed from the contemporary practical and social reality."[54] The reality that the councilor alludes to is one where church bells form a "neutral," in his words, background ambience, whereas Islamic calls to prayer violate the neutrality of public space. The issue was therefore not merely a matter of noise pollution but of Islamic noise pollution. This style of reasoning poignantly illustrates that which Nussbaum objects to, namely making difference in rights based on religious difference, a clear violation of Article 1 of the Constitution, which prohibits discrimination on the basis of religious preferences, and Article 6, which grants religious freedom.

Such arguments do not aim for strict neutrality but aim to neutralize religious practices in the public space, echoing a Netherlands tradition originating in the infamous "Protestant bias" that has been analyzed critically by scholars of religion.[55] Contemporary legal standards go beyond so-called Protestant preferences, as agreed upon in the Constitution as well as the Treaty of Rome, and now strictly expand equal religious liberty to Muslims and Catholics, atheists, dissenters, and traditions that were earlier in history deemed outside the scope of protection offered by the concept of religion.

Nijhuis too knew very well that the legal reality of public religion in the Netherlands differs from his description of Dutch common sense. Many mosques in the Netherlands already amplified calls to prayer, some going back to the 1980s. He therefore suggested a strategic compromise, to sound the call once a week for the Friday prayers and with a prior agreement on volume. His colleague Jeroen Hatenboer, an alderman also with the Liberal Party, was charged with the ungrateful task of ameliorating tensions between the Turkish mosque representatives and adhan opponents (which included whites as well as Syriac Dutch Christians). Just like colleagues of the same party in other cities, as an alderman he could not and undeniably did not distinguish Christian from Muslim rights or question the legal right to broadcast the Islamic call to prayer—in theory a right that allows for the five daily calls, including in the morning and the evening. Nevertheless, protests functioned to minimalize the strict neutrality principle's application in practice. Minute details were under negotiation such as whether the adhan would be amplified three times a week with a volume of fifty-seven decibels or only one time with a volume of sixty-three decibels. The mayor, a member of the liberal Democrats 66, warned local politicians that he would "defend the Constitution" in case the negotiations would lead to banning the call to prayer. In the final agreement, after months of negotiating, the mosque would amplify the call only once per week and with a maximum of fifty-seven decibels, exactly the outcome that was advocated by Nijhuis as a reasonable compromise.[56]

The result was disappointing for some mosque members, as it was for some opponents. It is important to ascertain, however, that such calls to prayer can be heard despite strong opposition and prevailing Islamophobia, which is fiercer in Enschede than for example in Utrecht, where the issue did not raise similar problems for the recently built Ulu Mosque. Those who had advocated against Islamic soundscapes, that is, right-wing liberals and conservative Christians but also the Enschede Labor Party and the Socialist Party in the nearby town of Zutphen, grudgingly accepted the agreement reached in Enschede. Importantly, no Dutch mosque has ever been taken to court on the issue. The Enschede mosque could have pressed further for its demand of a daily call by taking legal action but like other mosques chose not to do so, and accepted a compromise that a majority in the neighborhood could agree upon. Without the law on its side, backed by a Lockean principle of strict neutrality, the mosque could never have bargained as long as it did, in a situation where the minimal standard of equal rights—to ring church bells and to amplify calls to prayer—is openly disputed. Certainly, the application of strict neutrality remains contested, but adhan opponents do not have the legal prerogative to grant the mosque permission—much to their frustration—nor is the sounding of the call to prayer a case of exempting the mosque from a general rule.

THE CHOICE BETWEEN STRICT neutrality or accommodation is not simply one between mere formal, "cold" equality and sensitive, "warm" accommodation. We must recognize the two approaches without one superseding or overriding the other. From this perspective, it follows that their aims cannot be neatly divided as achieving formal versus substantive equality. Nussbaum holds such a position but acknowledges the thought that there are no easy answers when investigating poles of neutrality in evaluations of political secularism. She has, however, admonished Europeans for failing to fully apply the minimal Lockean standard to citizens who happen to be Muslims. Or, to put it differently, the partial failure here is caused by insufficient attention to the political standards of citizenship versus excessive attention for cultural identifications. It is not adequate to acknowledge this as a truism and then continue to conceptualize the harder cases of accommodation as being "really" determinative of equality or revealing the nature of religious freedom more precisely. By doing so, analytic efforts to understand the right of religious freedom and equality will fail to grasp what is at stake in Europe today and reduce this right to a plethora of exceptional cases rather than the mainstream issues of constructing houses of worship, sounding calls to prayer, and being free to dress as one wishes. This argument can also be extended to more difficult cases, such as the disputed right to unstunned ritual slaughter, which was not defended by the Dutch Council of State and the Senate on the basis of an idea of legal accommodation alone but on an overriding concern with equal rights as guaranteed under the Constitution and the European Convention on Human Rights.[57] In sum, in a Europe where xenophobia does not abate, and where people will continue to be trapped in civilizational identities offered by the so-called world religions, the political value of a rigid concept of equal rights matters a great deal, only to be underestimated at our own peril.

NOTES

This chapter is based on a Studium Generale lecture delivered in 2017 at Wageningen University, the Netherlands.

1   Talal Asad, *Formations of the Secular: Christianity, Islam, Modernity* (Stanford University Press, 2003); Saba Mahmood, *Religious Difference in a Secular Age: A Minority Report* (Princeton, NJ: Princeton University Press, 2015); Elizabeth Shakman Hurd, *Beyond Religious Freedom: The New Global Politics of Religion* (Princeton, NJ: Princeton University Press, 2015).

2   Christopher L. Eisgruber and Lawrence G. Sager, *Religious Freedom and the Constitution* (Cambridge, MA: Harvard University Press, 2007); Tariq Modood, *Multiculturalism: A Civic Idea* (Cambridge, UK: Polity Press, 2007); Tariq Modood, "Multiculturalizing Secularism," in *The Oxford Handbook of Secularism*, ed. Phil Zuckerman and John R. Shook (New York: Oxford University Press, 2016), 354–68; Veit Bader, "Postsecularism or Liberal-Democratic Constitutionalism?," *Erasmus Law Review* 5, no. 1 (2007): 5–26; Rajeev Bhargava, "States, Religious Diversity, and the Crisis of Secularism," *Hedgehog Review* 12, no. 3 (2010): 8–22; Craig Calhoun, "Rethinking Secularism," *Hedgehog Review* 12, no. 3 (2010): 35–48; Martha Nussbaum, *The New Religious Intolerance: Overcoming the Politics of Fear in an Anxious Age* (Cambridge, MA: Harvard University Press, 2012); Akeel Bilgrami, *Secularism, Identity, and Enchantment* (Cambridge, MA: Harvard University Press, 2014).

3   John Rawls, "The Idea of an Overlapping Consensus," *Oxford Journal of Legal Studies* 7, no. 1 (1987): 1–25.

4   Birgit Meyer, "Mediation and the Genesis of Presence: Towards a Material Approach to Religion" (inaugural lecture, Utrecht University, October 19, 2012).

5   Peter Geschiere, *The Perils of Belonging: Autochthony, Citizenship, and Exclusion in Africa and Europe* (Chicago: University of Chicago Press, 2009); Jan Willem Duyvendak, *The Politics of Home: Belonging and Nostalgia in Western Europe and the United States* (New York: Palgrave Macmillan, 2011).

6   This chapter was completed in 2018. The Partial Ban on Face-Covering Clothing Act (Wet gedeeltelijk verbod gezichtsbedekkende kleding) went into effect in 2019.

7   Rainer Forst, *Toleration in Conflict: Past and Present* (Cambridge: Cambridge University Press, 2013), 231; John Locke, *A Letter Concerning Toleration*, ed. James H. Tully (Indianapolis, IN: Hackett, 1983), 43.

8   Cf. Ernst van den Hemel's chapter in this volume.

9   Rob Wijnberg, "Waarom de vrijheid van godsdienst moet worden afgeschaft," in *Nietzsche and Kant lezen de krant: Denkers van vroeger over dilemma's van nu* (Amsterdam: De Bezige Bij, 2009), 50–54.

10 Cf. Annelies Moors, "The Dutch and the Face-Veil: The Politics of Discomfort," *Social Anthropology* 17, no. 4 (2009): 393–408; Adriaan Overbeeke, "Introducing a

General Burqa Ban in the Netherlands," in *The Burqa Affair across Europe: Between Public and Private Space*, ed. Alessandro Ferrari and Sabrina Pastorell (New York: Routledge, 2013), 101–26; Jill Marshall, "S.A.S. v. France: Burqa Bans and the Control or Empowerment of Identities," *Human Rights Law Review* 15 (2015): 377–89.

11 See, for example, Peter van Rooden, *Religieuze Regimes: Over godsdienst en maatschappij in Nederland, 1570–1990* (Amsterdam: Bert Bakker, 1996); Peter Jan Margry, *Teedere quaesties: Religieuze rituelen in Conflict; Confrontaties tussen katholieken en protestanten rond de processiecultuur in 19e-eeuws Nederland* (Hilversum: Verloren, 2000); Gloria Wekker, *White Innocence: Paradoxes of Colonialism and Race* (Durham, NC: Duke University Press, 2016); and Hans Blom, Hetty Berg, Bart Wallet, and David Wertheim, *Geschiedenis van de joden in Nederland* (Amsterdam: Balans, 2017).

12 Cf. Luca Mavelli and Erin Wilson, eds., *The Refugee Crisis and Religion: Secularism, Security, and Hospitality in Question* (New York: Rowman and Littlefield, 2016); Jennifer B. Saunders, Elena Fiddian-Qasmiyeh, and Susanna Snyder, *Intersections of Religion and Migration* (New York: Palgrave Macmillan, 2016); Ulrich Schmiedel and Graeme Smith, eds., *Religion in the European Refugee Crisis* (New York: Palgrave Macmillan, 2018).

13 Ernst Hirsch-Ballin and Paul van Geest, "Buma's Schoo-lezing: Maatschappelijke scheidslijnen mogen geen breuklijnen worden," *Christen Democratische Verkenningen* 3 (2017): 18–23.

14 Martha Nussbaum, *Liberty of Conscience: In Defense of America's Tradition of Religious Equality* (New York: Basic Books, 2008), 67.

15 Nussbaum, *New Religious Intolerance*, 87.

16 "Gemoedsbezwaren en ziektekostenverzekeringen," *Reformatorisch Dagblad*, September 29, 2005.

17 *Verzekerdenmonitor 2013* (The Hague: Ministry of Health, Welfare and Sport, 2013). See also *Uw registratie als gemoedsbezwaarde bij Zorginstituut Nederland* (Diemen: National Health Care Institute, 2016).

18 Ton Bernts and Joantine Berghuijs, *God in Nederland: 1966–2015* (Utrecht: Ten Have, 2016).

19 "Sarah Izat over een genderneutrale god, Koerdische feministen en 50 hoofddoeken," December 29, 2017, https://www.vice.com/be/article/43q339/sarah-izat-over-een-genderneutrale-god-koerdische-feministen-en-50-hoofddoeken.

20 Cf. Nussbaum, *Liberty of Conscience*, 228–29.

21 Aristotle, *The Nichomachean Ethics*, trans. J. A. K. Thomson, rev. Hugh Tredennick (London: Penguin, 2004), 1132b, 123.

22 Cf. Niklas Luhmann, *A Systems Theory of Religion*, trans. David A. Brenner, with Adrian Hermann (Stanford: Stanford University Press, 2013), 201–31.

23 Cf. Heiner Bielefeldt, "Freedom of Religion or Belief—A Human Right under Pressure," *Oxford Journal of Law and Religion* 1, no. 1 (2012): 15–35. I use the figure of the postsecularist only to indicate the normative move away from aggressive antipluralist conceptions of what political secularism should entail. This is in line with Jürgen Habermas's proposal for a postsecular society, which retains the normative priority for a secular constitutional state. See Jürgen Habermas,

"Religion in the Public Sphere," *European Journal of Philosophy* 14, no. 1 (2006): 1–25; Craig Calhoun, Eduardo Mendieta, and Jonathan Van Antwerpen, eds., *Habermas and Religion* (Cambridge, UK: Polity, 2013). For several critiques of the concept of the postsecular, see Veit Bader, *Secularism or Democracy? Associational Governance of Religious Diversity* (Amsterdam: Amsterdam University Press, 2012); James A. Beckford, "Public Religions and the Postsecular: Critical Reflections," *Journal for the Scientific Study of Religion* 51, no. 1 (2012): 1–19; and Stathis Gourgouris, *Lessons in Secular Criticism* (New York: Fordham University Press, 2013). Bader, for example, expands on Rawls's attempt to go beyond the secular-religious divide and convincingly shows why the very words *secular* and *secularism* should not be part of our legal or constitutional discourse at all. The main issue, from this perspective, is not whether the state is secular, since there are illiberal secular states, but whether it belongs to a liberal-democratic constitutional state that upholds basic liberties for all. In the Netherlands, the words *secular* and *secularism*, or even the famed phrase "separation of church and state," are indeed nowhere mentioned in the Constitution. A liberal priority for specifically spelled out rights, such as Article 6, *de vrijheid van godsdienst en levensovertuiging*, or the freedom to hold and express any religious or other comprehensive convictions, is what matters in actual governance.

24 Nussbaum, *Liberty of Conscience*, 229.
25 Nussbaum, *Liberty of Conscience*, 83.
26 Simon Critchley, *Infinitely Demanding: Ethics of Commitment, Politics of Resistance* (New York: Verso, 2007), 7.
27 Simon Critchley, "England Loses," *New York Review of Books,* June 28, 2016.
28 "Syrian Asylum Applications in Europe," UN Refugee Agency, accessed January 2018, http://data.unhcr.org/syrianrefugees.
29 Frans Timmermans, "Europaspeech," Maassilo, Rotterdam, February 19, 2014.
30 Edith Schippers, "De paradox van de vrijheid," H. J. Schoo Lecture, Rode Hoed Amsterdam, September 5, 2016.
31 Cf. Justus Uitermark, Paul Mepschen, and Jan Willem Duyvendak, "Populism, Sexual Politics, and the Exclusion of Muslims in the Netherlands," in *European States and Their Muslim Citizens: The Impact of Institutions on Perceptions and Boundaries*, ed. John Bowen, Christophe Bertossi, Jan Willem Duyvendak, and Mona Lena Krook (New York: Cambridge University Press, 2014), 235–55.
32 Ernst Hirsch-Ballin, *Citizens' Rights and the Right to Be a Citizen* (Leiden: Brill, 2014); Paul Scheffer, *De vrijheid van de grens* (Amsterdam: De Bezige Bij, 2016).
33 Cf. Philomena Essed and Isabel Hoving, *Dutch Racism*, Thamyris/Intersecting 27 (Amsterdam: Rodopi, 2014); Wekker, *White Innocence*; Achille Mbembe, *Critique of Black Reason*, trans. Laurent Dubois (Durham, NC: Duke University Press, 2017); and the chapter by Markus Balkenhol in this volume.
34 "Herontwikkeling II: Moskee in de stad," Pakhuis de Zwijger, Amsterdam, December 9, 2015.
35 See the YouTube channel for Westermoskee Ayasofya, February 17, 2016, https://www.youtube.com/watch?v=ZzDZoRdZoVs.

36 Tariq Modood, "Multicultural Nationalism, Political Secularism and Religious Education," in *Multiculturalism—How Can Society Deal with It? A Thinking Exercise in Flanders*, ed. Tariq Modood and Frank Bovenkerk (Brussels: KVAB Press, 2017), 13–42.

37 Kemal Rijken, *De Westermoskee en de geschiedenis van de Nederlandse godsdienstvrijheid* (Amsterdam and Antwerp: Atlas Contact, 2014), ch. 6. See also the interactive, online 2014 documentary *Mosque in Amsterdam* (*Moskee in de Stad*, in Dutch and Turkish with English subtitles), accessed January 2018, http://moskeeindestad.nl/site/en/.

38 Pooyan Tamimi Arab, *Amplifying Islam in the European Soundscape: Religious Pluralism and Secularism in the Netherlands* (London: Bloomsbury, 2017), 122, emphasis added. See also Daan Beekers and Pooyan Tamimi Arab, "Dreams of an Iconic Mosque: Spatial and Temporal Entanglements of a Converted Church," *Material Religion: The Journal of Objects, Art and Belief* 12, no. 2 (2016): 137–64.

39 "Een stukje Istanbul in Amsterdam," April 8, 2016, https://www.nrc.nl/nieuws/2016/04/08/een-stukje-istanbul-in-amsterdam-1605584-a372077.

40 The tension between Armenians and Turks of the Netherlands was beautifully captured by the widely discussed 2015 documentary *Bloedbroeders*, about the memory of the Armenian genocide among Dutch citizens of Armenian and Turkish descent.

41 "Greece and Turkey Spar over Ramadan Prayers at Hagia Sophia," *Religion News Service*, June 14, 2016. See also the Greek Foreign Ministry's announcement on its website, June 6, 2016, which promptly received a critical reply by the Turkish Foreign Ministry. https://www.mfa.gr/en/current-affairs/statements-speeches/foreign-ministry-announcement-regarding-the-scheduling-by-the-turkish-authorities-of-koran-reading-in-hagia-sophia.html. Under Atatürk, the call to prayer was explicitly mentioned in the national anthem of the new republic. However, it was banned in Arabic, to be replaced by a Turkish translation, between 1932 and 1950 as part of Kemalist secularism. Umut Azak, "Secularism in Turkey as a Nationalist Search for Vernacular Islam," *Revue des mondes musulmans et de la Méditerranée* 124 (2008): 161–79.

42 Cf. Elif Batuman, "Ottomania: A Hit TV Show Reimagines Turkey's Imperial Past," *New Yorker*, February 17, 2014.

43 Thijl Sunier and Nico Landman, *Transnational Turkish Islam*, Shifting Geographies of Religious Activism and Community Building in Turkey and Europe (New York: Palgrave Macmillan, 2015). This preference was visualized powerfully in a Dutch documentary on young Turkish Dutch supporters of President Erdoğan (*Erdogans aanhang*, VPRO Tegenlicht, broadcast on national television on November 19, 2016).

44 Cf. Tamimi Arab, *Amplifying Islam*, ch. 4.

45 Amartya Sen, *Identity and Violence: The Illusion of Destiny* (New York: Norton, 2006), ch. 1. See also Gerd Baumann, *Contesting Culture: Discourses of Identity in Multi-ethnic London* (Cambridge: Cambridge University Press, 1996); Paul Gilroy, *Postcolonial Melancholia* (New York: Columbia University Press, 2005); Kwame Anthony Appiah, *Cosmopolitanism: Ethics in a World of Strangers* (New York: Norton, 2007).

46 Nussbaum, *New Religious Intolerance*, 87.

47 An exchange between David Miller and Cécile Laborde on the Swiss minaret ban similarly shows the tension discussed in this chapter, between a majority-based notion of cultural belonging and equality guaranteed by citizenship. David Miller, "Majorities and Minarets: Religious Freedom and Public Space," *British Journal of Political Science* 46, no. 2 (2016): 437–56; Cécile Labord, "Miller's Minarets: Religion, Culture, Domination" (presentation at Oxford University and the European University Institute, Florence, April 2015).

48 Cf. Abdullah Saeed, "Secularism, State Neutrality, and Islam," in *The Oxford Handbook of Secularism*, ed. Phil Zuckerman and John R. Shook (New York: Oxford University Press, 2017), 188–200.

49 Eric Roose, *The Architectural Representation of Islam: Muslim-Commissioned Mosque Design in the Netherlands* (Amsterdam: Amsterdam University Press, 2009); Marcel Maussen, "Constructing Mosques: The Governance of Islam in France and the Netherlands" (PhD diss., Amsterdam School for Social Science Research, 2009).

50 Ernst Hirsch-Ballin, "De grondwet in politiek en samenleving: Rechtstaatlezing 2013," Felix Meritis, Amsterdam, October 11, 2013. See also Oskar Verkaaik and Pooyan Tamimi Arab, "Managing Mosques in the Netherlands: Constitutional versus Culturalist Secularism," *Journal of Muslims in Europe* 5, no. 2 (2016): 251–68.

51 Wet Openbare Manifestaties, artikel 10: "Klokgelui ter gelegenheid van godsdienstige en levensbeschouwelijke plechtigheden en lijkplechtigheden, alsmede oproepen tot het belijden van godsdienst of levensovertuiging, zijn toegestaan. De gemeenteraad is bevoegd ter zake regels te stellen met betrekking tot duur en geluidsniveau."

52 Tamimi Arab, *Amplifying Islam*, ch. 2.

53 A group of neo-Nazis was convicted for terrorism after an arson attack against another mosque in Enschede, believing that such acts would frighten the municipality into reconsidering plans to host refugees. See "Vier jaar cel voor aanslag op moskee Enschede," NRC Handelsblad, October 27, 2016.

54 Joost G. A. Nijhuis, "Geluidsversterkte azaan, mogen, moeten, willen," VVD Enschede, February 3, 2016, translation mine.

55 See, for example, Leigh Eric Schmidt, *Hearing Things: Religion, Illusion, and the American Enlightenment* (Cambridge, MA: Harvard University Press, 2000); and Isaac Weiner, *Religion Out Loud: Religious Sound, Public Space, and American Pluralism* (New York: New York University Press, 2014).

56 Tamimi Arab, *Amplifying Islam*, 148–49.

57 Cf. Sipco Vellenga, "Ritual Slaughter, Animal Welfare and the Freedom of Religion," *Journal of Religion in Europe* 8, no. 2 (2015): 210–34; Aleksandra Gliszczyńska-Grabias and Wojciech Sadurski, "The Law of Ritual Slaughter and the Principle of Religious Equality," *Journal of Law, Religion and State* 4, no. 3 (2016): 233–66; and Raad van State 2017, advies W15.13.0243/IV.

2. CONFUCIAN SECULARISM IN THEORETICAL AND HISTORICAL PERSPECTIVE

ALBERT WELTER

Secularism in the West was forged in relation/reaction to religious, specifically Christian, traditions. In this chapter, I find parallels with the role Confucian secularism played in the administration of religion, specifically Buddhism, in China. I argue that public and private realms were never thought of as distinct in China but as part of a continuum of harmonious, if sometimes contested, terrain where secular and sacred aims met. The chapter explores how the administration of Buddhism in China informs us about a Confucian secularism, especially notions of a "public" sphere (following Jürgen Habermas), and how distinctive these notions are in a Chinese context, where sharp distinctions between "public" and "private" break down in the face of an espoused harmony between secular and religious roles. In place of a "public sphere," I posit the notion of a "sphere of privilege" where interested parties are allowed access to the mechanisms of power and arenas of cultural privilege. In this way, I respond to questions about the nature of Confucian secularism by suggesting the unique species of secularism that the Confucian and Chinese tradition represents, where notions of the separation of church and state give way to administrative policies designed to manage religious forces, providing official support for sanctioned institutions and activities and proscribing beliefs and activities that run counter to government aims.

In addition to providing an alternate model for secularism, where secular and religious agendas are seen ideally as harmonious and complementary, the Chinese context challenges the master paradigm of the science of religion that provided the framework for Western modernity. Max Weber was instrumental in formulating a paradigm for academic knowledge about religion that claimed universal status regardless of time and place. In the concluding section, I take up the discussion of how Chinese secularism, in challenging Weber's presumptions, questions the very notion of the Western formulation of modernity as a universal, normative paradigm.

What Lies Beneath: Native Terminology Relating to "Religion" in China

Like many of the categories of knowledge systems that entered East Asia as part of a general acceptance of modernization and Westernization, the term "religion" received standard formulation in a Sino-Japanese logographic term coined in Meiji Japan as *shūkyō* (宗教), pronounced *zongjiao* in modern Chinese. The combination of these two logographs, *zong* and *jiao*, was almost entirely unprecedented, but each of the logographs taken independently had long-standing meanings in China and throughout East Asia. The combined logographs quickly formed a new category indicating the kind of exclusive allegiance or devotion to a tradition common to the definition of religion in the West. While religion in the West was understood as part and parcel of an exclusive faith to a single and universal creator, God, the concept of exclusivity, while not unknown in East Asia, was the exception rather than the rule. Nor was faith necessarily the primary concern, as praxis replaced dox as how one's relationship with a tradition was defined, and praxis in different traditions simultaneously was much more common than not. As the combined logographs *shūkyō* or *zongjiao* became the normative equivalent of "religion" in the East Asian context, the majority of practitioners began to see themselves as essentially "not religious," meaning "not religious in the Western sense of the term." This confusion, the association of religion with exclusive commitment based on faith, has marred the understanding of religion in the region to the present day.

One way of suggesting a possible inherent meaning for "religion" in the Chinese (and Japanese) context is to look at the latent native meanings of the logographs used to translate the Western term "religion." While it is not my intention to invoke an etymological reductionism in place of "religion" as an easy solution, I do contend that an etymological analysis of the two logographs, *zong* (宗) and *jiao* (教), reveals latent native understandings lurking beneath the surface of the modern normative category *zongjiao*.

The logograph *zong* (宗) is composed of two elements: the upper element (the "radical") 宀, signifying the "roof" of a building; and the lower element 示, which by itself is an independent logograph (pronounced *shi*) meaning "to show, reveal; to announce, report." Taken together, the upper element indicates the roof of an ancestral shrine, while the lower element indicates offerings presented to the ancestors while reporting (i.e., praying) to them. In short, the logograph *zong* is closely associated with the veneration of ancestors that forms the core of traditional Chinese expressions of religiosity.[1]

The logograph *jiao* (教) is likewise pregnant with embedded meanings that resonated in a traditional native context. It, too, can be broken down into two parts: a left element, 孝; and a right element, 文 (the "radical"), both of which form independent logographs when taken on their own. The left element, *xiao* (孝), refers to "filial piety," the cardinal Confucian virtue of respect for one's parents, exhibited through actions and attitudes exhibited both in this life and after they have departed, but broken down further into upper and lower subelements, one finds an abbreviated form of the character for "elder," *lao* (老), over the character for *zi* (子), "son" or "child." The right element, *wen* (文), contains a range of meanings: "letters, literature, writing, culture." Taken as a whole, *jiao* indicates the passing down of writings imbued with cultural values (i.e., traditions) from elders to children. It is hardly surprising to find Chinese, particularly Confucian, undertones lurking in the etymological analysis of these logographs. The logographs themselves exhibit a native understanding of attitudes and behaviors that approximate our category of "religion." The combination of these logographs as *zongjiao* reflects a newly coined term that transposes them into a Western category, one that has assumed normative status but is often confused by attitudes and actions suggested by their etymological origins.

The Metaphor of Proximity: The Confucian Rejection of Universalism, the "Public Sphere," and the "Sphere of Privilege"

Russell McCutcheon argues that modern European rhetorical innovations delimited religion as a private concept "in a way that was designed to sequester it from the state," creating the "public sphere" and the "private sphere" and establishing the "separation of church and state." However externalized, objectified, or reified as natural or eternal this order was suggested to be, there was nothing natural about it. Instead, it is a "fabrication" that segregates (or "straitjackets") the world, and although it might be a fabrication that benefited modern Europe, it is an ordering of the world that is hardly self-evident.[2]

According to Habermas, "The bourgeois public sphere may be conceived above all as the sphere of private people come together as a public; they soon claimed the public sphere regulated from above against the public authorities themselves, to engage them in a debate over the general rules governing relations in the basically privatized but publicly relevant sphere of commodity exchange and social labor. *The medium of this political confrontation was peculiar and without precedent*: people's public use of their reason (*öffentlich Rasonnement*)."[3] The public sphere as "a discursive space in which individuals and groups congregate to discuss matters of mutual interest and, where possible, to reach a common judgment," as "a theater in modern societies in which political participation is enacted through the medium of talk," or as "a realm of social life in which public opinion can be formed" draws on well-known notions put forth by Habermas of a public sphere that mediates between a "private sphere" and the "sphere of public authority."[4] According to Habermas, whereas "the private sphere comprised civil society in the narrower sense, that is to say, the realm of commodity exchange and of social labor," and the "sphere of public authority" dealt with the state, or realm of the police, and the ruling class, the public sphere crossed over both these realms and "through the vehicle of public opinion it put the state in touch with the needs of society."[5] In this sense, according to Nancy Fraser, "the public sphere is an arena conceptually distinct from the state," a "site for the production and circulation of discourses that can in principle be critical of the state." The public sphere "is also distinct from the official economy; it is not an arena of market relations but rather one of discursive relations, a theater for debating and deliberating rather than for buying and selling." These distinctions between "state apparatuses, economic markets, and democratic associations . . . are essential to democratic theory."[6] The people themselves came to see the public sphere as a regulatory institution against the authority of the state.[7] The study of the public sphere centers on the idea of participatory democracy, and how public opinion becomes political action. A basic premise of public sphere theory is a belief in the efficacy of enlightened debate. Political action is instigated by public sphere debate; the only legitimate governments are those that listen to the public sphere.[8] Accordingly, "Democratic governance rests on the capacity of and opportunity for citizens to engage in enlightened debate."[9]

This characterization invites comment in several respects. The discussion is framed essentially around Habermas's characterization of a "public sphere" drawn from eighteenth-century European bourgeois society. It is a category that presupposes a number of unique features pertaining to that society: participatory democracy, the role of public opinion, and attitudes toward citizen activism, not to mention the lack of regard for status (hierarchy) among participants, the domains of common ground over which private citizens could exercise authority, and ever-expanding notions of inclusivity that in principle could exclude no one, to name but a few. As a realm that mediates between the private sphere and the Sphere of Public Authority, the public sphere can hardly be said to exist outside modern democracies, so the first question that must be addressed is the applicability of a notion of the public sphere to a premodern or non-Western context. Clearly the term does not apply. Yet, to the extent that democratic forms of government provide a normative model against which modern governments are judged, one can hardly dismiss discussions of the public sphere out of hand, even in the Chinese context.[10] As with the case of democracy, even when it is not subscribed to, countries such as China are frequently forced in international forums to explain their actions against the norms that democratic value systems presuppose, so that even when China does not sanction a public sphere where democratic presumptions prevail, large portions of the rest of the world and even some of its own citizens presume that this is a model that China should aspire to. There are fewer arenas in China where this is more self-evident than in the arena of religion and the limits of China's tolerance toward its public display. The question thus turns to why there is such resistance to a public sphere in the Chinese context. How does Chinese thinking about things like a private sphere and the sphere of public authority work to inhibit the growth of a public sphere? To answer this question requires a shift away from the Western discourse surrounding a public sphere initiated by Habermas and an entry into the Chinese discourse that delineates how arenas of influence are apportioned and managed through bureaucratic apparatuses in the Chinese context.

As pointed out by Oskar Negt and Alexander Kluge, the German term for "public sphere" in Habermas's title *Öffentlichkeit* includes a variety of meanings but implies a spatial concept, social sites, or arenas where meanings are articulated, distributed, and negotiated, as well as the collective body constituted by "the public."[11] The public sphere as spatial concept provides a good entry point for understanding how the Chinese rationalize and manage the flow of public discourse on criteria different from the model assumed by Habermas. While Habermas's model of the public sphere is predicated on the creation of free and open public spaces, sites, or arenas where meanings are articulated, distributed, and negotiated, the Chinese model is built upon notions of symbolic spatial proximity, where distance from the center is viewed as a means to manage and control access and privilege. Chinese notions of "space" are thus managed on the basis of proximity that positions participants around a centrifugal force, creating a symbolic social universe that arranges and manages articulated, distributed, and negotiated spaces in relation to each other. Access to power and privilege is managed through proximity to the center. This includes the power to express oneself publicly, that is, to engage in public debate.

Chinese notions of proximity that govern access and privilege are firmly rooted in the Confucian tradition. These notions dominated the Chinese imperial state and continue to resonate to the present under different guises. It is not that the Chinese were unaware of alternatives. The Confucian consensus emerged out of a welter of intellectual turmoil, termed the "hundred schools of thought" (*zhuzi baijia* [諸子百家]) of the Spring and Autumn and Warring States periods of Chinese history (770–221 BCE). Among the schools of thought that challenged for supremacy was one instituted by the philosopher Mozi (墨子) (or Mo Di [墨翟]; 470–ca. 391 BCE) and his disciples, who became known as Mohists (*mojia* [墨家]). Mozi argued for a form of universalism whereby everyone is equal before Heaven, and of standards to be followed, "there is nothing better than following Heaven."[12] Mozi advocated that no distinctions based on kinship proximity were warranted, that freedom from partiality through "universal love" (*boai* [博愛]) would rid the world of chaos and friction. The universal standard provided by Heaven created norms applicable to all alike, and all became equal before Heaven.

The Confucian consensus actively disputed the model endorsed by Mozi and his followers. Whereas Mohists saw in their universal standard the seeds of social harmony, Confucians viewed it as a pretext for chaos. It was unnatural, the Confucians argued, to love another's parents as much as one's own, or to regard the members of others' families as the equal to one's own. Human relationships naturally followed a spatial proximity determined by kinship ties: those closer to one on the kinship scale were more deserving of affection and regard than strangers at a distance. The hypothetical standard that rendered everyone equal violated the law of natural human instincts, where love or affection was apportioned on a sliding scale based on relative proximity. In the Confucian constellation, filial piety was transformed from bland respect for one's parents to an ultimate mandate by which one's virtue was measured. Filial piety was thus not a voluntary choice but a mandate written into the order of the universe, the violation of which threatened the natural law of

Heaven. In this constellation, human relations became a finely tuned balancing act dictated by symbolic notions of proximity. Confucian texts provided the code books through which proximate human relations were understood and managed.

The influence of the Confucian kinship model did not stop with the family but was superimposed on the framework of society as a whole, whereby the entire population was regarded as the "Chinese family." The emperor, as patriarch of the nation, presided over the Chinese family, just as patriarchs presided over individual Chinese clans. Ministers of state proffered their obedience and respect to the emperor in a manner modeled on the filial respect learned as children toward one's parents. The deference ministers showed to the emperor was mitigated by the Confucian tradition of remonstration, whereby the minister also had a duty to respectfully guide imperial decision-making to the point of actively disagreeing with the emperor if the situation warranted it. This was a privilege accorded only to Confucian-educated advisors, who "earned" the right to remonstrate (i.e., express their "public" opinion, though the *public* in this case was restricted to the emperor and his court) through their command over the Confucian curriculum and the moral virtues it instilled in them. The hierarchy of the Chinese bureaucracy thus imitated the kinship proximity model that the Confucian tradition enshrined. Entrance into the bureaucratic constellation marked one as a privileged member of the ministerial family, where rank and position determined a relative scale to access and privilege. Gaining entrance to this world of access and privilege was an overwhelming preoccupation of the aspiring elite.[13]

How do these notions affect the way religion has been managed in the Chinese context? In the following section, I touch briefly on how Buddhism was managed in China, based on the notion of allowing and denying privileges based on the model of spatial proximity.

Administrating Religion in China: The Example of Buddhism

In the Chinese context, the template for managing religion was established with the entrance of Buddhism into China. Over the centuries, Chinese administrative practices and policies were formed to manage Buddhist institutions and the Buddhist influence, and this served as a prototype for managing other religions as they became established in China.

Some years ago, French Sinologist Jacques Gernet outlined a model for how Buddhism functioned in Chinese society based on material and economic criteria, the relevance of which is still evident.[14] While noting the great diversity that characterizes the Buddhist institutional presence in China, from great monasteries housing dozens of monks to village chapels and mountain hermitages with one or two inhabitants, Gernet also calls attention to a similar diversity in terms of status.[15]

> Some monasteries are official places of worship and are recognized as such. They have received their name [e (額)] by imperial bestowal as well as gifts of land, funds, servants, allotments of local families, and certain privileges. They are entitled to annual subventions from the court. Their monks have been selected and ordained by the emperor and are supervised by officially appointed clergy who are held accountable for their conduct. The other kind[s] of establishments are merely tolerated and are always the first to fall victim to repressions. These are private places of worship, serving the great families as well as the people.[16]

Following the distinction in status accorded Buddhist institutions, Gernet stipulates that there were three kinds of Chinese monks: "the official monk, maintained at state expense and responsible for the performance of ceremonies of the imperial cult"; "the private monk, fed and clothed by the great families"; and "the common monk who lived in the country side, either in isolation or as a member of a small group."[17] What Gernet indicates, in effect, is that there was great distinction between official and private monasteries and that private monasteries were also divisible into two types: those constructed by officials and members of prominent families and those erected to serve the interests of the common people. Great divides of privilege and power separated these three types of institutions and the monks who inhabited them. Rather than a single Buddhist institution in China, it is important to recognize the diversity among the types of institutions and monks who comprised the Buddhist world. The recognition of these distinctions weighed heavily on the fate of Buddhism in China. An imperial court that tolerated Buddhism and even one that identified with Buddhism was obliged to resist uncontrolled expansion of clergy and monastic constructions: expansion and construction perpetrated by imperial relatives and high officials, although highly visible, was difficult to control owing to the influence and privilege of the perpetrators; developments at the popular level occurred in response to diffuse forces and relatively anonymous patrons.[18]

Just as elite families coveted entrance into the privileged world of ministerial position in the government bureaucracy (ostensibly through the examination system but also through "backdoor" type connections), so did great families seek to convert their private monasteries into official establishments and exercise all their influence in order to do so. Similarly, clergy members whose ordinations had not been officially accredited benefited from imperial decrees sanctioning their ordained status. As Gernet notes, "This amounted to a steady and highly effective pressure exerted upon the religious policy of the court, tending to favor a development of Buddhism in China well beyond the bounds that governments might have reasonably wished to impose on it."[19]

In short, while religions like Buddhism faced serious challenges to gain acceptance in China, there did exist legitimate avenues whereby Buddhist institutions and clergy were allowed access to privilege. Official monasteries and clergy served at the behest of the emperor and were recognized as legitimate members of the bureaucratic establishment. Clergy residing in monasteries sponsored by the great families, protected by the prestige of their patrons, also enjoyed a kind of privileged status and held out the hope of conversion to official status. In times of suppression, however, these monasteries were vulnerable to the vagaries of imperial policy, and the protections afforded them by their patrons could easily evaporate. The "common" monasteries and the clergy who inhabited them were most vulnerable and least tolerated, but any of the private, nonofficial monasteries and clergy could be subject to closure at government whim. The elite Buddhism practiced at official monasteries, the reserve of a privileged few, was the "official" face of Buddhism and, as such, immune from persecution.

According to binary oppositions that divide reality into competing hierarchical spheres, monastics and their institutions can hardly fit anywhere but on the religious/sacred/church side, juxtaposed against the secular/profane/state, and with which there is little in common.[20] What do we make of the Buddhist monastery as government institution, or members of the Buddhist clergy as officials in the government bureaucracy? Such arrangements strike the modern reader as medieval, at best, and relegated to a dark age of confusion where the natural lines of demarcation separating (i.e., protecting) religion (the irrational) from the state (the rational) are not in force.

What the Chinese example suggests is that the conceptual categories of Western modernity separating the sacred and secular are not the only "natural" means available to adjudicate between rational and irrational. This is not to suggest that binaries do not also apply to the Chinese context, as even passing familiarity to *yin/yang* ideology attests. But borrowing the metaphor of proximity based on kinship, the Chinese paired their binaries to a model of spatial proximity. This produced not strict oppositions per se but graded distinctions of acceptance/tolerance based on symbolic proximity to a central authority. It was this model that was used to adjudicate between the various Buddhisms that existed in the Chinese context as described by Gernet, to determine and legislate between acceptable Buddhist "rational" behavior and unacceptable "irrational" and superstitious behavior. This does not mean that China was exempted from the "violent hierarchy" that, according to Jacques Derrida, such binaries suggest, but the model of spatial proximity did serve to soften the violence as binaries were regarded as less absolute and more tolerant.[21]

Chinese Secularism and Religion, or Secularism with Chinese Characteristics?

The experience of Buddhism in the Chinese context provides a clear glimpse into the principles guiding Chinese secularism (I use the phrase "Chinese secularism" here as interchangeable with the discussion on Confucian secularism, the overwhelming determinant of a Chinese secularism), and its management of religious affairs. While my specific comments here pertain to the Chinese state's management of Buddhism, the principles espoused are easily transferable to the management of other religious traditions and other religious activities. Even the modern policies on religion by the officially atheist Chinese Communist Party (CCP) may be seen as heir to these principles. According to current policy, religious activities are officially permitted for five religious groups: Buddhism, Daoism, Islam, Catholicism, and Protestant Christianity.[22] The activities of these groups are subject to CCP oversight, but they are also supported institutionally and financially. Members of officially acknowledged groups must abide by rules mandated by the CCP, including provisions regarding patriotism, and a key aspect of these groups is that they are regarded as patriotic associations.[23] Accounting for religious adherents who are not included as members of CCP-authorized groups is difficult and estimates vary widely, but the majority of religious practitioners (and by most estimates, the vast majority) operate in autonomous communities outside state sanction and authority. Toleration for these groups varies according to the public versus private nature of the activities engaged in (reprimands are less likely in the case of private, behind-closed-doors or "house" activities) and the vagaries of state tolerance. Beyond this are groups whose practices are labeled as "superstitious" (Falun Gong being the most noted example) and deemed to be intrinsically disruptive to the socialist aims and policies of the state and its citizens. Any activity so labeled is liable to be prohibited, at times forcefully, especially activities involving public performance.

It is easy to correlate modern CCP policy toward religion with traditional dynastic government policies toward Buddhism. Recall Gernet's tripartite division—"the official monk, maintained at state expense and responsible for the performance of ceremonies of the imperial cult"; "the private monk, fed and clothed by the great families"; and "the common monk who lived in the country side, either in isolation or as a member of a small group"—and we see a semblance of CCP policy toward religion: officially authorized religious groups, autonomous private groups, and groups branded as active in "superstition."[24] The concentric circles that radiate from the control mandated by central authority privilege an inside sphere, a "sphere of privilege," of sanctioned activities deemed to foster government aims, operating as legitimate organs of government policy. Beyond this, religious activities may be tolerated but not officially sanctioned. Any activities deemed to defy official policy are subject to censure.

As a result, some basic distinctions may be made between Western and Chinese definitions of secularism. Modern Western conceptions enshrine the principle of the separation of government institutions from religious institutions and religious dignitaries. They sanction the right to be free from religious rule and teachings, or from the imposition by government of religion or religious practices upon its people. They subscribe to the view that public activities and decisions, especially political ones, should remain uninfluenced by religious beliefs and/or practices.

In contrast to this Western definition, Chinese secularism, including the present government, advocates that the administration of religion falls fully within the purview of the state; that sanction and support of religious institutions and activities are provided for by the state, so long as they abide by the dictates of state policy; and that any public sphere is controlled by the state, while formulating a "sphere of privilege" that provides for earned access to the arena of cultural discourse and influence.

Chinese Secularism and Religion

On a more theoretical level, the discussion of Chinese secularism and its relation to the administration of religion raises important questions regarding the nature of religion in relation to modernity, as commonly understood. The discussion of "modern" or "modernity" invokes the spirit of Max Weber, especially Weber's formulations of modernity and its relation to tradition (especially religion) and the West's alleged uniqueness over the non-West, including China (the very essence of Weber's formulation of modernity).[25] While contemporary theorists have moved beyond Weber, Weber's formulations in this regard cast a long shadow over our understanding and may be used as a convenient touchstone in the discussion of formulations of secularism in China and the West. Weber, perhaps more than any other theorist on religion, was instrumental in forming a master paradigm for academic knowledge that claims universal status regardless of time and place. Weber's formulation of modernity derives from European Enlightenment notions of rationality and subjective freedom that grew out of Protestant Christianity and the rejection of "traditional" Christianity, or Catholicism, that preceded it. Weber's formulation essentially negates everything that is nonmodern: the past (medieval Europe) and the other (Asia). By necessity, Asia and medieval Europe are lumped together as lacking rationality and subjective freedom—the essential components of Weber's modernity ("rationality" is the Weberian term; "subjective freedom" is the functional equivalent term used by Habermas). In the Weberian project, the key concepts of modernity were products of Christian civilization, universalized as truths applicable to all times, all societies, and all civilizations.

Weber's notion of modernity was predicated on a notion of secularism that isolated and marginalized religion under the rubric of "separation of church and state," assigning religion a primarily private function and curtailing religious participation in the public sphere. By historicizing the Weberian project as a product of a particular time and a particular civilization (thus depriving it of its universalizing mission), we are forced to reconsider the fallacious underpinnings of Weber's "modernity" and how the conceptual framework deriving from it has tainted our understanding of the non-West, including China. In this regard, it is necessary to disassociate "'modernity' from its modern European origins" and "break the internal connections between modernity and the historical context of Western rationalism, so that processes of modernization can no longer be conceived as rationalization, [or] as the historical objectification of rational structures."[26]

What does this have to do with our understanding of religion and secularism, private and public sphere? Quite a lot, I contend, for the separation or noninvolvement of religion in the operation of the secular state is a normative principle of modern nation-states formed on the Western model, as is the subsequent privatization of religion. The Chinese model of Confucian secularism or "secularism with Chinese characteristics" seriously challenges the presuppositions of Western normative principles, allowing for, even encouraging, judicious participation of religious institutions and their representatives in the public sphere. Confucian secularist encouragement of religious participation does not tolerate the unbridled reign of subjective freedom but sanctions responsible religious expression that openly subscribes to government aims and sees religious participation as a fulfillment of such aims. Access to the public sphere is privileged, and entrance to it is determined by specific markers and conditions of acceptance. To the extent that Chinese governments incorporate traditional policies toward the administration of religious groups (and current CCP policies toward religion suggest that they do), we will see a new understanding of religion vis-à-vis the secular that challenges and supplants the hitherto normative pattern imposed by Western secularism.

By questioning the applicability of the Weberian project to cultures such as China, we are questioning Weberian notions of modernity itself, based as it is on concepts of allegedly universal applicability that privilege uniquely Western developments. In this regard, we must understand our new mission: to explain how the concept of rationalization has been employed for all societies and historical periods as a conceptual and theoretical principle, how it has organized and regulated our view of social and cultural history, and how it has managed to align all historical data into a seamless historical discourse—one that marginalized most human experience, especially Asian. Wang Hui's point is that the trope of Western modernization (following Weber) has been validated by a negation of the past and the non-West.[27] The rise of the non-West necessarily questions this premise, and confronting and challenging Weber is a step in this process. Beyond this, we must recognize a challenge to the entire European enlightenment project based on Georg W. F. Hegel's "principle of subjectivity," the notion that individual autonomy constitutes the essence of what it means to be human and entails freedom from all forms of external authority.[28] Religion, in the Chinese context, does not represent a notion of subjective freedom from all forms of external authority, a privileged private sphere. To the contrary, it represents the potential for privileged access to the levels of public participation, for full and inclusive membership in the execution of state policy.

My own contribution here, in some small way, hopes to engage this process by analyzing linguistic and conceptual concepts that are important to notions of religion and secularism, private and public, key components of the modernization project, as linguistic and conceptual concepts in their natural Chinese logographic habitat. Rather than invoking the normative frames of reference applied to "religion" and "secularism" as Western concepts based on Western modernization theory, I have looked at equivalent Chinese frames of understanding. Finally, I suggest that the Chinese frames of understanding not be simply relegated to a "past" or "other," Weberian markers of the absence of true "modernity," but viewed as indicators of an alternate modernity not indebted to Western frames of reference, with an accompanying alternate understanding of how relations between religion and secularism are adjudicated.

NOTES

An earlier version of this chapter appeared as "The Sphere of Privilege: Confucian Culture and the Administration of Buddhism (and Religion) in China," in *Religion, Culture, and the Public Sphere in China and Japan*, edited by Albert Welter and Jeffrey Newmark (London: Palgrave Macmillan, 2017), 1–12.

1. The etymological explanations of Sino-Japanese logographs provided in this section are by and large consistent throughout numerous dictionaries and other linguistic reference works. I have generally relied on the explanations provided in Ogawa Tamaki, Nishida Taichirō, and Akatsuka Kiyoshi, eds., *Shin ji gen* [新字源] (1968; Tokyo: Kadokawa shoten, 1988).
2. Russell McCutcheon, *The Discipline of Religion* (London: Routledge, 2003), chs. 11 and 12, 230–90, quoted in Craig Martin, "Delimiting Religion," *Method and Theory in the Study of Religion* 21 (2009): 173–74.
3. Jürgen Habermas, *The Structural Transformation of the Public Sphere: An Inquiry into a Category of Bourgeois Society*, trans. Thomas Burger (Cambridge, MA: MIT Press, 1989), 27 (emphasis added).
4. Gerard Hauser, "Vernacular Dialogue and the Rhetoricality of Public Opinion," *Communication Monographs* 65, no. 2 (June 1988): 86; Nancy Fraser, "Rethinking the Public Sphere: A Contribution to the Critique of Actually Existing Democracy," *Social Text*, no. 25/26 (2006): 57; Robert Asen, "Toward a Normative Conception of Difference in Public Deliberation," *Argumentation and Advocacy* 25 (Winter 1999): 117; Habermas, *Structural Transformation of the Public Sphere*, 30.
5. Habermas, *Structural Transformation of the Public Sphere*, 30, 30, 31.
6. Fraser, "Rethinking the Public Sphere," 57.
7. Habermas, *Structural Transformation of the Public Sphere*, 27.
8. Seyla Benhabib, "Models of Public Space," in *Habermas and the Public Sphere*, ed. Craig Calhoun (Cambridge, MA: MIT Press, 1992), 87.
9. Hauser, "Vernacular Dialogue," 83.
10. The impact of Habermas is described by Weidong Cao, "The Historical Effect of Habermas in the Chinese Context: A Case Study of the Structural Transformation of the Public Sphere," *Frontiers of Philosophy in China* 1, no. 1 (January 2006): 41–50.
11. Oskar Negt and Alexander Kluge, *Public Sphere and Experience: Toward an Analysis of the Bourgeois and Proletarian Public Sphere* (Minneapolis: University of Minnesota Press, 1993), translated by Peter Labanyi, Jamie Daniel, and Assenka Oksiloff. According to Cao ("Historical Effect of Habermas," 44), Chinese scholars also disagreed on how to translate "Öffentlichkeit" into Chinese. Some thought it should be translated as *gonggong lingyu* (公共領域) (public domain/sphere/field/territory/area), some thought that it should be translated as *gonggong lunyu* (公共论域) (domain/sphere/field of [critical] public discussion), while others thought it should be trans-

lated as *gonggong kongjian* (公共空间) (public space). The first alternative became the commonly accepted one. The second one preserves the polemical nuances that Habermas associated with the "people's use of reason" (*öffentlich Rasonnement*). Habermas, *Structural Transformation of the Public Sphere*, 27.

12 Mouzi [墨子], Bk. 1, "On the Necessity of Standards" [*fayi* (法儀)], section 4, 莫若法天, China Text Project, accessed June 28, 2012, http://ctext.org/mozi/on-the-necessity-of-standards.

13 The Confucian bureaucracy in premodern China approximates Habermas's description of the world of letters of courtly noble society, whose influence extended to the public sphere in the world of letters (*literarische Öffentlichkeit*). Habermas, *Structural Transformation of the Public Sphere*, 29–30.

14 Jacques Gernet, *Buddhism in Chinese Society: An Economic History from the Fifth to the Tenth Centuries*, trans. Franciscus Verellen (New York: Columbia University Press, 1995).

15 Gernet, *Buddhism in Chinese Society*, 3.

16 Gernet, *Buddhism in Chinese Society*, 4. I have added the Chinese character for the temple name tablet conferred by the emperor (額) and changed the pronunciation from Wade-Giles *o* to pinyin *e*.

17 Gernet, *Buddhism in Chinese Society*, 4. To give an idea of the relative numbers of institutions housing each of these three types, Gernet refers to the *Bianzheng lun* [辯正論] (T 52, no. 2110) by Falin [法琳] (572–640), which enumerates for the Northern Wei dynasty (386–534): 47 great state monasteries; 839 monasteries of princes, dukes, eminent families, and so on; and 30,000 or more monasteries built by commoners.

18 Gernet, *Buddhism in Chinese Society*, 5.

19 Gernet, *Buddhism in Chinese Society*, 5.

20 Jacques Derrida describes meaning in the West as defined in terms of binary oppositions, "a violent hierarchy" where "one of the two terms governs the other." Jacques Derrida, *Positions* (Chicago: University of Chicago Press, 1981), 28–30.

21 Derrida, *Positions*, 28–30.

22 There are far too many sources discussing the current state of religious practice in China, and government policies surrounding it, to list here. For a comprehensive, if slightly dated, overview, see the articles contained in Daniel L. Overmyer, ed., *Religion in China Today* (Cambridge: Cambridge University Press, 2003).

23 See, for example, Pitman B. Potter, "Belief in Control: Regulation of Religion in China," in Overmyer, *Religion in China Today*, 11–31. Potter characterizes CCP policy as an attempt to manage a balance between socioeconomic autonomy and political loyalty (12–13, 27), noting the inherent tension that "to the extent that policies on regulation of religion require a degree of subservience that is inconsistent with religious conviction, compliance will be elusive" (29).

24 Gernet, *Buddhism in Chinese Society*, 4. The sociologist Fenggang Yang uses a similar tripartite division to describe the administration of religion in contemporary China. Fenggang Yang, "The Red, Black, and Gray Markets of Religion in China," *Sociological Quarterly* 47 (2006): 93–122.

25 My thoughts on this topic have been informed by Wang Hui, "Weber and the Question of Chinese Modernity," trans. Theodore Huters, in *The Politics of Imagining Asia* (Cambridge, MA: Harvard University Press, 2011), 264–306.
26 Jürgen Habermas, *The Philosophical Discourse of Modernity*, trans. Frederick Lawrence (Cambridge, MA: MIT Press, 1987), 2.
27 Hui, "Weber and the Question of Chinese Modernity": 267–68.
28 As characterized by Habermas, *Philosophical Discourse of Modernity*, 7, 18.

3. FROM EXCLUSIVE TO INCLUSIVE SECULARITY
Religion, State, and the Public Space in Tunisia after the Revolution
MOHANAD MUSTAFA

This chapter examines the relationship between religion and politics in Tunisia after the popular revolution in 2010. Prior to the revolution, Tunisia was one of the most emphatically secular states in the Arab world; its government in the postcolonial period combined rigid authoritarianism with a radical secularization project. This combination resulted in the separation of church and state, with exclusion of religion from public spaces on the one hand and the exclusion and suppression of political Islam in public space and the political sphere on the other. The popular revolution led to the collapse of the authoritarian regime and began a process of democratization, the most successful such process following the eruption of popular Arab revolutions against authoritarian regimes. The Tunisian Revolution also rekindled the question concerning religion and politics' relationship in Tunisian public discourse, in the context of both the relationship between church and state and the status of religion in the public sphere. This chapter examines these developments using the postsecular literatures that have evolved over the past several decades. The chapter's main argument is that the rise of political Islam in the Tunisian public sphere, coupled with the Tunisian government's attempt to break off with the radical secularist legacy of the deposed authoritarian regime, have produced a compromise on the status of religion between secular and Islamist strands, namely the Islamic Ennahda movement. The two mainstays of the compromise are the Islamic strand's acceptance of separation between church and state and the secular strand's acceptance and inclusion of religion as an actor shaping the Tunisian public sphere. The Tunisian case study suggests that the broader questions circulating in Arab political discourse about democratization and modernity do not necessarily require religious answers. Rather, they provoke further questions about the nature of secularity and secularism in the Arab world.

Questions pertaining to secularity, the status of religion in public space, and the separation of church and state are among the key contentions in Arab and Islamic thought of the past two centuries, especially since the annulment of the Caliphate in the 1920s. The spectrum of debate on these three questions stretches from those who maintain that Islam is both a religion and a state and so separating the two goes against the very essence of Islam, to those who claim that Islam does not provide a sustained pattern of government and so matters of state are rational-political rather than religious or faith-based. In this chapter, I do not address the ongoing debate on Islam, politics, and the state, which is unlikely to ever be determined and which will most likely result in the creation of many more ideologically cohesive Islamic schools of thought and the evolution of Islamic political thought more generally. Rather, I show that a consensus exists between all Islamic schools—including several secular strands—on the importance of Islam in the public sphere in Arab society, and also to highlight the emergence of the notion of *al-dawla al-madaniya* (the secular state) in Islamic political discourse.

The chapter is divided into four parts. The first part introduces the debates on the relationship between religion and the public sphere and the role of civil society in this interaction. The second part describes the place of religion in the Tunisian postcolonial state. The third part analyzes the Tunisian political Islam movement and its views on democracy, civil society, and the place of religion in the modern state. The fourth part addresses the situation in Tunisia after the revolution, namely the relationship between religious actors and the secular state and its influence on democratization.

Political Islam, Democracy, and the Public Sphere

The rise of the postsecular paradigm and renewed attention to the dominant place of religion in even the ostensibly secularized European public sphere has engendered two schools of thought on the relationship between political Islam and democracy in Arab countries. The first school includes researchers such as John Esposito, James Piscatori, and John Voll, who maintain that the approaches of some thinkers affiliated with political Islam can be aligned with Western democratic principles. Moreover, they argue that the ideas promoted by some of political Islam's leaders and thinkers can assist in the reconceptualization of the democratic ideal in general and help amend some of the shortcomings of Western democracy in particular.[1]

By extension, several articles in Larry Diamond, Marc Plattner, and Daniel Brumberg's edited volume *Islam and Democracy in the Middle East* suggest that the presence of Islam in Arab states is not in and of itself a sufficient explanation for democracy's absence. Factors including economic patterns, the political elite, and the types of government and opposition are suggested as alternatives that offer more satisfying explanations.[2] Daniel Price, who conducted an empirical study on this very subject, also concludes that Islam cannot be considered the reason for the absence of democracy in Muslim states.[3]

The second school includes scholars such as Bernard Lewis and Samuel Huntington.[4] Despite considerable disagreements among themselves on key premises of Islam's role in Arab society, they are united in concluding that parties identified with political Islam are among the main obstacles to democratic change in the region and even threaten the democratic process itself. They draw their conclusion from an essential feature of Islam, which is the lack of distinction between the religious and political collectives and, unlike Christianity, between the kingdom of heaven and the temporal kingdom.[5]

However, neither school's arguments contribute much to an understanding of how the parties affiliated with political Islam participate in electoral processes at all. Nor do they offer clarity on the dynamic that steps toward democratization could engender in the region; they also fail to provide an adequate explanation of the factors that led to these steps in the first place. In sum, both schools suffer from the same flaw: they attempt to deduct the political behavior of movements and parties identified with political Islam directly from their long-term ideologies instead of from their political practices.

In addition to the aforementioned debates, postsecular literature has contributed to scholarly understanding of another aspect of the relationship between religion and democracy, namely the role of religion in the public sphere. It was a long-standing trend to uphold as normative the dichotomies pitting "religion/tradition" and "secular/modern" against one another. This dichotomous approach effectively ignored the historical and cultural specificity of secularism, religion, tradition, and modernity while simultaneously equating modernity and secularity, understood here as the disengagement and segregation of religion from the public sphere.⁶ This equation of secularity and modernity led to pervasive scholarly belief in the decline of religion in social and private life as well as the decline of religious institutions.

However, far from receding from the public sphere as anticipated by secularization theorists, religious actors and faith-based organizations appear to be growing in salience while revitalizing discourses on religiosity, spirituality, and morality in public life and policy.⁷ Specifically, since the rise of politicized Christianity and Islam in the 1970s, it has become increasingly difficult to theorize the complexity of religious phenomena from the lens of secularization theories.⁸

A nuanced understanding of the current relationship between religion and the public sphere is introduced by Jürgen Habermas, who differentiates between what he calls the formal and informal public/political spheres—the former consisting of parliaments, courts, and ministries and the latter as the appropriate setting for communication between religious and nonreligious people.⁹ He maintains that although political institutions need to maintain neutrality with respect to religion, discourse between secular and religious citizens and between those belonging to different religions can and should use religious language and arguments. Habermas and Reemtsma understood religion's reentry into the public sphere to be a shift into what they pronounced a "post-secular age."¹⁰ This was meant to insinuate that the world was returning not to a state where secularism and rationalism did not exist but to "one in which religious and secular worldviews could co-exist and even enter into dialogue with one another."¹¹ The until recently dominant liberal school of civil society excludes religious actors from this realm.¹² However, there is an evolving school of civil society that takes a more communitarian approach by understanding civil society as containing nonliberal groups, including religious ones.¹³

In literature more specifically oriented around the development of civil societies in the Arab world, there are two main approaches to understanding civil society's role and importance.¹⁴ Religious Islamic thought maintains that civil society existed in Islam well before it developed in Europe. According to this opinion, the role of Islamic civil society differed greatly from its Western counterparts.¹⁵ Counter to this, secular Arab opinion holds that civil society is a new development in the Arab world and should not be associated with the various civil and social structures that existed previously in Muslim societies.¹⁶

As such, Islamic thought perceives contemporary civil society organizations to be an influence of Western modernization on Arab society, which has successfully maintained its Islamic ideals. An examination of Islamic sources shows that at Islam's nascence, the prophet Muhammad formed the first Umma (political community) in Medina, the second-holiest city in Islam, where Prophet Muhammad is buried, and the site of the political and religious base of Islam in its formative period. This school of thought, however, does not differentiate between political community and civil society. Rather, the political community is referred to as a civil society in Islamic sources and is influenced by the Western social contract, which holds that the establishment of the state is in fact the establishment of civil society. In addition, this opinion does not recognize the separation that later formed between the state and the civil societies working within it.[17] It is worth mentioning that the definition and significance of civil society, including that of the Arab secular school, is not a political community but the existence and actions of social organizations that constitute a link in the chain connecting the state to the public.[18] Therefore, secular Arabs reject the claim that the Umma was in fact a civil society, arguing that the historical realities of political and social Islam do not reflect what is now called "civil society."[19]

Divergences between religious and secular approaches in modern Arab thought have resulted in markedly different perceptions of civil society. Those aligned with the secular approach reference "volunteer organizations," whereas those aligned with the Islamic approach view them as communitarian social organizations. The former group seeks to affect the state's political policies, while the latter group focuses on changing and galvanizing the community's character. Another contrasting characteristic between these two models is that the concept of the civil prioritized by the secular approach arises mostly in cities, whereas the notion of the communal valued by the religious approach arises primarily in villages or rural areas. The former expresses modern relations of power and production; the latter, however, represents the traditional relations of power and production (the tribe, clan, and ethnicity; the social and ethical structure).[20] Having introduced these key literatures and concepts, I now turn to the Tunisian case.

Church and State in Postcolonial Tunisia

Tunisia is considered a relatively homogeneous state compared to other countries of the Maghreb. The Tunisian state came into being in 1956 as a result of the independence agreement signed between France and the Tunisian National Movement's al-Dusturi al-Jadid (New Constitutional Party), led by Habib Bourguiba; this party represented secular forces in the Tunisian national movement.

With the triumph of the secular-modernist strand and the declaration of Tunisian independence, President Bourguiba turned to realize his vision for Tunisia's future through two principle moves: (1) establishing and solidifying a centralized authoritarian regime and (2) marginalizing Tunisia's Arab and Muslim identity, then replacing it with a new Tunisian nation culturally and politically detached from the Arab Muslim world. Bourguiba, influenced by his Western (specifically French) upbringing, wanted to build a Tunisian society that was modern in all respects. He was also deeply influenced by Mustafa Kemal Atatürk and his contributions to shaping modern Turkey.[21]

Tunisia was the most secular state in the Arab world in general and the Maghreb in particular, as demonstrated across fields like legislation, family law, freedom of worship and conscience, and overall cultural and institutional policy.[22] The struggle waged by Arab states at the time was against political Islam as a phenomenon, not against Islam as a religion or personal religious identity. In fact, Arab regimes cultivated and embraced institutional Islam as a counterbalance to the perceived threat of political Islam. In Tunisia, conversely, the regime waged a relentless war against Islam as a religion, marginalizing institutional Islam across the country and dispersing or shutting down its institutions—most notably the Ez-Zitouna. The state effectively nationalized religion, pushing the *ulama* (clerics) to the margins of social and public life.[23]

While other states of the Western Maghreb such as Algeria and Morocco nationalized religion without actually confronting it, Tunisia fought religion by adopting a radical secular ideology and fostering exclusivist institutional secularity. Esposito defines the type of secularism adopted in Tunisia as "secular fundamentalism," with secularism expressed not only in a rigid separation of church and state but through the adoption of aggressively antireligious, antifaith policies.[24]

The very first step undertaken by Bourguiba after independence was passing the marriage laws of August 1956, a move perceived as a blunt challenge to the Tunisian religious establishment of Ez-Zitouna and to the traditional and religious elite of the state. The new law endowed women with rights that contradicted Islamic law and religious texts. Inter alia, the law banned polygamy, banned men from divorcing their wives, banned underage marriages, and enshrined women's right to vote and be elected as well as their right to choose their own partners—even in opposition to family members or custodians. It also allowed Muslim women to marry non-Muslims.[25]

Bourguiba's next step was to wind down and eventually stop the project of instilling literary and cultural Arabic as the dominant language of Tunisia's public sphere. The ongoing use of French and the marginalization of literary Arabic was supported by the state, which saw it as an important step toward the modernization and Westernization of the country and its elite, which formed under colonialism and continued to manage the state under Bourguiba,to a large extent in French.[26]

Alongside the marriage laws, Bourguiba weakened the most important religious institution of Tunisia and one of the most important ones in the entire history of Islam—the Ez-Zitouna, an institution parallel to the al-Azhar clerical university in Egypt. In the early 1960s, the regime canceled junior high school studies in the institution, restricting it to an institution of higher education dedicated to teaching Islamic law on a modest scale. The government also barred graduates of the institution and other Islamic colleges from senior government roles.[27] The new regime's weakening of Ez-Zitouna was another move to marginalize Islam in Tunisian society, despite the important role that the institution played in the struggle against French colonialism.[28] This series of actions proved crucial to the emergence of political Islam, soon to rise from the ruins of moderate institutional religion.

In addition to the cardinal steps, the new president also undertook structural and symbolic moves to further marginalize Islamic identity and engender a complete separation of church and state.[29] They can be summarized as follows:

— Cancelling Friday as the official resting day of the week and replacing it with Sunday, to align with the West.
— Calls, in the early 1960s, to stop fasting during the holy month of Ramadan. Bourguiba was the first Arab president to eat publicly during Ramadan; he also asked Ez-Zitouna to produce a fatwa (edict) allowing eating during Ramadan for economic reasons, as he believed the fast harmed economic growth and the labor market. Unsurprisingly, Ez-Zitouna rejected the request, and the relationship between religious institutions and the state deteriorated further.
— Banning the women's head covering, the hijab.
— Closing the Islamic Waqf institution and banning Tunisians from consecrating assets to the Waqf.
— Framing the pilgrimage to Mecca as a squandering of foreign currency that the state should be using for national construction projects.
— Closely monitoring mosques and religious institutions, establishing state appointments of imams that preached the official ideology, and transforming mosques into prayer houses exclusively rather than

places of education and learning. The mosques were to open immediately before prayer and close immediately after.
— Closing the Shariʻa courts in 1956 and handing their functions over to the civil courts system.

The aim of Bourguiba's policies was to reduce the presence of religion in public and private life and to organize society along modern rather than religious principles. Rachid al-Ghannouchi, the leader of the Islamic movement in Tunisia, sharply criticized the political elites of the time. He argued that the elites were educated in France, influenced by French secularism, and bent on a total war against Islam. The Tunisian national movement, he argued, achieved what French colonialism could not: destroy religious institutions, including the Waqf, and abandon religious tradition—all in the name of modernization. Al-Ghannouchi believed that the independence was not a triumph, as the postcolonial political elite simply continued the work of French colonialism with considerably greater success. He also pointed out a paradox between modernization and authoritarianism in Tunisia: instead of producing a democratic state, as in France, the aggressive modernization movement produced a dictatorial regime.[30]

Political Islam and Democracy in Tunisia

The relationship between Islamic culture, Islam, and democracy has been the subject of considerable research. At first, literature tended to focus on studying the phenomenon of political Islam in the early twentieth century, and the number of works attempting to explain the complex and multifaceted phenomenon of the spread of political Islam has grown dramatically since the 1970s. Nevertheless, hardly any of the explanations offered strayed far from the central argument that all movements identified with political Islam rose in reaction to a state of deep crisis in Arab and Muslim societies, which is to say that political Islam is first and foremost a protest against the reality of crisis in the cultural and political fields.[31]

Political Islam in Tunisia was characterized by considerable flexibility and responsiveness to the demands of Tunisia's political regime, even if those sometimes contradicted the broader Islamic discourse. Furthermore, on both practical-political and ideological levels, the development of political Islam in Tunisia was dictated by its attempts to integrate into the secular political system despite its guardedness. In contrast to similar movements elsewhere, the development of political Islam in Tunisia occurred alongside the development of Tunisian society at large and in response to the challenges posed by the Tunisian intellectual elite, which had few reservations about criticizing and even attacking political Islam and Islam in general—an uncommon occurrence in other Arab states. Its characteristics evolved gradually over a period of two decades.

Islamic organization in the 1970s evolved against the backdrop of the financial crisis, caused by the adoption of free-market policies and economic liberalism. The crisis hit deep, particularly among strata already weakened by the new economic policy, including government officials, the petit bourgeoisie, and the middle class. Mark Tessler also argues for a direct relationship between the economic situation in Tunisia and the rise of political Islam; that is, he maintains that the rising popularity of the movement is best explained not by ideological drives but by the economic crises that occurred in the Arab states of the Maghreb throughout the 1960s and 1970s.[32]

Before 1978, Islamic activity in Tunisia was confined largely to school and universities—in other words, apolitical venues—and focused on religious preaching among high school and university students. The magazine *al-Maarfa* (Knowledge), which was produced from 1972 to 1979, made substantial contributions to the spread of Islamic thought among students by serving as an ideological, cultural, and social venue for political Islam. Its pages hosted debates and arguments against Western culture in general and institutional modernization in particular.

A political framework for Islam in Tunisia emerged contemporaneously with the Islamic Revolution in Iran in 1979. The revolution had a positive effect on political Islam in Tunisia, at least in the first two years; local Islamic leaders saw the Iranian situation as parallel to Tunisia's, with radical secularism excluding religion from public spaces.[33]

In April 1981, President Bourguiba announced a new era of political pluralism. He conditioned the licensing of new political parties and organizations on a commitment to renounce violence and honor the values of the constitution and the state. Al-Ghannouchi and his allies announced the establishment of the Mouvement de la Tendance Islamique (MTI, Islamic Tendency Movement) at a conference that same year. Most of MTI's leaders and members were university educated; 80 percent were graduates from all academic degrees and the rest were public servants or members of the free professions.[34]

A new stage in the history of Tunisian political Islam began in 1987, in the wake of Bourguiba's demotion and Zine El Abidine Ben Ali's ascent to power. The new president declared a new era under the motto "reconciling with identity," which entailed reconciling with the Islamic identity marginalized under Bourguiba.[35] This newfound atmosphere of political openness saw the rise of the Ennahda (Renaissance Movement) in 1989, which replaced the MTI movement. Ennahda is still viewed as one of the most moderate political Islam movements in the Arab world, with some scholars considering it a reformist movement in the context of political Islamic thought.[36]

The establishment of Ennahda signaled a transition to an Islamic movement that accepted the principles of pluralism and engaged in vigorous self-criticism of Islamic activities from the period preceding its establishment, the 1980s.[37] Ennahda's constitution defined its main political objective as follows: "The Ennahda movement fights to maintain the republican regime, while honoring the constitution, the realization of liberty, the independence of the courts, the neutrality of the administrative institutions of the state, and deepening cooperation with the Arab and Muslim states."[38] Nevertheless, Ennahda's application for recognition, filed with the Ministry of the Interior in February 1989, was rejected that June. After the parliamentary elections of 1989, Ennahda was forced to operate in the absence of its historic leader, al-Ghannouchi, who left Tunisia after the elections and did not return until after the 2010 revolution. The 1990s saw the regime continue to suppress Ennahda through arrests, surveillance of membership, and house arrests. According to an Amnesty International report, eight thousand members of the movement were arrested.

In light of this history, François Burgat and William Dowell conclude that the Islamic movement in Tunisia has adapted impressively to the local reality, and that compared to other strands of political Islam, it has undergone many political and ideological phases in the adaptation process.[39] In this regard, it is important to analyze and introduce the positions of Tunisian political Islam in relation to the democratic idea. I primarily focus my analysis on the writings of Rachid al-Ghannouchi, the leader of the Tunisian Islamic movement. It should be noted that after the political and security persecution that Ennahda faced in 1992, a new ideological era began for Tunisian political Islam. The new ideological revolution crystallized in al-Ghannouchi's most important book, *Public Liberties in the Islamic State*.[40] The book was an academic study combining modern philosophy and Islamic thought, with a view toward engaging with modern political ideas, including democracy, human and civil rights, citizenship, and the status of minorities.[41]

Al-Ghannouchi belongs to the moderate Islamic school on questions of democracy, pluralism, and public and personal liberties in society and the state.[42] Al-Ghannouchi believes that public, private, and human rights must be respected in the Islamic state. He argues that these liberties are recognized already in the Quranic text and stresses that the modern idea of human rights, including the Declaration of Human Rights, is in no way essentially contradictory to Islam. He also suggests that all rights and liberties concerning free expression, political organization, political participation, and dialogue should become cornerstones of the relationship between Muslims and society and the state.[43]

The "secular moderate" approach propagated by al-Ghannouchi can be observed long before the revolution. In an interview he gave in 2007, al-Ghannouchi stated that separating church from state but making religion present in public space does not harm the Islamic project. Quite the contrary:

> The state appropriated religion in Tunisia, but Turkish secularism, despite its radical and anti-Islamic beginnings, has evolved, with time, into moderation nationalism and allowed for the establishment of Islamic institutions and schools ... which means that the Islamic movement in Turkey was established outside the scope of the secular Turkish state, and religious institutions were founded as part of the separation of church and state. Religion was taken up by the people and the people eventually managed to establish schools and religious institutions, while in Tunisia none of this is allowed.[44]

In another interview, with the Egyptian daily *Al-Shaab* in October 1989, al-Ghannouchi reflected on the changes that political Islam in Tunisia underwent in the modern era: "The Islamic movement engaged in ideological self-criticism, which has led to a new policy based on deepening freedom and democracy as key to social reform, a key based on the principle of citizenship.... The project of the Islamic movement is the project of civil society, based on cultural and political pluralism, supportive of the lower strata of society and focusing on the social questions, while supporting professional associations and civil society organizations."[45] According to al-Ghannouchi, the political legitimacy of the regime stems from the scope of liberties that it allows, both constitutionally and practically, especially with regard to freedom of expression, freedom of political organization, and peaceful contestation between various movements, schools, and ideologies in the state—all this through the holding of free general elections. He argues that if any particular regime were to allow these liberties in the state, the Islamic movement would support it and see it as legitimate, even if secular or communist parties were to contest the elections.[46]

Al-Ghannouchi goes on to argue that the people endow the regime with legitimacy by voting for it in free and fair elections. He adds that the legitimacy of an elected regime is real, even if the people happen to choose a secular regime. He argues that freedom of conscience and pluralism are values that Islam protects and commands. Al-Ghannouchi employs a theological argument by saying that a religious text can be interpreted in many ways. While it is true that the text is one, its interpretation can be pluralist, changing from one person to another; therefore, political pluralism cannot be in contradiction with Islam, which already recognizes a plurality of interpretations for its own sacred texts.[47]

Aligned with general political Islamic thought, al-Ghannouchi agrees that Islam is both religion and state, but he argues that the Islamic state is not an autocratic state presuming to speak, judge, and rule for God. Rather, it is a state of civic institutions, expressive of the free will of its citizens and maintaining the vital interest of its people. Such a state will be established only when the people will it to be established.[48]

Furthermore, al-Ghannouchi believes that Muslims must integrate into the modernization project, albeit still within an Islamic framework. He argues that the political divide in Tunisia is not between a modernist movement and a traditional one but between two kinds of modernity, that which ignores Islam and that which attempts to bring Islam and modernity together. To this end, he maintains that there are a great variety of opinions on the status of the woman in Islam, and that the gates of *al-ijtihad* (interpretation) must be opened to reconsider the place of the woman in Islamic society.

Al-Ghannouchi draws a distinction between two concepts, *al-dini* (religious) and *al-siasi* (political). He argues that not all Islamic heritage is religious in the sense of absolutely sacred; rather, there are *farajat* (lacunae) that people need to fill in accordance with their needs and the context in which they live.[49] In other words, Islam offers Muslims the freedom to make rational decisions on political issues such as the character of the state and the structure and purpose of the regime. Issues in the realm of siasi are not considered sacred, which cannot be changed and where the text, rather than the context, is the determining factor.

Al-Ghannouchi argues that liberalism has two sides, enlightened and dark. The enlightened side includes the recognition and protection of civil rights and liberties, and the adoption of the democratic system. The dark side, however, includes liberalism's leaning on the absolute power of the mind and the neglect of faith as an important motivating force in life, an overemphasis on the individual at the expense of community and collective, and the exclusion of religious values from economic arrangements, social relations, politics, and international relations.[50]

Al-Ghannouchi's pluralism stems from the pressure applied by the secular Tunisian regime onto the Islamic movement, which led him to adapt pluralistic ideas and principles regarding the status of woman and non-Muslim minorities in society, democracy and democratic constitutions, equality, and the concept of citizenship. Moreover, his own difficult experience of exile and pressures on his movement have led him to adopt these principles, integrate them in his Islamic platform, and provide them with spiritual and religious basis drawn from Islamic thought.

Tunisia after the Revolution: Toleration between Religious and Secular Actors

Islam appears in postrevolutionary Tunisian discourse as a system of values and a component in the Tunisian social identity as well as a source of cultural inspiration and a factor in connecting with the broader Arab and Muslim region. Conversely, Islam does not emerge as a source of legislative or political authority, nor as an integral component of the new regime. Indeed, Alfred Stepan describes the Tunisian case as "the twin tolerations," namely, the Islamic movement and religious citizens' toleration of the state and the state and state law's toleration of religious actors freely expressing their views and values in the public sphere.[51] In this section, I identify this postrevolutionary tolerance through three primary analyses. To begin, I address the Ennahda movement's political conduct after the revolution and its contributions to the democratization process. I then analyze Ennahda's postrevolution political platform, followed by an analysis of the Tunisian constitution, as a product of compromise between the religious and secular forces in Tunisian society.

The fall of the authoritarian regime was followed by a transition period toward democracy in Tunisia. First, elections were held to set up a constitutional assembly that would articulate a new constitution and administrate the transition period. These elections saw Ennahda win 37 percent of the vote, far ahead of the next biggest party, at 28 percent. Having acquired 89 seats in the assembly, the movement went on to set up a coalition with the secular al-Tiqtal (Unity) party and the el-Mottamar (Congress for the Republic) party. The first postrevolutionary government based on this coalition was led by Hamadi Jebali of Ennahda, and Moncef Marzouki of Congress for the Republic became the first postrevolutionary president. These postrevolution developments show that political Islam was flexible and willing to cooperate with secular movements despite its electoral clout. After the constitution came into force in 2014, new parliamentary and presidential elections were held. Ennahda obtained 26.4 percent of the vote, which translated into 69 parliamentary seats out of 217, and it was overtaken by Nidaa Tunis, a coalition of secular and traditional parties, which obtained 35.7 percent of the vote, or 85 seats. In the presidential

TABLE 3.1 LEGISLATIVE ELECTION RESULTS, 2014

Candidate list	% of overall voters	Number of seats
Nidaa Tunis	37.50	86
Ennahda	27.70	69
Free Patriotic Union	4.02	16
Popular Front	3.60	15
Afek Tunis	3.02	8
Congress for the Republic	2.10	4
Democratic Current	1.90	3
People Movement	1.30	3
National Destourian Initiative	1.30	3
Current of Love	1.20	2
Republican Party	1.40	1
Democratic Alliance	1.20	1
National Salvation Movement	0.18	1
Movement of Socialist Democrats	0.17	1
Others (4)	1.00	4

Source: National Democratic Institute, "Final Report on the 2014 Legislative and Presidential Elections in Tunisia" (Washington, DC, 2014), 53, https://www.ndi.org/Tunisia-election-report-2014.

elections, Ennahda opted not to put forward a candidate, and these elections were won by Beji Caid Essebsi, a secular leader and member of the old elite. The Nidaa Tunis party led the government, and Ennahda remained in opposition. Subsequent developments and a succession of prime ministers have led the movement toward a historical turning point. In 2016 Ennahda's general conference decided to separate political activities from religious ones; the party became exclusively political and religious activity was relegated to civil society organizations.[52]

Ennahda's ideological and political orientation is reflected in its political platform, published ahead of the parliamentary and presidential elections of 2014 under the title "Electoral Platform: Toward a Developing Economy and a Secure Country.""[53] In the platform's foreword, al-Ghannouchi wrote that the new Tunisian constitution "bridged Islam and the essence of modernity and established the principles of the rule of law and respect for individual liberties and human rights."[54] After listing the achievements of past governments in which his movement played a pivotal role, he lists the movement's three ideological goals in the contemporary Tunisian context: "Recognizing the cultural primitivism compared to what other nations have obtained through progress that guaranteed their power, wealth and pride, and all because of the liberation of the mind from delusions and liberation of the government from tyranny"; "recognizing the need to bridge these gaps through acquiring modern sciences and technology, and developing administrative and political institutions . . . so as to preclude tyranny"; and "recognizing the validity of Islam and its tradition as a source of authority on values and culture, and a basis for a reformist project of modernity through interpretation and renewal and deliberation of the issues of a modern world and politics."[55]

Crucially, the platform identifies building democracy, and supporting democratic processes and core values, as the movement's central political goal.[56] As an extension of this main goal, the platform highlights the need for "completing the construction of democratic institutions, support for civil society, advancing the media and the party system, and advancing the Tunisian democratic experiment through debate, building relationships between political and civil movements based on mutual respect, cooperation, clean competition, with the aim of strengthening national unity, and fighting terrorism, the culture of hatred and violence and the fragmentation of society."[57] In another section, devoted to culture, education, and art, the platform identifies the need to advance culture by supporting both cultural institutions and the cultural producers themselves during their working lives and through their pensions, as well as the necessity of reforming Tunisia's general and higher education systems.[58]

Most of the remainder of the platform addresses economic issues as well as the terrorism problem in the state, propagated mostly by extreme Salafi factions; the platform offers social and military means to deal with the threat. On the social front, the platform promises to promote moderation, tolerance, and openness through changes to the educational system and to emphasize the value of work and the growth of cultural and sports activity in Tunisian society.[59]

The chapter on Tunisian society opens by detailing the movement's approach to the position of women in society: "Our belief is that the woman is a central partner in the building of a balanced society, developed economy and economic growth. We support equality between the sexes and will continue to fight against all forms of exploitation, marginalization and violence against women, and preserving family principles and promoting the family structure."[60] To this end, the platform proposes allowing the children of Tunisian mothers and foreign fathers to obtain Tunisian citizenship, to support programs for the advancement of women from rural areas, to extend maternity leaves from two months to three, and to establish the office of an ombudsman against gender discrimination. Here, we can see the influence of the legacy of the Tunisian women's struggle for civil and political equality in the Ennahda movement's platform, which manifests in greater involvement by women in the movement's political activities. For example, Ennahda made history when a female mayor from the movement won the council elections in the capital city, Tunis. Ennahda also separated the religious and political aspects of its work. In other words, the Islamic movement was activated in two arenas, the political in the governmental arena and the religious in the public sphere. As al-Ghannouchi stated, "Ennahda has changed from an ideological movement engaged in the struggle for identity, to a protest movement against the authoritarian regime, and now to a national democratic party. We must keep religion far from political struggles."[61]

Given how Ennahda's postrevolutionary political conduct and written political platform demonstrate a commitment to political pluralism and democratic values, I now examine the postrevolutionary Tunisian constitution to identify how it reflects the secular state's stance on Islam. The constitution, which was finally affirmed in 2014, was formulated by various political movements in Tunisia after the revolution. It is a new social contract, a foundational document of the postauthoritarian era that reflects compromises between the different political, social, and ideological movements in Tunisia. Although Ennahda was by far the largest party in the democratically elected Constitutional Assembly, the constitution, as articulated by the assembly, went on to shape a de facto secular state while respecting the status of religion in the public sphere and the importance of religion to Tunisian society's collective and cultural identity.

The words "Islam" and "Muslim" make seven appearances in the constitution. Islam appears twice in the context of Tunisia's social identity, in the phrase "Arabic Islamic identity."[62] It appears twice more to emphasize the bond with other Muslim societies, once in the formula "Arab and Muslim peoples" and once more in the formula "Muslim peoples," referring to non-Arab Muslim nations. "Islam" appears once as a means of determining Islam as the official religion of the state, and again in a requirement that the president must always be a Muslim (Tunisia's population is 99 percent Muslim). And finally, "Islam" appears once in the context of national values, in the formula "as an expression of our nation's retention of the values of Islam and its aims, characterized by tolerance and moderation." The rest of the text is articulated as a democratic, liberal, and secular constitution. In the remainder of this chapter, I consider only the constitutional clauses directly relevant to my topic.

In the first chapter of the constitution, which lists the general principles of government, the first article declares: "Tunisia is a free, independent, sovereign state; its religion is Islam, its language Arabic, and its system is republican." The second article reads: "Tunisia is a civil state based on citizenship, the will of the people, and the supremacy of law." The third states: "The people are sovereign and the source of authority, which is exercised through the peoples' representatives and by referendum." The fourth article notes that the motto of Tunisia is "freedom, dignity, justice, and order."

On the issue of religion in the new system of governance, Article 6 explains that "the state is the guardian of religion. It guarantees freedom of conscience and belief, the free exercise of religious practices and the neutrality of mosques and places of worship from all partisan instrumentalization. The state undertakes to disseminate the values of moderation and tolerance and the protection of the sacred, and the prohibition of all violations thereof. It undertakes equally to prohibit and fight against calls for Takfir and the incitement of violence and hatred." Unlike the Egyptian Constitution, for example, this first chapter does not reference Islamic law as a legislative source. Religion retains its place as a source of cultural inspiration, and the state guarantees both freedom of religion and freedom from religion.

In chapter 2, which deals with rights and liberties, Article 21 states that "all citizens, male and female, have equal rights and duties, and are equal before the law without any discrimination. The state guarantees freedoms and individual and collective rights to all citizens and provides all citizens the conditions for a dignified life." Article 31 guarantees "freedom of opinion, thought, expression, information and publication." Article 46 commits the state to "protect women's accrued rights and work to strengthen and develop those rights" and to work to "attain parity between women and men in elected Assemblies." In chapter 5, which deals with the judiciary, clause 102 notes that "the judiciary is independent. It ensures the administration of justice, the supremacy of the Constitution, the sovereignty of the law, and the protection of rights and freedoms."

Through these examples, we see that the Tunisian Constitution appears to be secular. Ennahda was the main movement to support and accept this constitution in the general assembly, which means that the Islamic movement accommodated the separation of religion from state. Ennahda's distinct religious and political vision began with al-Ghannouchi's thought in exile; continued through the movement's political platform, especially through its support for separating religious activity from the political; and culminated with its support of the Tunisian Constitution.

From Exclusive to Inclusive Secularism

Tunisia is the only Arab state to have succeeded, so far, in maintaining a steady pace toward democratization despite economic and security challenges and the historical legacy of religious-secular hostility. The Tunisian case is unique in two ways: First, it is the only Arab state to have established a radically secular regime along the French and Turkish models. Second, it is the only state in which an Islamist party has risen to make a decisive contribution to democratization in the state.

Independent Tunisia was built upon two axes: rigid authoritarianism and exclusive secularity. The authoritarian regime suppressed every attempt at multiparty political pluralism, including movements that identified themselves with the secular regime's own values. Tunisian exclusive secularity, meanwhile, rejected ideological and intellectual pluralism, with the exception of ideas closely identifying with the hard line of the regime. The idea of religion as a system of values of key importance in Tunisian history has been summarily excluded from both the formal and informal political arenas. The exclusion of political Islam was a double one: both political and because of the regime's hard-line secularism.

The link between authoritarianism and secularism espoused by the postcolonial and prerevolutionary regime in Tunisia was a challenge facing the 2010 democratic revolution, especially in light of the rise of political Islam, which manifested in the electoral power accrued by Ennahda and its contribution to the revolution's success. The secular strand of Tunisian society, and its multitude of political parties and movements, had to deal with the problematic legacy of radical secularism that could not have survived without an authoritarian regime—certainly not considering the key role religion played in the pre-independence Tunisian society, including in rallying support for the fight for independence. Only a rigid, hard-line regime could impose exclusive secularism in this context. Political and ideological developments in Tunisia closely followed the new religious and secular policies that emerged in the West. Political Islam detached itself from the political-religious tradition that held Islam to be both religion and state, while the secular strand distanced itself from the authoritarian legacy that held rigid, exclusivist secularism as a precondition for modernity. Tunisia's formula of inclusive rather than exclusive secularity, complemented by a mutually beneficial separation of church and state and the inclusion of religion in the public sphere, offer a model for democratization in the Arab world, where Islam remains an important component of individual and collective identity. The Tunisian case study underscores that the most pertinent questions in Arab politics, those pertaining to democratization and modernity, are not religious questions but secular first and foremost.

NOTES

1 John Voll and John Esposito, "Islam's Democratic Essence," *Middle East Quarterly* 1, no. 3 (1994): 3–11; John Voll, "Islam and Democracy: Is Modernization a Barrier?," in *Modernization, Democracy, and Islam*, ed. Shireen T. Hunter and Huma Malik (London: Praeger, 2005), 82–97; John L. Esposito and James P. Piscatori, "Democratization and Islam," *Middle East Journal* 45, no. 3 (1991): 427–40.

2 See, for example, Abdou Filali-Ansary, "The Sources of Enlightened Muslim Thought," in *Islam and Democracy in the Middle East*, ed. Larry Diamond, Marc F. Plattner, and Daniel Brumberg (Baltimore: Johns Hopkins University Press, 2003), 237–51.

3 Daniel Price, *Islamic Political Culture, Democracy, and Human Rights: A Comparative Study* (Westport, CT: Praeger, 1999), 153–54.

4 Bernard Lewis, "Islam and Liberal Democracy," *Atlantic Monthly*, February 1993, 89–98; Samuel Huntington, "Will More Countries Become Democratic?," *Political Science Quarterly* 99, no. 2 (1984): 192–218.

5 Lewis, "Islam and Liberal Democracy"; Samuel Huntington, *The Clash of Civilization and the Remaking of World Order* (New York: Simon and Schuster, 1996).

6 Sam Kaplan, "Religious Nationalism: A Textbook Case from Turkey," *Comparative Studies of South Asia, Africa and the Middle East* 25, no. 3 (2004): 668; Roger Friedland, "Religious Nationalism and the Problem of Collective Representation," *Annual Review of Sociology* 27, no. 1 (2001): 127.

7 Gerard Clarke, "Faith Matters: Faith-Based Organisations, Civil Society and International Development," *Journal of International Development* 18, no. 6 (2006): 835–48; Kenneth D. Wald, Adam L. Silverman, and Kevin Fridy, "Making Sense of Religion in Political Life," *Annual Review of Political Science* 8 (2005): 121–43.

8 Michael O. Emerson and David Hartman, "The Rise of Religious Fundamentalism," *Annual Review of Sociology* 32 (2006): 127–44; Darren E. Sherkat and Christopher G. Ellison, "Recent Developments and Current Controversies in the Sociology of Religion," *Annual Review of Sociology* 25 (1999): 363–94; Daniel Philpott, "Has the Study of Global Politics Found Religion?," *Annual Review of Political Science* 12 (2009): 183.

9 Jürgen Habermas, "Religion in the Public Sphere," *European Journal of Philosophy* 14, no. 1 (2006): 1–25.

10 Jürgen Habermas and Jan Philipp Reemtsma, *Glauben und Wissen: Friedenspreis des Deutschen Buchhandels* (Frankfurt am Main: Suhrkamp, 2001), quoted in Philip S. Gorski and Ateş Altinordu, "After Secularization?," *Annual Review of Sociology* 34 (2008): 55–85.

11 Jürgen Habermas and E. Mendieta, *Religion and Rationality: Essays on Reason, God, and Modernity* (Cambridge, MA: MIT Press, 2002), quoted in Gorski and Altinordu, "After Secularization?," 56.

12 Francis Fukuyama, *Trust: The Social Virtues and the Creation of Prosperity* (New York: Free Press, 1995).
13 B. Turam, "The Politics of Engagement between Islam and the Secular State: Ambivalences of 'Civil Society,'" *British Journal of Sociology* 55, no. 2 (2004): 259-81.
14 Kamil M. Al-Sayyid, "The Concept of Civil Society and the Arab World," in *Political Liberalization and Democratization in the Arab World*, vol. 1, *Theoretical Perspectives*, ed. Bahgay Korany, Rex Brynen, and Paul Noble (Boulder, CO: Lynne Rienner, 1995), 48-131.
15 Ahmad Moussalli, "Modern Islamic Fundamentalist Discourse on Civil Society, Pluralism and Democracy," in *Civil Society in the Middle East*, ed. Augustus Richard Norton (Leiden: Brill, 1993), 79-119.
16 Azmi Bishara, *Civil Society: Critical Study* [in Arabic] (Doha: Arab Center for Research and Policy Studies, 2012).
17 Saad El-din Ibrahim, *Egypt, Islam and Democracy* (Cairo: American University in Cairo Press, 2004).
18 Nadia Abu-zahir, "Civil Society," in *Between the Descriptive and the Normative: Deconstructing a Conceptual Muddle* [in Arabic] (Ramallah: Palestinian Institute for the Study of Democracy, 2008).
19 Seif Al-din Ismail, *Comparison between Civil and Communitarian Society from the Islamic Perspective* [in Arabic] (Damascus: Dar Al-fikr, 2003).
20 Nadia Abu-zahir, "Civil Society.," 179-185.
21 Derek Hopwood, *Habib Bourguiba of Tunisia: The Tragedy of Longevity* (London: Macmillan, 1992).
22 Katerina Dalacoura, "Islamist Terrorism and the Middle East Democratic Deficit: Political Exclusion, Repression and the Cause of Extremism," in *Democratization in the Muslim World: Changing Patterns of Power and Authority*, ed. Fredric Volpi and Francesco Cavatorta (London: Routledge, 2007), 158. Tunisia's secularism was pursued despite its constitution, which states that the official religion of the state was Islam and that the president of the state must be Muslim, a useful illustration of how meaningless a constitution of an authoritarian state is, for practical purposes.
23 Abdelbaki Hermassi, "The Political and the Religious in the Modern History of the Maghrib," in *Islamism and Secularism in North Africa*, ed. John Ruedy (New York: St. Martin's, 1996), 87-99.
24 John L. Esposito, "Islam and Secularism in the Twenty-First Century," in *Islam and Secularism in the Middle East*, ed. Azzam Tamimi and John L. Esposito (London: Hurst, 2000), 9.
25 Hermassi, "Political and Religious."
26 Charles Micaud, *Tunisia: The Politics of Modernization* (London: Pall Mall, 1964).
27 Mahmmod Al-Dawudi, "On Collective Identity and Its Problematics: The Modern Tunisian Society" [in Arabic], *Al-mustaqbal Al-arabi* 217 (1997): 29-50.
28 Norma Salen, *Habib Bourguiba, Islam, and the Creation of Tunisia* (London: Croom Helm, 1984); Emad Eldin Shahin, *Political Ascent: Contemporary Islamic Movements in North Africa* (Boulder, CO: Westview, 1997).

29 Kenneth J. Perkins, *Tunisia: Crossroads of the Islamic and European Worlds* (Boulder, CO: Westview, 1986), 118–24.
30 Rachid al-Ghannouchi, "Secularism in the Arab Maghreb," in *Islam and Secularism in the Middle East*, ed. Azzam Tamimi and John L. Esposito (London: Hurst, 2000), 107–9.
31 Hraia R. Dekmejian, *Islam in Revolution: Fundamentalism in the Arab World* (Syracuse: Syracuse University Press, 1995).
32 Mark Tessler, "The Origins of Popular Support for Islamist Movements: A Political Economy Analysis," in *Islam, Democracy, and the State in North Africa*, ed. John P. Entelis (Bloomington: Indiana University Press, 1997), 93–126.
33 François Burgat and William Dowell, *The Islamic Movement in North Africa* (Austin: University of Texas at Austin, 1993), 86.
34 Abdelbaki Hermassi, "The Rise and Fall of the Islamist Movement in Tunisia," in *The Islamist Dilemma: The Political Role of Islamist Movements in the Contemporary Arab World*, ed. Laura Guazzone (Berkshire, UK: Garnet, 1995), 105–28.
35 Al-Dawudi, "On Collective Identity."
36 Michael Collins Dunn, "The Al-Nahda Movement in Tunisia: From Renaissance to Revolution," in *Islamism and Secularism in North Africa*, ed. John Ruedy (New York: St. Martin's, 1996), 149–65; John P. Entelis, "Political Islam in the Maghreb: The Nonviolent Dimension," in *Islam, Democracy and the State in North Africa*, ed. John P. Entelis (Bloomington: Indiana University Press, 1997), 43–74.
37 Guddun Kramer, "Islam and Pluralism," in *Political Liberalization and Democratization in the Arab World*, vol. 1, *Theoretical Perspectives*, ed. Bahgay Korany, Rex Brynen, and Paul Noble (London: Lynne Rienner, 1995), 122.
38 Alya Alani, *Islamic Movement in the Arab World: Case Study Tunisia* [in Arabic] (Rabat: Point View, 2008), 122.
39 Burgat and Dowell, *Islamic Movement*.
40 Rachid al-Ghannouchi, *Public Liberties in the Islamic State* [in Arabic] (Beirut: Center for Arab Unity, 1993).
41 Azzam Tamimi, *Rachid Ghannouchi: A Democrat within Islamism* (Oxford: Oxford University Press, 2001).
42 Tamimi, *Rachid Ghannouchi*.
43 Al-Ghannouchi, *Public Liberties*.
44 Abd Hakem Mufid, "Interview with Rachid Ghannouchi," *Sawat al-haq wa-ahuriya*, December 17, 2007, 1–4. All translations are mine unless otherwise noted.
45 Faiz Sara, *Islamic Movement in Arab Maghrib* [in Arabic] (Beirut: Center for Strategic Studies, 1995), 78.
46 Al-Ghannouchi, *Public Liberties*.
47 Al-Ghannouchi, *Public Liberties*.
48 Voll and Esposito, "Islam's Democratic Essence."
49 Tamimi, *Rachid Ghannouchi*.
50 Al-Ghannouchi, "Secularism in the Arab Maghreb," 117.
51 Alfred Stepan, "Tunisia's Transition and the Twin Toleration," *Journal of Democracy* 23, no. 2 (2012): 89–103.

52 Al-Ghannouchi responds to this situation as follows: "It would be a grave mistake to respond to the threat of terrorism and extremism by forcibly excluding religious values from public life. This kind of repression has been at the root of terrorism in our region. Under the former presidents of Tunisia, the institutions of mainstream reformist Islamic thought were shut down or restricted, leaving the way for extremist ideas to fill the vacuum." Rachid al-Ghannouchi, "How Tunisia Will Succeed," *New York Times*, November 20, 2014.
53 Ennahda Movement, "Electoral Platform: Toward a Developing Economy and a Secure Country" [in Arabic] (Tunis: Ennahda Movement, 2014).
54 Ennahda Movement, "Electoral Platform," 6.
55 Ennahda Movement, "Electoral Platform," 10–11.
56 "We will maintain our efforts for democratization and for moving away from tyranny, corruption and human rights violations, and for building a democratic regime based on citizenship and honoring liberties and equality of rights and obligations and the rule of law. . . . The power of the state rests on the popular will, its elected institutions and commitment to the law, and its ability to enforce the rule of law to attain the political, cultural, and social aims of the revolution." Ennahda Movement, "Electoral Platform," 11.
57 Ennahda Movement, "Electoral Platform," 12.
58 Ennahda Movement, "Electoral Platform," 13.
59 Ennahda Movement, "Electoral Platform," 48.
60 Ennahda Movement, "Electoral Platform," 55.
61 Tarek Amara, "Tunisian Islamists Ennahda Move to Separate Politics, Religion," Reuters, May 20, 2016.
62 "Tunisia: The Constitution of 2014," ConstitutionNet, http://constitutionnet.org/vl/item/tunisia-constitution-2014.

4. NEOLIBERAL POLITICAL THEOLOGY

MARCIA KLOTZ AND LEEROM MEDOVOI

The past twenty years have seen a burgeoning field of studies that examines the rise of neoliberal thought and the growing influence of Chicago School economic theory on both government policy and subject formation in numerous social contexts around the globe. In this chapter, we offer some reflections on one question that has received relatively scant attention in this growing body of scholarship: why does neoliberalism, despite its radical reformulation of social life within an exclusively secular framework that is grounded in the economic science of rational decision theory, appear in many contexts to be deeply compatible with religious traditionalism in a variety of modes?[1] In a number of historical contexts, the rise of neoliberal regimes has gone hand in hand with a resurgence of culturally conservative religious movements. Within the United States, it was the presidency of Ronald Reagan, the first and greatest cheerleader of the neoliberal agenda in the White House, that also established a growing and long-lasting role of Christian evangelism within the political mainstream. In Egypt, the short-lived reign of the Muslim Brotherhood appeared equally devoted to a political practice of Islam within the

Egyptian state and to a radical restructuring of the Egyptian economy, according to neoliberal principles. As explored in Ori Goldberg's contribution to this volume, Israeli policies likewise unite the growing influence of conservative branches of Orthodox Judaism with a neoliberal discourse that justifies Zionist expansion into the Negev as an "opportunity for Bedouin-Israeli development" or that promotes the establishment of Jewish-owned "industrial zones" in the occupied territories. Or we could look to the election of Narendra Modi in India, whose far-right policies celebrate Hinduism while privatizing and deregulating the Indian economy as quickly and radically as possible. In all these instances, Chicago School economic policy and science appear deeply compatible on a political level with conservative religious movements, each drawing sustenance from the other.

While we lack the expertise to speak to the connections between neoliberalism, on the one hand, and radical Islam, Orthodox Judaism, or nationalistic Hinduism, on the other, we devote this chapter to an examination of the links between contemporary Christianity and the rise of neoliberalism within the United States. As Chris Lehmann's recent work demonstrates, the triumph of neoliberal thinking has been especially conducive to the rise of specific denominations within U.S. culture, especially those evangelical churches that embrace the doctrine of prosperity, along with Mormonism, in which the celebration of wealth as a sign of divine blessing has always played a strong role. Lehmann argues (contra Max Weber) that these religious movements, which actively embrace capitalist wealth, actually have a strong grounding in U.S. history. Capitalism has not advanced through a secularizing disenchantment of the world, as Weber imagined, but through borrowing and absorbing the theological magic of the divine into the money form itself. Prosperity-preaching evangelicals and Mormons, the modern Christian movements most comfortable with celebrating money as a sacred object, are the fastest-growing religious institutions in the country, Lehmann points out, while the less materialistically focused Christian denominations (old-school Methodists, Episcopalians, and Presbyterians, for example) are watching their congregations wizen and dwindle.[2]

While Lehmann presents a strong case for the centrality of a sacralized monetary role within the history of both U.S. Christianity and American political culture more broadly, we turn the question around, asking what the role of religion has been in economic theory, and how that role might be evolving with the advent of neoliberalism. This in turn, we believe, will show that neoliberalism grounds itself in theological concepts that prove attractive to certain forms of organized religion, and that grounding has facilitated precisely the kinds of political alliances capable of maintaining and sustaining neoliberalism. The durability of the neoliberal approach, which has survived severe economic crises, financial meltdowns, and waves of strong political opposition from all over the globe, may owe a great deal to its religious form of self-legitimation. In analyzing its promises and failures, we thus believe that economic and political approaches need to be supplemented by a methodology that attends to the religious.

Liberal Economic Theologies

The theological aspects of a specific organization of capitalism may strike some readers as a counterintuitive object of study. We are more accustomed to thinking of *political* than of economic theology, the divine model for sovereign state power and authority as theorized by Carl Schmitt, who famously argued that "all significant concepts of the state are secularized theological concepts."[3] Neoliberalism, in contrast, has often been described as a counterforce to the theologically grounded authority of the state, a process that celebrates a strictly secular form of market power that "hollows out" national sovereignty even as it redefines the subject as a rational market player, as entrepreneur rather than citizen. But on what basis does neoliberal authority ground itself; how is it legitimated? If the neoliberal market has been so successful in hollowing out state power, is that success likewise grounded in a secularized theological paradigm, and if so, what kind of political authorization does it constitute?

We begin with a brief outline of theological elements that have operated as central pillars of liberal economic thought, and then turn from there to how these elements are changing in the present moment, or in other words, to the question of what constitutes the "neo" in neoliberalism. Perhaps the most important point we can make in this chapter is that the liberal tradition has embraced a very distinct mode of political theology that deviates from the sovereignty model, as most famously elaborated by Carl Schmitt and Giorgio Agamben. The key move in Schmitt's well-known account was to distinguish the sovereign from the juridical order per se. While the sovereign establishes the law, he also stands above and beyond it as "he who decides on the exception."[4] Since we learn little about the exception from the vacuous universality of the rule, but everything about the rule from the concrete and revealing condition of the exception, Schmitt urges that we analyze sovereignty from the perspective of the latter, the legal breach that occurs in moments of crisis.[5] Both the rule and the exception operate, per Schmitt, through the rationality of a political theology in which the sovereign as "omnipotent lawgiver" is modeled directly upon God. The rule is encapsulated by the juridical order of the modern constitutional state, which is structured on direct analogy to God's natural laws. By contrast, argues Schmitt, "the exception in jurisprudence is analogous to the miracle in theology."[6] When a sovereign power suspends constitutional law, declaring a state of emergency in which it can exercise its omnipotent power without restraint, that sovereign power acts like God himself when he intervenes directly in the world. Schmitt mocks liberal jurists who, in their desire for a full rational order, have forgotten altogether about the state of exception, or who attempt to circumscribe it within the juridical order so as to eliminate its anomalous and mystical quality. While a certain fascistic fascination with the divine power that lies behind the state is obvious in his prose, Schmitt's political theology has proven useful to scholars and critics who wish to understand how the state's authority and capacity for action extends well beyond the exercise of its laws.

However, Schmitt's caricature of liberal theories of the state as ignorant of the theological mysteries of modern politics deserves reconsideration. For Schmitt, who is interested only in state power, the domain of the economy hardly enters the analysis, existing simply as an extension of juridical order, a technocratic space bound by rules within which liberals (and even socialists or anarchists) pathetically demand that the "biased rule of politics over unbiased economic management be done away with."[7] What Schmitt misses here is any consideration of the tradition of political *economy*, which, like jurisprudence, concerns itself with rules and exceptions that have long operated as secularized theological concepts.

In his outstanding study *The Illusion of Free Markets: Punishment and the Myth of Natural Order*, Bernard Harcourt has argued for an enduring relationship between economic liberalism's enshrining of the market as a space of natural order and a related notion of "legal despotism" that concerns the exercise of carceral punishment against those who have violated natural law.[8] Beginning as far back as the Physiocrats of the eighteenth century, continuing through Adam Smith, Jeremy Bentham, and even the Chicago School of the twentieth century, Harcourt demonstrates an ongoing concern in liberal political economy with maintaining the freedom of the marketplace from state intervention. From François Quesnay's notion of "ordre naturel" through Friedrich Hayek's concept of "spontaneous order," we find a zone of social activity that is organized not by human design but by natural order.[9] Within this model, state intervention is at best redundant, merely reiterating the laws by which economic transactions will be conducted anyway, or at worst disruptive, a misguided "policing" that produces disorder and damages market efficiency.

This understanding of the economy affords both similarities to and differences from Schmitt's observations regarding the state. Both models assume a zone of jurisprudential order. Like the domain of law, the modern economy represents a realm ordered by rules that apparently run themselves. There is, however, a difference: the legal domain, even if assumed to be modeled on divine morality, is humanly given, designed. The domain of political economy, by contrast, is understood to be naturally given (like the law of gravity or perhaps the law of large numbers). Intervention by state power into the domain of the economy, therefore, is not the case of a human sovereign suspending its *own* rules. It is rather the case of a human sovereign attempting—and failing—to suspend the rules of nature, an attempted miracle that can only fail.

Harcourt further notes that liberal political economy's account of natural order in the market has always been accompanied by a related but distinctive analysis of the politics of penality, which serve to manage those whom Quesnay, the leading Physiocrat, called the "hommes pervers" and defined as a man "perverted precisely because he does not abide by the natural order of free exchange. Being 'out of order' or 'déréglé' translates today into this idea of bypassing an orderly market." Precisely because their "disordered passions" lead such criminal individuals to attempt to bypass the natural law of the market, the state must indeed intervene, policing these evil individuals by providing "severe punishments."[10]

Is this policing of the homme pervers a case of what Schmitt would call the rule or the exception? That depends on one's frame of reference. From the perspective of the state, it would appear to be the rule, requiring laws that prohibit, police who enforce, prisons that incarcerate. One of Harcourt's key points is that our notion of the free market as maximizing freedom becomes curiously compatible with the carceral state, the legalized imprisonment of massive segments of the population. On the other hand, if one's frame of reference is the *natural law* of the market, then the policing of the homme pervers becomes instead a state of exception, a situation (admittedly ongoing) where the natural laws have been suspended, both because the homme pervers does not obey them and because the liberal state must suspend its normal laissez-faire policy, precisely in *not* letting things take their natural course. In every incarceration, the state steps in to intervene, enacting a miracle of divine punishment that comes from outside the natural economic order. For the Physiocrats, this action should ideally come from the "legal despotism" of an "absolute, hereditary monarch founded on divine right," and so operates very much on the model of a political representation of divine authority.

Harcourt does not directly entertain the implications of liberalism's natural ordering of the market as a matter of political theology, although in at least one moment he observes that "the political, moral and economic realms were governed, the Physiocrats believed, by fundamental natural laws established by an almighty being in order to best promote the interests of mankind."[11] In short, he acknowledges that the liberal concept of a natural economic order derives from a deistic vision of a beneficent but noninterventionist God who grants us the power of reason to discover the goodness of his laws and the ability to honor them. The question that arises here is what, exactly, is *political* about this theological vision.

Some interesting answers to this question are suggested by Elizabeth Pritchard's *Religion in Public: Locke's Political Theology*. John Locke's philosophy of natural order would seem to have anticipated the Physiocrats insofar as, for him too, God has set in motion natural laws that humans are required to understand and obey: "The State of Nature has a Law of Nature to govern it, which obliges every one and Reason, which is that Law, teaches all Mankind, who will but consult it, that being all equal and independent, none ought to harm another in his Life, Health, Liberty or Possessions. For Men being all the Workmanship of one Omnipotent, and infinitely wise Maker; All the Servants of one Sovereign Master, sent into the world by his order and about his business, they are his property."[12] Pritchard sharply distinguishes Locke's political theology from that offered by Schmitt, wherein the sovereign always stands outside and beyond the law. For Schmitt, because liberals mistakenly view sovereignty as emanating from and coterminous with the law, they inevitably fail to see its structural relationship to a transcendent God. In short, liberals assert no political theology. In Pritchard's analysis, however, Locke asserted a "covenantal theology" drawn from biblical notions of covenant between human beings and God (whether with Noah, Abraham, David, the people of Israel, or all humanity through Jesus).[13] The key point about covenantal theology is that it maintains a distinction between God's absolute and ordained power: absolute power represents what God can do as the sole transcendent and omnipotent being, while ordained power expresses what God can do within the limits he has chosen for himself in entering a covenant. This distinction neatly solves Schmitt's problem, showing how liberals can indeed maintain a transcendent God even while imagining natural law as a limit (the terms of the covenant) that both God and humanity will respect. Quoting Perry Miller on Puritan covenantal theology, Pritchard notes that these natural laws also represent a sacred agreement within which God's power is "constrained to be moral, committed to sweet reasonableness."[14]

Within this covenantal framework, humans submit themselves as God's property, but at the same time, God's miracles take shape as purely beneficent acts. Contra Schmitt, for whom the miracle is an explosive act of arbitrary power that shatters quotidian life *and* human bodies when it suspends the law (killing the enemy and destroying the wicked), for Locke, it is Jesus's miracles of healing bodies, multiplying loaves, and resurrecting the dead that represent the new role of divine intervention.

Neoliberal Political Theology

Before returning to neoliberalism, let us sketch what this means in terms of grasping the political theology of liberalism. In Schmittian political theology, the key secularized concept is that of the sovereign himself, who stands in for a transcendent God who has provided us with laws. Liberal political theology, however, is more complex, because there are at least two important secularized concepts at play: that of the sovereign, albeit one who is here bound by a covenantal agreement; and that of natural law itself, the order of the marketplace, whose wisdom can only be fully realized if the state abides by its covenantal agreement not to disrupt the working of those laws, while the people abide by their side of the agreement to operate in accordance with them.

Each side of the covenant, of course, can be violated, and it is here that a dual concept of the enemy emerges for liberalism. People who fail to follow natural law, seeking to bypass the market due to their disordered passions, become the violators of a divine covenant (hommes pervers). In dealing with them, the state must make an exception to its secularized deism, its nonintervention into the economic business of humans, by stepping in to punish the violators. But the state itself can also violate this covenant by seeking to intervene in the laws of the market. Here we face what will be understood not merely as an inefficient or ineffective form of government but a government that is itself an *état pervers*, an unnatural state that violates a sacred agreement and thereby proves itself arbitrary and coercive, tyrannical or even totalitarian, given its interference in the freedoms of property, enterprise, and exchange that form the basis of natural economic law.

Indeed, Hayek's *The Road to Serfdom*, a founding text of neoliberal thought if ever there was one, serves as a broad polemic against the perverse state. Writing at the height of World War II, Hayek takes as his starting point a deep revulsion for Adolf Hitler's Germany—the very example that inspired Schmitt's (generally positive) theorization of the political theology of the state, extrapolated into a universal theory of state power. The odious nature of the Third

Reich leads Hayek to an equally generalized theory; he portrays *all* government intervention into economic matters—every intervention, that is, that does not adopt the limited aim of maximizing competition—as a fundamental assault on freedom, a privileging of the collective at the expense of the individual.[15] Such intervention constitutes the first step on the slippery slope toward totalitarianism, in which the government controls all social and political life. The Keynesian welfare state thus finds its place on a continuum with the socialist planned economy of the Soviet Union, and ultimately with the *National Socialism* of Hitler's fascist dictatorship.

If the "misguided" understanding of the role of state government was triumphing around the world in Hayek's day—in its infantile stage in Franklin D. Roosevelt's New Deal, or the more developed manifestation of the Soviet Union, and fully mature in Benito Mussolini's Italy or Hitler's Germany—Hayek and his followers placed their faith in a countervailing force: the "*spontaneous order*" (consistently italicized in his text) of the market. Admittedly, as a secular rationalist, Hayek never claims an overtly *divine* role for this ordering principle, yet he describes it in highly theological terms. Indeed, he celebrates a state of devout subservience to the market system as the only moral position for the contemporary individual, the only means to defend against the gradual descent into the tyranny of fascism. We must accept *on faith* that the market is far beyond human comprehension and give ourselves over to it: "The refusal to yield to forces which we neither understand nor can recognize as the conscious decisions of an intelligent being is the product of an incomplete and therefore erroneous rationalism. . . . The only alternative to submission to the impersonal and seemingly irrational forces of the market is submission to an equally uncontrollable and therefore arbitrary power of other men."[16]

The faith professed here by Hayek must have felt like a call in the wind in 1944, when state power was at its zenith, with the muscular state authorities of Germany and Italy still at war with the centralized economic model of the Soviet Union, while the free-market democracies of Europe and the United States were still heavily leaning on New Deal policies to mitigate against the economic collapse of 1929. But Hayek's faith in the ordering principles of the marketplace was to find devout followers in George Stigler and especially Milton Friedman, whose tireless evangelizing in the three decades following the war finally bore fruit when Reagan declared his own faith in the "magic of the marketplace" in the 1980s.

During his presidency, Reagan pushed forward four distinct but related policy positions. First, following the Chicago School, he framed government as the problem standing in the way of the social panacea of market freedom. Second, he reinstalled the Cold War through a militant foreign policy of confrontation with the Soviet Union. Third, he promoted a "war on drugs" and "law and order" campaign that vastly accelerated the state of mass incarceration in America. And finally, espousing the Christian underpinnings of American freedom, Reagan incorporated the evangelical right into a winning political hegemony for the first time in the nation's history.

Only the first of Reagan's four positions would be foregrounded by a more conventional understanding of neoliberalism (whether Marxist or Foucauldian) that revolves around economic deregulation and the marketization of society. By framing neoliberalism within the covenantal perspective of liberal political theology, however, we can see the coherence in all four legs of Reagan's platform. In his May 1983 national radio address on the topic of small business, for example, he made a strong pitch for tax cuts and deregulation while celebrating America's entrepreneurs as the "faithfuls who support our churches, schools, and communities, the brave people everywhere who produce our goods, feed a hungry world, and keep our homes and families warm while they invest in the future to build a better America."[17] What interests us here is the economic theology with which he grounds such entrepreneurial faithfulness. On the one hand, he explains, America's entrepreneurs are driven by "self-interest." But self-interest alone cannot produce the beneficence of the market because the entrepreneur must simultaneously wed his self-interest to a successful anticipation of what the consumer wants or needs. In this regard, Reagan suggested, "entrepreneurs intuitively understand one of the world's best kept secrets: Capitalism begins with giving. And capitalism works best and creates the greatest wealth and human progress for all when it follows the teachings of scripture: Give and you will be given unto . . . search and you will find . . . cast your bread upon the waters and it will return to you manifold." The invisible hand that guides the natural law of the marketplace, in other words, is itself associated with a divine promise of abundance generously awarded to those who will cleave to the "morality" of expanding exchange.

Just two months earlier, in a speech to the National Association of Evangelicals, Reagan had already clarified his views on this covenantal blessing of economic natural law, which God established between himself and entrepreneurial humanity, while also calling for militant anticommunism abroad and for a war at home against drugs, abortion, and other unruly, immoral behaviors. Earlier in the speech, Reagan introduces this point by arguing that "freedom prospers only where the blessings of God are avidly sought and humbly accepted."[18] The problem with secular (Keynesian) liberal Americans, by contrast, was that even as "they proclaim that they're freeing us from superstitions of the past, they've taken upon themselves the job of superintending us by government rule and regulation." Reagan here compliments the Christian right for understanding the divine status of the economy's natural law. It is their godliness that shields them from the modern secular temptation of the *état pervers*, the government whose hubristic interference with the market's natural laws shatters the covenant that would guarantee "the blessings of God" and whose most extreme exemplar was, for Reagan, the "evil empire" (a term first used in this speech) of the atheistic Soviet Union. Godliness likewise protects us from the sinful path of the homme pervers, who, unlike the covenant-honoring entrepreneurial subject, relents to the unruly passions associated with "adultery, teenage sex, pornography, abortion, and hard drugs." When it comes to either the perverse state (communist or Keynesian) or the perverse individual (the criminal, sexually profligate, or the drug user), government has a legitimate function in Reagan's view: "There is sin and evil in the world, and we're enjoined by Scripture and the Lord Jesus to oppose it with all our might." While Reagan endorsed a neoliberal ideology of the market's rationality, therefore, his politics were neither secular nor technocratic. His wars on communism, big government, and crime were inextricably tied to his market fundamentalism, functioning as holy struggles against subjects and powers understood as the enemies of an underlying political theology of covenant.

In several important respects, Reagan's version of neoliberalism should be seen as merely transitional. On the surface, his policy assertions hardly differed from classical liberalism's call for a government withdrawn from the economy but zealous in punishing the unruly criminal others of the *homo economicus*. From this perspective, all that made Reagan *neo*liberal was his revivalist moment in history: he called for a return to the "free market" and minimalist government of the nineteenth century, because the twentieth century had taught us that Keynesianism was not only a policy failure but the first leg on the road to Soviet totalitarianism.

Nevertheless, Reagan's classical liberal rhetoric was tacitly accompanied by major shifts in regulatory policy that did in fact lead toward a substantive mutation of liberalism. Above all, Reagan began to refocus the economy away from the production of goods and services and toward financial activities. As Greta Krippner shows, two major decisions contributed to this process, which followed on and intensified the deregulation of financial markets that had occurred in the 1970s.[19] First, Reagan funded his campaign promise to cut taxes without corresponding spending cuts by a new reliance on foreign credit. And second, he directed the Federal Reserve System to relinquish its Keynesian efforts to manage the money supply, permitting markets to determine the availability of credit on their own instead. The result was more than an enormous burgeoning of global credit structures or even the extraordinary empowerment of the banking industry; these new policies ultimately enacted an enormously consequential shift in the *object of economic faith*. The "invisible hand" was no longer responsible for simply coordinating the supply and demand of goods and services; it jumped the frame, so to speak, metamorphosing into a divine arm for harmonizing global credit and futures markets on a grander scale than had ever before existed.

Reagan also enacted another important policy decision that radically shifted corporate culture on the domestic level, abandoning the enforcement of antitrust laws. As a result, even as financial institutions took on a far more influential role in the global economy, corporations were beginning to behave more and more like financial institutions internally.[20] Investment bankers, for the first time, could attempt a new moneymaking strategy in which they used one firm's capital to buy a controlling interest in a competitor, absorbing some of its parts while liquidating and selling off others, often for more than the company's overall stock value. The so-called mergers and acquisitions mania of the 1980s, while roundly criticized at the time for its cold-blooded dismantling of perfectly profitable corporations, marked the beginning of what would come to be more euphemistically known as the "shareholder revolution," a development that would force corporate managers to defend against hostile takeovers by operating their companies from the perspective of the investment value they represent for shareholders rather than from the perspective of their customers, employees, or communities.[21] This substantially shifted corporate focus away from the actual production of goods and services and toward whatever financial transactions might maximize payoffs to shareholders. As Warren Buffett phrased it, "You've now got a body of people who've decided they'd rather go to the casino than the restaurant" of capitalism.[22]

The most noteworthy aspect of this development, for us, is the profound transformation of the very concept of the "market" that took place through this substantive neoliberal turn to financialization. Whereas within the model of classical liberalism, the market represents a place for the buying and selling of commodities, a setting where the entrepreneurs Reagan extolled met the customers whose needs they so brilliantly anticipated, the new financialized neoliberal market of the 1990s was a venue that *invested now in commodities to be produced in the future* as opposed to the *selling now of commodities produced in the past*. Trade in derivative markets gradually came to dwarf trade in goods and services. Indeed, by the beginning of 2015, only 15 percent of all money in the market system was circulating in the so-called real economy; the remainder was locked away within the futures markets of financial institutions.[23]

By the 1990s onward, then, anyone "in the market," including the growing number of Americans whose retirement accounts were kept in equity funds, was participating as an individual in the permanent "shareholder revolution." On the most quotidian level, those retirement accounts enacted a faith that one could make rational and successful calculations to assure *future* wealth for both oneself and society at large through seizing sound investment opportunities today. On a larger, more abstract level, those investments transformed the "invisible hand" into a kind of intelligent design lying behind corporate evolution, a Darwinian principle that unerringly guided corporate America into more efficient and competitive waters.

This insight suggests an important revision to Michel Foucault's otherwise prescient analysis of the subject of neoliberalism in his *Birth of Biopolitics* lectures. Foucault suggested that neoliberalism installs a new sense of the homo economicus, no longer the huckster and trader of Adam Smith but now an "entrepreneur of the self" who seeks to maximize his human capital in all social domains. While we agree with this general observation, we would suggest that Foucault's allusion to the "entrepreneur," which invoked (as did Reagan's use of the term in the same era) a producer of commodities, misses the critical financial turn that would accelerate only in the decades subsequent to Foucault's lectures.[24] The emergent neoliberal subject of the 1990s through the 2010s is more accurately characterized not as an "entrepreneur of the self" but as an *investor in the self*, or perhaps as a *shareholder of one*. Investing in yourself, not just for the long term but also in terms of immediate return (maximizing shareholder value), means doing everything possible to attract investment from others right now: from colleges, employers, or partners of all possible kinds. The successful self, one of Reagan's "faithful," no longer creates something that the consumer wants but presents himself as an opportunity that no smart investor could pass up. This represents an important shift in neoliberalism, one in which the subject is no longer liberal in accordance with Weber's paradigm: how can I show myself to be productive, so as to earn the faith of creditors and God? Rather, the subject of the new paradigm asks: How can I show myself to provide an excellent return, competing successfully against all the other options on the market, both now and in a future ensured by providence?

The turn toward a logic of investment over exchange has likewise shifted the understood purpose of the state under neoliberalism. From an institution that once ensured the free exercise of the laws of supply and demand in a marketplace of goods, the state now aims to protect the free and efficient flow of credit in a marketplace without which rational decisions to invest in the future cannot occur. Successful government is now defined in relation to a new goal: maximizing efficiency in order to bring transaction costs for investors as close to zero as possible.

Joshua Ramey has recently suggested that these behaviors constitute a disavowed form of the cultural practice of divination.[25] Under neoliberal conditions, Ramey proposes, markets are understood to offer us the deeper meaning of events, but only in a highly monotonous register, since neoliberalism reads every successful turning of a profit as a sign of efficient market operations and every failure to do so as a sign that we face interference with market mechanisms that need to be eliminated. This "theodicy of chance," as Ramey terms it, constitutes neoliberalism's peculiar political theology, providing us with a retroactive religious meaning for life events while simultaneously enshrining a specific concept of the future-oriented individual as the intrepid entrepreneur who is an "ersatz combination of the prophetic and the authoritarian, the gambler and the rational planner."[26] What Ramey's account does not address, however, is how this orientation toward the future might serve to bind the subject politically, or even contractually, to neoliberalism. This results from Ramey working with a thinner concept of religion than we are using; divination, as he understands it, is nothing more than an explanatory framework that offers meaning and understandable order in a chaotic universe. In contrast, we see in neoliberalism a religious framework that is substantively closer to Judeo-Christianity in its emphasis on covenantal theology. The neoliberal subject promises to approach life as an investor in herself. From the perspective described by Ramey, this can be understood precisely as a commitment to taking actions (signing up for an internship, going to college, marrying someone, and of course investing in a 401(k)) that bet on a positive market outcome, that is, that this action *will have been profitable* at some unspecified point in the future. Meanwhile, the state must work to eliminate all possible transaction costs on those investment opportunities. In cases of economic emergency such as financial meltdown, meanwhile, the equivalent of the Schmittian miracle no longer means the propping up of demand (as it did under Keynesian liberalism). Instead, it takes the forms of the Troubled Asset Relief Program (TARP) bailouts: the state suspends the law in order to unlock liquidity to maintain the investment stream, the deus ex machina salvation of those too big to fail.[27]

We conclude by returning to our point of departure, with the question of how best to explain neoliberalism's ability to win political durability through alliances with religious movements. We suggest that, within U.S. culture, this tendency is not limited to the "prosperity gospel" that establishes the rapprochement in recent decades between evangelical Christianity in the United States and neoliberal imperatives for the economy, the state, and the subject. While there are certainly many denominations that have thrived by promising that religious faith will automatically lead to economic success, we are suggesting a deeper if hidden harmonics between Christian faith and neoliberal economics—both in the self and in the market.

The first element that strikes us as essential here is the pacification of opposition to the neoliberal paradigm that has grown from the evisceration of the labor movement, on the one hand, and the proliferation of private debt, on the other. Regarding the former, Lehmann addresses the proliferation of the "Walmart model," an explicitly Christian style of management that celebrates the ideal of the "good wife" praised in Proverbs 31 as emblematic of both the Walmart workforce and the kind of customer Walmart hopes to attract: hardworking, not given to complain, efficiently making the most of her income.[28] If Christian passivity is celebrated in Walmart's rhetoric as an ethos of the new labor system, Lehmann's analysis seems to imply that this kind of religious injunction may have contributed to the general weakening of labor in the economy as a whole.

While the importance of such rhetoric may be hard to gauge in the context of a globalized labor force and a concerted effort on the part of the U.S. government to weaken union power, the influence of Christianity appears far stronger in the ethical language associated with the general proliferation of indebtedness that has occurred since the 1970s, with the broad dissemination of credit cards to the populations of Europe and North America. Even as wages have stagnated or even fallen throughout the Global North, consumption has continued to rise, funded largely on credit. The evisceration of labor power has been accompanied by a skyrocketing level of consumer debt, allowing corporate culture to profit more directly from the interest individuals pay on the amount they owe than from the surplus value of the labor they invest in the job. This shift has resulted in a political climate in which resistance becomes far more difficult, as strikes become less frequent and often ineffectual under a system that has organized a concerted assault against organized labor, and as a generalized state of indebtedness emerges as a broad strategy of political control. As David Graeber writes, "If history shows anything, it is that there's no better way to justify relations founded on violence . . . than by reframing them in the language of debt—above all, because it immediately makes it seem that it's the victim who's doing something wrong."[29] Even in the wake of the Occupy movement, in which thousands of people gathered in streets, parks, and town squares around the world to protest against the power of financial institutions, a movement to pledge a debt strike to protest student loans failed to draw more than a few thousand signatories. The imperative to repay money that has been voluntarily borrowed is strong and ubiquitous, even when the loans were made under coerced or dishonest conditions. The strength of that imperative has everything to do with a strong tradition linking monetary debt to sin. Contemporary debt theorists invariably mention that the words for "debt" and "guilt" or "sin" go back to a common etymological progenitor—not just the German *Schuld* of Friedrich Nietzsche's *Genealogy of Morals* but extending all the way back to the very roots of Christian culture; religious and financial moralities have been intertwined for at least two millennia.[30]

If the broad practice of political control through debt marks a cite where the relationship between Christianity and the neoliberal economic order becomes apparent as it relates to the theme of punishment for our sins, then the discourse of investment illustrates neoliberalism's strategy of control through the promise of reward. One of the most perplexing characteristics of neoliberal thinking is its dogged faith in the act of investment, even in the face of numerous economic crises. Since the 1980s, neoliberalism has borne witness to one crisis after another of the new futures markets that it sanctifies, from the crash of high-tech stocks in the late 1990s to the post-9/11 market collapse and finally, of course, the bursting of the real estate bubble in 2008 and resulting global recession. It would seem that we have entered a state of permanent crisis, or what Lauren Berlant calls "crisis ordinary."[31] Yet remarkably, we have seen very little effective challenge to neoliberalism as a result.[32]

This neoliberal faithfulness to the future reward of investment may be read as a political theological element that is striking for its historical congruency with the rise in the American evangelical movement of apocalyptic thinking. If economic liberalism had once aligned with Christianity primarily through libertarian notions of God-given freedom and classical Lockean covenantal thinking that looked backward to a moment of contract and a present of promised abundance, the past fifty years have seen this model metamorphose into a markedly different inflection of Christian thinking, beginning perhaps with the extraordinary success of Hal Lindsey's *The Late, Great Planet Earth* of 1970 but accelerating since the 1980s, and indeed throughout the decades of the neoliberal ascendancy.[33] An intense focus on end times, impending apocalypse, and the Book of Revelations within evangelical Christianity has gone hand in hand with the rise of neoliberal faith in the future rewards of investment in a volatile and precarious present.[34] Apocalyptic evangelicalism is marked by a kind of eschatological urgency that reads the chaos of the present as a sign for the faithful to gather themselves for the ultimate separation of the goats and the sheep. This shift marks a crucial element in the harmonics between apocalyptic Christianity on the one hand and a new mode of covenantalism specific to neoliberal doctrine on the other. The two share a homeostatic circuit of divine authority that actually *increases* their efficacy as the future grows more uncertain. The more unstable life becomes, the more compelling the call for faith in the coming apocalypse and the theology that grounds it. For neoliberalism, meanwhile, whose covenant concerns the future blessings that the market will bring to those who invest wisely today, every market crisis becomes not a reason to *question* the system but an opportunity to wager on the profits that lie on the other side of the secular apocalypse, profits that others less faithful might find too risky to pursue. Precarity becomes, in short, a special opportunity to renew vows of faith. The proper neoliberal subject is one who, refusing panic, cleaves to the vision of a providential future in troubled times. But this entails a theological shift: we have moved from a classical liberal gospel derived from the economistic teachings of the Book of Proverbs (or perhaps the Deuteronomistic history's promise of abundance to the faithful who keep the mitzvot) toward a celebration of risk in uncertain times most prominently associated with the apocalyptic future orientation of the Book of Revelations, which prophesies that the redeemed will be saved at the expense of the whole.

In conclusion, it is not merely a "prosperity gospel" that has aligned evangelical Christianity in the United States with neoliberalism. Rather, these harmonics concern first and foremost a shared religious notion of investing in one's acts of faith through uncertain times. If the market volatility of contemporary capitalism increases our sense of personal precarity, then, like passengers in a turbulent aircraft, we find prayer to be an increasingly obvious course of action. Neoliberalism asks us not only to invest in ourselves and to accept full responsibility for the debts we cannot pay when those investments prove unfruitful; it also demands that we keep faith in the providential outcome of that effort, renewing our commitment to the covenantal promise that the future will redeem those who do not lose hope. The more frightening the impending cataclysm, the louder the call.

NOTES

1   Exceptions to this rule include Jason Hackworth, *Faith Based: Religious Neoliberalism and the Politics of Welfare in the United States* (Athens: University of Georgia Press, 2012); and Chris Lehmann, *The Money Cult: Capitalism, Christianity, and the Unmaking of the American Dream* (New York: Melville House, 2016). Hackworth's book examines the importance of evangelical religion in undermining the welfare state in the

United States as George H. W. Bush celebrated the "thousand points of light" that could take on the government's task of caring for the poor; Lehmann's book (which we engage more fully below) offers a broader discussion of the historical link between Christianity and capitalism in the United States.

2   Lehmann, *Money Cult*, 14-15.
3   Carl Schmitt, *Political Theology: Four Chapters on the Concept of Sovereignty*, trans. George Schwab (Cambridge, MA: MIT Press, 2006), 6.
4   Schmitt, *Political Theology*, 5.
5   Schmitt, *Political Theology*, 36.
6   Schmitt, *Political Theology*.
7   Schmitt, *Political Theology*, 65.
8   Bernard Harcourt, *The Illusion of Free Markets: Punishment and the Myth of Natural Order* (Cambridge, MA: Harvard University Press, 2011), 94-97.
9   François Quesnay, *Analyse de la Formule Arithmétique du Tableau Économique de la Distribution des Dépensees annuelles d'une Natione Agricole* (1766), accessed September 10, 2020, https://www.taieb.net/auteurs/Quesnay/t1766t.html; Friedrich Hayek, *Studies in Philosophy, Politics and Economics* (New York: Touchstone, 1969), 97.
10 Harcourt, *Illusion of Free Markets*, 38, 95.
11 *Harcourt, Illusion of Free Markets*, 93.
12 Elizabeth Pritchard, *Religion in Public: Locke's Political Theology* (Stanford: Stanford University Press, 2013), 62.
13 Covenants express reciprocal sacred agreements across the human/divine divide that might be understood as the basis for the "secularized theological concept" that becomes the social contract. It therefore makes sense that "covenant" represents the religious form that will lead to the political theology of Enlightenment thought in general and liberalism in particular.
14 Pritchard, *Religion in Public*, 69.
15 Friedrich Hayek, *The Road to Serfdom* (Chicago: University of Chicago Press, 1944), 41-42, 83-90.
16 Hayek, *Road to Serfdom*, 210.
17 Ronald Reagan, "Radio Address to the Nation on Small Business," May 14, 1983, https://www.presidency.ucsb.edu/documents/radio-address-the-nation-small-business.
18 Ronald Reagan, "Remarks at the Annual Convention of the National Association of Evangelicals in Orlando, Florida" [aka "Evil Empire Speech"], March 8, 1983, https://www.reaganfoundation.org/media/50919/remarks_annual_convention_national_association_evangelicals_030883.pdf.
19 Greta R. Krippner, *Capitalizing on Crisis: The Political Origins of the Rise of Finance* (Cambridge, MA: Harvard University Press, 2011), 10, 58. See also Gerald H. Davis, *Managed by the Markets: How Finance Reshaped America* (Oxford: Oxford University Press, 2009), 31-40.
20 Rana Foroohar, *Makers and Takers: The Rise of Finance and the Fall of American Business* (New York: Crown Business, Penguin, 2016).
21 William Lazonick and Mary O'Sullivan, "Maximizing Shareholder Value: A New Ideology for Corporate Governance," *Economy and Society* 29, no. 1 (2000): 13-35;

Mary O'Sullivan, *Contests for Corporate Control: Corporate Governance and Economic Performance in the United States and Germany* (Oxford: Oxford University Press, 2001); Karen Ho, *Liquidated: An Ethnography of Wall Street* (Durham, NC: Duke University Press, 2009).

22 Quoted in Foroohar, *Makers and Takers*, 10.

23 Foroohar cites a study that shows $630 trillion to be caught up in credit default swaps and derivatives trades at the beginning of 2015, while the gross market value of those same contracts was $21 trillion. Bank for International Settlements, "OTC Derivatives Statistics at End-December 2014," April 2015; Foroohar, *Makers and Takers*, 194-95.

24 Michel Foucault, *The Birth of Biopolitics: Lectures at the Collège de France, 1978-1979*, ed. Michel Senellart, trans. Graham Burchell (Basingstoke, UK: Palgrave Macmillan, 2008), 230.

25 Joshua Ramey, "Neoliberalism as a Political Theology of Chance: The Politics of Divination," *Palgrave Communications* 1 (2015), https://doi.org/10.1057/palcomms.2015.39.

26 Ramey, "Neoliberalism."

27 We would argue, however, that the neoliberal state remains equally committed to the incarceration of the homme pervers. Market bypass by unruly subjectivity remains a threat that any kind of liberal state is expected to punish. Wall Street criminals, meanwhile, avoid jail time because they can afford attorneys to argue this is a class of people who (all in all) should not be punished for technical mistakes made while investing in the future.

28 See also Bethany Moreton, *To Serve God and Wal-Mart: The Making of Christian Free Enterprise* (Cambridge, MA: Harvard University Press, 2009).

29 David Graeber, *Debt: The First 5,000 Years* (Brooklyn, NY: Melville House, 2011), 5.

30 Gilles Deleuze, "Postscript on the Societies of Control," *October* 59 (1992): 3-7; Maurizio Lazzarato, *The Making of the Indebted Man: An Essay on the Neoliberal Condition* (Los Angeles: Semiotext(e), 2012); Richard Dienst, *The Bonds of Debt* (New York: Verso, 2011); Friedrich Wilhelm Nietzsche, *On the Genealogy of Morals* (Oxford: Oxford University Press, 1996).

31 Lauren Berlant, *Cruel Optimism* (Durham, NC: Duke University Press, 2011), 5.

32 Mark Fisher, *Capitalist Realism: Is There No Alternative?* (New York: Zero Books, 2009).

33 Hal Lindsey, *The Late, Great Planet Earth* (Grand Rapids, MI: Zondervan Academic, 1970).

34 Matthew Avery Sattun, *American Apocalypse: A History of Modern Evangelicalism* (Cambridge, MA: Belknap Press of Harvard University Press, 2014); Angela M. Lahr, *Millennial Dreams and Apocalyptic Nightmares: The Cold War Origins of Political Evangelicalism* (Oxford: Oxford University Press, 2007); Richard D. Kyle, *Apocalyptic Fever: End-Time Prophecies in Modern America* (Eugene, OR: Cascade Books, 2012).

5. "CHRISTIAN ATHEISM" ON TWITTER
Dutch Populism and/as Culturalized Religion

ERNST VAN DEN HEMEL

The Netherlands is undergoing an influential turn to the right, and it is not alone. Whether one considers the proposal of the Dutch Partij voor de Vrijheid (PVV, Freedom Party) to ban the Qur'an and close all mosques, the German Patriotische Europäer Gegen die Islamisierung des Abendlandes (PEGIDA, Patriotic Europeans against the Islamisation of the Occident) movement's paradoxical call to save religious toleration by limiting migration from Islamic countries, or the French National Front's call to defend "sacred laïcité," it is clear that the success of contemporary Europe's burgeoning right-wing movements depends on their ability to mobilize public hostility toward the Islamic faith of immigrants.

What actually motivates the religious focus on this hostility, however, is a matter of significant debate. Some scholars argue that right-wing populism is riding a more general secular counterreaction to the resurgence of religion in the twenty-first century.[1] In this narrative, populists exploit the discomfort felt by a largely secular European culture when confronted with the religion of migrants.[2] Other scholars, such as Nadia Marzouki, Duncan McDonnell, and Olivier Roy, argue, however, that this position fails to account for populism's own investments in and uses of religion. For instance, in *Saving the People: How Populists Hijack Religion* (2016), Marzouki, McDonnell, and Roy have traced the populist fascination with making religious appeals. In this same volume, Roy argues that populists approach religion as "essentially a matter of identity for populist parties," noting that Church leaders are concerned about how to relate to populist references to religious identity.[3] As the volume's subtitle indicates, it is not uncommon for scholars to suggest that populist references to religion constitute a "hijacking," an abuse, or a perversion of religion. Other scholars, meanwhile, have highlighted that populist references to religion fit into a longer tradition of political theology. For instance, in "Political Theology and Populism," Andrew Arato observes that a political theological notion is cited in the populist invocation of "the people."[4] These authors open up a new field of inquiry wherein it is understood that references to religion play an important role in populist discourse. What precisely this role is, however, is the subject of an ongoing academic debate. This chapter contributes to this debate by providing a contextualized discourse analysis of populist social media discourse on religion. In so doing, I address the roles of religion and secularity in contemporary Western European populist discourse and thus contribute to an understanding of the resurgent roles of and conflicts concerning religion and secularity.

Populist Religious Secularity / Secular Religiosity

Part of the reason why there has been little attention paid to populist discourse on religion thus far is its seemingly contradictory dimensions. As illustrated by Geert Wilders's letter to Pope Francis in 2013, is not uncommon to see secular values associated with Judeo-Christian culture. In this letter, the leader of the Freedom Party (PVV) indicates that "atheists ... owe their freedom and democracy to the West's Judeo-Christian civilization."[5] This is just one example of the many secular values that are attributed to the religious cultural roots of the West in populist discourse. At other moments, the PVV has included feminism, gay rights, freedom of speech, and the separation of church and state as values arising out of a religious cultural framework. At play in this selective approach might be a strong presence of "methodological secularism." That is to say, populist discourse on religion has been disqualified from being material for investigation on the basis of explicit normative judgments using a secular separation of categories. For instance, from a perspective that defines religion as the conscious adherence to a series of dogmas and the secular as separation between religion and nonreligion, populist talk of Judeo-Christian secularity claims seem to have little to do with religion. In short, from a perspective in which religion and secularity are distinct domains, "Christian atheism" can be nothing but paradoxical. But from a perspective that sees these religion-secularity relations as considerably more complex, things become more challenging.

Already in Samuel Huntington's "The Clash of Civilizations?" the struggle between "Western" civilization and "Islamic civilization" contains some interesting slippages. Although the societal blocks in which Huntington divides the world carry such evocative names as "the West" and "Islam"—note the opposition of a neutral geographical term, the "West," with a term that indicates a religion, "Islam"—Huntington borrows his description of Western culture from Bernard Lewis: "This is no less than a clash of civilizations—the perhaps irrational but surely historic reaction of an ancient rival against our Judeo-Christian heritage, our secular present, and the worldwide expansion of both."[6] The West is secular, but its secularity is related to its "Judeo-Christian" heritage. By extension, Islamic rage comes from an "irrational" reaction to secularity and Judeo-Christian heritage. As I argue in this chapter, this small excursus into Huntington's 1993 text shows something that is often overlooked in debates concerning the rise of populism in Western Europe: the conflation of religious roots and present-day secularity is not necessarily contradictory but part of a wider conservative mode of speaking about religion and secularity.

The implications of these fusions are considerable and can be felt in legislation, debates, and everyday speech. When secular values are both rational, universal values and explicitly rooted in Western religious history, universality becomes accessible only to those who share these roots. The remainder of this chapter is oriented around the correlated conflations between universality and locality, between ideals and cultures, between the empty appeal of seemingly neutral values and the culturalized backgrounds that explain their meanings. Specifically, I focus on a case study from the Netherlands. But first, let me situate the PVV's discourse in a short history of the Netherlands' turn to the right.

The Dutch Turn to the Right

It is frequently stated that Dutch national identity is characterized by secularity. More particularly, the Netherlands is known both among its own population and abroad as simultaneously the epitome of secularity and tolerance and as having an absence of national pride or national identity. One could point to deeper historical roots of Dutch antinationalist sentiments, including famed historian Johan Huizinga, who in his overview of Dutch national identity described the Netherlands as "relatively disinclined to sing its own praise."[7]

To the surprise of many, the Netherlands became a frontrunner in the development of the populist radical right. This turn to the right in the Netherlands has been the subject of many hypotheses and studies. For this chapter, I limit myself to the role of religion in these populist movements. A famous beginning point of the Dutch integration debate is liberal *coryfee* (and mentor of Geert Wilders) Frits Bolkestein's 1991 lecture in Lucerne on the end of the Cold War and its impact on Europe. The lecture was part of a conference on the future of Europe, and for Bolkestein this entailed a reflection on the West's cultural identity. For Bolkestein, the most important cultural principles of the West are "separation of church and state, freedom of expression, tolerance, and non-discrimination."[8] A remarkable conflation takes place in this discourse: "We maintain that these principles hold good not only in Europe and North America, but all over the world. Liberalism claims universal value and worth for these principles. That is its political vision. Here there can be no compromise." In more or less the same breath, Bolkestein cites a report from the Netherlands Scientific Council for Government Policy (Wetenschappelijke Raad voor Regeringsbeleid, WRR): "Very important aspects of our Western culture, such as individual freedom and equality are under attack from another culture. . . . No choice exists but to defend our culture against competing pretensions."[9] By these "attacks," Bolkestein means debates on headscarves, and so forth. "Here again our law must take precedence over their custom." Note the conflation between universal and cultural values, as secularity is presented as simultaneously universally valid and culturally rooted. It is worth pointing out that for Bolkestein, these values are both "valid everywhere" as well as geographically located. They are presented as universally validated common sense, yet they are simultaneously rooted in a certain region and culture.

In a newspaper article that accompanied the Dutch release of this lecture, Bolkestein continues to reflect on these roots of liberal values, identifying them as stemming from "Judaism, Christianity and humanism." In subsequent interviews, Bolkestein stated that in order to keep these values alive, you need a form of religion: "The shared myth [of Christianity] is gone. And now the question is whether we can function without that myth. . . . We can say: 'Hurray! We are no longer Christian!' but I wonder whether that attitude will be sufficient. I'm afraid not. Some intellectuals converted to Catholicism for that reason. For me that would be too artificial, because I am not a religious person, but culturally speaking, I am most certainly Christian."[10] Thus we have the secular liberal Bolkestein stating that a form of cultural religion is necessary to keep a society together. This is a form of religion that, not unlike Robert Bellah's civil religion, does not need to be predicated on personal faith.[11] What is important here is that universal values of liberalism are presented as intrinsically connected to religious roots. In addition, the religious past is not properly located in the past. It has shaped the present, much like roots shape a tree (with all the difficulties involved in uprooting as a result). We now get to a notion of how liberal politicians in the Netherlands square religion with secular values. According to Bolkestein, cultural cohesion is a necessary dimension of secular society, and fidelity to a shared, implicit, religious framework is integral to cultural cohesion.

Pim Fortuyn

Similarly, if we move on in our little pantheon of populism, there is an important insistence on religion and secular culture in the thought of Pim Fortuyn. Pim Fortuyn is widely credited as shaping the "integration debate" in the Netherlands. He launched a political party based on a program in which cultural identity and religion played a central role. His assassination in 2002 further polarized and engulfed Dutch society in an emotional political debate. Yet in spite of his crucial role in the Dutch "turn to the right," a detailed analysis of his thought is rare. As a result, the complex role of religion and secularity in Fortuyn's thought is seldom highlighted. Take a look, for instance, at the following quotation from one of Fortuyn's major works, *De verweesde samenleving* (The orphaned society): "Problems concerning integration and mutual acceptance are centered on the relation between the dominant Judeo-Christian humanistic culture on the one hand and Islamic culture on the other. I consciously speak in the broad terminology of culture rather than of religion. One can leave a religion, as we can see happening massively in our country, *a culture however, one cannot leave behind.*"[12] The word "Judeo-Christian" plays an important role here. In this quotation, Judeo-Christian culture is associated with leaving religion behind, whereas Islamic culture is seen as inherently capable of leaving religion. Judeo-Christian culture is thus associated with secularization. Yet, as Fortuyn also highlights, this does not mean that Judeo-Christianity is merely the disappearing historical background of contemporary secular Dutch society. According to Fortuyn, cultural roots are to be cherished, venerated, and maintained. In subsequent chapters in Fortuyn's book, the central position of a religious cultural framework for Dutch society is outlined. The religious past lives on, for Fortuyn, not in spite of but as the core of secular values.

PVV

When Pim Fortuyn was assassinated in 2002, there was a question of who would take over as the most visible exponent of populism in the Netherlands. After a number of years of turmoil, Geert Wilders, a politician from the secular liberal Volkspartij voor Vrijheid en Democratie (VVD, People's Party for Freedom and Democracy) and tutee of Bolkestein, formed his own political party explicitly resonating with Fortuyn. His first party program included references to Dutch Judeo-Christian-Humanist culture, and references to it have been a frequent hallmark of the PVV, or Freedom Party, of Wilders ever since.[13] For instance, in 2006, the PVV proposed to replace Article 1 of the Dutch Constitution with a reference to Judeo-Christian roots; in 2013, Wilders wrote an open letter to the pope wherein Wilders claimed that atheism is a Christian invention. In recent parliamentary debates, the PVV regularly states that "protecting one's own culture" is a Christian value.

This is, of course, merely a preliminary sketch of the role that religion played in the beginnings of the Dutch integration debate. Against this backdrop of changing narratives and approaches, I argue two major points. First, in the contemporary rise of populist right-wing discourse, religion plays a more important and challenging role than is often thought. And second, in order to understand the role of these references, it might be more productive to start from the bottom up and to focus on how references to religion function in populist discourse. We have highlighted so far *that* religion plays an important role and that the links between emptiness and fullness are complicated. But we have done little in examining *how* religion plays a role.

Quantifying "Judeo-Christianity"

This approach has led me to focus on the role of religion in the construction of the national self in contemporary populist social media activity. At the time of writing, the PVV is the second-largest party in Dutch parliament. The party, though successful in elections and highly visible in public debates, has been something of a puzzle for academics and commentators. For instance, PVV politicians are not inclined to speak to the press very often, let alone to academics. The party also does not have a scientific bureau and rarely engages in publications. However, the party—especially its leader, Geert Wilders—uses Twitter extensively.

There is an oft-noted connection between contemporary populist movements and online media. The debate on Twitter about populism has been highlighted by Benjamin Moffit and Simon Tormey and more recently in an extensive volume edited by Mojca Pajnik and Birgit Sauer.[14] In considering questions such as "How is the web used to spread ideas, mobilize supporters, and disqualify adversaries?" commentators have highlighted that social media allows populist movements to bypass print media and classical journalism outlets and address their followers directly. Pajnik and Sauer's analytical approach, the "critical frame analysis," is of particular interest for this chapter. As Pajnik and Sauers explain, a critical frame analysis "organizes ideas that provide coherence to a designated set of elements. . . . In other words, frames are forms of explanation or sensemaking cognitive structures."[15] Reflections on religion play an important role in the frame of Dutch right-wing populism. In the next segment, I focus on this role by mapping references to religion in PVV's Twitter activity. Particularly, I query the references to institutionalized Judaism and Christianity. This allows me to provide a preliminary yet more detailed answer to the kind of questions outlined by Marzouki, McDonnell, and Roy in their volume *Saving the People*, primarily, how does the populist claim to defend a religiously defined people relate to "real" religions?[16]

My Twitter analysis was conducted in collaboration with Emile den Tex from the University of Amsterdam–based Digital Methods Initiative and presented in the light of a workshop at the Ian Ramsey Center, Oxford University, in the summer of 2016. Our intention was to combine a qualitative diagnosis with qualitative focus in order to determine (1) the role of religion in PVV discourse and (2) what things are associated with these terms. Using the Twitter Capture and Analysis Toolkit (TCAT), we collected and categorized more than 100,000 tweets that were sent from seventy-seven official PVV Twitter accounts from May 2009 through June 2016. We queried the tweets for a lexicon consisting of terms normally associated with religion. We divided the 11,172 religiously oriented tweets into three main subcategories: Islam, Judaism, Christianity. Our analysis found that 9,085 tweets included content related to Islam, 1,505 tweets to Judaism, and 582 tweets to Christianity.

Several findings are important to highlight at the outset. First, a significantly higher number of tweets by the PVV are devoted to religion than tweets by liberal or social democrat parties. This indicates that religion plays a larger role in populist movements than in other political parties. Second, most tweets are focused on Islam. This is hardly surprising for a party known for its harsh stance on Islam. However, the tweets about Christianity and Judaism are more significant for this particular case study.

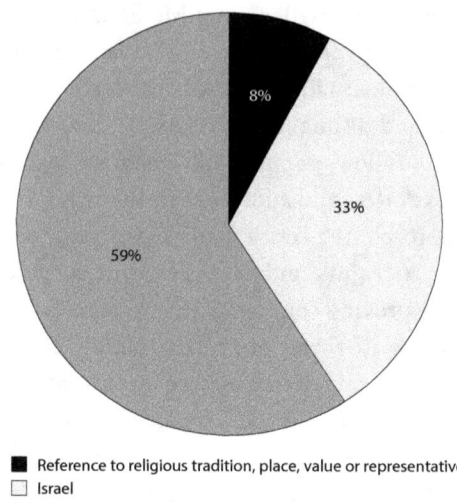

FIGURE 5.1. PVV Tweets Referencing Judaism, May 2009–June 2016.

Judaism

Data related to Judaism has one-click depth, meaning that we frequently see links to news items. Tweets were understood as relating to Judaism if they referenced one or more related words from our assembled lexicon. The result is that 59 percent of tweets about Judaism are focused exclusively on anti-Semitism (see figure 5.1). Of these tweets, 77.3 percent focus on anti-Semitism related to Islam. That is, these tweets make a direct association between an act of anti-Semitism and "Islam." If we then focus on the tweets covering Israel, which amount to 33 percent of all tweets referencing Judaism, 61.2 percent directly relate to Islamic anti-Semitism. Finally, 8 percent of the tweets address Jewish religion, rites, values, or representatives.

If we then combine our findings, we can see that of all PVV tweets on Judaism, 76 percent primarily address Islam-related antisemitism. What is strikingly absent is references to religious traditions or actually existing influence of Judaism on Dutch national culture. Judaism is predominantly depicted as a victimized religion in need of protection from Islamic intolerance.

Christianity

When we move on to the tweets that cover Christianity, we see that a majority of tweets reference Islam (see figure 5.2). We also see that there are few references to "actual" religion, meaning that there is very little debate on religious practice, dogma, or places. However, as we can also see, there are

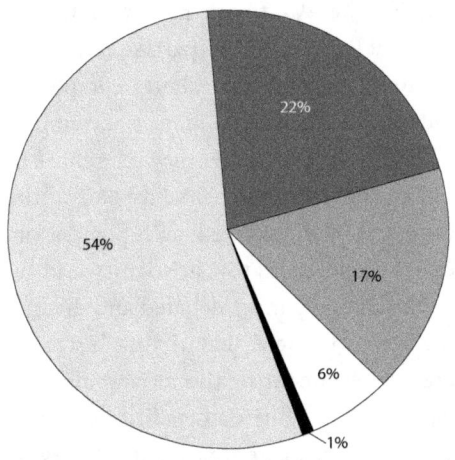

- Reference to religious tradition, place, value, or representative
- Criticism of "the Leftist Church"
- Catholicism
- Christian Democrats
- Criticism of "Islamic attacks on Christianity"

FIGURE 5.2. PVV Tweets Referencing Christianity, May 2009–June 2016.

more and more diverse references to actually existing Christian culture and influences.

In contrast to Judaism, we can see that there is a lively and quite diverse debate as to *what constitutes Dutch Christian values*. We see a lot more debates on a variety of historical and current forms of Christianity, and many more of these debates do not seem to be linked as directly to Islam as we have seen with the tweets on Judaism. These tweets that discuss Christianity are very rarely predicated upon concepts associated with faith; rather, we see a wide-ranging interest in cultural influences of Christianity (e.g., we see tweets with passionate pleas to protect Easter as a public Dutch holiday or to protect a historical church from being torn down). Also, quite a large number of tweets enter into criticism of what is perceived to be the permissive attitude of present-day Christians in times of multiculturalism.

PVV Tweets on Religion

In reflecting upon these preliminary findings, a series of trends emerge. First, not surprisingly, Islam is presented as a central antagonist of Western culture. Judaism and Christianity are presented as the hallmarks of Western identity, which is under attack. However, upon considering the particular roles played by Judaism and Christianity, one notices that there is little reference to "actual religion" when they are invoked. Although the PVV tweets more about Judaism and Christianity than even confessional Dutch political parties, references to theological concepts or personal testimonies of faith are almost completely absent. There is, however, a clear tendency to discuss the impact and importance of religion for Dutch culture. The PVV tweets show that references to Christianity and Judaism are intended to convey fundamental aspects of the cultural identity, cohesiveness, and interests of the native Dutch population. When parsing out differences between the references to Christianity and Judaism, the references to Christianity are strikingly more detailed and diverse. It is, for instance, not uncommon to see PVV tweets identifying historical religious figures as hallmarks of tolerance, or lamenting the tearing down of church buildings or the alleged disappearance of Christian traditions such as Easter. In contrast, the PVV's invocations of Judaism are almost entirely devoid of references to Jewish contributions to Dutch culture, such as the value of Jewish traditions or buildings.

Methodological Reflections

This methodological approach raises some important questions for future research, including the following:

— The definition of religion: I have, in my approach, taken a series of classical indicators of religion ("church," "Bible," etc.). However, scholars have expressed the need for sensitivity to a more distributed definition of religion. For instance, scholars could focus on more incident-oriented approaches. What, in a certain incident, is seen as religious?
— Creative spelling: Another limitation of this research is that I focused on existing lexicon, whereas populist movements excel in inventing language. What do we do with the many slurs, slang expressions, and ever-changing lingo of populism? In my opinion, this points to the necessity to combine data analysis with more embedded practices of research such as fieldwork or more qualitative discourse analysis.
— Irony: Automated queries tend to not pick up on irony. What do we do with ironic references to religion? Collaboration with emotion-recognition specialists would seem promising, provided it is combined with an emphasis on embedded research practices such as fieldwork.
— Medium specificity: In order to more meaningfully appreciate the circulation and impact of religion on Twitter, we would need to further

consider Twitter's medium-specific dimensions, for example the significance of a "retweet."

Global Implications

These considerations notwithstanding, the Twitter analysis provides insights into one of Dutch society's most divisive discursive contestations. Instead of seeing the PVV's tweets as expressions of "mere populism," a relatively simple mapping exercise allows us to identify dominant associations, which in turn can aid in predicting future directions and polarizations. While this chapter is about the Dutch context, there are wider implications of and applications for this analysis. As Twitter is a global medium, it would be, for example, quite an interesting exercise to compare PVV's invocation of religion with that of, say, PEGIDA in Germany or the alt-right in the United States.

Taking a wider purview, we live in times in which the lines between culture and religion are part and parcel of polarizing public and political debates. Whether it is the rise of Hindu nationalism and the concomitant claims of Hindu nationalists that Hinduism best safeguards secular tolerance, or the conflation of Russian orthodoxy and national identity in Russia, or the ongoing debate within the alt-right in the United States about Christianity and the attack on American culture by political correctness, the lines between religion, culture, and national identity across the globe are as divisive as they are fluid and confusing. Instead of approaching this through methodological secularism, a top-down "neutral" conceptual apparatus in which religion and secularity are seen as separate spheres, an approach is needed that is more sensitive to the intermingled, muddy, and interconnected identifications that generate emotional conflicts. A "bottom-up" approach is more suitable to exploring the intricacies in each national context. This would mean as well that "populism" as a term becomes less useful. The word is frequently used, both in colloquial language as well as in academic explorations of the Dutch turn to the right, in order to separate populist discursive practices from "normal" political discourse. As populist parties have become a permanent factor in Dutch politics, the line between populist and nonpopulist discourse becomes more difficult to draw. It would be more productive, as the agendas of populist movements are becoming more widely embraced and discussed, to map and identify certain discursive shifts (like the rise of "Judeo-Christian" to describe the West) as part of a broader reconfiguration of the roles of religion and secularity in national imagination, even if this means that the word *populism* becomes less useful.

Far from being neutral descriptive terms, "religion" and "secularity" tend to blend and perhaps have always blended into matters of cultural identity and division. Unpacking the emotional, polarizing, including, and excluding discursive practices they are a part of and placing them in a wider global point of view is an increasingly urgent task.

NOTES

1. See Ian Buruma, *Murder in Amsterdam: Liberal Europe, Islam, and the Limits of Tolerance* (London: Penguin Books, 2007).
2. Werner J. Patzelt and Joachim Klose, PEGIDA: *Warnsignale aus Dresden* (Dresden: Thelem, 2016).
3. Nadia Marzouki, Duncan McDonnell, and Olivier Roy, eds., *Saving the People: How Populists Hijack Religion* (London: Hurst, 2016), 11.
4. Andrew Arato, "Political Theology and Populism," *Social Research* 80, no. 1 (Spring 2013): 143–72.
5. Geert Wilders, "Open Letter to His Holiness Pope Francis," 2013, accessed February 15, 2018, www.geertwilders.nl.
6. Samuel P. Huntington, "The Clash of Civilizations?" *Foreign Affairs* 72, no. 3 (1993): 32.
7. Johan Huizinga, "Nederland Geestesmerk," in *Verzamelde Werken*, vol. 7, *Geschiedwetenschap: Hedendaagsche cultuur* (Haarlem: Tjeenk Willink and Zoon, 1950), 291. All translations are mine unless otherwise noted.
8. Frits Bolkestein, "De integratie van minderheden," in *Woorden hebben hun betekenis* (Amsterdam: Promotheus, 1992), 5.
9. Bolkestein, "De integratie van minderheden," 6.
10. Frits Bolkestein, 'Frits Bolkestein vreest Europa zonder Christendom,' *Nederlands Dagblad*, May 23, 2009.
11. Robert N. Bellah, "Civil Religion in America," *Journal of the American Academy of Arts and Sciences* 96, no. 1 (Winter 1967): 1–21.
12. Pim Fortuyn, *De verweesde samenleving: Een religieus-sociologisch traktaat* (Uithoorn: Karakter, 2002), 83, emphasis added.
13. Meindert van der Kaaij, "Grondwet wijzigen om islam," *Trouw*, March 21, 2006.
14. Benjamin Moffitt and Simon Tormey, "Rethinking Populism: Politics, Mediatisation and Political Style," *Political Studies* 62, no. 2 (2014): 381–97; Mojca Pajnik and Birgit Sauer, *Populism and the Web: Communicative Practices of Parties and Movements in Europe* (New York: Routledge, 2018).
15. Pajnik and Saure, *Populism and the Web*, 13.
16. Marzouki, McDonnell, and Roy, *Saving the People*, 8–9.

PART II.
RELIGION

Keyword: Nationalism

ERNST VAN DEN HEMEL AND MARKUS BALKENHOL

Now, the essence of a nation is that the people have many things in common, but have also forgotten much together. No French citizen knows if he is Burgundian, Alain, Taifale, Visigoth; every French citizen must have forgotten the St. Bartholomew's Day massacre and the massacres in the Midi in the 13th century.—ERNEST RENAN, "What Is a Nation?"

Since the earliest conceptualizations of nationalism, scholars have identified a complicated relation with religion and secularism.[1] Nationalist projects arose in collaboration, alongside, and in competition with religion.[2] The ways in which nationalism is seen as connected to the regulation of religion, in short, differ drastically. In this lexical entry, we chart some major connections between these notions as they have been identified by scholars, and we conclude with a reflection on the value of these terms for understanding a variety of current affairs.

Nationalism is frequently seen as intimately connected to the rise of secularization, where the influence of religion in the public sphere subsides and is replaced with civic values and a pluriform public sphere.³ We can see that a number of approaches to nationalism stress this relationship with religion. For Ernest Renan, whose famous definition of a nation is quoted here, "forgetting" religious strife such as the St. Bartholomew's Day Massacre was a central ingredient for a coherent national community. On the basis of this definition of the nation, nationalism can be conceptualized as connected to a demise or at least a curbing of the political influence of religion. Proponents of this view, which is still highly influential in approaches to nationalism, focus on the way in which nationalist projects explicitly orient themselves toward effacing religious strife by instituting some sort of civic imagination. This has led scholars to state that nationalism offers an alternative imagined community for the religious community. The choice in this framework is nationalism *or* religion. These lines of thought are of relevance to our contemporary world: even today, religions are frequently seen as threats to civil order, and a separation of the spheres of influence of religious institutions from political life is frequently seen as one of the core principles of contemporary polities. What is more, nationalism has historically presented itself as the harbinger of modernity.⁴

This supposed neutrality of nationalism with regard to religious matters, and the belief that nationalism constituted "progress" over and against other forms of political organization, has deep and deeply problematic roots with Western expansionism and colonialism. Nations and empires have not only been built at the same time; they are two sides of the same coin.⁵ For instance, many of the most prominent Enlightenment philosophers developed their theories of the state with regard to a variety of encounters with colonial others. Examples of this are Jean-Jacques Rousseau's natural man, the role of Africa in Georg W. F. Hegel's theses on history and the world spirit, Voltaire's *Candide*, Montesquieu's *Lettres Persanes*, and the encyclopedias of Denis Diderot. It was to a significant extent through their engagement with reports of colonial encounters that these philosophers developed the political theories that would form the basis for the modern nation-state, such as the figure of the citizen. This is why scholarship on citizenship, one of the most eminent forms of political association with the nation-state, increasingly turned to "citizenship after Orientalism."⁶

Despite the way in which nationalism can be seen as an attempt to replace the potentially unruly "vertical" fidelity of the believer to his deity with "horizontal" fidelity to the state and the nations that belong to it, it is also possible to identify a vertical dimension intrinsic to nationalism itself. Proponents of this view argue that nationalism is not characterized by the "ebbing of religious belief" as Benedict Anderson states but by a *migration* of belief.⁷ In this view, nationalism actively *uses* religious dimensions. Nation-states can often be seen demanding allegiance or subscription to their creeds, and they can obtain a cultlike status through martyrs, sacred documents, and the veneration of flags. It is this dimension that has led people to speak of nationalism *as* religion.[8] These considerations are worthwhile for our present to the extent that they focus on how nationalisms present and legitimize themselves as a transcendental belief pattern. This might also shed new light on what has been called "the culturalization of citizenship."[9] This notion can serve to highlight the often highly exclusionary ways in which membership of the polity is recognized. This is particularly poignant in critiques of gendered and sexualized citizenship. Works by Joan W. Scott and Judith Butler, for instance, elaborate how secular nationalism entails not just the liberation of women from religious oppression but also how nationalism entails the regulation of gender and sexuality.[10]

However, nationalism as religion might not only be framed in terms of exclusion. Recently, the notion of civil religion has resurfaced as a way to speak about and stimulate the core beliefs that underlie ideals of inclusivity and tolerance.[11] For authors such as Robert Bellah and Philip Gorski, civil religion can exist alongside or independent of one's chosen religion.[12]

Finally, there are also examples of nationalisms that closely align themselves with a single particular religious creed as one of their core defining characteristics. "Religious nationalism," as this has been described, is characterized by the conflation of religious and national identity.[13] There have been, and there are, movements that state that certain nation-states should be seen as, for instance, explicitly and exclusively Christian, Islamic, Jewish, or Buddhist. These religious nationalist movements view exclusive religious identification as one of the prerequisites for full participation in the polity and they do not see religious dissenters as equal members of the polity.

Contemporary Returns and Limits of Nationalisms

This incomplete sketch of a variety of positions gives both an idea of the historical complexity of this question as well as a point of departure from which we can approach contemporary questions concerning nationalism and religion. On the one hand, the narrative that predicts a decline of importance on the global level of individual nation-states because of globalization still contains some force. Globalizing currents in economy, law, culture, and religion are actively challenging the coherence and imaginative capacities of geographically oriented identities.[14] However, on the other hand, the nation remains one of the most central traits of self-identification for peoples all over the world, and in many regions, nationalism is on the rise.

Indeed, many of the most recent nationalist movements have emerged as a response to an early form of globalization: colonialism. Nationalism was a central ingredient in the struggle of many societies for colonial independence. Seen in this light, it is perhaps less surprising that some of the most eminent late modern works on nations and nationalism have been produced by studying processes of decolonization. Anderson, for instance, developed his influential idea of the "imagined community" through an analysis of the Indonesian struggle for colonial independence. This nationalist movement strove to replace the colonial state with a new form of political association that could nonetheless encompass the diversity of people contained under colonial rule. More complex still, the diasporas that emerged from the transatlantic slave trade have found alternative modes of binding that both embrace their belonging to a nation and undermine the idea of territorial coherence.

Perhaps it makes more sense, echoing William Cavanaugh, to speak of the migrations of nationalism rather than of a decline. Investigating how religion and secularism are caught in processes of national belonging remains an urgent question. In what follows, we give two examples and an afterthought.

European Union

In the case of the European Union, there were those who expected and hoped that the role of the nation-state would subside and be replaced by a more internationalist form of solidarity.[15] Specifically after World War II, the goal of European integration was to create an international community in which national identification would increasingly become a less divisive factor of influence. Even today, spokespersons for the European Union credit the EU with preventing war on the European continent.[16] At the same time, there are perpetually recurring debates concerning the religious identity of "Europe." From Robert Schuman's idea of a Christian Europe to debates concerning the inclusion of Turkey and potential references to Christian roots in a hypothetical European Constitution, there are recurring discussions concerning the interaction between the secularity of Europe and its religious roots.[17]

After a time in which nationalism was expected to withdraw (and to be replaced by European ideals), it is now common to see parties explicitly calling for a return to the nation to safeguard national and cultural identity. These calls must be understood not only in the context of European unification but also as a mode of engaging with the decline of European empires. Hence, the flip side of anticolonial nationalist movements are the responses to decolonization in the former metropoles. There, the decline of colonial empires has often been experienced as a sense of loss, what Renato Rosaldo has called "imperial nostalgia," as their self-understanding as colonial powers has been thrown into crisis.

Religion plays an important part in these developments. Many Western European parties are actively concerned with the question of whether Islam is compatible with national values, and some parties are actively demanding pledges of allegiance from Muslims to the nation-state.[18] Religion is not just an "Other" for these nationalist movements. References to a "shared" religious cultural heritage are frequently used to define national communities. British prime minister David Cameron's statement that Great Britain should cherish its Christian heritage is illustrative of this development, as is the indicative use of "Judeo-Christian" to describe Western nation-states.[19] The question of religion and nationalism is once again wide open in contemporary Europe.

Central here is also a debate concerning the European project's capacity to capture the imagination. As Rosi Braidotti and others have argued, there is a tenacious tendency to associate the imagination of communities with roots. Nonetheless, one could also imagine a form of political imagination that breaks with the idea that a historical national community is the only way to forge collectivity.[20]

Islamic State?

In September 2014, U.S. president Barack Obama called the Islamic State (IS) "not Islamic and not a state." This was followed by statements of a similar nature by other politicians.[21] This disavowal of the religious violence and the state-building claims of the Jihadist organization seem to imply a number of things concerning both states and religions. For instance, by fully distancing Islam from the activities of the Islamic State, a criterion concerning what counts as Islam and what does not is applied. Apparently, the group's claims notwithstanding, the aspirations of IS to create an Islamic caliphate falls outside warranted religious political claims. What are the recognized and contested roles of religion in contemporary state-building practices? What is the place of movements such as IS in the development of thought concerning state-religion interactions? In its rhetoric, IS criticizes the artificial nature of many Middle Eastern nation-states and relates these borders to colonialism. By giving shape to an alternative polity, shouldn't IS be seen as a combination of the theological concept of the caliphate and the modern notion of religious nationalism rather than outside political theological thought?

Politics of Belonging?

Although the national register is dominant in addressing which forms of religion belong and which do not, it is important to resist isolating this connection between secular national recognition and religious practice. As suggested by Nira Yuval-Davis in *Politics of Belonging: Intersectional Contestations*, it might be worthwhile to approach practices of belonging through the prism of intersectionality.[22] By extension, we might ask: What are modes of belonging that go beyond the nexus of regulating religion in the nation-state? What are ways of religious or secular organizing that move independently from or parallel to nationalist identifications? Here, we might look to religious diasporas. And finally, what are ways in which religion can play a role in identity formations that are not limited to, or that interact creatively with, the nation-state?

NOTES

1 Cf. influential definitions of the nation such as Ernest Renan, "What Is a Nation?" (1882), reprinted in *Qu'est-ce qu'une nation?*, by Ernest Renan (Paris: Presses-Pocket, 1992), trans. Ethan Rundell, http://ucparis.fr/files/9313/6549/9943/What_is_a_Nation.pdf; and Ernest Gellner, *Nations and Nationalism*, New Perspectives on the Past (Malden, MA: Blackwell, 2005). For an overview, see Erica Benner, "Nationalism: Intellectual Origins," in *Oxford Handbook of the History of Nationalism*, ed. John Breuilly (Oxford: Oxford University Press, 2013).

2 Debates concerning and definitions of nationalism fall outside the scope of this lexical entry. We sketch here some issues that have been of influence to us: Nationalism should be seen in connection to the rise of the nation-state. The nation-state is usually defined as a political entity that ties cultural or ethnic groups in a certain territory (the nation) to a polity that governs this territory (the state). Nationalism can be seen as a way in which this remembering and forgetting—in short, the belonging of groups to the state—is generated, maintained, and regulated. Anthony Giddens, for instance, has defined nationalism as "a phenomenon that is primarily psychological": "the affiliation of individuals to a set of symbols and beliefs emphasizing communality among the members of a political order." See Anthony Giddens, *The Nation-State and Violence* (Berkeley: University of California Press, 1985), 2:16. In what follows, we approach the idea of nationalism with these concerns in mind: nationalism is about the ways in which the nation-state is imagined.

3 Many classical approaches to nationalism take this point of view. Ernest Gellner, for instance, sees the rise of nationalism as occurring simultaneously with the demise of religion. Gellner states that nationalists value religion "as an aid to com-

munity, and not so much in itself." Gellner, *Nations and Nationalism*, 77. Similarly, Benedict Anderson states in his influential *Imagined Communities: Reflections on the Origin and Spread of Nationalism* (New York: Verso, 2006) that nationalism is inherently linked to the "ebbing of religious belief" (11).

4   For an overview, see Liah Greenfeld, "Nationalism and Modernity," *Social Research* 63, no. 1 (April 1, 1996): 3–40.

5   See, for instance, Paul Gilroy, "Nationalism, History and Ethnic Absolutism," *History Workshop*, no. 30 (October 1, 1990): 114–20.

6   See Engin Isin, ed., *Citizenship after Orientalism: Transforming Political Theory* (London: Palgrave Macmillan, 2015). See also "Oecumene: Citizenship after Orientalism," accessed September 11, 2020, www.oecumene.eu.

7   See William Cavanaugh, *Migrations of the Holy: God, State, and the Political Meaning of the Church* (Grand Rapids, MI: Eerdmans, 2011). One can also think of Carl Schmitt's famous statement that "all significant concepts of the modern theory of the state are secularized theological concepts." Carl Schmitt, *Political Theology: Four Chapters on the Concept of Sovereignty*, Studies in Contemporary German Social Thought, trans. George Schwab (Cambridge, MA: MIT Press, 1985), 31.

8   See Carlton Hayes's *Essays on Nationalism* (New York: Macmillan, 1933), which includes a chapter titled "Nationalism as a Religion." Anthony Smith argues that nationalism is "a new religion of the people." According to Smith, nationalism is a religion because it offers a form of collective salvation but also because it relates to "a system of beliefs and practices that distinguishes the sacred from the profane and unites its adherents in a single moral community of the faithful." Anthony D. Smith, *Chosen Peoples: Sacred Sources of National Identity* (New York: Oxford University Press, 2003). As Roger Friedland states, a form of religion might be fundamental to all authority: "Faith, beyond reason and proof, thus undergirds the performativity of [any] authority, the saying so that makes it so." Roger Friedland, "Religious Nationalism and the Problem of Collective Representation," *Annual Review of Sociology* 27 (2010): 132. Jan Assmann highlights the religious dimension of national thought: "Nationalism is . . . a political religion that does not tolerate other religions besides itself." Jan Assmann, "Monotheism and its Political Consequences," in *Religion and Politics: Cultural Perspectives*, ed. Bernhard Giesen and Daniel Suber (Leiden: Brill, 2005), 150. José Llobera even states that "nationalism is the god of modernity": "in modernity, nationalism has become a functional equivalent of religion: nationalism has become a religion—a secular religion where god is the nation." José Llobera, *The God of Modernity: The Development of Nationalism in Western Europe* (Oxford: Berg, 1994), 143.

9   Jan-Willem Duyvendak, *The Politics of Home* (London: Palgrave Macmillan, 2011), 92–93.

10 See Joan W. Scott, "Sexularism" (RSCAS Distinguished Lecture, Robert Schuman Centre for Advanced Studies at the European University Institute, Florence, Italy, April 23, 2009); Judith Butler, "Sexual Politics, Torture, and Secular Time," *British Journal of Sociology* 59, no 1 (2008): 1–23.

11 "Civil religion" was originally coined by Rousseau to describe what he saw as a necessary ingredient to uphold the social contract. It was used by Robert Bellah in

1967 to describe what he saw as the religious belief in the national identity of the United States. This "civil religion," upheld by a variety of "typical" American values and rituals such as holidays, flag ceremonies, and the veneration of foundational documents and martyrs, runs parallel to or independent of the chosen religion of a certain individual. See Robert N. Bellah, "Civil Religion in America," *Daedalus* 96, no. 1 (1967): 1–2.

12 Philip S. Gorski has stated, for instance, that Barack Obama's election is part and parcel of a return of a notion of civil religion that succeeds in bringing together a nation that was divided. See Philip S. Gorski, "Civil Religion Today" (ARDA Guiding Paper Series, Association of Religion Data Archives, Pennsylvania State University, 2010), http://www.thearda.com/rrh/papers/guidingpapers.asp.

13 "Religious nationalists," according to the definition used by Gorski, "advocate a total fusion between a religious creed and a political community." Examples include the conservative right in the United States as well as a variety of historical attempts to construct a state out of believers of the same type. Gorski, "Civil Religion Today," 7.

14 Philip L. White, "Globalization and the Mythology of the 'Nation State,'" in *Global History: Interactions between the Universal and the Local*, ed. A. G. Hopkins (New York: Palgrave Macmillan, 2006), 257–84.

15 For an overview of these arguments, see Karl Dieter Opp, "Decline of the Nation State? How the European Union Creates National and Sub-National Identifications," *Social Forces* 84, no. 2 (2005): 653–80.

16 See Paul Rohan, "The Nation State: Is It Dead?," BBC, 1998, http://www.bbc.co.uk/worldservice/theneweurope/wk18.htm. Indeed, the EU was even awarded the Nobel Peace Prize in 2012.

17 See Gary Wilton, "Christianity at the Founding: The Legacy of Robert Schuman," in *God and the EU: Retrieving the Christian Inspirations of the European Project*, ed. Jonathan Chaplin and Gary Wilton (New York: Routledge, 2015); Srdjan Cvijic and Lorenzo Zucca, "Does the European Constitution Need Christian Values?," *Oxford Journal of Legal Studies* 24, no. 4 (2004): 739–48.

18 See Geert Wilders's proposal to oblige all Muslims in the Netherlands to swear an oath of allegiance to the Netherlands. Geert Wilders, "Stop Denying the Obvious: Islam Is a Problem," Gatestone Institute, September 26, 2014, http://www.gatestoneinstitute.org/4733/stop-denying-the-obvious-islam-is-a-problem.

19 Rowena Mason, "David Cameron: I Am Evangelical about Christian Faith," *The Guardian*, April 17, 2014.

20 See Rosi Braidotti, "Nomadism: Against Methodological Nationalism," *Policy Futures in Education* 8, nos. 3–4 (2010): 408–18.

21 Michael Wilner, "UK's Cameron on Islamic State: They Are Not Muslims, They Are Monsters," *Jerusalem Post*, September 14, 2014.

22 Nira Yuval-Davis, *The Politics of Belonging: Intersectional Contestations* (London: SAGE, 2011).

Keyword: Fundamentalism
LEEROM MEDOVOI

In the spirit of genealogical inquiry, this chapter asks not what is the truth of fundamentalism but instead what work is performed by the truth claims about it. We are therefore focusing less on those whom we call "fundamentalists" than on what calling them (or sometimes ourselves) fundamentalists might accomplish, particularly when contrasted to alternative terminologies one could deploy, such as Scripture-affirming or conservative on the one hand and militant or extremist on the other. Why fundamentalism?

A political concept no more than a century old, "fundamentalism" typically evokes what the *Oxford English Dictionary* (OED) describes as a "strict adherence to ancient or fundamental doctrine."[1] To call someone or something "fundamentalist," therefore, is to represent them as "dogmatic" in a literal sense: as the embracers of a dogma. But this is a dogmatism of a particular sort: first, it is religious; and second, fundamentalism's embrace of doctrine is said to offer "no concessions to modern developments in thought or customs" (OED). Fundamentalism is therefore defined as that which disavows the changes demanded by modernity. In its derogatory uses, this connotation comes to represent the fundamentalist as a dangerously militant anachronist.

Examining the genealogy of how the term *fundamentalism* has been used in the United States over the past century highlights the complicated relationship of religion, secularism, and political belonging in recent American history. While the earliest use of the term signified a rejection of liberal religions' "concessions" to secular modernity, the reframing of the term in the late twentieth century not only did the work of demonizing communism and anti-U.S. Islamic movements but also helped integrate conservative Christians (the original "fundamentalists") into the stronghold of American neoliberalism.

The word "fundamentalism" was coined in the 1920s as a self-description by certain American Protestants who, in contrast to their liberal Protestant counterparts, continued to champion what they understood to be the "fundamental" tenets of Christianity, tenets that at that time appeared under assault by Darwinism and especially biblical "higher criticism."[2] Curtis Lee Laws, a Baptist editor, made the first known use of the word in 1920, offering a strikingly military image of fundamentalists like himself who were ready, as he put it, to "do Battle Royal for the Fundamentals." First among these tenets worth fighting for, of course, was the divine inspiration and inerrancy of Scripture, followed by particular Scriptural claims (Mary's virginity, the ex-nihilo creation of the world) that now appeared in dispute.

While "fundamentalism" was born as an affirmative if combative statement of commitment to reveal biblical truth, it was quickly resignified by an alliance of secularists and liberal Protestants as a derogatory term for aggressive theological rigidity. What follows is an investigation into the basis of this derogation. The idea of what the OED calls making "concessions to modern developments" contains within it a rich set of theopolitical implications that trace back to the early stages of liberalism.

In his "Letter Concerning Toleration," John Locke famously argued that only ancient Jews had possessed a true theocracy, while Christianity has always maintained a separation between worldly and spiritual authority. In the Christian context, Locke claims, it has always been inappropriate to force others "by fire and sword to profess certain doctrines."[3] While Locke acknowledges the deep importance of arriving at spiritual truth for the sake of one's soul, he insisted that it was not appropriate for worldly authority, the government or commonwealth, to impose this truth. It has often been assumed that this argument in Locke implies a case for the privatization of religion. In fact, as Elizabeth Pritchard has convincingly shown, Locke was arguing for just the opposite, the *making public* of religion as it moves into a public sphere construed as a marketplace of religious ideas, a competition of churches in civil society. Religion, for Locke, should no longer serve as a pretext for violent conflict but become instead a site for demonstrating the profound spiritual value of public debate, persuasion, and the development of opinion.[4]

Seen from this liberal perspective, fundamentalists are people who refuse to let their religious opinions enter the Lockean "marketplace of ideas," to entertain and engage with arguments that might lead to "concessions" that count as responses to the natural development of modern thought and practice. Instead, they become figures for intolerance and even war. As Karen Armstrong dramatically puts it, fundamentalists engage a battle that they do not regard "as a conventional political struggle, but experience [it] as a cosmic war between the forces of good and evil."[5] The fundamentalist embodies a perpetual threat to the authority of the state that is mounted in the name of allegedly embattled religious truths.

Had "fundamentalism" simply remained a term for marginal American Protestant groups, its significance would be quite limited. In the late 1970s, however, prominent conservative evangelical leaders such as Jerry Falwell began reclaiming the term even while insisting on its compatibility with active engagement in American politics.[6] At almost the same moment, the term began to go global, acquiring in the process a certain utility for naming the enemy of a world civil society that was characterized (in Lockean fashion) by the mutually tolerant coexistence of modern secularists and "good" (i.e., liberalized) forms of religion. As religious historian David Harrington Watt has noted, "fundamentalism" received its intellectual debut as a global concept with Martin Marty's 1980 proclamation that Jerry Falwell and the Ayatollah Khomeini were essentially kindred spirits who were "militantly antimodern, fanatical, and [who] hold in contempt the separation of church and state. Every day, it seems, brings forth new evidence of the growing power and determination of the religious recalcitrant."[7] In establishing the influential Fundamentalism Project at the University of Chicago, Marty sought to produce scholarship in support of a liberal political culture that might push back against an international upsurge in religious conservatism. It is ironic, therefore, that the chief beneficiaries of his arguments were themselves ultimately conservatives. By redeploying the concept of "fundamentalism" onto the terrain of the Islamic world, Marty ironically helped shore up what might be called the political theological basis for an alliance between market neoliberalism, hawkish neoconservatism, and the Christian evangelical right.

Ronald Reagan, elected in no small part against the backdrop of Jimmy Carter's impotence in the face of the Iran Hostage Crisis, brought Evangelists and free-market neoliberals together in a hegemonic coalition that was united through an explicit Lockean theology of liberalism (America's liberal freedoms are grounded in Christian faith in God's natural laws, including those of the market). At the same time, as can be seen in his famous cold war "Evil Empire Speech," notably delivered at the 1983 annual meeting of the American Association of Evangelicals, Reagan added militancy to this assemblage by redefining communism as a *theological* enemy and redescribing it as a secular variant of what Marty had called "fundamentalism." Reagan was continuing a narrative initiated by Reverend Billy Graham during the Dwight D. Eisenhower administration, according to which the United States' battle against the Soviet Union was not a conflict between two secular powers but a battle between Christian truth and atheism. After Reagan's 1980 election, American evangelical hostility toward atheistic communism moved into a new phase, as it became commonplace for conservative evangelicals to see Reaganomics as an integral component of the Christian worldview. In Reagan's account, of course, it was not Falwell who was akin to Khomeini but the likes of Soviet leader Yuri Andropov, leader of a militant and rigidly dogmatic totalitarian party whose members "preach the supremacy of the state, declare its omnipotence over individual man, and predict its eventual domination of all peoples on the earth."[8] Reframed in this way, Christian Evangelicals became theological partisans of the market, inclusive of the marketplace of ideas and thus *not* fundamentalist, while secular communism, paradoxically, became the true site of a theological dogmatism whose deep threat to global civil society necessitated an ardent defense.

In the post–cold war environment, and especially since the September 11, 2001, terrorist attacks, this notion of fundamentalism has reverted not only to the site of Islam but also to other religiosities construable as a civil threat. George W. Bush's "global war on terror" replayed Reagan's themes by describing jihadism as a kind of totalitarian "Islamofascism" continuous with both Nazi and Soviet doctrinalism.[9] Marty's compatriots at the Fundamentalism Project have continued to write in ways that ultimately support these political effects when, as recently as 2003, in *Strong Religion: The Rise of Fundamentalisms around the World*, they describe contemporary fundamentalism as the "third rebuff" of Enlightenment expectations, a social phenomenon that follows in the footsteps of Burkean conservatism/clericism in nineteenth-century Europe, and then the "totalitarian Bolshevism" and "clerical-authoritarianism of fascism and Nazism in the twentieth century."[10]

As a discourse of scholarship, "fundamentalism" presents the apparent advantage of being genuinely comparative in its effort to identify "family resemblances" among religious political forces situated across globally diverse regions, cultures, and histories. In this sense, the study of fundamentalism is ineluctably appealing for a project like RelSec, the Religion, Secularism, and Political Belonging program whose translocal approach spawned this book.[11] On the same grounds, it can be positively compared to a term such as "Islamism," which risks the collapsing together of very different kinds of political projects as well as making religious politics a problem exclusive to Islam. At the same time, however, it is critical to observe that "fundamentalism," though comparative, is not a neutral term but one that produces an antimodern figure through the trope of a violent rejection of the exchange of ideas and a vision of modernity as essentially characterized by the give-and-take that finds its institutional archetype in the market. None of this is to say that the various religiously grounded forms of political belonging today do not need explanation. Yet there are alternatives to the "fundamentalist thesis" in the form that Martin Marty and R. Scott Appleby have conceptualized it. Faisal Devji, for example, has analyzed jihadist movements by developing comparisons, not to Protestant evangelicals but to vanguardist and humanitarian movements.[12] Kamran Talattof has shown how the politics of "fundamentalist" Islam constitute a reworking of the themes of revolutionary Marxist movements.[13] Likewise, interpreting the "Hindutva" phenomenon in India as "fundamentalist" risks obscuring some of its most interesting features, such as the movement's strong association of Hinduism with key liberal values, including tolerance, religious freedom, and the nation-state.

Novelist Mohsin Hamid arguably gets the last laugh when, in *The Reluctant Fundamentalist*, he narrates the story of a formerly Westernized Pakistani who comes to reject his work on Wall Street and returns to do political work in his homeland.[14] If at first we assume that the fundamentalism of the novel's title must be Islamic, presaging the protagonist's reactive and violent return to his Muslim roots, the novel eventually comes to suggest something quite different, namely that the fundamentalism at the heart of the story is "market fundamentalism," a faith in the commandment to practice a cost-benefit analysis that should, in fact, have steered him away from love of country and family and toward a life that honors only the natural law of financial valuations. As Hamid's novel cleverly confirms, in the final analysis the antifundamentalist is himself tacitly modeled upon the fundamentalist. To create a theological fundamentalist enemy of modernity, one must embrace with "no concessions" the political theology of liberalism, a theology that asserts spiritual enmity against those whom it views as the world's militant anachronists.

NOTES

Feedback from multiple team members was critical to the writing of this lexical entry. Special thanks to Marcia Klotz, Karen Seat, Caleb Simmons, Max Strassfeld, and Kamran Talatoff.

1. *Oxford English Dictionary*, s.v. "fundamentalism," accessed September 7, 2018, http://www.oed.com.
2. See Simon Wood, "Rethinking Fundamentalism: Ruholla Khomeini, Mawlana Mawdudi, and the Fundamentalist Model," *Journal for Cultural and Religious Theory* 11, no. 2 (Spring 2010): 171; David Harrington Watt, "Muslims, Fundamentalists, and the Fear of the Dangerous Other in American Culture," *Journal of Religion and Society* 12 (2010): 3; and Malise Ruthven, *Fundamentalism: The Search for Meaning* (Oxford: Oxford University Press, 2004), 17–18.
3. John Locke, *A Letter Concerning Toleration* (New York: Hackett Classics, 1983), 25.
4. Elizabeth Pritchard, *Religion in Public: Locke's Political Theology* (Stanford: Stanford University Press, 2014), 1–13.
5. Karen Armstrong, *The Battle for God: A History of Fundamentalism* (New York: Random House, 2011), xiii.
6. See Ed Dobson, Jerry Falwell, and Edward Hindson, *The Fundamentalist Phenomenon: The Resurgence of Conservative Christianity* (Garden City, NY: Doubleday, 1981), which proudly reclaims the term from its history of abuse even while repoliticizing it. See also Susan Friend Harding's ethnographic study of this moment in the surge of the American Christian right, *The Book of Jerry Falwell: Fundamentalist Language and Politics* (Princeton, NJ: Princeton University Press, 2001).
7. David Harrington Watt, "Muslims, Fundamentalists, and the Fear of the Dangerous Other in American Culture," *Journal of Religion and Society* 12 (2010): 5–6; Martin E. Marty, "Fundamentalism Reborn: Faith and Fanaticism," *Saturday Review*, May 1980, 37.
8. Ronald Reagan, "Remarks at the Annual Convention of the National Association of Evangelicals in Orlando" [aka "Evil Empire Speech"], March 8, 1983, https://www.reaganfoundation.org/media/50919/remarks_annual_convention_national_association_evangelicals_030883.pdf..
9. Although David Horowitz was probably the most responsible for the recycling of "Islamofascism," his term circulated widely on the political right during the early years that followed the 9/11 attacks. Even Bush eventually referenced the term in an interview as one of several competing terms for Islamic "radicalism." "Transcript: Bush Discusses War on Terrorism," *Washington Post*, October 6, 2005.
10. Gabriel A. Almond, R. Scott Appleby, and Emmanuel Sivan, *Strong Religion: The Rise of Fundamentalisms around the World* (Chicago: University of Chicago Press, 2003), 5.
11. For a fuller description of the RelSec project, see https://chcinetwork.org/programs/relsec, accessed July 18, 2020.
12. Faisal Devji, *Landscapes of the Jihad: Militancy, Morality, Modernity* (Ithaca, NY: Cornell University Press, 2005).
13. Kamran Talattof, "Comrade Akbar: Islam, Marxism, and Modernity," *Comparative Studies of South Asia, Africa and the Middle East* 25, no. 3 (2005): 634–49. See also Devji,

Landscapes of the Jihad; and Faisal Devji, *The Terrorist in Search of Humanity: Militant Islam and Global Politics* (New York: Columbia University Press, 2008). Talattof, while accepting the term "fundamentalism," uses it quite differently (as a form of engagement *with* revolutionary modernity) in his article "Comrade Akbar." See also Wood, "Rethinking Fundamentalism," in which the author shows that even the archetypal Ayatollah Khomeini does not truly fit the fundamentalist bill when his words and actions are considered carefully.

14   Mohsin Hamid, *The Reluctant Fundamentalist* (New York: Harvest Books, 2008).

6. RELIGION, POLITICS, AND NATIONALISM, A CASE STUDY
The Palestinian Islamic Jihad Movement
RAEF ZREIK AND MOHANAD MUSTAFA

This chapter addresses the ways in which religious discourse is presented and appropriated in the Palestinian national movement. For the moment, we assume that such a division between religious and national dimensions is possible—even if only in the form of an ideal. The chapter is divided into three parts. In the first part, we describe the development of the Palestinian national movement, depicting major moments of overlap between its religious and national dimensions. The second part, the heart of the chapter, focuses on the Islamic Jihad movement and the philosophy of the movement's founder, Dr. Fathi Shaqaqi, who was assassinated in the 1990s—apparently by Israeli forces. We primarily focus on his writings and less on his political activities. The third part is an epilogue wherein we more expansively examine the interplay between religion and nationalism within and beyond the Palestinian context.

The Palestinian National Movement and Its Religious Context

The presence of religious discourse in the Palestinian national movement is a complex matter that is influenced by at least five overarching and interconnected historical factors. The first factor is the Palestinian national movement's close and reciprocal relationship with the Arab national movement. The fluctuations in the Palestinian movement between pan-Arab and Islamist approaches were to some extent paralleled by similar changes in the Arab world.[1] A second factor is ideological evolution in the Islamic world. Although in many cases the Islamic influence was transmitted through the broader filter of the Arab world, the influence could sometimes be direct. This is the case regarding the Iranian Revolution's influence on the birth and development of the Islamic Jihad movement.[2] The third factor is Zionism's emergence as a settler movement and, at a later stage, the State of Israel and its influence on the Arab world and the Middle East.[3] A fourth factor is Palestinian society's ideological and political pluralism, as it includes all the ideological currents that existed in the Arab world in the first half of the twentieth century, including the pan-Arab, the local national, and the Islamic religious. A fifth factor is the central position of Palestine in Islamic religious discourse, as Palestine is considered holy Islamic terrain that contains some of the holiest Muslim sites after Medina and Mecca. The fact that these holy sites are under occupation and non-Muslim control has augmented the Israel-Palestine predicament's religious dimensions and has turned the liberation of Palestine into a central matter in Islamic religious discourse.[4] And finally, religion's prominence should be understood vis-à-vis internal Palestinian political dynamics. For example, one of the reasons for Hamas's rise during and following the 1990s relates inter alia to increased financial and political corruption within the Palestinian Authority. In other words, Hamas's rise signified a vote of no confidence in the corrupt regime of the Palestinian Authority more than a preference for Islam as an ideological or political frame.[5] A more detailed history of the Palestinian National Movement identifies various exigencies for the Islamic Jihad Movement's eventual emergence.

The Palestinian national movement, like the Arab national movement, emerged toward the end of the nineteenth century and the beginning of the twentieth century.[6] The Arab national movement, for as long as the Ottoman Empire existed, conceived of itself through its differentiation from the Turkish Ottoman regime in the Holy Land. As a national movement acting in opposition to an Islamic regime, it was natural that the Arab national movement would raise the national Arab flag based on Arabic language and Arab culture.⁷ In this setting, nationalism appears as a phenomenon separate from religion and even in competition with it, and so it is understandable that Arab nationalist circles such as those led by Butrous al-Bustani and Satea al-Hosari, among others, emphasized their nationalism's separation from any religious affinity.⁸ It is also worth noting that many of those in Arab nationalist circles were of Christian origin. Given these various factors, it is unsurprising that at this stage in Palestinian national history, religious discourse emerges primarily as a reform discourse that attempts to cope with challenges that the modern "West" poses for reforming existing structures rather than a revolutionary discourse that aims to fundamentally alter things.⁹

The reform approach was not sustained in the aftermath of World War I. A multitude of factors—including the destruction of the Ottoman Empire, British and French colonialism in the region, the annulment of the Turkish Caliphate, the Balfour Declaration, and increased Jewish immigration to Palestine—transformed the Palestinian national movement's confrontation with the "West" in general and with Zionism in particular into a direct conflict. It is not surprising that in 1928, four years after the demise of the Caliphate, Hassan al-Banaa created the Muslim Brotherhood in Egypt.

Over the British Mandate years, the Palestinian national movement was led by Haj Amin al-Hosseini, who also served as the chairman of the Supreme Islamic Council. While Mufti al-Hosseini primarily saw his leadership in national terms, it was not lacking in religious motives; under his guidance, the Palestinian national movement was presented as a national struggle with a religious flavor. It is worth noting that a central reason for al-Hosseini's leadership was that the Mandate refused to hold any elections that would allow Palestinian leaders to be selected on a nationalist basis. Generally, the Mandate recognized Arabs only as a religious minority and not as a national group, an approach that emerged in the Balfour Declaration. As such, the religious character of Palestinian representation at the time was something of a colonial imposition.

Following the war of 1948 and the Nakhba, secular national movements arose across the Arab world in Egypt, Syria, Tunisia, Algeria, and Iraq. The secular Palestinian national movement first emerged during this same period, the 1950s and early 1960s, primarily among a group of young graduates of the American University in Beirut who were students of Dr. Constantine Zuriq, a secular national leader who coined the term "Nakhba" for the mass exodus of Palestinian Arabs. Together, they founded the Arab National Movement (ANM).¹⁰ As young intellectuals who were drawn to the Arab national ideology, they approached the Palestinian issue as part of a pan-Arab national issue, and as such they were in close contact with the Gamal Abdel Nasser regime in Egypt.¹¹

In the 1960s, the Palestinian national movement was at its peak. This was one of the periods of intensified tension between the Islamic and national streams, and it was also the same period when the Muslim Brotherhood was persecuted and imprisoned in Egypt. It is worth noting that during this time, Sayed Qutb rose to prominence as a philosopher of the Muslim Brotherhood and as the author of *Milestones*, written while he was in prison. Its publication marked a watershed moment in the evolution of the Muslim Brotherhood's thought due to its political-activist-revolutionary tone, which is quite evident when contrasted with the social reform tone of previous writings by Muslim reformers in the Arab world.[12]

During these years, ANM activists were not involved in actions against Israel and they did not organize the Palestinian refugee masses. Some scholars suggest that this was because they saw the Palestinian issue as intertwined with broader Arab nationalism and in turn as necessitating Nasser's leadership. From this historical perspective, the ANM activists waited for an act of opposition from Nasser that did not happen, a period in which the Palestine issue also gradually grew less relevant for them.[13]

At this point, a group of young people—mostly Muslim Brotherhood activists under the leadership of Abu Jihad and Yasser Arafat—established the Palestine Liberation Organization (now known as Fatah). They commenced military operations against Israel in 1965.[14] Fatah's establishment and military operations against Israel constituted a turning point for the Palestinian national movement as it implicitly expressed a lack of trust in the Nasserian pan-Arab national project. These Fatah activists did not need the burning defeat of 1967 in order to shoulder their political mission and diverge from the Nasserian and Baathist Arab regimes, and it is possible that their religious background and affiliation with the Muslim Brotherhood helped them more easily delink from the chains of the Nasserian national project.[15]

From the end of the 1960s to the 1980s, Fatah led the Palestinian national movement. While during this period there was no lack of religious practices and ceremonies in Palestinian politics, Fatah overwhelmingly conducted a nationalist discourse—a sensibility that is reflected in the 1968 Palestinian National Charter.[16] This approach became even more pronounced after 1974, the year in which the Arab League recognized Fatah as the sole representative of the Palestinian people and also implicitly recognized the Israeli state as part of the "Ten-Point" program. From this point forward, through the 1988 Palestinian Declaration of Independence in Algeria and ending with the Oslo Pact in 1993, the Palestinian issue was presented as a national struggle, drawing upon the rhetoric of a nation's right to self-determination so that its goals were defined as the end of the occupation, political independence, the establishment of a state, and the return of refugees.[17] Put differently, the Palestinian struggle was not defined in religious terms or as an intercultural war between West and East but as a war against occupation and colonialism.

During this period, the Muslim Brotherhood, in both Palestine and Jordan, did not participate in the fight against Israeli occupation or initiate any real actions against it.[18] It believed that the time was not right for such actions, for Islamic society's awareness must first be aroused, and only afterward would it be possible to wage an armed struggle for Palestine.[19] But many years before Hamas's entry into Palestinian politics, signs of change emerged among Muslim Brotherhood activists who were dissatisfied with the movement's inaction on the Palestinian issue and who urged the Muslim Brotherhood to take a central role in the resistance against Israeli occupation. These activists felt that they could not join the Palestinian national movement in its existing form since it had abandoned its connection to Islamic religious ideology. For these reasons, the political choice seemed to fall between two problematic extremes: either an Islamic movement without Palestine (the Muslim Brotherhood) or a Palestinian national movement that forgot its Islamic context (Fatah). Islamic Jihad intended to fill this political void.

The Islamic Jihad Movement: Beginnings

The Islamic Jihad movement emerged toward the end of the 1970s, and it was established by several central Palestinian activists who were then studying in Egyptian universities.[20] They were intellectual, reading revolutionary literatures of the period, including Marxist and existentialist works.[21] Prominent among them was a medical student named Fathi Shaqaqi, who would later lead the movement. They had all previously been active in the Muslim Brotherhood in Palestine and they were in close contact with Sheikh Ahmed Yassin. Immediately after their graduation from the university, they returned to the occupied territories, both Gaza and the West Bank, and began activities against the occupation that included military activities. This move marked a detachment from the Muslim Brotherhood—which in their opinion was not sufficiently militant and did not fight against the Israeli occupation—and an increased closeness to the Palestinian national movement. Therefore, it could be argued that the nationalist aspect of Islamic Jihad was stronger than it was among Hamas operatives.

Like other political Islam movements, the Islamic Jihad movement was strongly influenced by the Iranian Revolution, even though Iran was a Shiite state and they were Sunni Muslims. Shaqaqi devoted one of his first books, *Al-Khomeini and the Alternative Islamic Solution*, to the imam Khomeini, and he drew inspiration from how the Islamic religion was harnessed for revolution as a means of enlisting the masses, enabling a state such as Iran to stand at the forefront against a world power such as the United States of America.[22] While the book was printed and distributed in Iran, the proximity between Islamic Jihad and Iran led to Shaqaqi losing his membership in the Muslim Brotherhood, and he was even forced to flee from Egypt following its publication.

These events occurred at the end of the 1970s and beginning of the 1980s, when the Palestinian national movement under Fatah began to hint at its willingness to compromise with Israel. It also coincided with the rise of various political Islam movements in Egypt, Afghanistan, and Syria, and perhaps most importantly the "Amal" movement in Lebanon, followed immediately by the Hizballah movement. In this sense, the rise of the Hizballah was in many ways the parallel Shiite movement to the rise of Islamic Jihad in the region.[23]

Ideological Profile: Shaqaqi and His Writings

General Attitude Concerning Islam

As expressed in his writings, Shaqaqi saw Islam as his starting point and derived his principles from it.[24] Undoubtedly in this sense, Shaqaqi aligns with the Muslim Brotherhood, as it also approached Islamic texts as its starting point.[25] Shaqaqi identified the fall of the Ottoman Caliphate as the point of collapse and major defeat of Islam in the modern era.[26] Here, Shaqaqi can also be understood as continuing the lineage of the Muslim Brotherhood—more specifically, as the scion of Sayed Qutb.[27]

It is clear that for Shaqaqi, Islam was not only a religious system that conceptualized the relationship between individuals and their creator but a complete cultural and moral system that constituted one side in a cultural war between the Orient and the colonial West: "since Napoleon's campaigns and until the First World War, the West has attempted by all means to break up the rigid Islamic barrier that prevented it from controlling the world's treasures."[28] In turn, Shaqaqi viewed Islam as the sole unifying and enlisting force against Western colonialism and Christian aggression. Shaqaqi understood the genesis of the Muslim Brotherhood as a reaction to the end of the Caliphate and attacks from the West.[29] He felt that Arab nationalism's prior attempts to fight Western aggression had failed and that "Islam remains alone and isolated in the struggle to defend the nation's culture and its unity began from Palestine and runs through Sudan, ending with the Hizballah in Lebanon."[30]

Shaqaqi also believed that the Islamic religion could serve a constructive role beyond enlisting forces to resist and control Western hegemony, noting that "Islamic ideology is a divine, practical and moral approach and a worldwide one that includes solutions to all the problems of contemporary society."[31] Shaqaqi did not want to free himself from the West in order to tag along behind it or to create a state in the image of Western states and cultures. According to his argument—in which he followed the path of Sayed Qutb—the West, with its two primary forms of regimes, democratic liberalism and Marxist socialism, was in a deep state of crisis in terms of both values and ideology.[32]

Shaqaqi followed Qutb's revolutionary conception of the connection between religion and politics.[33] Unlike Muslim Brotherhood leaders with reformist or gradated perspectives, Qutb envisioned a dichotomized, revolutionary world split between "Jahalia" (the period of time before Islam) and Islam, which necessitated a sharp transition from one to the other.[34]

The main principle behind Shaqaqi's revolutionary approach to Islamic ideology was "Hakemia," the belief in God's sovereignty and supremacy.[35] Building upon this principle, Shaqaqi argued for a revolutionary stance "against the sovereignty of man in all its forms and situations."[36] Invoking a liberatory and universalizing rhetoric, Shaqaqi envisioned the creation of "a Muslim society where people will be liberated from slavery one to the other by transforming everyone into slaves of God alone."[37] A dependence on God unmediated by human sovereignty engenders liberation, equality, and independence, similar to how obedience to the rule of law releases people from their dependence on the will of others. It is not surprising that Shaqaqi emphasized the universal and egalitarian character of Islam, since according to his argument about Islam, "the universal context is the only relevant context—not blood ties neither nationality nor color or ethnicity."[38] For Shaqaqi, Islam is not just political but revolutionary and universal.

CRITIQUE OF THE MUSLIM BROTHERHOOD. If Shaqaqi's starting point was the religious text and he was motivated by the desire to resurrect the Caliphate, then how did he differ from the Muslim Brotherhood? Useful here is an overview of Shaqaqi's critiques, addressing his interpretations of the Islamic project in general and his role and tasks in Palestine in particular. We also touch upon the dynamic correlations that emerge in Shaqaqi's thought between history and revolution, modernity and heritage, nationalism and religion, secularism and nationality, and reform and revolution.

THE ROLE OF HISTORY, CRITIQUE, AND THE REVOLUTION. Shaqaqi had a critical attitude toward those Muslims who studied abroad in Europe and returned dazzled by its supposed superiority and advancements. Nevertheless, he was no less critical toward conservative Muslims who resisted innovation and were skeptical toward criticism. Although Shaqaqi continually declared that he was religious, he also felt that it was important to understand history, and he often deployed Hegelian dialectical terminology in his understanding of history. In a paper titled "History—Why?" Shaqaqi argues that history is not some sort of reiteration of past achievements or "a subject for entertainment and pleasure and awe regarding the stories of our illustrious past. Rather, it is a step subject to learning and analysis and criticism through a special method."[39] Studying religious texts alone is insufficient; religious insights and wisdom also emerge through history and therefore it is one's duty to study history. History helps reveal the absolute, which is also in the Qur'an.[40] In this vein, Shaqaqi strongly criticized the Muslim Brotherhood since it lacked "historic consciousness."[41]

For Shaqaqi, history should not only be studied but it should be approached critically as a subject for interpretation rather than literal adherence.[42] This approach grants the subject—the reader and interpreter of the text—a more central and active status. Thus there is also a revolutionary dimension to Shaqaqi's thought in that he grants significant importance to praxis. As he explains, "Islam is a serious dynamic practical approach. It is an approach that copes with the reality and not only a theory concerned with duties."[43] For Shaqaqi, it is impossible to separate theory from practice—only correct practice can lead to correct theory. It is not difficult to identify traces of Marxist thought in Shaqaqi's writing on praxis, wherein religion takes the place of the conceptual philosophy that emerges in Marxist writings on revolutionary political activity.

THE TERRITORIALIZATION OF FAITH AND THE CENTRALITY OF PALESTINE—THE DUTY OF JIHAD. We often think of religion as a transcendental phenomenon that floats above territory, whereas territorial thinking is the very core of national thinking. But Shaqaqi's thought demonstrates the limitations of this widely understood distinction. Shaqaqi's religious thinking leads him to Palestine and his thinking about Palestine leads him to the Islamic religion.

In his book *The Centrality of Palestine and the Contemporary Islamic Project*, Shaqaqi approaches the establishment of Israel as a core component of the West's all-encompassing war against the Islamic nation: "The establishment of

Israel is the most important and dangerous part of the general war, and with its establishment in the very heart of the Islamic world, the Western attack achieved one of its main missions."[44] In the eyes of the Muslim Brotherhood, the Palestinian issue was simply one more issue in the Islamic world like Kashmir, the Philippines, or Eritrea—but it should not be so.[45] And so, one of Shaqaqi's main criticisms of the Muslim Brotherhood was its overall neglect of the Palestinian issue and its failure to enlist in a full military struggle against Israel. The Muslim Brotherhood claimed that it had not yet reached the time for a jihad in Palestine and that it first had to educate people in Islamic principles. In contrast, Shaqaqi felt that there was a duty to set Palestine at the center of the Brotherhood's thinking and actions.[46] According to his understanding, the struggle for Palestine was a condition for the development of Islamic consciousness, since this consciousness could only develop through the practice of struggle.

This reading offers a new interpretation of the Palestinian question and, at the same time, a sort of renewed reading of the substance of Islam itself. The centrality of Palestine is seen as of primary religious importance in that Palestine is lacking without Islam and Islam is lacking without Palestine.[47]

The Palestinian issue's priority, therefore, stemmed from religious reasons because of the centrality of Palestinian land but also political reasons because of Israel's significance as a threatening and divisive entity. Shaqaqi's approach to Israel and Palestine integrated political-historical and religious analyses derived from Qur'anic texts. Shaqaqi understood Palestine to be the primary, burning point of confrontation between the Muslim Orient and the West's colonial project, as reflected by the alliance between Zionism and European colonialism. Thus the battle for the future of the Islamic nation and the resurrection of the Caliphate depended on Palestine, since Israel's existence constituted a real block to the unification of the Islamic world and the return of the Caliphate.[48] It is therefore very difficult to identify whether Shaqaqi affiliated with a particular religious, national, anticolonial, or cultural struggle, as all these elements are interwoven in his theories and analyses.

ON POLITICS AND THE ISSUE OF PERSONAL LIBERTY. One of the questions that occupies political philosophers today is the relationship between the political domain and ideological assumptions. Does a particular political viewpoint necessitate a particular ideological perspective, and does a particular ideology necessitate a particular type of politics?

Shaqaqi presents a complex approach in response to this question. On the one hand, he was an Islamic ideologist, guided by his perception of Islam as both a religion and a more general inclusive ideology. Shaqaqi assumed that politics were the continuation of ideology and that it is impossible to talk about the Islamic religion without its social-political context. Thus, in a certain sense, his politics are deeply enmeshed with ideology. But at the same time, Shaqaqi understands that the political world has a certain independent existence, so he was not interested in examining the motives or ideological convictions of people and groups with political attitudes similar to his own. Shaqaqi therefore had no problem cooperating with different streams in the Palestinian national movement, noting that "the main disputes will continue even within the streams themselves, but politics is the entry point that unites us all in a confrontation with the West, and Palestine is situated at the very core of politics."[49] In this sense, Shaqaqi viewed politics as to some extent autonomous, and political exigency led him to bracket all ideological disputes to advance a particular political program or goal.

The Palestinian issue in particular justified the postponement of all ideological disputes. For Shaqaqi, it was clear that all the different streams were being threatened, so there was a duty to give priority and preference to politics.[50] Consequently, in Shaqaqi's text "What Is the Jihad Movement?" he explicitly forbids violence between the different factions in the Palestinian national movement despite the deepest ideological disputes: "all disputes with the national movement will be resolved in discussions and it is forbidden to use force-violence except against the Zionist enemy."[51] For Shaqaqi, "Islamists must not relinquish the nationalists and nationalists must not relinquish the Islamists since there is not one side that is capable of managing the struggle alone."[52] The urgency and centrality of revolutionary politics also led the Jihad movement—and Shaqaqi in particular—to not attribute much decisive importance to how members or supporters led their private lives, nor was the movement interested in obliging supporters to undertake a religious lifestyle.[53]

THE IRANIAN REVOLUTION AND THE SHIITE ISSUE. Shaqaqi presented a consistent stance on the centrality of the political moment and its distinction from the ideological dimension, and also a consistent willingness to minimize religious dispute in service of political enlistment. In this vein, Shaqaqi wanted to minimize the Shiite-Sunni dispute and put it into proportion in relation to the opposition to the United States, the West, and Israel.

Shaqaqi enthusiastically supported the Iranian Revolution and devoted a book on the revolution to Imam al-Khomeini. He also did not lack praise for the ideologist of the Iranian Revolution, Ali Shariati. Shaqaqi was very enthused by revolutionary passion and in his essay "Iran, the Revolution and the State," he describes the capture of the U.S. embassy as "an earthquake. . . . Everything shakes as if a strong powerful hand grasped the world and shook it strongly."[54] In another essay, "Two Years after the Revolution," Shaqaqi expressed excitement at the revolution's ability to integrate theory with practice "in a dialectic manner."[55] Thus it is clear that for Shaqaqi, the revolution was not just a local event but an event of central significance to the entire Islamic world. As a result of the revolution, "life returned to this body which had been considered a dead body" and "we revealed ourselves."[56] This bodily rejuvenation was not religious but political: "in the consciousness of the world's Muslims and of those who had been weakened in general it wiped out the fear of strong and powerful states."[57] The revolution therefore was not a religious revelation or new theological insight but primarily a display of strength and self-confidence for the downtrodden.

It is therefore clear that the ethnic or sectarian aspect of the revolution being Shiite was not significant for Shaqaqi. Shaqaqi viewed the revolution as an event against Western powers and the United States and not against the Sunnis. The revolution offered a new path for all Muslims and not only for the Shiites among them. He emphasized the fact that the revolution itself relied on the words of Sunni philosophers such as Sayed Qutb and Hassan al-Banna, and he called the purported conflict between Sunnis and Shiites and the issues that arose in some Sunni nations "a stimulated and imaginary storm." He also presented the works of the aforementioned Sunni philosophers, and even those of Alkhardawi Sheikh of al-Azhar, alongside works by Shiite philosophers such as Imam Khomeini, demonstrating how each of the two sides views the other as partners in Islam and brothers in the same religion.[58]

Arab Nationalism

Shaqaqi is an outstanding case of a thinker who tried to reconcile Arab nationalism with Islam and Islam with Arab nationalism. In his essay "The Alternative Islamic Solution," Shaqaqi rejected the writing of several Arab nationalist thinkers and especially Christian nationalist thinkers, mainly those from the nineteenth century who identified tension between Arab nationalism and Islam.[59] According to Shaqaqi, the person who began this stream of Arab nationalism was the Christian philosopher Anton Farrah, although he was later joined by Muslim scholars such as Ali Abed al-Razeq, Taha Hussein, and Ahmed Lutfi al-Sayed.

Shaqaqi reasoned that a version of Arab nationalism that acted in detachment from or competition with Islam was problematic—even dangerous—because it sowed seeds of division within the body of the Islamic nation. As he argued in "Encounter of the Streams," "the West encourages the disintegration of the Islamic framework, not because it is interested in an active nationalist framework but out of the intention to break up the region into even more fragments until they form an ideological and conceptual void that will cause conceptual dependence on the West."[60]

According to this line of thought, an Arab nationalism that is detached from Islam plays a fragmenting and divisive role somewhat similar to the role played by Zionism and Israel. This is Shaqaqi's argument in his essay "The Palestinian Issue": "the Arab national movement was born as a legitimate son of the West's attack on the Islamic homeland, and Zionism began as part of the same attack in all its manifestations."[61] This Arab national trend, which began at the beginning of the twentieth century, adopted an antireligious tone during particular periods—especially in the Ba'ath party and certain periods of the Nasserian regime—and that proved to be its disastrous failure, ending with the defeat of 1967. For Shaqaqi, this series of events indicated that a national opposition or national socialism that turned its back on Islam was doomed to fail.[62] From Shaqaqi's viewpoint, those sixty years of national ideology were sixty lost years, and now the time had come for the nation to restore itself and embrace its religious past. This was also one of the problems of the Palestinian national movement more specifically, which thought that it could fight against Zionism alone without all-out war against the British and Western cultural colonialism and while not equipped with Islam.[63]

Thus Shaqaqi wanted to develop a national approach in harmony with religion rather than in opposition to it. In "Concerning the Renewed National Project," Shaqaqi wrote that "the contradiction between nationalism and religion is an imaginary contradiction and it began at the beginning of the twentieth century and this imaginary contradiction must be halted."[64] He further envisioned a major role for religion in the national project and the project of opposition to Western colonialism and Israel: "We believe that given the balance of tyrannical powers that tend in favor of the United States and Israel for the past decades in this region, then there can be no possibility of opposition unless it is through 'Almukdas' [the holy one]—since only 'The Holy' is capable of such confrontation and opposition, and if the national movement maintains that same element of 'holiness' then it will be able to resist and continue the struggle."[65]

SECULARITY AND SECULARISM. Shaqaqi claimed that there was a mistaken understanding of secularity and its meaning, and that as a result, secularity became an obstacle that intervened between religion and nationalism. When we approach secularity in its historical context, Shaqaqi argued, we see that it is possible to connect Arab nationalism and the Islamic religion.⁶⁶

In "Encounter of the Streams," Shaqaqi argued that "there is no necessary connection between Arab nationalism and secularism. Secularism means separation of the religion from the state, which is a Western fact that is unsuitable for Arab Islamic experience. . . . Nationalism is a separate stance from secularism and there is no need to create an artificial connection that has no logical foundation."⁶⁷ For Shaqaqi, secularism is not a neutral or ideology-void phenomenon. He viewed secularity in the European historical context as a fighting ideology, a practice of liberation from the tyrannical power of the church. That was its essence for him: "Secularism was born as a theory against the control of the church in society and in politics. . . . It was not religious values that were the problem but the church's control of social matters and over the state."⁶⁸ However, in the Islamic world, religion was always against the state and against the controlling regime, and so there was nothing to be liberated from. Shaqaqi viewed the problems in the Arab Islamic world as completely different from those of Europe: "The problem in the Arab and Islamic world is the control of the state and its hegemony in society. . . . Secularism liberated the society in the West from the power of the church but in Islamic society, secularism caused the disintegration of Islamic society in the face of the state and so it legitimized the complete control of the state over society, and thus allowed and contributed to the continuation of the patriarchal regime's control instead of contributing to man's liberation."⁶⁹ According to Shaqaqi, the Islamic religion played—and still plays—the role of limiting the power and tyranny of the state. In "Fundamentalism and Secularism," Shaqaqi writes: "Islam created a sort of society which resists the state's complete domination and hegemony and offers alternative to it, rendering it weaker and responsive to it, even if there be the strongest of sultans and rulers."⁷⁰ Weakening the power of religion in such a case actually weakens the power of civil society that stands opposite the state and its tyrants.

It is therefore evident to Shaqaqi that there is a distinction between what he calls "politics" and "religion," but he is also clearly aware of the presence of religion in politics. In "The Terror of Intellectuals against Islam," he ponders: "Should we relinquish everything religious if we enter the world of politics and should we relinquish everything political if and to the extent that we have entered the world of religion?"⁷¹ According to Shaqaqi, politics without religion is devoid of content since "politics is not created except through deep beliefs and the creed [Akida] of the society. Otherwise politics becomes a sort of self-negation and negation of the national identity."⁷²

Epilogue: Concerning Religion and Nationalism

The case of Fathi Shaqaqi and Islamic Jihad raises certain points about the connection between nationalism and religion. Religion is in this world, not outside this world. Even when it tries to tell us something about the world to come, it tells us about this world, the here and now, through language, symbols, sounds, and myths made of this material world. Yet on the other hand, nationalism always held a spiritual element that went beyond the mere aggregate of flesh-and-blood human beings. This process of pouring meaning into the collective body called nationality or nation is formed from materials that resemble those materials employed for religious discourse. What is known as the secularization process was not completed and will apparently not be completed.[73]

As a normative system, religion competes for the shaping of our moral and normative image and tries to shape our behavior, similar to the attempts of other systems such as morality, ideology, politics, and law. Many liberals tried to produce a theory of political liberalism without a thick worldview of ideology and morality.[74] But any political thesis is anchored in an ideological worldview that is beyond politics itself and allows us to attain political attitudes. In this context, religion is another ideology and to think that it is possible to separate the ideology from politics is simply a mistake, for it is hard to cut this Gordian knot. But even when it is cut, one must be aware that this cut has in itself an ideological/moral aspect to it.

Nevertheless, and despite the intimacy between the two concepts, we continue to talk about religion and nationalism as two distinct concepts or ideal types. We do not relinquish—nor can we relinquish—one of these concepts, and so the fact is that both concepts are alive and active and neither of them is consumed by the other concept, nor is there a total convergence between the two. Even those who reason that they are connected—because separation is problematic, because they were once one, and because each of them constitutes the other—still find it difficult to manage them in the conceptual realm without relying on their separation. This can be understood in analogy with other conceptual relations: the relationship of law to politics or knowledge to power.[75] That said, one should avoid an approach that collapses the two concepts or that views modern nationalism or the idea of sovereignty merely through the lenses of political theology, for this misses the uniqueness of the modern sovereign nation.[76] Another danger emerges from any opposing theory that sees both phenomena as unfolding on two separate domains, which risks missing the mutual constitution of the phenomena at hand.

The study of Islamic Jihad in particular and of Palestinian nationalism in general helps clarify these insights. Islamic Jihad was simultaneously an intervention in the discourse and praxis of the Palestinian national movement that was until then dominated mainly by Fatah. It deployed religion and mobilized it for the goals of Palestinian national movement. It enlarged the scope of the confrontation between the Palestinian national movement and Zionism / the State of Israel, locating it within a global struggle against colonialism and an attack on the Muslim world writ large. It believed that Palestinian nationalism should incorporate this understanding within its ideology and view this incorporation as an ideological guide. It also aimed at recruiting the "sacred" and the "holy" in service of the national cause of Palestine. In this regard, the Jihad offered a new framework for Palestinian nationalism, but still it was a form of Palestinian nationalism after all. Palestinian nationalism can work within a pan-Arab ideological umbrella or a communist ideology, and it can work within an Islamist frame as well. In this sense, the role of religion in Islamic Jihad in particular and Palestinian nationalism in general is more akin to that of Irish nationalism, not British (religion as mere explanation), nor Zionist (organic nonseparable intimacy).

On the other hand, Shaqaqi and the Jihad offered a new interpretation of the Muslim Brotherhood doctrine. In this regard, Islamic Jihad could be viewed as an intervention in the interpretation of religious texts and the canonical texts of Muslim Brothers themselves. The Islam that emerges from their writing is different from, though continuous with, other prior practices and interpretations of Islamic texts. This proves the mutual constitution of nationalism and religion. Religion is not a given category; rather, it is shaped and reshaped by nationalism, and so is nationalism by religion. The case of Shaqaqi and Jihad demonstrates how this happened, when, and under what circumstances. The circumstances are a matter of contingency, but the mutual constitution amounts to more than that.

NOTES

1 Mahar al-Sharif, *The Search for an Entity: A Study of Palestinian Political Thought* [in Arabic] (Nicosia: Center for Socialist Studies in the Arab World, 1995), 59–62. All translations are mine unless otherwise noted.
2 Khaled Alhroub, *Hamas: Thought and Political Practice* [in Arabic] (Beirut: Institute of Palestine Studies, 1997), 9–22.
3 The 1948 and 1967 wars undoubtedly had a significant impact on the formation of the Palestinian national movement. See Yazid Sayigh, *Armed Struggle and the Search for State: The Palestinian National Movement, 1949-1993* [in Arabic] (Beirut: Institute of

Palestine Studies, 1997). And in later years, while the Oslo accord at first reinforced the Palestinian Liberation Movement, its failure or the causing of its failure led to the weakening of the Palestinian Liberation Movement and its organization, which pinnacled with the victory of the Hamas movement in the 2006 Palestinian elections. George Giacaman, "Elections for the Palestinian Legislative Council and Political Transformation in Palestine," *Majallat al-Dirasat al-Filastiniyya* [in Arabic] 65 (2006): 60–68.

4   Abdallah Azzam, "Hamas: Historical Origins and the Charter" [in Arabic] (Office of Mujahdun Service, Bishawer, 1989).

5   As'ad Ghanem, *Palestinian Politics after Arafat: A Failed National Movement* (Bloomington: Indiana University Press, 2010).

6   Rashid Khalidi, *Palestinian Identity: The Construction of Modern National Consciousness* (New York: Columbia University Press, 1997).

7   Muhammad Abid al-Jabiri, *Issues in Modern Arab Thought* [in Arabic] (Beirut: Center for Arab Unity Studies, 1997).

8   Satea al-Hosari, *On Arab Nationalism* [in Arabic] (Beirut: Center for Arab Unity Studies, 1987). On Butrous al-Bustani, see George Antonius, *The Arab Awakening: History of Arab Nationalism Movement* [in Arabic] (Beirut: Dar Al-elm, 1969), 112–20.

9   Jamal al-Din al-Afgani, Muhammed Abdu, and Muhammed Rashid Reda constitute significant examples of this reform discourse. See Ibrahim M. Abu-Rabi', *Intellectual Origins of Islamic Resurgence in the Modern Arab World* (Albany: State University of New York Press, 1996). Of course, this story is not valid for the entire Arab nation and Islam. Thus, for example, in the states of North Africa (Morocco, Tunisia, and Algeria), the situation differs in two senses. First, all the population was Muslim and there was no presence of Christian Arabs as in the Middle East. Second, these states fell at a very early stage under Western colonial domination characterized as Christian. The combination of these two components led to the Islamist religious rhetorical part of the anticolonial discourse. Mohanad Mustafa, "Islamic Opposition and Democratization in Authoritarian Arab Regimes" [in Hebrew], in *Comparative Studies: Egypt and Tunisia* (Haifa: University of Haifa, 2012).

10 Helga Baumgarten, "Three Faces\Phases of Palestinian Nationalism," *Journal of Palestine Studies* 34, no. 4 (2005): 25–48.

11 Baumgarten, "Three Faces\Phases," 28–30.

12 Sayed Qutb, *Milestones* [in Arabic] (Cairo: Dar El Shourok, 1973).

13 Baumgarten "Three Faces/Phases," 31.

14 Soud al-Mulah, "Palestine between Muslim Brotherhood and Fatah," *Majallat al-Dirasat al-Filastiniyya* [in Arabic] 93 (2013): 138–71.

15 In Ronit Marzen's book on Arafat, she analyzes his speeches from the 1960s until his death. She found many religious motifs in his speeches: the sacred nature of Palestine and Jerusalem, the national and religious duty of the Arab and Muslim nation to Palestine, the call for "jihad" to liberate Palestine, sacrifice and hallowed death, and religious tolerance of Islam. Ronit Marzen, *Yasser Arafat: The Rhetoric of a Lonely Leader* [in Hebrew] (Tel Aviv: Riesling, 2016). In this context, it is difficult to determine whether Arafat used religious motifs in parallel to the rise in Islamic

discourse in the Arab world since the 1970s or if he believed in the religious significance of Palestine as a religious issue alongside its national significance.
16 Marzen, *Yasser Arafat*.
17 This final demand has become less dominant over the years.
18 Alhroub, *Hamas, 18-23*.
19 In this belief, members of the Muslim Brotherhood were to an extent similar to ANM members of the 1950s and 1960s, in that they saw the Palestinian issue as part of a more general issue and waited for changes and events to occur before liberating Palestine. ANM members waited for Nasser to act, and the Muslim Brotherhood believed that Islamic society's awareness must first be aroused.
20 Ziad Abu-Amr, *Islamic Fundamentalism in West Bank and Gaza: Muslim Brotherhood and Jihad* (Bloomington: Indiana University Press, 1994); Hatina Meir, *Islam and Salvation in Palestine: The Islamic Jihad Movement* (Tel Aviv: Tel Aviv University, 2001).
21 Nicolas Dot-Pouillard and Eugénie Rébillard, "The Intellectual, the Militant, the Prisoner and the Partisan: The Genesis of the Islamic Jihad movement in Palestine (1974-1988)," *Muslim World* 103, no. 1 (2013): 61-65. In the writings of Fathi Shaqaqi, it is possible to find references to Jean-Paul Sartre, Vladimir Lenin, Friedrich Engels, Erik Rollo, Noam Chomsky, Fyodor Dostoevsky, and so on.
22 Fathi Shaqaqi, *The Journey of the Pen That Defeated the Sword: The Collection of Fathi Shaqaqi's Writings* [in Arabic], 2 vols. (Cairo: Jaffa Center for Thought and Research, 1997), 1:434-59. The two volumes of this book contain all the books, research, lectures, speeches, and declarations of Fathi Shaqaqi.
23 Both movements grew out of activist actions in religious movements and adopted the resistant practices of militant national movements like those that arose in the Third World in the fight against colonialism: Fatah in the case of Islamic Jihad; and in the case of Hizballah, the Lebanese national movement that began as resistance against the Israeli invasion of Lebanon. Dot-Pouillard and Rébillard, "Intellectual," 161.
24 Shaqaqi, *Journey of the Pen*, 1:348. This even appears in one of the basic documents of the movement—although the movement is not occupied a lot with founding texts. Fathi Az-Aldin, *Milestones of Milestones* [in Arabic] (Ramallah: Afaq, 2004).
25 From his viewpoint, "to understand Islamic creed (as binding)—as well as Fikh, Shariya and sources of the religion—is the starting point." Shaqaqi, *Journey of the Pen*, 1:348.
26 Shaqaqi, *Journey of the Pen*, 1:200-201. As he argues, "The end of the Islamic Caliphate that was officially proclaimed in 1924 by Kemal Atatürk in Turkey is the tragic and sad end to the tradition of Islamic rule of 1,400 years."
27 James Toth, *Sayyid Qutb: The Life and Legacy of a Radical Islamic Intellectual* (New York: Oxford University Press, 2013).
28 Shaqaqi, *Journey of the Pen*, 1:173.
29 Shaqaqi, *Journey of the Pen*, 1:472.
30 Shaqaqi, *Journey of the Pen*, 1:418.
31 Shaqaqi, *Journey of the Pen*, 1:473.
32 Shaqaqi, *Journey of the Pen*, 1:436.

33 Abd-Hamid al-Wahid, *The God Sovereignty (Hakkimiya) in the Quran* [in Arabic] (Nablus: Al-Najah University, 2005).
34 Rashid Taha, Hassan al-Banna, and Sayed Qutb all saw the centrality of Islam but in a different manner. While Taha was mainly a reformist, al-Banna understood the importance of the political world, and so there was no room to suffice with the performance of religious duties. In his opinion, "a Muslim cannot complete his Islam if he is not political." Hassan al-Banna, *The Collections of Writing* [in Arabic] (Cairo: Dar El Shourok, 1992), 159.
35 Al-Banna, *Collections of Writing*,:240.
36 Al-Banna, *Collections of Writing*,:24.
37 Shaqaqi, *Journey of the Pen*, 1:237.
38 Shaqaqi, *Journey of the Pen*, 1:205.
39 Shaqaqi, *Journey of the Pen*, 1:319.
40 Shaqaqi, *Journey of the Pen*, 1:709.
41 Shaqaqi, *Journey of the Pen*, 1:327.
42 Shaqaqi was therefore not full of praise for some of the Muslim Brotherhood's writings and instructions, which he viewed as dogmatic analyses. Shaqaqi went even further in critiquing those streams of the Brotherhood that dealt solely with textual reading of the religious texts, arguing that "the Qur'anic system is a living and realistic system and no ready-made theory to be found between the leaves of a book or in an intellectual argument based on formative logic of 'Tauhid science' nor theology that focuses on dark corners is appropriate for it." Shaqaqi, *Journey of the Pen*, 1:242.
43 Shaqaqi, *Journey of the Pen*, 1:242. Heartfelt faith is insufficient as well: "Muslim society is not realized by good intentions and not in the realization of heartfelt theories of people, however many they may be." Shaqaqi, *Journey of the Pen*, 1:245.
44 Shaqaqi, *Journey of the Pen*, 1:432.
45 Shaqaqi, *Journey of the Pen*, 1:710.
46 Shaqaqi, *Journey of the Pen*, 1:429.
47 While Shaqaqi drew upon Qur'anic knowledge to demonstrate the centrality of Palestine in Islamic religious texts, he also moved beyond religious texts to integrate them with politics and history to form one unity, claiming that "the unity revolving on the Palestinian issue is historic unification with the Qur'an. It is a unification for the resurrection project [Alnahada] in its entirety." Shaqaqi, *Journey of the Pen*, 1:433.
48 Shaqaqi, *Journey of the Pen*, 1:423. Conversely, the traditional Muslim Brotherhood considered the establishment of Israel as an issue that it could delay coping with until there was a change in Islamic society itself. First, it had to raise its awareness and morality, and the restitution of the Islamic world needed to be given priority and even the return of the Caliphate as a condition for the liberation of Palestine. Shaqaqi saw this viewpoint as mistaken from its very foundations since there was no possibility that the Caliphate could be resurrected and no revival of the Islamic project as long as Israel continued to exist as the spearhead of the "West."
49 Shaqaqi, *Journey of the Pen*, 1:424.

50 Shaqaqi, *Journey of the Pen*, 1:421.
51 Shaqaqi, *Journey of the Pen*, 1:355.
52 Shaqaqi, *Journey of the Pen*, 1:423.
53 To the credit of the movement, it publicly protested in a clear way against the death sentence for the Sudanese philosopher Mahmoud Taha, who was put to death by the Numeiri regime following his rejection of the Islamic religion.
54 Shaqaqi, *Journey of the Pen*, 1:196.
55 Shaqaqi, *Journey of the Pen*, 1:223.
56 Shaqaqi, *Journey of the Pen*, 1:219.
57 Shaqaqi, *Journey of the Pen*, 1:224.
58 Shaqaqi, *Journey of the Pen*, 1:273–77.
59 Shaqaqi, *Journey of the Pen*, 1:469.
60 Shaqaqi, *Journey of the Pen*, 1:420.
61 Shaqaqi, *Journey of the Pen*, 1:174. This is not an original argument, of course, and similar arguments by the Muslim Brotherhood can be found in Yosef al-Kardawi, "Imported Solutions and How They Bestowed Calamity on Our Nation" [in Arabic] (Al-Rassala Institute, Al-Doha, 1971).
62 Shaqaqi, *Journey of the Pen*, 1:179.
63 Shaqaqi, *Journey of the Pen*, 1:176.
64 Shaqaqi, *Journey of the Pen*, 1:603.
65 Shaqaqi, *Journey of the Pen*, 1:714.
66 Al-Jabri, *Issues in Modern Arab Thought*. Shaqaqi makes a similar argument here regarding the relationship between religion and science. Shaqaqi, *Journey of the Pen*, 1:242.
67 Shaqaqi, *Journey of the Pen*, 1:426.
68 Shaqaqi, *Journey of the Pen*, 1:589.
69 Shaqaqi, *Journey of the Pen*, 1:426.
70 Shaqaqi, *Journey of the Pen*, 1:590.
71 Shaqaqi, *Journey of the Pen*, 1:406.
72 Shaqaqi, *Journey of the Pen*, 1:406.
73 Charles Taylor, *A Secular Age* (Cambridge, MA: Harvard University Press, 2007); Jose Cassanova, *Public Religions in the Modern World* (Chicago: University of Chicago Press, 1994).
74 John Rawls, *Political Liberalism* (Cambridge, MA: Harvard University Press, 2005).
75 Duncan Kennedy, *Legal Reasoning: Collected Essays* (Aurora, CO: Davies Group, 2008); Michel Foucault, *Power/Knowledge: Selected Interviews and Other Writings, 1972–1977*, ed. and trans. Colin Gordon (Brighton, Sussex: Harvester, 1980).
76 Carl Schmitt, *Political Theology* (Chicago: University of Chicago Press, 1985).

7. TRAINS ON TIME
Faith, Political Belonging, and Governability in Israel
ORI GOLDBERG

Belonging was, at first, an exercise in sovereign imagination in Israel. The National Religious Party, known as Mafdal, was founded in 1956. It was the result of a union between two other parties that defined themselves as "religious Zionist." Religious Zionism began with secular Zionism. Most of the world's Jews did not become fervent Zionists when the movement began to form in late nineteenth-century Europe. Most of the Jews who became Zionists preferred the vision of a national community to that of a religious community. The founding fathers of Zionism saw themselves very much as Jews in terms of identity, culture, and faith. Their model of community, however, was predominantly secular and socialist. They were eager to incorporate Judaism into their national vision as culture but not as a rationale for a legal or political order.

Only a small group of Zionists could not forgo their faith when they joined the movement of national revival. The new national community of the secular Zionists stood proudly at one end of a Jewish communal spectrum. This was a modern community, a vision of normalcy and order. It had functioning institutions and feasible political goals. The secular Zionists saw redemption for the Jews in normalization. A national movement culminating in statehood was the epitome of the normal.

At the other end of the spectrum stood the ultra-Orthodox community, the community of the European diaspora. This was a community of believers. It followed a well-known maxim from *Pirkei Avot* (Ethics of the Fathers), a Talmudic text providing the Torah's views on ethics and interpersonal relations. The sages offered three rules for a virtuous life:

> Love work. Hate the rabbinate. Do not become a familiar of the authorities.
> (Avot, 1:10)

A commentary on *Pirkei Avot* offers the following explanation: "Why should you not become a familiar of the authorities? If the authorities know your name, they will ultimately seek you out, kill you and take all your money" (Avot of Rabbi Natan, chapter 11).[1]

This sort of distrust extends beyond a response to anti-Jewish sentiment. It amounts to a suspicion of any institutional authority. This is how institutions work, the text seems to say. Once an individual is known to them, authorities will need to exercise their sovereignty and empty individuals of their own sovereignty. A community is united by faith. Faith affirms God's sovereignty, and those who share this faith are certain in their disdain for human power struggles. Redemption for this community would come directly from God.

The religious Zionists needed to create a community that would incorporate elements of both models. They were a part of the national revival, but they could not sever their bond with the religious community, the community of the faithful. The religious Zionists saw themselves as a bridge between the two communal models, an attempt to have the best of both worlds. The seculars considered them unable to hitch their wagon to the progress train, wallowing in obsolete superstitions. The ultra-Orthodox considered them either weak or messianic. The religious Zionists sought their own definition of the Jewish condition, being unable to accept both "normalcy" and "isolation." An additional dimension of their middle-ground status is apparent in their denial of a Palestinian peoplehood and, in fact, of a unique Israeli-Palestinian conflict. The Palestinians, as far as Mafdal was concerned, constituted a physical threat to Jewish lives, regardless of Israel's occupation of Palestinian territories since 1967. As such a threat, the Palestinians were simply "Arabs" who could choose to leave Israel and live in any other "Arab" country. The urgency of their proximity to Israel was simply a challenge of homeland security. As the Palestinians were the ones who "lost," they also served as a constant vindication of the Israeli state's cosmological and institutional propriety.

Mafdal, "their" party, accepted the institutionalism of the state. In fact, Mafdal saw itself as the keeper of a heritage compatible with the practices of the State of Israel. A constant of coalitions led by the right-wing Likud (Consolidation) party since 1977, Mafdal consistently demanded (and often received) control of the Ministry of Education. Alongside being Israel's largest public sector employer (and thus able to provide jobs for deserving, and less-deserving, party members), the Ministry of Education is charged with shaping curricula for Israeli state schools of all sectors. Still in keeping with the Ottoman model, Israeli citizens' matters of personal status are regulated and enforced based on their religious affiliation. Marriage and divorce, probate, adoption, and other such issues depend on the religion a person bears, usually by birth. Education is administered, by extension, according to similar logic. Mafdal ministers saw themselves as the common thread tying different strands of Judaism (secular, religious Zionist, ultra-Orthodox), as well as other religious traditions, into an "Israeli" whole. Their role in creating an "Israeli" Judaism, bringing together the national community and the community of believers, was first and foremost in their minds.

The intentional creation of a community, this exercise in conscious belonging, had a theological grounding in the writings of Rabbi Yitzchak Ya'akov Reines. Dov Schwartz, an influential scholar of religious Zionism, describes Rabbi Reines's thought as follows: "The uniqueness of the people of Israel could be defined through the conceptual array of modern nationalist theory. 'The Chosen People' represent the extreme manifestation of national uniqueness, an emotional bond accompanied by total loyalty to the unique national foundations anchoring the very peoplehood of the Jews—people, land, Torah. This loyalty, claimed Rabbi Reines, even while it may be explained and described in rational and psychological terms, is unparalleled among the nations."[2]

This uniqueness, then, requires contrast (and context) provided by the modern world. Jews are an unparalleled exemplar of national excellence, so validated by belonging within the world and its conventions and criteria. Such a project demands constant engagement and work within the world, an acceptance of the world's rules. Engaging with the world requires that Jews consciously distance themselves from a heritage of separation and tension, perhaps their dominant historical trajectory over recent millennia. Belonging to the world, even if from a peak of excellence, becomes a mindful endeavor. Jewishness *is* the consciousness of being Jewish in the world.

This notion of belonging—conscious, in context, instrumentally modern— was the choice of most religious Zionist leaders. Still, from its very beginning, religious Zionism also belonged in a very different way to a very different world. The dynamic of redemption moved this world rather than the relational logic of excellence. How else could one understand the fulfillment of so many biblical prophesies, all specifying that the return of the Jews to the "Land of Israel" would signal the reconciliation of God with his Chosen People, the Jewish equivalent of the end times?[3] The returning Jews belonged to this divinely inspired emergence, not to the stable routines of the modern world.

Rabbi Avraham Yitchak Hacohen Kook, Harav ("the" Rabbi) Kook, led those who emphasized the divine nature of Jewish national revival. In his view, divine existence was the heart of all things, the truth of them. While the surface of everyday life was not a lie, it was a diminished truth. Jews were God's most perfect creation because their existence in the world was the closest of all to the divine fountain of being. Rabbi Kook was a Kabbalist, a thinker and scholar of a powerful Jewish mystical movement.[4] He saw the Jewish people as a conduit for the channeling of the divine into the surface world. Jews accomplished this through their innate capacity for faith. This faith placed Jews closer than any other people to the beating divine heart of being.[5]

The national revival of the Jews was a surface manifestation of a redemptive dynamic unleashed at the divine heart. The defining Jewish trait was not excellence (as in the Reines approach) but authenticity. Jews were not a bridge, reconciling the best of devotion with the best of national thought. Rather, Jews reflected the whole of being by being the most transcendent element of being. Jews conferred transcendence upon the rest of creation. Zionism, the rebirth of Jews as a nation, was, according to Rabbi Kook, a movement of tension and appropriation. Because so much of the Zionist movement was secular, Zionism heightened the tension between the surface of human events and the underlying divine presence and providence. This tension, however, would ultimately be resolved as the undeniable truth of divine redemption emerged and appropriated the seemingly complete practical approach toward Jewish nation building. Belonging to the Jewish people, according to Rabbi Kook, required an attunement to different (often contrasting) levels of reality. The sustained imaginative endeavor suggested by Rabbi Reines was seen as a compromise, an unrequited reticence to accept both worldly tension and extraworldly redemption/resolution.

In the hands of his son, Rabbi Tzvi Yehuda Kook, Harav Kook's theology became the ideological pillar of the settler movement. This wing of religious Zionism seeks to establish Israeli presence and effective dominion over territories occupied by Israeli military forces since the 1967 Six-Day War. What began as an effort marginal to the mainstream adaptability of religious Zionism grew gradually into a force of equal stature and influence. The "Young Turks" of the movement viewed their elders' imaginative quietism with great disdain. The mundane was no match for the miracle.

For a long while, this tension seemed irresolvable. After all, each version of the religious Zionist truth uses a different bonding mechanism inherent in Judaism, and perhaps in monotheistic religion. The original spirit of Mafdal defines belonging to the Jewish polity as a matter of consciousness. A life of faith is meant to be a worldly life, with all the faults and limitations of this world. Faith is an instrument for steering oneself through this worldly life, making decisions and preferences in full knowledge of their potential cost. The logic of the settlers anchors political belonging in what I call "dynamic submission." The clashes between the earthly and the eternal are part of a script. Believers choose to participate in the drama, to have its logic become their logic. The moment of assent and the acceptance that events are being directly driven by divine determination allow the believer freedom to move and maneuver in this world.

The difficulty of reconciling these two notions of political belonging within a single party, like Mafdal, is clear. Where pragmatism stays the course, redemption takes the plunge. Mafdal did, indeed, splinter in 1999. Several radical leaders of the settler movement left it to form a party called Tkumah (Revival). Tkumah later allied itself with an amalgam of other right-wing parties, renaming itself the National Union.[6] The splinters did not do well in parliamentary elections, securing only minimal (and highly sectorial) representation. Mafdal also faltered. The party was torn between its competing visions of religious Zionism, wistful for its heritage of insider influence while in thrall to newer, more proactive visions of transforming the secular Jewish state. This debate, over the nature of the relationship between religious faith and political belonging, limited the party's appeal to the broader Israeli public.

Transformation

In the parliamentary elections of 2006, Mafdal joined forces with the National Union. Together, they received a disappointing total of nine seats. Before the elections of 2008, Mafdal elders decided to rebrand their party, naming it Habayit Hayehudi—Hamafdal (the Jewish Home—Mafdal).[7] An internal committee, staffed by the eternal elders, chose a respected scientist, Daniel Hershkowitz, to head the new party. This selection was meant to project a new image, one transcending sectorial squabbles and reconciling Mafdal's religiosity with a "scientific" (i.e., value-neutral) approach to Israeli politics. As such superimposed power plays often will, this one failed as well. The National

Union withdrew from the Jewish Home, and Mafdal received just three seats in the Knesset, its poorest showing in decades. The crossover appeal of science as a symbol of openness and inclusivity was, apparently, somewhat limited.

Four more years of infighting plagued the party. In 2012, for the first time in its history, Mafdal held open primaries for its leadership and places on the party's Knesset slate. The incumbent leader of the party, MK Zevulun Orlev, a long-standing elder, was trounced in the leadership election by Naftali Bennett.[8] The new leader projected a very different image from both of the previous leaders. He was born to immigrants from the United States and grew up in Haifa. Bennett served in various Israel Defense Force (IDF) special forces units and later became a successful high-tech entrepreneur, selling his cybersecurity firm, Cyota, for $145 million. He entered politics in 2016 and served as chief of staff for Benjamin Netanyahu. With Ayelet Shaked, he founded an extraparliamentary movement, My Israel.[9]

Bennett was (and remains) a paragon of personal success and public commitment in present-day Israel. For many Israelis, his service in the special forces units demonstrates a willingness to sacrifice one's own welfare for the good of the nation. High-tech entrepreneurship not only reigns as the embodiment of the collective Israeli dream during the first decades of the twenty-first century but also signifies personal strength, purpose, and capability.[10] These are much-valued qualities in an Israel consciously and quickly ridding itself of its socialist heritage and welfare state.[11]

Interestingly, the prominent portion of his Wikipedia bio does not mention that he also served as the secretary-general of the Yesha Council, a political arm of the settler movement. This fact is mentioned later on in the entry, indicating an understanding that settler credentials remain outside the stable pale of generic Israeli identity. His work for Benjamin Netanyahu, Israel's longest-serving prime minister, is prominently displayed and establishes Bennett as reliably right wing, a necessity in a political climate that views "leftist" as a pejorative term. Bennett emerges as a leader, a doer, and a decision maker. One needs to be both resolute and quick on one's feet in order to succeed in the special forces as well as in the high-tech world. The assumption is that both traits carry well into the political arena. Bennett leads by personal example. Belonging to his Jewish Home requires less thought and participation than emulation.

Bennett's campaign ads stressed his all-encompassing (and therefore to be emulated) Israeli appeal. His potential voters were addressed as "brothers and sisters," and he emphasized his love for all things Israeli, from the Torah to the IDF.[12] His overhaul of Mafdal seemed to suggest a radical blurring of lines between religion and secularity. The Israeli state had struggled with the relationship between its Judaism and its democracy since 1948. If Israel is a state for Jews, how would its non-Jewish citizens fare? If Israel is a democracy, first and foremost, how can it fulfill its self-perceived mission as a Jewish homeland? Bennett's Jewish Home appeared to create a synergetic effect generated by pride and success. Everyone (everyone Jewish, that is) belonged to the Jewish Home by default, because everyone was part of the success that was Israel. Individual belonging came about through emulation; collective belonging occurred through self-acceptance and validation. "We really are terrific," Bennett seemed to say. "Let's own it together." In the 2012 elections, his Jewish Home party received twelve Knesset seats, the best showing in the history of a religious Zionist party.

Ideological Coalescence

Bennett's appeal lay in his seamless realization of the Israeli dream. He *was* what he was, and he needed to expend no conscious effort in order to belong or draw others to him. In other words, ideological articulation on his part might have detracted from the immediacy of his presence. He left the ideological maturation of his new "movement" to his most visible partner and ally, Ayelet Shaked.[13]

Shaked, born in 1976, experienced a meteoric rise through the Israeli political system. She was appointed as Israel's minister of justice in 2015.[14] A computer engineer by training, she became involved in politics after several years spent working for Texas Instruments. Shaked was a formidable presence in Israeli right-wing circles, and she soon attracted the attention of Netanyahu. She worked as his office manager at the prime minister's office between 2008 and 2010. Her alliance with Bennett was formed during this period.[15] After leaving the PM's employ, she and Bennett formed My Israel. Shaked continued to be active in Likud, Israel's ruling party led by Netanyahu, but then joined Bennett when he took the Jewish Home / Mafdal by storm, becoming his second-in-command.

Shaked is an emphatic standout on the Israeli political scene. In a system besotted with stereotypes and labels, Shaked has made a career of defying conventional wisdom. First and foremost, she identifies herself as a secular woman, despite being a senior leader of a religious Zionist party. This is an iconoclastic move in Israeli politics, where "tribal" affiliation is often a crucially defining feature of careers. The unified and united statist vision remains the dominant paradigm in Israel, considering the Zionist project of national Jewish revival paramount over particular ideological agendas. Zionism is considered to be a secular movement, a revolt against the conventions of "diaspora Judaism," which emphasized community and religion over the blunt obviousness of state nationalism (in the eyes of the state's citizens, that is). This overarching quality of Zionism, its secular revolt, has prevented a continuum of secularisms from taking form in Israel. Secular Zionism remains a point of origin for any Israeli endeavor, even ones that are directed against this secular Zionism. One is either for it or against it, and there is no room for deviance, as gradated and diverse as such deviance might be.

Israeli identity politics thus become powerfully static. In such circumstances, a clear label both distinguishes one from others and certifies the same one as a legitimate piece of the greater puzzle. Conscious detachment from default definitions is remarkably rare. The religious divide is, perhaps, the deepest fault line of Israel's collective consciousness. The debate between "normal" and "holy" nationalism is potentially disturbing to the extent that it remains effectively untouched. The religious stay religious and the secular, secular. Shaked's choice to transcend this gap is thus even more remarkable than defense doves transforming into hawks or capitalists turning into ardent social democrats.

Shaked's image stands complementary to Bennett's figure. Where he leads by emulation, she seeks to lead by conscious example. Despite his credentials with Netanyahu and the settler movement, his political stance is fixated in, and on, the present. That is, Bennett's notion of political belonging is anchored in a sense of normalcy and this normalcy's immediate, self-explanatory appeal. Why fix something that is not broken? Shaked, perhaps in an attempt to balance her irreverence, consistently provides ideological justifications for her praxis. These endeavors, as well as her unique brand, make her stand out in the Israeli political field.

The seminal text she has produced is a programmatic article published in the first volume of *Hashiloach*, an intellectual journal launched in 2016 and devoted to right-wing essays on Israeli politics, history, and society. Generally, the current Israeli right is not known for excessive intellectualization. The country's founding socialist fathers produced lengthy, elaborate ideological justifications for Judaism's double billing as religion and nationality. The Israeli right treats this duality as a point of strength and pride. This national religious starting point leads to a conception of Jewish sovereignty and executive power that is holistic in its self-assertion.[16]

Shaked's article is therefore another convention-defying attempt on her part. We have, so far, considered the emerging lines of religious Zionist models of political belonging through an evolving interplay of identities, Israel's defining struggle between Judaism as religion and Judaism as secular nationalism. Shaked attempts to reconcile these traditionally opposing strands into a broad vision that combines Judaism as nationality and religion with free-market neoliberalism. Her programmatic approach complements Bennett's immediate, emulation-based concept of both authority and political belonging. I next consider her argument in some detail, translating passages from the Hebrew original and placing them in the political and cultural context we have already woven.

Pathways to Governability: Political Belonging as a Trip to Nowhere

One of the concepts that has recently become significant in Israeli political discourse is "governability." Good governability is often described as a powerful engine leading the governmental train; as a powerful political engine successfully pulling a long row of cars until they reach their destination quickly and effectively. Good governors are, in accordance, seen as those capable of carrying out decisions successfully and effectively; as those who know the efficient, quick and safe ways to move on the public railroad from point A to point B.

But this analogy is completely mistaken. Good governability is not blind intensity, and it certainly is not just a powerful, mute engine. The ability to execute goals as defined is a necessary condition for good governability, but it is by no means sufficient: Good governability is measured, first and foremost, by the possibility government ministers have to determine the destination [and goals] themselves. A political leader, senior as she may be, who knows how to deliver the train at its destination but is incapable of determining the destination itself, that leader does not govern. Rather, she is a contractor performing a service. She may have been appointed minister, she may be cutting ribbons at the end of the road, but she is no more than a contractor.

Moving on a railroad laid by someone else does not require leaders; drivers would do it just as well. The essence of governability is one: Establishing the direction of progress and setting goals.—AYELET SHAKED, "Pathways to Governability"

Shaked anchors her argument in a concept and an analogy. The concept is "governability." The analogy likens the business of state government to the driving and leading of a train. The analogy provides a context for the concept. The reader is allowed to inhabit "governability," to see it as relevant to her life, through an image of dependence and motion. "Governability" becomes a mechanism of bonding, describing a relationship between engine and cars on the road to a shared, if unspecified, destination.

Governing is not like driving a train engine. When you drive, you accept certain rules and conventions. As your engine moves on the railroad, you (as the driver) know at any point in time and space if you are moving forward or backward. Your motion has meaning because it has context and structure. The engine moves in a certain way, on a spectrum of potential speed, toward a certain point and away from another point. If belonging is defined as a "close and intimate relationship," then governability provides a platform for a political belonging.[17] Passion for the future or the unknown can kindle a sense of adventure or manifest destiny. Nothing is more intimate than the knowledge that "you are here," particularly when shared with other people, regardless of where "here" might be.

Nonetheless, as soon as we have established the analogy, we learn that it does not really exist. There is no immediacy and there are no conventions. In fact, there is no belonging. Leadership is an exercise in strength and sovereignty, lived and executed individually. The leader is the strongest, most sovereign individual, provided by the other (weaker) individuals with the prerogative of setting their goals. In fact, even that formulation does not accurately describe the power of the leader. Leadership allows one to determine which way is forward and which backward. Orientation is a virtue of strength and self-sufficiency rather than a hallmark of intimacy and shared consciousness.

Still, the power of the leader does not come from the hallowed status of "leadership." The leader is simply the most powerful and sovereign individual. Shaked's article is, as it turns out, an attempt to define this individuality as a Jewish ideology. In terms we have already discussed, Shaked sees this individuality as a possible bridge between the alternative identities of Judaism—religion and nationality. Her goal then resonates in the context of religious Zionist politics. This bridge may be the holy grail of Israeli politics, preceding even Israel's half century of conflict with the Palestinians. Harnessing the tension between "Jewish" and "Democratic," religion and nation, may be the most effective guarantee of Israeli coherence, necessary for the continued existence and flourishing of the Israeli state.

Shaked's argument is based on a heated critique of Israel's legislative and judicial politics. Before proceeding with this critique, however, she makes a meaningful rhetorical gesture in order to solidify her claim for the status of "ideology." Shaked does so by channeling the thought of Milton Friedman. In a special preface written for the Hebrew translation of *Capitalism and Freedom*, Friedman says of Israel's predicament,

> I first visited Israel 37 years ago, when I served as a visiting professor at Hebrew University for several months. I summarized my impressions

and remarked that I thought two Jewish traditions struggled in Israel, one against the other. [The first was] a century-old tradition of faith in paternalist, socialist rule, along with a rejection of Capitalism and the free market; [the second was] a two-thousand-year-old tradition that had developed out of the necessities of the diaspora: A person's reliance on himself along with free cooperation; a talent for circumventing government oversight; using all aspects of Jewish invention in order to capitalize on market opportunities, such that had been overlooked by shortsighted government administrators. I reached the conclusion that fortunately for Israel, it has been demonstrated that the more ancient tradition is the more durable one.[18]

Friedman sees Israel as a test case for his broader economic outlook. Judaism provides him with a fairly unique history, a people surviving for millennia without the regulating mechanism of the state. If Friedman suggests a Jewish notion of belonging, one that possesses sufficient depth and inertia to create intimacy, it consists of belonging to the antistate. Jews share a sense of invention most clearly seen and used in the evasion of government regulation. The vision of the Israeli state, according to Friedman, was hatched in a collectivist movement, devoted to the drudgery of institutionalism. Fortunately, Israel is also a conglomeration of Jews and is thus capable of fending off the incursions of centralized statehood. Friedman is not interested in governability or in social convention but in the indomitable spirit of *homo economicus*. For Shaked, however, he provides the historical and philosophical depth she requires for her ideological undertaking.

Ideologies often begin with a critique of current reality. Shaked seems to do so. "I wish," she writes, "that today I could share Friedman's confidence in the certain victory of the values of freedom our people upheld throughout 2,000 years of life in the diaspora, [values] which brought us to the amazing prosperity we enjoy today."[19] Ideological discourses, however, segue from critique to the formulation of a corrective vision, a desired reality. That is not Shaked's case. In real life, she and her colleagues are winning the good fight: "When I examine the bills that reach the ministerial committee for legislation, I find that without the powerful pressure we apply to the engine's brake pedal, week after week, the bills would have created a different world for all of us, one parallel to our own world."[20]

Shaked is no longer demanding the right to steer the engine in any direction she prefers. Her leadership, and that of her friends, is now focused on applying pressure to the brake. The freedom of which she speaks is a negative freedom, a freedom from the restrictions of rules and regulations. This freedom may provide an incentive, at the individual level, for creativity and innovation. At the level of leadership, and also in the context of community, such freedom serves mostly to limit and curtail. In other words, Shaked hits the brake to keep the engine moving and because of this constant motion, she has neither need nor inclination to steer. The integrity of motion becomes dependent on the inevitability of its direction. Belonging implies a certitude born of experience, an intimate familiarity with emerging reality. The passengers aboard Shaked's train are locked into a moving car, shuttling between a glorious past and a glorious future. Their present motion, dependent on constant braking, assures them only an extremely bumpy ride.

Threats and Resolutions

Shaked brakes in response to two main threats. The first is the prevalent misconception among Israeli legislators with regard to the proper place of parliament in a functional state. According to Shaked, Israeli parliamentarians in search of media attention inundate the executive with countless irresponsible bills. They are irresponsible because they limit the individual freedoms of landlords, employers, and corporations, along with the discretion of law enforcement personnel. For example, attempts to freeze rent fees for several years would, according to Shaked, cause landlords to initially set prices higher but would also make apartments less desirable investments. The supply of apartments would decrease and prices would rise as a result. The dynamic, breaking to move in a single direction (the one established by the free market's invisible hand), becomes apparent once again.

Another interesting example has to do with a bill proposing the compulsory arrest of any person against whom two complaints have been made regarding the violation of a restraining order. Shaked writes, "Of course, such a law would encourage making false complaints in case of a familial feud because, in such a state, any complaint, even if it is baseless, amounts to an arrest order." In this case, the attempt to force a police officer's hand is thwarted in order to keep everyone in the moving car. Feuds are irrelevant to quest for constant motion. The proposed bill, I assume, sought to address a reality of prevalent domestic violence. For Shaked, the only constant of the present is its capacity for motion. No lingering malaise is vile enough to force the creation of a cure, because a cure might cause the engine to falter.

The Life of the Law

Shaked quotes Oliver Wendell Holmes's famous saying "the life of the law has not been logic; it has been experience." Hebrew lacks the continuous tense, and in Shaked's translation the phrase is rendered in the straight present: "The life of the law is not logic, but experience."[21] The experience, she says, is the accumulated experience of numerous engagements between individuals, as opposed to abstract legal logic, which has no relation to the "dynamics of the real world."[22]

Her main rival, in this respect, is Aharon Barak, formerly the chief justice of Israel's Supreme Court. Barak is credited with masterminding Israel's "Constitutional Revolution," asserting the claim that Israeli courts hold the power to oversee, and potentially overturn, the laws of the Knesset. While Israel does not have a constitution, it has a series of Basic Laws ultimately meant to adhere into a constitution when consensus is reached on various core issues. Barak read the court's prerogative into two of these laws, both of which passed in the early 1990s.[23]

According to Shaked, Barak created the sort of alienation that allows bills as curious as those described here to be put forth by members of the Knesset. His notion that the courts are capable of reviewing and canceling legislative decisions is a debilitating blow to what Shaked understands as Israel's national cohesion.

Barak's approach allows him, according to Shaked, to cleave Israel's "Democratic" elements from the state's "Jewish" identity. She suggests that for Barak, the Jewish tradition is a burden to be shed quickly, because it impedes the abstract, universal rationality of "Democracy" and its laws. Shaked, however, suggests that it was Jewish tradition that guided John Locke, Thomas Jefferson, and "countless revolutionaries, pursuers of justice and opponents of tyranny."[24] She believes in "the wisdom of the people; in the history of the People of Israel that has proven, in contrast to the histories of other people, that our popular . . . and national wisdom are to be trusted."[25] In the very same paragraph, however, national wisdom and Jewish tradition find their "most justified and correct" expression in the decision of the people, expressed by electing representatives. Ultimately, of course, the decision of these elected representatives becomes the clearest distillation of Jewish history, tradition, and values. "I believe," she writes, "that the people and its representatives are those who should express [the people's] will, and that their decision should be the final word at the public level."[26]

Shaked's railroads run in a circle. Every four years (or whenever elections are held), tradition and history are nullified. There can be no movement forward because there is no momentum. Values do not accrue and neither do practices. The only mark of merit is election. Her argument offers a vicious take on Friedman's existential observation. For him, Jews excel at maneuvering and outsmarting. This is a problematic statement because it seems to corroborate base anti-Jewish sentiments. Still, it seeks to identify shared qualities in Judaism, qualities that would allow for a sense of communal identity, a foundation of belonging. For Shaked, Jews are always and only Jews. As such, they may be the ideal subjects of a truly free market, but that is of no consequence. Their Jewishness is not even a quality, because it has no features other than its sheer existence. Jewish leadership in the Jewish state moves the train by constantly pressing the brake pedal, preventing any value of substance from penetrating this sheer existence.

The circle, as circles will, is closed. Integration with the world is impossible. As minister of justice, Shaked played a leading role in flouting international law when she promoted policies meant to impose full Israeli sovereignty on the occupied territories.[27] But the circle is also empty. Shaked's rails run a circumference. The state is a minimalist regulator (applying the brake) of free, sovereign individuals, who are indubitably Jewish yet are so in no substantially discernible way. There is nothing to which a Jew can belong, because a person's Jewish identity defies communication. Nothing is shared, and as a result, nothing is intimate.

Shaked's ideology perfectly complements Naftali Bennett's leadership. All you need in order to belong to their Jewish state is a desire to be like the leader combined with the knowledge that you are isolated just as you are, in isolation. Trains, particularly as an image of punctuality, carry significant connotative force in the collective Israeli psyche. Evoking the Nazis' transport of Jews from all over Europe, in wartime, to the concentration camps, trains are a synecdoche of the Holocaust, particularly of the Nazi penchant for systematic efficiency. Trains are not easily used as a vision of such efficiency in Israel's political rhetoric. Shaked's insistence on them is an acute demonstration of belonging without belonging.

NOTES

1. All translations are mine unless otherwise noted.
2. Dov Schwartz, *Challenge and Crisis in Rabbi Kook's Circle* [in Hebrew] (Tel Aviv: Am Oved, 2001), 216–17.
3. "Land of Israel" is a phrase used to connote continuity between divine promise and actual fulfillment, preceding "state" and focusing on physical (and mythical) space.

4 Kabbalah is, of course, the subject of an immense scholarly literature. For a concise, illuminating introduction, see Joseph Dan, *Kabbalah: A Very Short Introduction* (Oxford: Oxford University Press, 2007).
5 See Schwartz, *Challenge and Crisis*, 233–36.
6 See "Mafdal" [in Hebrew], Israel Democracy Institute, accessed September 17, 2020, https://www.idi.org.il/policy/parties-and-elections/parties/mafdal/.
7 Israeli coalition governments are notoriously unstable and short-lived.
8 Hershkowitz had departed earlier, assuming the presidency of Bar Ilan University.
9 "Naftali Bennett," Wikipedia, accessed September 17, 2020, https://en.wikipedia.org/wiki/Naftali_Bennett. See also Eithan Orkibi, "'New Politics,' New Media—New Political Language? A Rhetorical Perspective on Candidates' Self-Presentation in Electronic Campaigns in the 2013 Israeli Elections." *Israel Affairs* 21, no. 2 (2015): 277–92.
10 *Start-Up Nation: The Story of Israel's Economic Miracle* (New York: Twelve, 2007), a book by Dan Senor and Saul Singer, exemplifies the personal and public infatuation with the narrative of high-tech success. The book has been embraced by the Israeli establishment, presented (for example) by Israeli ambassadors to local dignitaries in their countries of service as an introduction of sorts to present-day Israel.
11 Most emphatically, Bennett's prevailing in a personal, open contest is as far removed as possible from the backroom committees that dominated religious Zionist politics before his rise.
12 See, for example, "You Have a Home—Jewish Home Election Broadcast" [in Hebrew], posted by Naftali Bennett on January 8, 2013, https://www.youtube.com/watch?v=ntItSIV8tus.
13 Israeli politics, perhaps in deference to its Zionist tradition, is partial to "movements."
14 For a concise biography, see "Ayelet Shaked," Wikipedia, accessed September 17, 2020 https://en.wikipedia.org/wiki/Ayelet_Shaked.
15 Shaked and Bennett were fired by Netanyahu, reportedly after a major falling out with Sara Netanyahu, the prime minister's wife. For an interesting profile of Bennett, Shaked, and the new leadership of the settler movement, see David Remnick, "The Party Faithful," *New Yorker*, January 21, 2013.
16 Sovereignty and executive power had been absent from Jewish historicity for millennia before the foundation of Israel.
17 *Merriam-Webster's*, s.v. "belonging," accessed September 17, 2020, https://www.merriam-webster.com/dictionary/belonging.
18 Milton Friedman, *Kapitalism Ve-Cherut* (*Capitalism and Freedom*) (Jerusalem: Shalem, 2002), 14. Shaked quotes most of this text in her article "Pathways to Governability" [in Hebrew], *Hashiloach* 1 (October 2016): 40. I did not have access to the English original of Friedman's work, and my translation is from the quotations in Hebrew in Shaked's article.
19 Shaked, "Pathways to Governability," 40.
20 Shaked, "Pathways to Governability," 40. The ministerial committee for legislation is chaired by the minister of justice and decides on governmental support or rejection

for bills proposed by members of the Knesset. In Israel, such governmental support is crucial for a bill to become law.

21 Shaked, "Pathways to Governability," 43.
22 Shaked, "Pathways to Governability," 43.
23 For a succinct summary of interpretative and legislative revolution by Barak himself, see Aharon Barak, "A Constitutional Revolution: Israel's Basic Laws," *Forum Constitutionnel* 4 (1992–93): 83–84, http://digitalcommons.law.yale.edu/cgi/viewcontent.cgi?article=4700&context=fss_papers.
24 Shaked, "Pathways to Governability," 51.
25 Shaked, "Pathways to Governability," 55.
26 Shaked, "Pathways to Governability," 54.
27 See, for example, "Regulation Law," Wikipedia, accessed August 12, 2020, https://en.wikipedia.org/wiki/Regulation_Law.

8. MAKING SENSE BY COMPREHENDING SENSIBILITY
A View of Chinese Religions
MU-CHOU POO

The terms of religion, secularism, and political belonging are problems that have generated vast amounts of debate, misunderstandings, polemics, and even hostilities in the modern world, not least in purely academic discourses. Since the participants of this project have been genuinely interested in seeking mutual understanding in a most amicable fashion, and even in the end certain areas that these terms encompass may still seem less comprehensible than others, we could all appreciate the basic idea that plurality and respect for individuality is a basic attitude and value that we should abide by. We acknowledge that the meanings of religion, secularism, and political belonging may have specific local nuances in each culture and in different times, yet we also do not want to go to the extreme by saying that translation is ultimately impossible. The fact that a chapter on Chinese religion is now written in English forces us to at least admit that translation of ideas is possible over language barriers. It of course raises the question of whether one can completely be free from the numerous ideological and semantic assumptions or misunderstandings that language learning necessarily implies. It is completely possible that one scholar may be able to overcome these barriers of translation better than another, thus what we are able to present here can only be open to further discussion and debate.

This chapter discusses the characteristics of Chinese religions and what the term "secularism" could mean in the Chinese context both historically and contemporarily. In addition, the chapter explores how political belonging could be understood in the context of a strong state and a long historical and cultural heritage that tend to engulf or overshadow any religion and render the term less an effective idea to describe something that is "nonreligious."

So, what is religion in the Chinese world?[1] We encounter a translation problem immediately. Before the nineteenth century, there was no common term in Chinese that referred to "religion" in general, and each religion would be referred to as the teachings of so-and-so. What we call religion today, such as Buddhism and Daoism, were called "teachings of the Buddha" or "teachings of the Dao." The Japanese first translated the term *religion* into an invented term, *zongjiao* [宗教], which literarily means "lineage teaching." This translation was accepted into the modern Chinese vocabularies and was used widely. This translation of religion, moreover, carried with it an understanding of religion with its Judeo-Christian assumptions into the Japanese and Chinese world of thought in the modern era. This was also the origin of the idea that "China did not have religion" that some early twentieth-century Chinese intellectuals pronounced. What most of the scholars, East or West, now consider as religion, such as Daoism, Buddhism, and sometimes even Confucianism, were for a time regarded as either philosophies or superstitions. It took the Chinese intellectuals almost the entire twentieth century to first accept that there were religions in Chinese history and then to disentangle from the imported assumption of what religion was and why Chinese religions did not quite qualify as true religion—often in the measurement set by the standard of the Judeo-Christian definition of religion, especially the Protestant branch of Christianity, whose missionary schools had played an important educational role for the Chinese intellectuals in the first half of the twentieth century.

This situation was caused jointly by Western scholars who study Chinese religions, many of them with a missionary background, and Chinese intellectuals who received Western-style education in China or abroad. The trend to study Chinese religions and analyze Chinese religions using intellectual tools that were a product of the Judeo-Christian tradition was a worldwide phenomenon in most of the twentieth century.

The Study of Chinese Religion in the West: A Product of the Western Intellectual Tradition

Riding with the same intellectual current that prompted Western scholars to study the non-Judeo-Christian religions, the study of Chinese religion in the West has also gone through several phases. It is now well known that the Jesuits who came to China in the seventeenth century, for tactic reasons, represented the Chinese state religion as monotheistic, therefore compatible with Christianity, while Buddhism and Daoism and other forms of popular cults were regarded as idolatrous. This view had influenced generations of European intellectuals until modern times.[2] Late in the nineteenth century, the Dutch scholar J. J. M. de Groot wrote a monumental work, *The Religious System of China*.[3] The tremendous energy he spent and the breadth of knowledge of the Chinese classics that he demonstrated could still impress us today. No one can say that he was not enthusiastic about China. Yet he was also the one who said that "as with semi-civilized peoples in general, so in China religious ideas and usages pervade social life to its inmost recesses."[4] Moreover, "many rites and practices still flourish among the Chinese, which one would scarcely expect to find anywhere except amongst savages in a low stage of culture."[5] De Groot used ancient documents to demonstrate that the Chinese religion that he saw in the late nineteenth century did not change fundamentally, which meant that the Chinese society that he saw was mostly in a "low stage of culture." The kind of continuation de Groot mentioned cannot be described as completely wrong. For even today, the farmers' almanacs that one can find in Taiwan or Hong Kong still contain many similarities in content and vocabulary with the "Daybook" (i.e., a text that identifies good and bad days to do certain things according to the calendar) that was unearthed in a third-century BCE tomb in Hubei province.[6] It is also true that many Chinese people still believe in the art of geomancy and in burning paper money for their ancestors. Yet it is problematic if we refer to these activities as something that can only be found among savages and in a more primitive society. In any case, even if we admit that there is a high degree of continuity of Chinese culture—which we should—similar religious activities do not necessarily mean the same religious mentality at work. Time has worked wonders to transform the content of a culture. De Groot's view can only be one of the views among many observers. For example, James Legge (1815–97), the great translator of Chinese classics whose work is still useful today, believed that the ancient Chinese religion was monotheistic, because the concept of "heaven" that the Confucians propagated was undoubtedly the worship of the only High God.[7] His idea, of course, was not too different from that of the Jesuit missionaries who came to China two hundred years before him.

This is not the occasion to fully discuss the implications of either de Groot's or Legge's works, such as if they were "Orientalists" in the Edward Said sense or else. But they demonstrated a rationalist and positivist attitude to their subject, an attitude that later can also be found in the work of Max Weber. For Weber, religion is the result of rationalization of the world around us, and Chinese religion is no exception. Although Weber wrote a famous treatise on Confucianism and Daoism, his real intention was probably not to understand Chinese religions for their own sake but to answer his question of why China did not develop the kind of capitalism that Western Europe had been able to accomplish.[8] His discussion of China, in the end, was only part of his grand scheme to demonstrate his sociological methodology.

A contemporary of Max Weber, the French scholar Marcel Granet, who was under the influence of Émile Durkheim and paid special attention to the role of religion in social structure, inaugurated a new wave of interest in Chinese religion.[9] He did not seem to agree with de Groot's view about the primitiveness of Chinese religion; neither did he agree with Legge to see Chinese religion through the glasses of Christian theology. What he wished to do was use the example of Chinese religion or Chinese society as a test ground to employ Durkheimian sociological theories to understand human society. It was a very far-sighted view during the early twentieth century. As Maurice Freedman later reflected, Granet was a scholar who cared about the whole of humanity. The reason for his studying China was because he wished to find a path to break the parochial European localism and reach out to the other cultures in the world.[10] In Granet's own words, "By its extent, its duration, its mass, Chinese civilization is one of the most powerful creations of mankind; none other is richer in human experience. Yet it is infinitely less familiar to the public than the Mediterranean civilizations. . . . Nevertheless, every cultivated man is today aware of the narrowness of the world circumscribed by classical studies. Why should China remain alien to him if nothing human should remain alien?"[11]

These words are still valid even today. Under the influence of Granet, French Sinologists launched an important movement to study Chinese religions, especially Buddhism and Daoism, and made tremendous contributions to the understanding of China and Chinese religions in the twentieth century. Looking at Granet's ideas a century later, I am not sure whether Granet was not more interested in applying Durkheimian social theory than understanding Chinese society and religions. According to Freedman, Granet himself once said: "'La Chine, je m'en fous. Ce qui m'intéresse, c'est l'Homme' (If I must translate: 'I don't give a damn about China. What interests me is Man')."[12] However one may interpret his words, one cannot help but suspect that he had a primary motivation to establish a sociological model by employing material from China. Thus eventually he and Weber belonged to the same category of Western scholars who were more interested in finding universal patterns in Chinese religion than understanding Chinese religion per se.

The second half of the twentieth century saw in the Western study of China a change from the emphasis on political and socioeconomic aspects of China in the period from the 1950s to the 1970s, to a cultural turn after the 1980s when more and more efforts have been devoted to discover the cultural foundations that lie beneath the facade of political events: issues of science, medicine, literature, education, gender, social life, local community, and, not least of all, religion received unprecedented attention. It is undeniable that this trend was a reflection of the problematiques current in the Western intellectual world. The study of Chinese religion in recent scholarship would strive to discard most of the Eurocentric or Judeo-Christian perception of what a religion means in a living society (as spiritual guide for individual moral life or salvation, for example) and try to reach a less ideologically laden view—if possible. It has often been suggested that instead of stressing the importance of belief, it is perhaps ritual actions that we should emphasize in characterizing Chinese religion. For example, according to Daniel Overmyer, the local religious activities in Chinese society were the factors that defined and secured the Chinese cultural tradition for centuries, as they provided people with a sense of identity. This identity was built on a common local ritual tradition, the worship of gods and ancestors, the celebration of yearly festivals, and various ways to foretell the future and drive away evil spirits.[13]

Overmyer's view was representative of many contemporary Western scholars who study Chinese religion. By emphasizing the importance of ritual activities, one may avoid using the Judeo-Christian concepts and values to evaluate the religions of other cultures. That is, Overmyer tried to separate "faith"—the paramount characteristics of Judeo-Christian religion—and "religious activities/rituals" that he thought are more important elements of some other religions, including not only Buddhism or Daoism but also the so-called popular religion that consisted of the worship of various deities. For all their importance, religious ideas cannot survive or be transmitted without the practice of the living person, and it is through ritual practice that a religious culture and community is formed and sustained. While agreeing with all these, one can still ask: After learning all the ritual traditions, have we reached the end of our inquiry? Can we really comprehend the sentiments of those people who built the temples, carved the divine statues, and organized festive parades? Are we not facing the problem that, by stressing the ritual characteristics of Chinese religion, one nevertheless falls into another trap that somehow played down the importance of religious sensibility?

In sum, whether as a preparation for imposing a hegemonic order such as Christianity on another or as a means to counter Eurocentrism or Orientalism, or as a useful tool to construct postcolonial discourse, or even as simple (or not so simple) sinophilic passions, one has the impression that the study of Chinese religion in the West has inevitably been the product of or influenced by the changing Western worldview and discourse on civilization.

The most difficult task for us now should be to discover and to acknowledge such invisible colored glasses. Many scholars would certainly think that this is already commonsense knowledge and that the scholarship in religious studies has gone over this issue many times and surpassed the stage of "recognizing the colored eyeglasses." Yet it is an undeniable fact that, in the twenty-first century, when many scholars around the world expressed increasing interest in the religion and history of China, this interest was a direct reflection of the increasing power of China as a nation or as a culture in the contemporary international scene. If this point has some value, then this increasing interest in China can also be seen as a kind of colored glasses: it was when China grew into a strong international power that Western scholars were obliged to show more interest. When Granet addressed his Western audience and argued for an equal weight of China compared with the West, he asked, "Why should China remain alien to him if nothing human should remain alien?"[14] The logical conclusion is that the interest in or importance of China and Chinese religion should not be based on the size, population, national power, or even history but on the fact that what had happened in China historically and contemporarily was also part of the phenomenon of the entire human society. One cannot expect to have a comprehensive understanding of humanity without understanding the example of China.

The Study of Chinese Religion in Modern China: From Superstition to Local Culture

The study of Chinese religion in modern China was also a story inseparable from the intellectual current that swept the world since the early twentieth century, when Chinese intellectuals were confronted with unprecedented national crises both politically and culturally. Leaders of the iconoclastic new culture movement were mostly ardent believers of Western ideas and values, including the philosophy of John Dewey and the doctrine of Marxism. They regarded religion as the synonym of superstition and a symbol of backwardness. The president of the Beijing University, Cai Yuanpei (1916–27), for example, propagated the idea of using aesthetics to replace religion as the basis of education for the modern citizen. Among all the turmoil of the 1930s and 1940s, ironically, protestant Christianity received some patronage from political leaders such as Chiang Kai-shek, partly because of its association with science, modernity, and Western powers. But the general attitude of the Chinese government and intellectuals remained critical of religion, especially during the turbulent years of the 1950s and 1960s, until the collective sentiments began to change after the mid-1970s. Religion became a legitimate subject of study again. It was not an easy transition, however, as old antireligious ideology needed to be explained away. The best justification for Chinese scholars to study religion, it seems, was linking religion with the value of "serving the people." The usual argument goes as follows: In traditional times, the feudal landlords exploited the livelihood of the people, yet despite this disadvantage, the people strived to find expressions for their religious sentiments. These religious sentiments, though originated from fear of the unknown and ignorance of nature, nonetheless possessed some good qualities, such as maintaining family and social stability, or the virtue of honesty and working hard. For some Chinese scholars, therefore, to study the religious activities of the people is to confirm the conviction that "the people" are the center of history. Many books published in recent years took pride in presenting the rich fabric of local religious customs and regarded them either as part of the local culture or as keys to understand local culture, a very legitimate subject at a time when local identity was enhanced as China's economic boom trickled down into local societies. Particularly worth mentioning is the fact that this trend of studying local religions was partly encouraged by and in cooperation with an increasing number of Western scholars, thus in a sense it was the result of international cooperation.[15] It would be interesting to see how this tide of new localism with input from the West can bring the study of religion in China onto a different level. For the time being, however, I notice a conspicuous lack of treatment of the sentiments of the believers. Instead, the excitement of the Chinese scholars is often exuberantly expressed, for now they have the chance to study and, as is often said, "to keep the essence and discard the dreg." This type of attitude inadvertently reveals the top-down mentality of researchers toward their subjects. Such mentality may even be more prevalent among the Chinese scholars, because it would be easy for them to assume that since they are studying their own culture, they are entitled to have the authority to make proper judgments about which is the essence and which is the dreg. The traditional hierarchical relationship between Chinese literati and the commoners may easily be inherited by contemporary scholars, a point worth considering.

The Chinese State and Religion

The attitude of the Chinese state toward religion, however, is another matter that had little to do with whatever understanding of religion there was but had everything to do with the authority of the state. No religion is to have the authority, moral or political, over the state, that is, the mechanism that controls the operation of the entire country. In the imperial period, from at least the establishment of the Qin-Han empire in the third century BCE, the state had taken claim of the most supreme power there was in the world, represented by the emperor, whose title, the "Son of Heaven," pointed to an unchallengeable authority over the rest of the world. This authority, boosted by a series of exclusively imperial ritual performances such as the worshipping of heaven and earth, which confirm or confer the divine status of the emperor as the mediator between heaven and man, helped with a mantel of moral-ethical superiority constructed by "Confucian" scholars over the centuries, so that the emperor possessed this status of a divine being and a living saint. At least this was the official line of argument that the state sold to the common people. This official facade was at no time truly believed by the people at the core of the game: the ministers, the courtiers, the bureaucrats. It was also because of this fact that corrupted regimes were able to be replaced by another who could claim to have the Mandate of Heaven, the only claim that could supersede the authority of the current Son of Heaven. Thus the transition of political power, although mostly done by military force, was always done under the pretext of a celestial authority. The source of this authority, that is, the heaven, was not a "God" in the sense of the Judeo-Christian religion, yet the quality and power associated with this heaven, such as benevolence and justice, point to a moral agency that assumes almost a divine personhood. This idea of a heaven that was the last resort of worldly justice was actually always there in the common mentality of the population since as early as the time of the *Book of Poetry*, or the eighth to sixth centuries BCE. Thus one could not say that there was not an element of belief in a power that was above the human world and somehow controlled human destiny.

The relationship between the imperial authority, the Mandate of Heaven, the popular conception of a just and benevolent heaven, and the ultimate authority of the emperor over any form of religion makes an understanding of what a religion is or was in China a challenge. Furthermore, a clear distinction between what is religious and what is secular in the sense of the secularism that our colleagues from the Netherlands were discussing could not easily be achieved. The Chinese state / imperial house gained the claim to power by being able to manage the peace and prosperity of the society, which was "secular" in the sense that no religious ideology was involved in the actual management. Yet the state and the imperial house could not totally abstain from association with something sacred, that is, the ultimate source of legitimacy, the Mandate of Heaven, even though this mandate could be gained by force. Moreover, if the state is secular in the sense of actual management of peace and prosperity, it nonetheless took the various religions under its protection. Buddhism, Daoism, and local religious cults each received state sanction from time to time, and sometimes simultaneously.[16] Thus in a sense, the state in China could be said to be secular in the aspects of social and political management but religious in the aspects of upholding a supreme power that was bestowed by heaven and concentrated in the one person of the emperor. The state was therefore both a secular and a religious institution.

In this regard, the relationship between political belonging and religious piety in traditional China appears to be an entangled one. The people were demanded to pledge loyalty to the ruler on the premise that the ruler received the Mandate of Heaven. Thus the loyalty was an expression not merely of political belonging but also of religious piety. While this belonging may be indisputable, it may still be subject to the sanction of the Mandate of Heaven. When we consider the contemporary situation in China, such an observation may provide some insight into the issue of the relationship between state power and religions.

Chinese Intellectuals and Religions

If the authority of the state over religions was never a question, the attitude of the elites in society toward religious activities in Chinese society was not without debate and questioning, as there has always been a confrontation between the sober-minded views of intellectuals and the passionate need of the multitude. A famous third-century BCE Confucian philosopher, Xunzi, once commented on the common practice of divination and magic in society.

> You pray for rain and it rains. Why? For no particular reason, I say. It is just as though you had not prayed for rain and it rained anyway. The sun and moon undergo an eclipse and you try to save them; a drought occurs

and you pray for rain; you consult the arts of divination before making a decision on some important matter. But it is not as though you could hope to accomplish anything by such ceremonies. They are done merely for ornament. Hence the gentleman regards them as ornaments [*wen*], but the common people regard them as supernatural [*shen*]. He who considers them ornaments is fortunate; he who considers them supernatural is unfortunate.[17]

Xunzi's rational analysis represented the Confucian attitude that influenced generations of intellectuals. He believed that the religious activities such as divination and ritual acts were decorations of social life. They were ornaments that could add to the benefit of the community, yet it was not advisable to assume that there were really gods or spirits in charge of things in the world, otherwise such religious activities would be harmful to society.

During the Han dynasty (220 BCE–212 CE), the intellectuals who constituted the majority of state officials held a consistently condescending attitude toward religious activities at local communities. Stories were told about how upright officials cracked down on shamans who performed fraudulent tricks to the credulous commoners and benefited from the extravagant cult expenditures. The official attitude was that any cult unsanctioned by the state was to be expunged—which sounds very familiar even today.[18] When Buddhism and Daoism became better established in society, the state, for one reason or another, chose to promote them yet insisted that Confucian learning remained the foundation of state ideology. Existing local cults learned to associate themselves with either Buddhism or Daoism, or both, by adopting their rituals and incorporating or being incorporated into the constantly growing pantheon. Critical voices from the elite against religious activities never ceased to be spelled out: one could criticize Buddhism for its "barbarian" origin, or criticize Daoism for its association with exorcism and superstition, or criticize both for their other-worldly outlook against the presumably humanistic and this-worldly outlook of the Confucian learning.

It became clear, therefore, that the antireligious or agnostic attitude that modern Chinese intellectuals exhibited was not merely a modern phenomenon in response to the challenges of the Western powers and the influence of Western ideas but had a deeper root in Chinese history. It is also clear, however, that religious activities never ceased to exist in Chinese society. There was another side of the conflict between the intellectuals and the popular need of religion. The overarching term "the intellectuals/elite," which we often view as one social stratum as opposed to the common people, actually represented a not very clearly circumscribed segment of society that was far from being homogeneous. Even from the early imperial period, not all intellectual officials adopted a prohibitive attitude toward local cults, and some of them even participated in the worship when they found it useful or agreeable to do so. Moreover, there were various degrees and shades of rationalist attitudes, even in one person facing different situations.[19]

For example, many literati wrote dry and formal dynastic history during the day while reading and collecting ghost stories at night. Indeed, the reading, collecting, and disseminating of ghost stories, proliferating among the literati society since the late third century and lasting until the modern times, could be revealing indications regarding the attitude of many intellectuals toward things supernatural. It seems that the ghost stories were not only for entertainment but also carried certain sentiment that inclined toward another world that may administer a different set of social justice, as illustrated in an often-quoted story (ca. third century CE) about a certain Zong Dai.

> Zong Dai was the Inspector of the Commandery of Qingzhou. He abolished the excessive cults and wrote a fine treatise on the nonexistence of ghosts, which no one could refute. One day a scholar wearing a gray headcloth and carrying a name card came to visit Dai. They discussed various issues and when they began to talk about the nonexistence of ghosts, the scholar shook his robe and left, saying, "You have terminated our blood offering for twenty-some years, but since you had a black cow and a bearded servant, we could not bother you. Now your servant has abandoned you and the cow is dead, today we are able to get the better of you." As soon as he finished speaking, he disappeared. Dai died the next day.[20]

On the surface, the most important message of this story is perhaps to show in a humorous way that it is useless to repudiate the power of ghosts or that of the popular beliefs. Yet the story also reveals some subtleties. Dai's abolition of the excessive cults was ostensibly the act of a responsible Confucian scholar-official. As far as Confucian ethics is concerned, therefore, his death was unjustified. Yet for a believer in ghosts, Dai deserved to die, since he had made livelihood difficult for the ghosts. The story can thus be understood as a sarcastic view of those self-righteous officials who, disregarding people's emotional attachment to the cults, took away people's livelihood in the name of high-minded moral principles. The words spoken by the ghost, therefore, could be construed as a sympathetic expression of the sentiment of the suffering people.[21]

This hidden implication contained in the story may not be something that the official Confucian ideology would like to encourage. Yet all along there was a subterrain in the intellectual world that was close to the common people and local cults. In fact, it has been demonstrated that the so-called popular religions in Chinese society have always had a close symbiotic relationship with literary activities. One can trace this relationship as early as the third-century BCE almanacs, down to the protective and ritual texts found in Han dynasty tombs, the Daoist talismans and liturgical texts of the Six Dynasties period, the transformation literature (*bianwen*) of the Tang dynasty, and the various Precious Volumes (*baoquan*) of the Ming-Qing period, to the contemporary morality books and spiritual writings. All these could not have existed without the active participation of literati or literate personnel at various levels of literary accomplishment. Thus one can hardly make a clear-cut distinction between the world of the intellectuals and that of the common religious populace.

With this understanding of the history of the confrontation, coexistence, and intermixture between the intellectuals and religions in Chinese society, it became clear that the elite rationalist attitude, although exhibiting a strong aversion toward things supernatural, could also have kept a lenient position toward the religious activities of the commoners, as they acknowledged or even approved, as Xunzi did, the difference between the gentleman and the "little man." In other words, there was indeed a tendency among the intellectuals—whatever their level of sophistication—to accept, though perhaps not necessarily comprehend, the religious sentiments of the commoners.

The Characteristics of Chinese Religions

What could be summarized as the characteristics of Chinese religions that could make a contrast to the Abrahamic religions? From the earliest time onward, the Chinese perceived the world as full of extrahuman beings. All religious behaviors were in a sense reactions to these extrahuman beings or forces associated with them.[22] Until the arrival of Islam and Christianity in China, the basic cosmology of most of the Chinese people remained polytheistic, and the dominating issue for the Chinese believers was not whether there was one god, but which god or spirit was more powerful or efficacious. The element of morality that students of other religious traditions might consider inseparable from religious life, that is, the idea that religion was about leading a good moral life, was not a major issue in the case of ancient China. This is not to say that morality was unimportant, for no society can survive without a common moral system, but there was a side of the Chinese religious mentality that could be seen as operating outside the sphere of morality and in the sphere of efficaciousness.

This observation implies that the religious activities in ancient China were utilitarian in nature. In order to improve personal welfare and avoid misfortune caused by the extrahuman forces, people chose to perform various rituals, some propitiatory, some exorcistic, but basically techniques with little connection to an individual's personal morality. In a text found in a late third-century BCE tomb, for example, people were instructed to take all sorts of exorcistic rituals to ward off various ghosts and spirits.[23] No mention was made suggesting one's own moral behavior as a possible source of the attack of ghosts and spirits. In other words, there was no "crime and punishment" in the imagined relationship between human and extrahuman.

Of course, it can be argued that there was no lack of moral element in Chinese religions. One can point out that early in the Zhou dynasty (ca. 1046–256 BCE), the concept of the Mandate of Heaven had already emerged as a moral concept that linked the behavior of the sovereign to his legitimacy to rule. The *Book of Poetry* also exhibited a sentiment that craved heavenly justice. However, it was only in the early Daoist movement in the late third century CE that morality became an integrated element in religious teachings. The leader of the early Daoist movement stipulated the rule that an adept should act with honesty and faithfulness and repent on his wrongdoings in case he fell ill. The assumption was that the spirits (gods and ghosts) would punish a person with illness should the person act with dishonesty and deceit.[24] The Buddhist idea of hell as a place of punishment for the morally corrupted, moreover, needs no more emphasis.

Despite this moral turn in religious sentiment, the amoral mentality still constituted an underlying base that reveals itself from time to time in Chinese popular religious mentality. For example, the idea that by reciting the name of the Buddha or a certain sutra many times, one can gain access to the Western paradise, despite the possible psychosomatic experience one can derive from such actions, can easily become a mechanical number counting. The calculation of the number of merits in the "Merit Counting Book" prevalent in the Ming and Qing period, for another example, reduced or transformed immaterial piety and compassion into material commodity, like the accumulation of credits in a bank, which can be drawn when needed. Indeed, the combination of this amoral mentality with the often-stereotypical moral teaching—that the good gets rewarded and the evil gets punished—created a kind of religious sensibility that may at times be difficult to comprehend.

This description of the nature of Chinese religions, with all its possible biases, while not meant to be comprehensive, could serve as an example that shows how one should not employ without judicious precaution the Judeo-Christian standard of religious piety to measure the Chinese religious sensibility. The most important message, from a cross-cultural point of view, is that apparently the usual approaches to the study of religion, such as the contrast between "secularism" and "religion," or what "religion" means, cannot be applied without considering the case of China. Chinese rulers, although some might be ardent followers of Buddhism or Daoism, were to a large extent secular as head of the government. Yet at no time did the rulers of China ever give up their role as Son of Heaven, thus occupying a central position in all the religions of the land. Moreover, the mainstream Confucian philosophy had an essential role in shaping a secular moral code with its emphasis on a higher level of "heaven" as the universal moral standard. Therefore, religion—if the idea of Son of Heaven represents a type of religion, and the Mandate of Heaven promoted by Confucianism also belonged to the realm of religious belief—was inseparable from the "secular" world in China.[25] If this case with China can be considered as a useful example of the study of religion and secularism in a global context, it could at least complicate the theoretical foundation of the very concepts of religion and secularism, as the authors of this volume have strived to demonstrate.

NOTES

1. The term *Chinese religions* merely refers to the religious activities that happened in the area that historically belongs to the Chinese cultural sphere. It usually includes so-called indigenous beliefs such as the worship of natural spirits and various deities, or the kind of organized religions such as Daoism and Buddhism. Other religions that later came to China, such as Christianity, Islam, Judaism, or Manicheism, lie outside the scope of this chapter. Here I am mainly concerned with the religious life of the people in traditional societies.
2. See Jordan Paper, *The Spirits are Drunk* (Albany: State University of New York Press, 1995), 4–5; and John Lagerwey, *China: A Religious State* (Hong Kong: Hong Kong University Press, 2010). For Christianity in China, see Nicolas Standaert, ed., *Handbook of Christianity in China*, vol. 1, *635–1800* (Leiden: Brill, 2001). For the Jesuits, see Jiam M. Borckey, *Journey to the East: The Jesuit Mission to China, 1597–1724* (Cambridge MA: Harvard University Press, 2007); and Ronnie Po-chia Hsia, *A Jesuit in the Forbidden City, Matteo Ricci, 1552–1610* (Oxford: Oxford University Press, 2010).
3. J. J. M. de Groot, *The Religious System of China: Its Ancient Forms, Evolution, History and Present Aspect; Manners, Customs and Social Institutions Connected Therewith*, 6 vols. (1892; Leyden: Brill, 1972).

4   De Groot, *Religious System of China*, 1:x.
5   De Groot, *Religious System of China*, 1:xi.
6   Mu-chou Poo, "Popular Religion in Pre-Imperial China: Observation on the Almanacs of Shui-hu-ti," *T'oung Pao* 79 (1993): 225–48.
7   James Legge, *An Argument for Shang-te as the Proper Rendering of the Words Elohim and Theos in the Chinese Language* (Hong Kong: Hong Kong Register, 1850); James Legge, *The Religions of China: Confucianism and Tâoism Described and Compared with Christianity* (London: Hodder and Stoughton, 1880).
8   Max Weber, *The Religion of China: Confucianism and Taoism*, ed. and trans. Hans H. Gerth (New York: Macmillan, 1964).
9   Marcel Granet, *Danses et légendes de la Chine ancienne* (Paris: F. Alcan, 1926).
10 Maurice Freedman, "Marcel Granet, Sociologist," in *The Religion of the Chinese People*, by Marcel Granet, trans. Maurice Freedman (New York: Harper Torchbooks, 1975), 28.
11 Freedman, "Marcel Granet," 28.
12 Freedman, "Marcel Granet," 29.
13 Daniel L. Overmyer, introduction to *Ethnography in China Today: A Critical Assessment of Methods and Results*, ed. Daniel L. Overmyer (Taipei: Yuan-liu, 2002), 10.
14 Freeman, "Marcel Granet," 28.
15 Notable among Western scholars are Daniel L. Overmyer, John Lagerwey, and Kenneth Dean.
16 See Anthony C. Yu, *State and Religion in China: Historical and Textual Perspectives* (Chicago: Open Court, 2005).
17 B. Watson, *Hsün Tzu* (New York: Columbia University Press, 1963), 85.
18 Mu-chou Poo, *In Search of Personal Welfare: A View of Ancient Chinese Religion* (Albany: State University of New York Press, 1998), ch. 8.
19 Poo, *In Search of Personal Welfare*, ch. 8.
20 *Peizi yulin* [裴子語林], in Lu Xun, *Gu xiaoshuo gouchen* (Taipei: Tangshan Publishing, 1986), 28, translation mine.
21 See further discussion in Mu-chou Poo, "Justice, Morality, and Skepticism in Six Dynasties Ghost Stories," in *Interpretation and Literature in Early Medieval China*, ed. Alan Chan and Yuet-keung Lo (Albany: State University of New York Press, 2010), 251–71.
22 Poo, *In Search of Personal Welfare*, ch. 2.
23 Poo, *In Search of Personal Welfare*, ch. 4.
24 Isabelle Robinet, *Taoism: Growth of a Religion*, trans. Phyllis Brooks (Stanford: Stanford University Press, 1997), 66.
25 For a bold and stimulating discussion along this line, see Lagerwey, *China*.

9. EVANGELICAL CHRISTIANITY, BIG BUSINESS, AND THE RESURGENCE OF AMERICAN CONSERVATISM DURING THE 1970S

DAVID N. GIBBS

The 1970s brought a major ideological shift in the United States, moving the political agenda decisively to the right. At the domestic level, economic policy became increasingly market-based, eschewing the Keynesian proclivities of an earlier period, while at the international level, there was renewed emphasis on confrontation with the Soviet Union. The conservative shift was evident in both political parties. This chapter assesses how the rise of evangelical Protestantism influenced the political shift of this period. The term *evangelical* will be used as denoting variants of Christianity that emphasize literal interpretations of the Old and New Testaments; the importance of personalized and emotional relationships between individual Christians and Jesus Christ; hostility toward secularist political tendencies; and the salience of life-transforming "born again" experiences.

The overall conservative shift was led by business elites, who sought free-market economic policies and military expansion. In seeking these objectives, they established common cause with evangelical Christians, and the resulting business-Christian alliance offered advantages to both groups: From the standpoint of the evangelicals, business support enhanced their power and better enabled them to lobby for the "traditional values" that the evangelicals favored. From the standpoint of business elites, the coalition with evangelicals offered a mass base, which included millions of conservative voters. The glue that held together this disparate alliance was funding, supplied by business figures and expended by church clergy. The combination of money, votes, and religious fervor, which resulted from this alliance, was a significant factor in producing the rightward shift of the era. At an affective level, the new Christian conservative identity created a strong sense of "belonging" among its adherents, in a culturally unstable era, which helped make this identity an especially potent force for the political right. The public role of Christian conservativism has remained a distinctive feature of U.S. politics, one that endures to the present day.

The Crisis of the 1970s

During the post–World War II era, a "class compromise" emerged in the United States, which entailed government regulation of the macro-economy, a federal welfare state of moderate size, and mass labor unions—a state of affairs that came to be accepted by most business interests.[1] After 1970, however, the class compromise was undermined, as business gradually withdrew support from the project. This withdrawal of support was based on changed circumstances: During the 1970s, profit rates declined in multiple sectors and reached historically low levels, a process that has been well documented by economic historian Robert Brenner.[2] This decline in profitability was a matter of grave concern for corporate executives and was probably the most important factor undercutting the class compromise. Second, sizable elements of U.S. youth were becoming politically radicalized and associated with a New Left that first emerged on college campuses during the 1960s and remained a potent force into the early 1970s; this too was a source of apprehension among business elites. Third, the 1975 defeat in Vietnam generated reluctance on the part of the U.S. public to countenance new overseas interventions, which left multinational companies concerned that their investments in unstable regions, such as the Persian Gulf, lacked military protection.[3]

The rise of business anxiety during this period was most clearly explicated by a memorandum written by Lewis Powell, a Virginia corporate attorney who would later serve on the U.S. Supreme Court. Originally written as a confidential strategy paper for the U.S. Chamber of Commerce in 1971, the document was leaked to the press and published in the *Washington Post*. In this memorandum, Powell emphasized the danger of growing antibusiness attitudes among the general public. He focused especially on the influence of political activist Ralph Nader, whose criticism of U.S. corporate power was considered especially threatening. Powell also noted criticisms of business emanating from academia, mainstream clergy, and the mass media. Overall, the Powell memorandum advanced the notion that the American business class faced an unprecedented attack on its practices and the free-market ideology that undergirded it. In response, the Powell memorandum advocated an extended campaign by business to counter this perceived attack and laid out a proposed program of corporate lobbying, aimed not only at policy makers but also at the general public. The lobbying effort was to be backed by "generous financial support from American corporations."[4] In retrospect, its wording may seem shrill and overstated, but there is no doubt that Powell expressed a widespread sentiment among U.S. business figures, and this sentiment deepened over time.

The memorandum coincided with a massive lobbying campaign by business interests that also began during the early 1970s and continued throughout the decade, and aimed at curtailing the New Deal legacy of regulated capitalism. While there was a substantial augmentation in the scale of business involvement in politics, the *character* of the involvement also changed: During the 1970s, business increasingly sought not merely to influence specific legislation—as it had done in the past—but also to engineer a fundamental shift in the political climate, in a laissez-faire direction.[5] New business lobbies were founded, such as the Business Roundtable, while preexisting lobbies, such as the National Association of Manufacturers and the U.S. Chamber of Commerce, were reinvigorated with increased financial support.[6] The business mobilization would in time generate a sea change in U.S. politics that culminated in the election of Ronald Reagan in 1980. This business mobilization also funded a growing network of highly talented conservative intellectuals, associated with such corporate-funded think tanks as the Heritage Foundation, the American Enterprise Institute, and the Hoover Institution.[7] Among the most important of these rising conservative intellectuals was Paul Weyrich of Heritage, who would play a key role in planning and orchestrating the mass mobilization of conservatives among the general public.

The 1970s also was a decade of mass religious mobilization, which some authorities have termed America's "fourth great awakening."[8] The most distinctive feature of this awakening was a rapid growth in fundamentalist sects, outside the more established Protestant churches. By 1976, one-third of the U.S. adult population reported that they had experienced being "born again" with Jesus Christ.[9] At the same time, more mainstream congregations, such as the Episcopalians, Lutherans, Methodists, and the United Church of Christ (as well as the Catholic Church), all saw significant declines in membership, consistent with a more generalized loss of public confidence in established institutions that was one of the hallmarks of public opinion at this time. Just as people were losing confidence in established political institutions due to military failures in Vietnam and the Watergate scandal, the public was also losing confidence in established religion.[10] Among the more mainstream churches, the only one that registered major growth during this period was the Southern Baptist Convention; and fittingly, the Baptists were among the most evangelical of all the purportedly mainstream Protestant groups.[11] The burgeoning movement of fundamentalist churches had thus emerged as a powerful and potentially decisive electoral force.

The Evangelical Mobilization Begins

While political conservatives in the Republican Party did not create this evangelical awakening, they were clearly prepared to mobilize the evangelicals and fortify their efforts, beginning during the presidency of Richard Nixon. The president himself was irreligious, and "church worship bored him," according to one study.[12] Yet he clearly understood the potential of Christianity to rally large numbers of voters against the antiwar movement, the "hippie" counterculture," and the Democratic Party, which was increasingly viewed as embracing these heretical tendencies. Nixon made a special effort to mobilize not only Christian voters but also Christian businessmen. At one point, Nixon directed an aide to "develop a list of rich people with strong religious interest to be invited to the White House church services."[13]

The most important element in Nixon's religious strategy was his alliance with charismatic Baptist pastor Billy Graham, who held mass rallies that were widely televised. These rallies combined emotional commitment to Jesus with support for President Nixon and his political agenda; they also showcased mass contempt for Nixon's secularist enemies. Graham played a prominent role in Nixon's first inauguration ceremony in 1969. His religious invocation was considered by *Time* magazine to be a "mini-inaugural address," in which Graham condemned the "materialistic and permissive society," as well as "crime, division, and rebellion"—a thinly veiled criticism of the counterculture.[14] Nixon's own inaugural address was filled with religious references.[15] In response to mass student demonstrations against the Vietnam War in 1970, Graham helped sponsor an "Honor America Day," with a mass rally of conservatives in Washington, DC, to support the president's war effort.[16]

From Nixon's standpoint, the affiliation with the Baptist preacher was a stroke of genius, as it added a populist and even anti-elitist character to his administration. It also generated political support for Nixon from among Graham's numerous admirers, many of whom were working-class southerners, who had traditionally voted Democratic. In encouraging a social backlash, Nixon was subtly appealing to racist sentiment, since much of the backlash was against racial integration. Graham himself generally opposed segregation and racism, but this was not necessarily true of his overwhelmingly white followers.[17] Overall, the whole operation fit in well with the Nixon administration's "southern strategy," which sought to forge a new Republican majority in this traditionally Democratic region.

Despite his populist image, Graham also had impressive connections to conservative businessmen, which no doubt increased his value to the Republican Party. Throughout his career, Graham had combined his religious proselytizing with strident anticommunism, as well as free-market and anti-union ideas. As early as 1952, Graham stated that in the Garden of Eden there were "no union dues, no labor leaders, no snakes, no disease," and similar themes were reiterated throughout his long career.[18] He attracted considerable corporate support. According to one biography, "Graham enjoyed numerous long-standing relationships with men of great wealth," including such prominent figures as J. W. Marriott, H. L. Hunt, Clint Murchison, Sid Richardson, and J. Howard Pew.[19] Oilman Pew seems to have been an especially important figure in supporting Graham; Pew also supported *Christianity Today*, a Graham-affiliated publication that became one of the leading voices of evangelical Christianity. In 1971, the executive editor of *Christianity Today* wrote to a colleague that Pew was a "great benefactor" of the publication as well as "one of the most wonderful men I have ever known."[20] By affiliating his presidency with Graham, Nixon could further cement his ties to corporate America while at the same time broadening his electoral appeal among social conservatives.

Nixon's association with religion paid rich dividends, especially in light of the Democratic Party's shift toward a more secular direction. The rise of the women's movement, with its associated ideas of gender equality and abortion rights, was embraced by the Democrats, at least at the national level. The 1972 Democratic convention was widely viewed as a "secularist putsch," a point that Nixon did not fail to emphasize in his reelection campaign.[21] The Republicans' strategy produced a large swing of religious Protestant voters away from the Democrats and toward Nixon, contributing to Nixon's landslide victory over George McGovern in the November election. Nixon's support among white southerners who regularly attended church reached 86 percent—in a constituency that traditionally had voted Democratic.[22]

In the long run, the Nixon presidency would end in disgrace, with the Watergate scandal and Nixon's humiliating resignation in 1974. On the other hand, the Nixon administration's mobilization of religion would prove useful as a model to rising New Right activists in private industry and also in industry-funded think tanks, such as the Heritage Foundation. Building on Nixon's approach, the New Right would use religion to drive a conservative realignment in U.S. politics, one that was to go far beyond the tepid conservatism of the Nixon administration itself. And if Graham was no longer available to lead this movement, there existed a coterie of ambitious preachers who would eagerly replace him while building on the idea of the corporate-friendly religious figure that Graham helped pioneer. And finally, the Nixon–Graham concept of combining the mobilization of religion with the simultaneous mobilization of business interests, and fusing the two sets of interest groups, would prove instructive for New Right strategists such as Weyrich, who would avidly adopt this strategy as well.

Evangelical Politics after the Nixon Presidency

A remobilization of evangelicals began almost immediately after Nixon's demise. Spearheading this remobilization was Bill Bright, who in 1975 founded the Christian Embassy in Washington, which sought to "evangelize members of Congress, the military, the judiciary, and the diplomatic service," as well as the Here's Life, America organization, to evangelize the general public.[23] Bright's endeavors combined religious and economic conservatism, and they attracted financial support from the Coors (of Coors Brewing), the Hunts (of Hunt Oil), and the DeVos family (Amway Corporation) as well as Mobil Oil, PepsiCo, and Coca-Cola. Bright also founded a Christian publishing company, Third Century Publishers, which distributed copies of conservative tracts that combined religious piety with economic conservatism and praise of the free market. Third Century's editor in chief, Rus Walton, also served as a director at the National Association of Manufacturers.[24] Meanwhile, the evangelical Fellowship Foundation "tapped wealthy businessmen" and with these funds organized prayer groups among members of Congress and other high-ranking government officials.[25] In Texas, pastor James Robison gained a large following for his sermons against both "demonism and liberalism." He was funded by the Hunts, the owner of the Texas Rangers baseball team, and a prominent Houston banker.[26] In southern California, fundamentalist leader Demos Shakarian "continued to recruit the Sunbelt's merchants and financiers" into his church while he advanced "pro-capitalist politics."[27] The wealthy DeVos family helped underwrite the Christian Freedom Foundation, which sought to "further religious right organizing efforts."[28]

Perhaps the most important evangelical leader of the 1970s was Jerry Falwell, who led a congregation in Lynchburg, Virginia, and whose radio and television show *The Old Time Gospel Hour* had a national audience. Falwell also established the fundamentalist Liberty Baptist College (later Liberty University), which offered a Christian college experience to the faithful. A strong believer in capitalism, Falwell affirmed that "the free enterprise system is clearly outlined in the Book of Proverbs."[29] He also preached anti-union views. One researcher dryly observed that Falwell's position "coincides with the interest of local business owners and managers far better than it does with those of most people in his own congregation."[30] With his fervently probusiness position, Falwell attracted many wealthy benefactors.[31]

At least some of the business funders were acting on the basis of cynical realpolitik rather than religious commitment. One of the major supporters of the evangelicals was Hunt Oil patriarch H. L. Hunt, who was merely a "nominal believer, who had a regular mistress and a healthy gambling habit."[32] For some, religion was simply a useful vehicle for advancing the conservative ideology that many businessmen supported instinctively, as a matter of self-interest. But this was not always the case. There also emerged during the 1970s a group of Christian business interests, whose executives combined an authentic religious fervor with entrepreneurial activity, including the Amway Corporation, Days Inn, Chick-Fil-A, and Mary Kay Cosmetics. The burgeoning market for Christian music produced several highly profitable companies. All these interests became ready sources of support for Christian causes.[33]

The Christian conservatives engaged the culture wars that were sweeping through the United States during the mid-1970s. One of the first major flare-ups occurred during 1974–75 in Kanawha County, West Virginia, where evangelicals protested against public school textbooks that contained excerpts from works by Mark Twain, Bernard Malamud, Eldridge Cleaver, and James Baldwin. The protests continued over a period of months and entailed repeated acts of violence, bombings, and shootings. The Ku Klux Klan mobilized to bolster the protesters—thus giving the overall movement a racist tinge—while coal miners staged a supportive strike. Local ministers led the protests and insisted that they were upholding "the infallible word of God."[34] The Heritage Foundation immediately saw an opportunity for using this dispute to curry favor with evangelicals. Accordingly, Heritage offered support to the Kanawha

County protesters, including free legal assistance as well as help presenting their cases to the national media.[35]

The culture wars continued throughout the decade with gathering intensity, and they would play out around issues of school curriculum, homosexuality, feminism, and abortion rights, often led by right-wing female activists, such as Anita Bryant and Phyllis Schalfly.[36] The ubiquitous Coors family helped fund Schlafly's activism, notably her crusade against the pending Equal Rights Amendment to the constitution, which proposed equality of the sexes.[37] Throughout the decade, these populist movements were integrated into the larger conservative movement, with its probusiness agenda, all of which formed a broad coalition. And these mobilization efforts produced a basic shift in the political orientation of evangelicals, who became far more engaged in politics than previously. This shift began around the middle of the decade, as described by political scientist Robert Putnam: "Prior to 1974 . . . most studies found evangelicals less disposed to political participation than other Americans—less likely to vote, to join political groups, to write to public officials, and to favor religious movements in politics. After 1974, by contrast, most studies have found them *more* involved politically than other Americans."[38] Evangelicals were indeed forming into a mass movement, one that would influence the U.S. political system well into the twenty-first century.

The Presidency of Jimmy Carter

The 1976 election constituted yet another setback for the New Right. The favored conservative candidate, Reagan narrowly failed to gain the Republican nomination, and the Democrats ultimately won the presidency while retaining their overwhelming majorities in both houses of Congress. Though the conservative defeat would prove only temporary, it seemed devastating at the time. And the new president, Jimmy Carter, threatened to co-opt culturally conservative issues, being both a southerner and an evangelical Christian himself, one who regularly taught Bible classes and embraced the mantle of having been born again. During and after the election, Carter had gained support from prominent evangelical ministers while winning nearly all the southern states; it briefly appeared that Carter could reintegrate these key constituencies back into the Democratic Party while holding the support of the party's more secular, northern wing.[39] Among his cohorts, the new president seemed the ultimate centrist, who would reconcile the divide between the religious and the secular and thus overcome or at least attenuate the culture wars. Carter would surely find some middle ground, or so it was hoped.

In reality, the middle ground did not exist. Carter's alliance with the evangelicals did not last long, and the failure of this alliance helped undermine his presidency. Some of Carter's problems resulted from questionable judgment: After his inauguration, Carter distanced himself somewhat from the ministers who had helped him win the election and generally held the evangelical movement at arm's length. He evaded several requests to speak before evangelical organizations or attend their public functions. It appears that the president felt secure in the knowledge that he himself was an evangelical. Carter believed he had no need to make special efforts with these groups—a strategy that had the predictable effect of alienating the evangelicals over time.[40] The president made more strenuous efforts to cultivate secularists, especially those in the burgeoning women's movement, who had always distrusted him to some degree. Key figures in the women's movement were appointed to the administration. Several of these appointments, notably the former Congresswomen Bella Abzug, were undiplomatic in their manner; they clashed repeatedly with the Christians, especially with regard to abortion rights and the still-pending Equal Rights Amendment. Particularly damaging to Carter's standing among evangelicals was a 1978 ruling by the Internal Revenue Service that threatened to strip the tax-exempt status from many Christian schools, which were considered racially discriminatory.[41] After 1979 Carter made feeble efforts to appease the evangelicals and repair the damage, but it was clearly too late.[42]

Amid the deterioration of Carter's relationship with evangelicals, New Right activists recognized an organizing opportunity. In 1979, they helped create the Moral Majority, an overtly political Christian group headed by Virginia pastor Jerry Falwell. The Moral Majority and its affiliated organizations held mass rallies and also coordinated networks of local Christian activists, virtually acting as a religious wing of the Republican Party. Perhaps the most important function of the Moral Majority was a mass voter registration campaign, which is believed to have successfully registered some two million voters for the 1980 election.[43] The new organization gained substantial business support. According to one account: "Falwell's high-flying profile with Republican leaders and the Moral Majority attracted a new kind of contributor: the superdonor. Texas oil billionaire Nelson Bunker Hunt had given millions to the Moral Majority. [Other contributors included] life insurance moguls Arthur Williams and Art DeMoss, cotton magnate Bo Adams, and a wealthy Pennsylvania poultry farmer, Don Hershey."[44] The Coors family also provided funds.[45] And the corporate-backed Heritage Foundation was instrumental in founding the organization, with Weyrich playing an especially central role.[46]

Consistent with the New Right philosophy of "fusionism," evangelical Protestants began forming alliances with diverse religious groups, including conservative Catholics and Orthodox Jews.[47] Despite his segregationist past, Falwell's Moral Majority was open to all races and gained some limited support among socially conservative black people.[48] A particularly striking feature of this period was the rise of "Christian Zionism," which became influential among evangelicals. The Christian Zionists were staunch supporters of the State of Israel, based on a biblical prophecy that the Jewish state anticipated the Second Coming of Jesus. Jewish groups responded with some trepidation to the evangelical support—considering the long history of antisemitism that had been associated with Christian awakenings in the past—but ultimately welcomed the prospect of forging new alliances for the pro-Israel project.[49] And finally, the evangelicals established common cause with corporate lobbyists seeking an expansion of the U.S. military: The president of the American Security Council, a trade group of weapons manufacturers, developed close ties to one of the Moral Majority's affiliated organizations, the Religious Roundtable.[50] Accordingly, many Christian conservatives advocated for an aggressive U.S. military stance and justified this advocacy is theological terms. According to Falwell, "Jesus was not a pacifist. He was not a sissy."[51]

During the 1980 election campaign, the evangelicals played prominent public roles, overwhelmingly in favor of the Republican candidate, Reagan. In the end, the evangelical mobilization was not decisive in Reagan's election, given his substantial, ten-point margin of victory over Carter. While the Moral Majority brought new voters to the Republican Party, especially among the vast numbers that the organization registered, it also probably alienated a sizable number as well. Overall, the net electoral benefit of the evangelicals to the Republican Party in 1980 was actually less than it had been in the earlier 1972 election.[52] However, the religious mobilization helped create a new and enduring force in U.S. politics for the long term whose strength grew over time. Pollster George Gallup would later remark that "religious affiliation remains one of the most accurate and least appreciated political indicators available."[53] Christian conservatism has proven an enduring and essentially permanent feature of the U.S. political landscape.

Conclusion

Superficially, the right-wing shift at the end of the 1970s resulted from massive investments by business interests that had turned against the postwar class compromise and sought more business-friendly policies. And indeed, we have seen that there is a good deal of truth in this explanation. The turn of evangelicals toward conservative politics and the Republican Party was surely influenced by sustained business funding. But there is another factor that should not be overlooked: the New Right developed a highly effective political strategy, which entailed the formation of broad coalitions integrating disparate groups, including socially conservative Christians and economically conservative business executives. The idea of blending together these groups was advocated by Ronald Reagan in 1977: "The time has come to see if it is possible to present a program of action . . . that can attract those interested in the so-called 'social' issues and those interested in 'economic' issues. In short, isn't it possible to combine the two major segments of contemporary American conservatism into one politically effective whole?"[54] The willingness to engage in such coalition building—and to do so as part of an overarching political strategy—accounts for much of the conservative success in this era, just as much as the massive infusion of money that undergirded that success.

The political left consistently avoided coalition building, and this avoidance points to a broader political failure. In some respects, the left's inability to check the rightward shift seems surprising, since labor unions remained large and powerful during the late 1970s, still accounting for a major share of the work force. In addition, the new social movements of the era held considerable sway among America's youth, and these included environmental, antinuclear, gay, and women's organizations. There also were African American, Chicano, and Native American political organizations, with substantial followings. While the left may have lacked corporate money, it could have compensated with broad popular support. The problem is that the progressive groups had little capacity to work together; the American Federation of Labor and Congress of Industrial Organizations (AFL-CIO) and other major unions were viewed with suspicion, because of their earlier support for the Vietnam War. And the social movements each had a single-issue focus, which prevented them from even considering significant cooperation with groups emphasizing different issues. There was also a profusion of small Marxist groups that sought revolutionary change, and they attracted some of the best and brightest among politically engaged young people. But these groups produced no realistic programs.

During the 1970s, the left seemed to reject the very idea of coalition building or majoritarian politics, almost as a matter of principle, a political stance that dovetailed with postmodernist theories that were just becoming popular in academia at the time. According to Marshall Berman, postmodernists "generally pushed their movements in the separatist and sectarian directions, away from broad civil rights coalitions and from human bonds that could transcend group boundaries."[55] Such attitudes go a long way toward explaining the New Right's success. Indeed, one of the most striking features of the New Right is the way it followed a political script of forming mass movements that had been pioneered by the *left*, from an earlier period. By the 1970s, however, the left had abandoned the idea of broad mass movements and strategic thinking more generally.

Stated simply, the right had a strategy for political success, whereas the left had none. It should come as no surprise that the conservative alliance of religion and money was so successful. When looking back at the story of religious mobilization during the 1970s, it appears that the outcome was not predetermined but was the result of specific political decisions that, for better or worse, ended with a victory by ultraconservatives in 1980. This victory has resonated in American politics ever since.

NOTES

1. On "class compromise," see Adam Przeworski, "Social Democracy as a Historical Phenomenon," *New Left Review*, no. 122 (July/August 1980): 27–58; and Robert M. Collins, *The Business Response to Keynes, 1929–1964* (New York: Columbia University Press, 1981).
2. Robert Brenner, *Economics of Global Turbulence: The Advanced Capitalist Economics from Long Boom to Long Downturn, 1945–2005* (London: Verso, 2006).
3. Regarding business concern about perceived U.S. military weakness, see "The Decline of US Power: The New Debate over Guns and Butter," *Business Week*, March 12, 1979.
4. Lewis Powell, "Attack on the Free Enterprise System: Confidential Memorandum for the US Chamber of Commerce," August 23, 1971, Lewis Powell Papers, Washington and Lee University, http://law2.wlu.edu/deptimages/Powell%20Archives/PowellMemorandumPrinted.pdf.
5. Dan Clawson, Alan Neustadtl, and James Bearden, "The Logic of Business Unity: Corporate Contributions to the 1980 Congressional Elections," *American Sociological Review* 51, no. 6 (1986): 797–811.
6. Benjamin C. Waterhouse, *Lobbying America: The Politics of Business from Nixon to NAFTA* (Princeton, NJ: Princeton University Press, 2013); Allan J. Lichtman, *White Protestant Nation: The Rise of the American Conservative Movement* (New York: Atlantic Monthly Press, 2008), 338.
7. On the larger context of right-wing think tanks during the 1970s, see Kim Phillips-Fein, *Invisible Hands: The Businessmen's Crusade against the New Deal* (New York: W. W. Norton, 2009), chs. 7–11; David Brock, *The Republican Noise Machine: Right-Wing Media and How It Corrupts Democracy* (New York: Crown, 2004); and Alan Crawford, *Thunder on the Right: The "New Right" and the Politics of Resentment* (New York: Pantheon, 1980).
8. Robert William Fogel, *The Fourth Great Awakening and the Future of Egalitarianism* (Chicago: University of Chicago Press, 2000).

9 Daniel K. Williams, *God's Own Party: The Making of the Christian Right* (New York: Oxford University Press, 2010), 160.
10 David Frum, *How We Got Here: The 70's; The Decade That Brought You Modern Life—For Better or Worse* (New York: Basic Books, 2000), 148–55.
11 Jerome L. Himmelstein, *To the Right: The Transformation of American Conservatism* (Berkeley: University of California Press, 1990), 115.
12 Williams, *God's Own Party*, 94.
13 Quoted in Dominic Sandbrook, *Mad as Hell: The Crisis of the 1970s and the Rise of the Populist Right* (New York: Knopf, 2011), 177.
14 Kevin M. Kruse, *One Nation under God: How Corporate America Invented Christian America* (New York: Basic Books, 2015), 246.
15 Richard M. Nixon, "First Inaugural Address," January 20, 1969, American Presidency Project, University of California, Santa Barbara, http://presidency.proxied.lsit.ucsb.edu/ws/index.php?pid=1941&st=&st1=.
16 Kruse, *One Nation under God*, 263–73.
17 Regarding Graham's attitudes toward racial segregation and his complicated relationship with Martin Luther King Jr., see Steven P. Miller, *Billy Graham and the Rise of the Republican South* (Philadelphia: University of Pennsylvania Press, 2009), 90–92.
18 Kruse, *One Nation under God*, 37–38
19 Grant Wacker, *America's Pastor: Billy Graham and the Shaping of a Nation* (Cambridge, MA: Belknap Press of Harvard University Press, 2014), 154. See also Jane Wolfe, *The Murchisons* (New York: St. Martin's, 1989), 233.
20 Lemuel Nelson Bell to Frank P. Stelling, December 18, 1971, Lemuel Nelson Bell Collection, Box 41, Folder 19, Billy Graham Center, Wheaton College. See also Darren E. Grem, "Christianity Today, J. Howard Pew, and the Business of Conservative Evangelicalism," *Enterprise and Society* 15, no. 2 (2014): 337–79.
21 The quoted phrase is from a study by Louis Bolce and Gerald De Maio, as presented in Kevin Phillips, *American Theocracy: The Peril and Politics of Radical Religion, Oil, and Borrowed Money in the Twenty-First Century* (New York: Viking, 2006), 184.
22 Phillips, *American Theocracy*, 184.
23 Robert C. Liebman, "Mobilizing the Moral Majority," in *The New Christian Right: Mobilization and Legitimation*, ed. Robert C. Liebman and Robert Wuthnow (New York: Aldine, 1983), 51.
24 Liebman, "Mobilizing the Moral Majority," 50–53. See also John G. Turner, *Bill Bright and Campus Crusade for Christ: The Renewal of Evangelicalism in Postwar America* (Chapel Hill: University of North Carolina Press, 2008).
25 Lichtman, *White Protestant Nation*, 342.
26 Darren Elliott Grem, "The Blessings of Business: Corporate America and Conservative Evangelicalism in the Sunbelt Age, 1945–2000" (PhD diss., University of Georgia, 2010), 199.
27 Darren Dochuk, *From Bible Belt to Sun Belt: Plain Folk Religion, Grassroots Politics, and the Rise of Evangelical Conservatism* (New York: Norton, 2011), 386. These activities were also undertaken by Bill Bright, according to Dochuk.

28. John S. Saloma III, *Ominous Politics: The New Conservative Labyrinth* (New York: Hill and Wang, 1984), 54.
29. Lichtman, *White Protestant Nation*, 347. Regarding the history of Falwell's relationship with the local business community, see Daniel K. Williams, "Jerry Falwell's Sunbelt Politics: The Regional Origins of the Moral Majority," *Journal of Policy History* 22, no. 2 (2010): 125–47.
30. Frances Fitzgerald quoted in Michael Lienesch, *Redeeming America: Piety and Politics in the New Christian Right* (Chapel Hill: University of North Carolina Press, 1993), 11.
31. Dirk Smillie, *Falwell Inc.: Inside a Religious, Political, Educational, and Business Empire* (New York: St. Martin's, 2008), 105.
32. Grem, "Blessings of Business," 199.
33. Grem, "Blessings of Business," 159, 161, 187, 191, 203, 210–11. Additional information on business funding can be found in Deborah Huntington and Ruth Kaplan, "Corporate Ties to the Evangelical Christian Groups: A Report to the World Student Christian Federation," August 28, 1980, unpublished report in Group Research Inc. Papers, Box 125, Folder 8, Columbia University, New York.
34. Lichtman, *White Protestant Nation*, 313–14.
35. Lichtman, *White Protestant Nation*, 314.
36. Regarding Bryant's and Schlafly's activism, see Anita Bryant, *The Anita Bryant Story: The Survival of our Nation's Families and the Threat of Militant Homosexuality* (Grand Rapids, MI: Revell, 1977); and Donald T. Critchlow, *Phyllis Schlafly and Grassroots Conservatism: A Woman's Crusade* (Princeton, NJ: Princeton University Press, 2008).
37. Russ Bellant, *The Coors Connection: How Coors Family Philanthropy Undermines Democratic Pluralism* (Boston: South End, 1991), 56.
38. Robert D. Putnam, *Bowling Alone: The Collapse and Revival of American Community* (New York: Simon and Schuster, 2000), 161.
39. J. Brooks Flippen, *Jimmy Carter, the Politics of Family, and the Rise of the Religious Right* (Athens: University of Georgia Press, 2011), 108–11, 210–11, 321.
40. Flippen, *Jimmy Carter*, 161, 250.
41. See Robert Freedman, "The Religious Right and the Carter Administration," *Historical Journal* 48, no. 1 (2005): 238–39; and Joseph Crespino, "Civil Rights and the Religious Right," in *Rightward Bound: Making America Conservative in the 1970s*, ed. Bruce J. Schulman and Julian E. Zelizer (Cambridge, MA: Harvard University Press, 2008), 97–105.
42. Flippen, *Jimmy Carter*, 157, 166–67, 250.
43. Liebman, "Mobilizing the Moral Majority," 54. The two million registered voters included those registered by the Moral Majority as well as its affiliated organizations Christian Voice and Religious Roundtable.
44. Smillie, *Falwell Inc.*, 105. Note that the time frame for these contributions is not specified.
45. Bellant, *Coors Connection*, 50.
46. Jerome L. Himmelstein, "The New Right," in *The New Christian Right: Mobilization and Legitimation*, ed. Robert C. Liebman and Robert Wuthnow (New York: Aldine, 1983), 26.

47 Himmelstein, "New Right," 19; Laura Kalman, *Right Star Rising: A New Politics, 1974–1980* (New York: Norton, 2010), 273–74.
48 Clyde Wilcox, "Blacks and the New Christian Right: Support for the Moral Majority and Pat Robertson among Washington, DC Blacks," *Review of Religious Research* 32, no. 1 (1990): 43–55.
49 On Christian Zionism, see Joe. L. Kincheloe and George Staley, "The Menachem Begin-Jerry Falwell Connection: A Revolution in Fundamentalism," *Journal of Thought* 17, no. 2 (1982): 35–39. See also "For AJC," memorandum from Irving Kristol, undated, probably 1981, Box 9, Folder 28, Irving Kristol Papers, Wisconsin Historical Society, Madison.
50 John Fisher, president of the American Security Council, was "one of the political members of the [Religious] Roundtable's 'Council of 56,'" according to Saloma, *Ominous Politics*, 61. For more information on Fisher and the Roundtable, see "A Third Religious Force Is Organized by the Right Wing," *Group Research Reports*, November 28, 1979; and Bellant, *Coors Connections*, 50. Regarding the close connections between the Religious Roundtable and the Moral Majority, see Robert Wuthnow, *The Restructuring of American Religion: Society and Faith since World War II* (Princeton, NJ: Princeton University Press, 1988), 205.
51 Quoted in Fred Halliday, *The Making of the Second Cold War* (London: Verso, 1983), 116.
52 Phillips, *American Theocracy*, 192.
53 Quoted in Phillips, *American Theocracy*, 124.
54 Ronald Reagan, "The New Republican Party" (speech at the 4th annual CPAC Convention, February 6, 1977), https://patriotpost.us/pages/430-ronald-reagan-the-new-republican-party.
55 Marshall Berman, "Postmodernism," in *Oxford Companion to Politics of the World*, ed. Joel Krieger (New York: Oxford University Press, 2001), 686.

10. AMONG NEW BELIEVERS
Religion, Gender, and National Identity in the Netherlands
EVA MIDDEN

The perceived struggle between so-called Western secular values and non-Western Islamic extremism is one of the most divisive political issues in contemporary Western Europe. The influx of refugees from Africa and the Middle East and violent attacks in Paris and Brussels have fueled harsh debates about the possibility of integration and about the centrality of values such as "emancipation" and "freedom" to national identity. Amid this heated sociopolitical context, there is a growing number of women converting to Islam across Europe.[1] As religion is generally not registered, there is no exact information on the number of converts, but it is estimated that there are approximately seventeen thousand in the Netherlands alone.[2] These converts occupy a controversial position in European societies, as they are often born and raised in Europe and have voluntarily chosen a religion that is heavily scrutinized in public debates. Women who convert to Islam are often confronted with questions about both national identity (are they still "French," "English," or "Dutch"?) and emancipation (are they making conscious and freely willed choices?).

In this chapter, I analyze the Dutch television show *Van Hagelslag naar Halal* (*From Dutch Chocolate Sprinkles to Halal*) to demonstrate what popular representations of women converts can teach us about the gendered entanglements of religion and national identity in the Netherlands. On this show, a group of Dutch converts to Islam and their mothers travel to Jordan, to work on their strained relationships and to develop mutual understandings. Their conversations are staged by the producers, so while the program does not necessarily accurately represent the women's opinions and experiences, it is an important example of how religion (especially Islam) is represented in the Netherlands' mainstream media. By enforcing the narrative arc of "turning away from," the TV show *Dutch Sprinkles* demonstrates how in/exclusion from the Dutch national body increasingly hinges upon Islam's supposedly fundamental incompatibility with Dutch culture and values—especially the value of "emancipation." In converting to Islam, converts are represented as having lost their emancipated "Dutchness." Drawing attention to (and deconstructing) this relationship will make it possible to produce alternative theories about the gendered politics of emancipation and their relationship to religion, secularism, and national belonging.

From Dutch Chocolate Sprinkles to Halal through Critical Discourse Analysis

In the television program *From Dutch Chocolate Sprinkles to Halal*, three young Dutch women who have converted to Islam travel to Jordan with their mothers. According to the website of the broadcasting organization, conversion has serious consequences for family relations: converts often feel rejected and misunderstood and parents are worried about the future of their children. Since the conversions, the mothers and daughters in the show find it difficult to communicate with each other, and they fight about many issues. While to a certain extent these fights and misunderstandings are related to the new daily practices of the daughters, such as prayer and eating halal food, their staged discussions also reflect larger sociopolitical issues that are currently at stake in the Netherlands. Throughout the program, the women talk about their personal experiences and relations while they visit various sights and people in Jordan. The end goal of the show is for the mothers to be present when their daughters pronounce their love for Allah at the Abu Darweesh mosque in Amman.[3]

The show was presented by Arie Boomsma, a famous Dutch television host with a Christian background, who is known for his television work on charged societal issues and for breaking certain taboos. Prior to *Dutch Sprinkles*, he made

De Roze Wildernis (*The Pink Wilderness*), for which he traveled to Argentina with four gay boys and their fathers with a similar intention of improving strained parent-child relationships but in relation to the boys' sexualities. The first episode of *Dutch Sprinkles* was aired in 2015 and had approximately 420,000 viewers, which is rather average in the Netherlands.[4] But while the show was not extremely popular, it addressed a theme that was highly contested in the Netherlands at the time. There was also a good deal of public discussion after the first episode, including reports by several online media outlets in which viewers criticized the show, as they "could not understand" the choices of the converted women.[5]

I draw upon Critical Discourse Analysis (CDA) to investigate the assumptions behind the show's representations of gender, national identity, and religion/secularism. The use of CDA, particularly the work of Norman Fairclough, is helpful for its emphasis on the power relations that underlie social relations. Particularly relevant is Fairclough's perspective on "common sense," which he defines as "an implicit philosophy in the practical activities of social life, backgrounded and taken for granted."[6] Dominant ideologies become common sense through processes of naturalization and standardization, whereupon they often invisibilize and sustain unequal power relations in discourse. This insight is crucial as I consider the ideologies that inform and underlie the commonsense standpoints and arguments advanced in *Dutch Sprinkles*.

Turning to and Turning From: The Gendered Politics of Conversion

Recent scholarship on conversion to Islam challenges popular understandings of the intentions and processes behind conversions as well as their varied impact on converts' identities. Contrary to what many believe, people do not only convert for a possible romantic partner but also because an independent search brought them to Islam. Moreover, while it is often believed that changes related to the conversion to Islam are radical and instantaneous, more recent scholars refer to conversion as a process, even though there are differing options as to how to understand this process.[7] In this vein, Oskar Verkaaik argues that scholars should not approach conversion as a "turning from and to," as Lewis Rambo defines it; converts do turn to something new, but they do not always reject something old. Conversion is very often a bricolage, in which old and new practices of faith are brought together. Understood as such, converts may be much more flexible than they are often given credit for, and regularly alternate between phases of faith and doubt.[8]

This nuanced conception of conversion is largely absent in *Dutch Sprinkles*, which primarily advances a "turning from and to" perspective on conversion wherein "old" identities are rejected and lost as "new" identities are embraced. This approach is rhetorically and gastronomically gestured toward in the show's title, as Dutch chocolate sprinkles are cast aside in favor of halal food, even though halal-observant Muslims have no religious imperative to stop eating chocolate. By extension, the converts' acts of "turning to" Islam are framed as acts of "turning from" not only their families but also the Dutch nation and its core values. The sections that follow are oriented around several of the key value-laden terms and debates that emerge throughout the show and shape this overarching perspective.

Dutchness as Secular

Dutch Sprinkles primarily emphasizes the perspectives and feelings of the mothers who have supposedly been "turned away" from. These mothers repeatedly define their concerns as a matter of not only personal but also Dutch national identity. To this end, they often frame their critiques of Islam and their daughters' practices as more general critiques of religion and its encroachment upon the secular values and spaces that they perceive as foundational to Dutchness. This emphasis underscores the grand finale visit to the mosque in Amman that the show has presumably been building toward all season, where the mothers are invited to join their daughters in prayer. This trip is framed as not only about mother-daughter support or tourism but about the mothers' willingness to engage, or reconcile themselves with, their daughters' religion. Religion is cast as something undesirable that the mothers have been forced to deal with, either positively or negatively, because of their daughter's choices. Several of the mothers will only attend reluctantly, if at all. Their hesitancy, and the reconciliatory framework more generally, resonates with Dutch debates about religion in the public sphere, where it is often argued that people do not want to "encounter" (or be bothered with) other people's faiths, especially Islam.

Mother Ingrid's comments about a visit to the mosque demonstrate how valuing secularism and a secular/religion binary is a vehicle for critiquing Islam and expressing concerns about its incompatibility with Dutch national identity. Ingrid begins more neutrally: "I am not a visitor of houses for prayer. I am not religious, I do not have any affection for any religion, so I do not really have any reasons to go to a mosque."[9] Ingrid proceeds to establish fundamental incompatibilities between Dutch culture and Islam. For example, when the mothers are asked at the end of the show to join their daughters at the mosque, she says, "When I cannot walk in as Ingrid, and cannot walk out as Ingrid, I am not going to do it. I am very attached to my own identity, I just am a Dutch woman, and I do not wear a headscarf."[10] Here, Ingrid makes connections between her personal (gendered, national) identity and its incompatibility with Muslim practices: as a Dutch woman she does not wear a headscarf. She claims not to have a problem with the headscarf itself, but she does describe it as something that is incompatible with her particular identity. A few minutes later, she adds, "This is my daughter's faith, even though I respect her wishes and happiness. If they would ask me in the Netherlands to go to a Reformed Church, wear a hat, and a long dress with flowers, I would also not do it. . . . I will not wear a headscarf for anyone."[11] Hence, Ingrid suggests that it is not just Islam she wants to distance herself from but any form of religion that tells her how to dress and behave. To an extent, Ingrid's standpoint can be viewed as a more general secular resistance against all religious institutions, a perspective that dissolves the specificity of Islam. Ingrid's defense, however, reflects a fairly common critique of Islam, as it is often considered the faith that challenges secular values the most. As Verkaaik explains, the desire for freedom and individualism in the Netherlands is for a large part defined as antireligious, and this antireligious attitude now turns against the "religion of migrants": Islam. Secularism, therefore, defines both the Dutch self and religious intolerance toward the Muslim Other.[12]

Emancipation and Loss

The mothers in the show consistently express the fear that their daughters will lose aspects of their identities through adherence to Islam, while their daughters explain that converting to Islam—and honoring modesty laws more specifically—is not about becoming another person but about being a better person. The fear of "identity loss" therefore becomes an affective and ideological framework for the mothers (and also arguably the show's producers) to link their daughters' newfound Muslim practices with broader national political debates and issues. When referencing their daughters' supposed "identity loss," the mothers generally do not invoke previously held religious identities but the intertwined gender and national identities that Islam presumably threatens. According to Karin van Nieuwkerk, the image of the Muslim woman without rights is ingrained in Dutch people's perceptions of Islam and at the same time explicitly opposed to a Dutch self-image of being liberal, free, and emancipated.[13] The values of emancipation and equality are linked to a European Dutch secularism, while Islam is equated with oppression and gender inequality, and therefore incompatible with Dutchness.

Unsurprisingly, the converts' clothing and approach to modesty emerge as a touchstone for conversations about "identity loss" and "emancipation." For example, in episode 2, heated conversations emerge around the hijab or headscarf, one of the most prominent symbols of Islam that is often stereotyped in the Netherlands as both "non-Dutch" and a "sign of oppression."[14] Exemplifying these views, two mothers explicitly express fear that their daughters will "lose their identity" by wearing headscarves.[15] Nour's mother, Petra, says she is afraid that when her daughter starts wearing a headscarf, she will not be allowed to express her opinion anymore.[16] In Petra's eyes, the headscarf is inherently oppressive; it therefore follows that her daughter cannot be emancipated (i.e., free to express her ideas) while wearing one. These concerns are further linked to "Dutchness"; because emancipation is considered to be a central Dutch value, Nour's mother believes that her daughter risks losing part of her Dutch national identity. Ingrid adds that she feels shame when she walks next to her daughter, who is wearing a headscarf. She explains that the headscarf is not something she wants to be associated with.[17] In both examples, the headscarf is viewed as a symbol that represents values that are in tension—and even incompatible—with the mothers' Dutch values. In contrast, Nour talks about the headscarf in very practical terms, describing it as something that protects her from harassment and makes men more inclined to listen to her as a person rather than look at her appearance. Unlike her mother, Nour does not make a connection between the headscarf and her national identity, nor does she describe it as limiting her freedom of expression but as enabling it.

Questions of "emancipation" and "loss" return in episode 4 when the mothers and daughters discuss Islam's rules and rituals. Several of the mothers do not understand why Dutch girls, who presumably enjoy great freedom, would choose the restrictions of Islam. In response, Nour explains that what the Dutch generally consider to be "freedom" does not feel like freedom to her: "I have always been bothered by the pressures of society. Going out is not pleasurable for me. I find it very negative and banal. When I am in Amsterdam, it makes me sad. I do not see it as freedom that women have to be naked all the time. I see freedom as something else and I find that difficult in the Netherlands."[18] The fact that women in the West can show nudity is not freedom to Nour; she wants a different kind of freedom. Lorena expresses similar views in episode 5, asking, "What is the value of wearing a miniskirt?"[19] Hence, Lorena also tries to point out that different women might want or value different things, and that what is important for some women might not be for others.[20]

The connection between conversion and loss, therefore, hinges in large part on a particular, secular European interpretation of women's emancipation. By choosing a faith that is considered to be particularly at odds with secularism, the converts are automatically understood to have lost or given up their "emancipated" status and values. This binary can be complicated by pointing to the emancipatory and even *self-identified* feminist struggles of some religious Muslim women, for whom emancipation is not necessarily secular in character and for whom religion is often an important source of inspiration in the struggle for emancipation.[21] In some cases, Muslim women also explicitly redefine what emancipation means by focusing more on sexual difference and less on equality as sameness, or by shifting attention away from the individual by recognizing women's positions within the family.[22] In other words, gender oppression can mean different things to different women, but emancipation can also be defined in different ways (i.e., having the choice to do what you want or being equal to). Some Muslim women in the Netherlands indicate that for them, emancipation has to take place in cooperation with their husbands and children, that emancipation also entails other things than merely paid work, and that they are not prepared to give up their religion in exchange for emancipation.[23]

The converts in *Dutch Sprinkles*, however, are given little opportunity to expound upon these or other experiences and perspectives. The prescribed narrative of "turning away" frames them through their deviation from the secular norm and largely prevents more complex and multifaceted perspectives on religion and gender from coming to the fore. They are mostly confronted with challenging questions about "why" they do certain things, wherein they must explain how their faith relates to the secular norm. These concerns dovetail with Saba Mahmood's famous assertion that religious women's experiences and strategies should not be simply interpreted as either resistance or submission. Rather, scholars should redefine the concept of agency and adjust it to a situation in which "the subject's own desires and socially prescribed performances cannot be easily presumed and where submission to certain forms of (external) authority is a condition for achieving the subject's potentiality."[24] This sense of religion as a means of "achieving potentiality" is at times gestured toward in the Dutch converts' explanations to their mothers. As in the modesty-related conversations, the daughters attempt to frame their conversions as a means of improving their lives, not turning away from them. This outlook, and the fundamental difference between the mothers' and daughters' perspectives, emerges in a conversation between Nour and a Jordanian woman who tells Nour, "I don't think you should ever stop being who you are. You were a beautiful person before. Why should you stop?"[25] This affects Nour's mother, Petra, who is afraid that Nour will become a different person. But both Nour and the Jordanian woman also explain that their faith is not about being a *different person* but about becoming a *better version of yourself*.[26] Converting to Islam, Nour explains, enriched her life. The Islamic faith provides her with strength and hope. When given the opportunity, the other daughters also state that their conversions reflect what they always believed or have felt coming for a long time rather than sudden or radical transformations.

Religion as Culture

As the mothers repeatedly frame the Islamic religion as fundamentally at odds with Dutch national culture, they often read their daughters' religious practices through a flattened, monolithic conception of both Islam and the "East." In one exemplary exchange, Petra says she is afraid that her daughter, Nour, might want to wear a burqa in the future, and Nour responds that such an interpretation of Islam does not fit the cultures she lives in and identifies with. Nour describes herself as part of both Dutch and Moroccan cultures, as her boyfriend is Moroccan, and says that the burqa and niqab are too far removed from both cultures.[27] In a letter to her mother, Nour again attenuates the difference between national culture and religion when she says: "You have many questions about faith, but most of the time they are actually about culture. When you for example ask me why certain women are oppressed, I cannot give any answers to you, because I do not know those countries and cultures. You can better ask me whether I am oppressed, so that I can talk about myself."[28] Nour not only states that there are differences between Muslim women's positions in different countries, but she also requests that her mother see her as the individual she always has been and still is. Public discourse on Islam arguably shapes this conversation: one could say that Nour is asking her mother to look at how she practices Islam rather than adhere to generic Dutch public discourses on Islamic practices. In light of the previously identified cultural emphasis on emancipation, it is also worth noting that Nour suggests that her mother is not letting her speak for herself, so Nour is reclaiming her individual agency by asking (or challenging) her mother to "ask me . . . whether I am oppressed."

The conflation of religion, nationality, and culture that Nour struggles to address—and find her place within—dovetails with research on the societal pressures faced by many European converts to Islam as they attempt to navigate prescribed relationships between religion and secularism, culture and nationalism. As Tina Jensen argues, converts to Islam in Denmark often describe themselves as "being squeezed between two sides," or "split between national culture and the culture of Muslims."[29] They do not feel they fully belong to the Muslim community because they are still seen as Danish, and they feel, and are treated as if, they lost their Danish identity after conversion to Islam.

These converts, it should be noted, can reify troubling European prejudices and racism when faced with these pressures; Esra Özyürek argues that because of the marginalization of Islam and Muslims, German converts to Islam often dissociate themselves from Muslim *migrants* and deliberately present themselves as *German* Muslims, or even denationalized and detraditionalized Muslims. However, Özyürek also observes that converts' renegotiation of various identities can, in Fatima El-Tayeb's terms, "queer ethnicity" by building communities based on the shared experience of multiple contradictory positionalities.[30] This multivalent perspective on identity and community is gestured toward in Nour's assertion that she (together with her boyfriend) affiliates with both Moroccan and Dutch cultures. But it is mostly impossible to read the *Dutch Sprinkles* converts' choices and experiences as "queering ethnicity," since the televised narratives about their conversion are structured as a "turning away from" the Netherlands and a "taking a step backward" from the enlightened secular present. Asking the converts questions about "how" they have dealt with conversion, or what they believe they have gained from their conversion, would make their perspectives and opinions more visible.

Islam and Conversion through a Secular Gaze

Dutch Sprinkles frames and interprets the converts' experiences not only in relation to secular Dutch nationals but also in relation to Muslims from Jordan during their trip. While the purpose of the trip was purportedly to bring the women closer together through the process of getting to know other Muslim women and families, the Dutch visitors and program viewers are also confronted with what is arguably an Orientalist perspective on the Middle East and Islam. The image of the Orient is probably the deepest and most recurring image of Europe's Other. As Edward Said famously observed, "European culture gained in strength and identity by setting itself off against the Orient as a sort of surrogate and even underground self."[31] Jordan is cast as a place for the Dutch Europeans' self-discovery and exploration as well as for observing the "authentic home" of the Muslim faith that the mothers find so unnerving. On the trip, differences between Western Europe and the Middle East, urban and rural, secular and religious, are often flattened and framed temporally as matters of "progress."

A gendered Orientalist perspective on Jordanian Muslim women emerges through the visit that the program organizes to "Jordanian families in the countryside." Although the Dutch women praise these families' hospitality, their contact is also difficult because of language issues and cultural differences. It is not entirely clear whether the program producers intentionally obfuscate the differences between culture and religion and the varieties of Islam in different geographical regions, but through the staged visits to these specific families, Islam is associated with "backwardness" and misogyny. These stereotypes emerge through the Dutch mothers' questions and declarations about Islam's "harmful practices." For example, during their visit with a Jordanian family, Nour's mother proclaims, "The men seem to decide everything and the women are in the kitchen and do not even come to see us. I see oppression here."[32] She compares the lives of these Jordanian women to life in prison and expresses fear for her daughter's future. To the Dutch mothers, the rural Muslim Jordanian women are emblematic of the "backwardness" of Islam and the Orient.[33] To the converted daughters, however, the visit seems out of place. They do not identify with these Jordanian families, their faith, or their practices, and they wonder aloud why they should engage with them. They do not, however, differentiate themselves from the Jordanian families in a derogatory way. The daughters explain on several occasions that for them, Islam is something else; they do not experience Islam as something that limits them but as something that enriches their lives.

The Dutch women later meet with Jordanian women again, but this time in the city of Amman, where each mother-daughter pair is connected with an "independent Muslim woman from Amman."[34] These women are highly educated, have careers, do not wear headscarves, and seem to have a more liberal interpretation of Islam than the Dutch converts, whose mothers were very excited about meeting the women from Amman. During a group discussion, Ingrid says she found the meeting very refreshing: "The woman called herself a liberal Muslim, . . . did not pray five times a day. . . . I loved to hear this, and I told her I love her, this was completely my style, this is also a possibility!"[35] One of the Dutch converted daughters, Lorena, says that her mother also loved the Jordanian woman from Amman: "My mother was completely . . . yes. . . . She would have loved to take Arouk home. . . . Thank you, Arouk [*she says cynically*]."[36] After the visit, the Dutch mothers state that they would like to see a bit more flexibility in how their daughters practice their faith, but the daughters are very clear about the fact that they want to practice how they see fit. In a discussion at the end of the episode, the show's presenter asks the daughters if the fact that they were not born as Muslims makes them more insecure about their faith, suggesting that this is the reason why they are stricter practitioners.[37] The daughters fiercely disagree for several reasons. Nour argues that for her, conversion was actually a very slow process and she is still thinking about how to deal with issues like veiling. Lorena argues that the Qur'an forbids certain things for a reason and that is why she follows these restrictions. When the presenter asks them whether faith is a set of rules or something in their hearts, Saroya says that she follows the rules with love. For her, there is no opposition between the "set of rules" and her heart.

How can we understand these two different meetings with Jordanian people? One could argue that by bringing the women in contact with both more conservative families from the countryside and more liberal women from the city, the program viewers are presented with different interpretations of Islam and hence not just the prejudiced understanding of Islam that I touched upon. However, when we look at the various meetings from the perspective of the converted daughters, another argument emerges. In neither of these meetings is the viewer encouraged to identify with the converts. When they visit the countryside, the converts' choices are questioned through what could be called an Orientalist perspective on Islam. Why would they want to live a life in which they will never be equal or free anymore? When they meet the "liberal Muslim women" from the city, the converts are questioned again. This time, they are represented as rigid and insecure because of their conversion. For the first time in the program, the topic of debate was not Islam and how it relates to other aspects of their identity but conversion itself and how this process influenced the way the daughters practice and experience their faith. Hence, conversion itself is presented as inherently conservative.

The daughters strongly disagree with this representation and talk about their conversion much more in relation to hope and strength. They also describe the strict regulations of the Qur'an as helpful to them rather than restrictive. Hence, almost never during the show is the converted women's faith discussed in positive terms or as something that the women themselves can endow with meaning. Moreover, only rarely during the show are the viewers encouraged to identify with the converted women; the gaze is always a voyeuristic gaze, through which they are subjected to control and curiosity.[38] The viewer, in turn, does not get to see the converted women as active agents who consciously give new meaning to their lives.

Conversion in the Netherlands

The religion/secularism divide in the Netherlands produces specific ideas about what it means to be Dutch, and gender plays a crucial role in these processes of identity formation and in/exclusion from the national body. It is often assumed that gender emancipation is inextricably linked to both secularism and Dutch national identity, while religion is viewed as a threat to emancipation and therefore Dutchness.

When we look at how the TV show *From Dutch Chocolate Sprinkles to Halal* framed and organized the trip to Jordan and the discussions, several things stand out. First, throughout the show, conversion to Islam is presented and discussed as something through which people, in this case the three girls, turn away from something and thus lose something. Rather than focusing on what the women gain from their conversion, or how they practically negotiate their new positions in society, the converts are scrutinized for choosing a religion that makes them "turn away" from old identities, most of all when it comes to gender. Second, on several occasions the show approaches Islam more as a culture than a religion, or at least the differences between culture and religion are conflated. Finally, the gaze in this show is a voyeuristic one. The converted women are subjected to control and curiosity; never does the viewer get to identify with these women. Asking the converts questions about how they dealt with conversion, or to describe their desires in life and what they believe they have gained from converting, would show a deeper interest in these women's choices. Instead they have to repeatedly explain themselves to the non-Muslim program makers and by extension to an intended, presumably non-Muslim Dutch audience.

Untangling debates about national identity and emancipation makes it possible to understand how secularism and religion are defined as each other's opposites. The anxieties and fears that played a role throughout the TV show were mainly focused on the convert's futures as Muslim women (i.e., the assumption that Muslim women cannot be emancipated) and the idea that the converts supposedly lost a part of their identity (i.e., by becoming Muslim, they became less Dutch). In this context, the choice for Islam is seen as a choice for not only a specific religion but also a specific gender regime, one that is considered incompatible with Dutch values. One could say that explicitly choosing Islam makes them challengers of the secular values that are considered such an important part of Dutch identity. By extension, it would be interesting to investigate to what extent people respond differently to men who convert to Islam. Further research is also needed on the relationship between religion/

secularism, emancipation, and national identity in different national contexts, but from the analysis given here it becomes clear that in order to understand the divide between religion and secularism in the Dutch context, emancipation is a key concept that helps us understand how the dichotomy is produced and what its effects are.

NOTES

1. See, for example, Karin van Nieuwkerk, "Gender, Conversion, and Islam: A Comparison of Online and Offline Conversion Narratives," in *Women Embracing Islam: Gender and Conversion in the West*, ed. Karin van Nieuwkerk (Austin: University of Texas Press, 2006), 95–120.
2. "Aantal Bekeerlingen in Nederland en België (Statistiek)," *Stichting Bekeerling* (blog), accessed July 24, 2020, http://www.stichtingbekeerling.nl/aantal-bekeerlingen-in-nederland-en-belgie/.
3. *Van Hagelslag naar Halal*, accessed July 24, 2020, http://www.npo.nl/van-hagelslag-naar-halal/POMS_S_KRO_2466706.
4. "*Van Hagelslag naar Halal*, het Nieuwe Programma van Arie Boomsma, Is Dinsdag van Start Gegaan Met 420.000 Kijkers," NU.nl, November 25, 2018, https://www.nu.nl/media/4171435/420000-kijkers-nieuw-programma-arie-boomsma.html.
5. Kirsten Zijderveld, "Onbegrip Voor Bekeerde Moslima's Bij 'Van Hagelslag naar Halal,'" Linda.nl, November 25, 2015, https://www.lindanieuws.nl/nieuws/fragmentgemist/onbegrip-voor-bekeerde-moslimas-bij-van-hagelslag-naar-halal/.
6. Norman Fairclough, *Language and Power* (London: Longman, 2001), 70.
7. See, for example, Anna Mansson McGinty, *Becoming Muslim: Western Women's Conversions to Islam* (New York: Palgrave Macmillan, 2006); Nieuwkerk, "Gender, Conversion, and Islam"; Najem V. Vroon, "Sisters in Islam: Women's Conversion and the Politics of Belonging; A Dutch Case Study" (PhD diss., University of Amsterdam, the Netherlands, 2014).
8. Oskar Verkaaik, *Ritueel Burgerschap: Een Essay over Nationalisme en Secularisme in Nederland* (Amsterdam: Amsterdam University Press, 2009), 132.
9. *Van Hagelslag naar Halal*, episode 6, min. 1.
10. *Van Hagelslag naar Halal*, episode 6, min. 12.
11. *Van Hagelslag naar Halal*, episode 6, min. 13.
12. Verkaaik, *Ritueel Burgerschap*.
13. Karin van Nieuwkerk, "Veils and Wooden Clogs Do Not Go Together," *Ethnos* 69, no. 2 (2004): 229–46.
14. Nieuwkerk, "Veils and Wooden Clogs," 235.
15. E.g., *Van Hagelslag naar Halal*, episode 2, min. 18.
16. *Van Hagelslag naar Halal*, episode 2, min. 22.
17. *Van Hagelslag naar Halal*, episode 2, min. 22.
18. *Van Hagelslag naar Halal*, episode 4, min. 28.
19. *Van Hagelslag naar Halal*, episode 5, min. 14.

20 See also Saba Mahmood, *Politics of Piety: The Islamic Revival and the Feminist Subject*. (Princeton, NJ: Princeton University Press, 2005).
21 Eva Midden, "Rethinking Dutchness: Learning from the Intersections between Religion, Gender and National Identity after Conversion to Islam," *Social Compass* 65, no. 5 (2018): 684–700.
22 Eva Midden and Sandra Ponzanesi, "Digital Faiths: An Analysis of Online Practices of Muslim Women in the Netherlands," *Women's Studies International Forum* 1, pt. 3 (2013): 197–204.
23 Eva Midden, "The Arena of Religion: Malala and Contemporary Feminism," in *Doing Gender in Media, Art and Culture*, ed. Rosemarie Buikema and Liedeke Plate (London: Routledge, 2018), 24–36.
24 Mahmood, *Politics of Piety*, 31.
25 *Van Hagelslag naar Halal*, episode 5, min. 19.
26 *Van Hagelslag naar Halal*, episode 5, min. 21.
27 *Van Hagelslag naar Halal*, episode 6, min. 8.
28 *Van Hagelslag naar Halal*, episode 6, min. 9.
29 Tina G. Jensen, "To Be 'Danish,' Becoming 'Muslim': Contestations of National Identity?," *Journal of Ethnic and Migration Studies* 34, no. 3 (2008): 400.
30 Esra Özyürek, *Being German, Becoming Muslim: Race, Religion, and Conversion in the New Europe* (Princeton, NJ: Princeton University Press, 2015); Fatima El-Tayeb, *European Others: Queering Ethnicity in Postnational Europe* (Minneapolis: University of Minnesota Press, 2011).
31 Edward Said, *Orientalism* (New York: Pantheon Books, 1978).
32 *Van Hagelslag naar Halal*, episode 4, min. 10.
33 Meyda Yeğenoğlu, , "Sartorial Fabric-ations: Enlightenment and Western Feminism," in *Postcolonialism, Feminism and Religious Discourse*, ed. Laura E. Donaldson and Kwok Pui-Lan (New York: Routledge, 2002), 83.
34 *Van Hagelslag naar Halal*, episode 5, min. 10.
35 *Van Hagelslag naar Halal*, episode 5, min. 24.
36 *Van Hagelslag naar Halal*, episode 5, min. 23.
37 *Van Hagelslag naar Halal*, episode 5, min. 25.
38 Laura Mulvey, "Visual Pleasure and Narrative Cinema," in *Film Theory and Criticism: Introductory Readings*, ed. Leo Braudy and Marshall Cohen (New York: Oxford University Press, 1999), 833–44.

PART III.
POLITICAL BELONGING

Keyword: Faith
ORI GOLDBERG

When asked to explain "time," Saint Augustine famously said: "What then is time? If no one asks me, I know what it is. If I wish to explain it to him who asks, I do not know."[1] This "explanation" rings true when one wishes to explain "faith" as well. In fact, it rings even truer when one wishes to consider how faith inspires political belonging in the modern world.

It has been common, in monotheistic traditions over the past 250 years, to think of two main dynamics through which faith engenders political belonging—universalism and ideology. Perhaps we could think of these two ways as two attempts at a definition of truth, each validated by the act of believing. This act creates a place for these two truths in the world, reinforces them and manifests them in their purest form. Faith is the *phronesis* of both ideological truth and universal truth, the quality that, through practice, establishes real and binding concepts of right and wrong.

Universalism is predicated by the abstract, inviolate, and sovereign individual subject. Universal status can be safely accorded only to abstractions, to existence steeped in solitude. Individuals are defined by the sphere that marks their inviolability rather than by the possession of a clearly defined trait or conviction. One of the first freedoms such an individual enjoys is the freedom to believe; indeed, modern thought is premised on the understanding of religion qua faith, as it allows the exercise of religion within the liberal framework of "the freedom of belief." This freedom is also a necessity, for without a leap of faith, the existence of other members in a political community (all sovereign individuals) would be dubious at best. In order to belong, one must believe; or yet, in order to belong, one can believe one does not believe at all. In both cases, one acknowledges one's own freedom to believe, and through it, the universality of the individual capacity to believe. This faith must be transubstantiated into conviction, lest the universal turn into the always already flawed, the contextual. Faith allows individuals to forgo their shuttered existence, even if they can only fly upward and outward on the wings of belief. From this vantage point above, they can verify, or more securely believe, that others such as they do exist.

The truth of ideology does battle with the realness of reality. An ideology dismantles this realness, the mass quality of existence, in favor of a vision of reality that claims to be "historically bound," "cost effective," "benefit maximizing," and so on. Existing reality is shown to be securely "happening" within one of two vectors. Reality may simply be the progression of humanity (or a people, or class), beginning from a fixed point far in the past and due to culminate in the less-than-foreseeable future. Reality may also (just as simply) reflect the straying of humanity from its proper path, the subversion and deterioration of a proper reality that must be restored and revalidated. The truth of ideology is the truth of obedience to a vision at odds with things as they are. Faith in the alternative is necessary for it to successfully sweep reality aside. There is no difference if such sweeping is corrective (redirecting strays) or progressive (moving along at the required pace). Persons, societies even, must believe that what they know is not right or sufficient. They must also believe with all their hearts that something else is required, and that they must devote themselves wholeheartedly to the realization of this "something." Faith in ideological truth enables political belonging through obedience. In contrast to universalist faith, ideological faith is not freedom. It is an essential requirement. It is a harness, but it is also a motor.

Both of these truths, the universalist and the ideological, are modernist truths. They are two ways of defining the modern subject—the subject of (the universal subject) and the subject to (the ideological subject)—that is, the Janus face of subjectivization (or *assujetissement*), which portrays the twofold relationship of the subject to truth. Returning to Augustine, proponents of these truths do not know how to explain them, least of all as creators of political belonging. These truths must be accepted as utter truths in order to be true. Faith is either extrapolation or obedience. In both cases, it inspires belonging by default by recognizing hierarchies of being that automatically negate one's own. With universalism, a sovereign believing subject must come to terms with unshakable loneliness along with unending (and incommunicable) similarity. In the case of ideology, the believing subject must obey the dictate of doing away with reality itself in favor of a new and improved version. The first is the work of the Self (vis-à-vis other selves); the second is the work of the Other (through the Self's complex appeal to it).

Universalism and ideology define a spectrum of political belonging currently created or accessed through faith. Is there a way out of this dichotomy between the two poles? What middle ground stretches between them? We can assume that within this middle ground, the instrumentalization of faith is diminished. Unlike the high ground of the ends, within the middle ground, faith is not a vessel for inviolable individual sovereignty or an optimal reality (both abstract by definition).

Middle-ground faith imbues what is, and it is imbued by that which is. This dual relationship allows it to escape the deepest pitfall of the real—succumbing to a static vision of being. It aims to escape the polarization between faith as the fully internal (placed within the self's interior) and faith as the necessarily external (the outside of ideology)—between consciousness and practice. For believers who do not opt for either universalism or ideology, faith is an axis. It occurs and is performed in the world, and as such is both social and grounded in difference. Simultaneously, faith acknowledges and affirms the existence of larger truths, of realness as a continuum. Ensuing political belonging thus takes place in two dimensions at the very least, or more likely in two (to the second power) dimensions. No clear hierarchy exists between abstract principles and concrete practices. When neither is avoidable or deniable, both become desirable.

The real challenge offered by middle-ground faith is a challenge of reacquisition. Before the advent of the political as abstract/concrete, political belonging was a demonstration of actuality rather than a paean to possibility. Its double mode of being was the gold standard of ethics and institutions. The desire to set back the clock is, of course, the epitome of empty modernity. One cannot renege on history. Still, the syntax of middle-ground faith persists. The resurgence of theological politics has recast this middle-ground syntax as a potent generator of power and belonging, confusing a "West" addicted to universalism and ideology. Engagement with this new/old sense of political belonging is essential for effective policy. The barren ends of ideology and universalism grow less and less alluring for more and more people. Belonging as an axis, a multitude of political voices and dimensions, offers a real chance for (dare we say it?) redemption.

NOTE

1 Philip Burton, *The Confessions*, Everyman's Library (New York: Knopf, 2001).

Keyword: Civil Religion
MU-CHOU POO

Before discussing civil religion in the context of Chinese history, a look at Jean-Jacques Rousseau's concept of "civil religion" should be of some help, since it intersects with all three of this volume's overarching themes, namely "religion," "secularism," and "political belonging."

> It follows that it is up to the sovereign to establish the articles of a purely civil faith, not exactly as dogmas of religion but as sentiments of social commitment without which it would be impossible to be either a good citizen or a faithful subject.... While the State has no power to oblige anyone to believe these articles, it may banish anyone who does not believe them. This banishment is not for impiety but for lack of social commitment, that is, for being incapable of sincerely loving the laws and justice or of sacrificing his life to duty in time of need. As for the person who conducts himself as if he does not believe them after having publicly stated his belief in these same dogmas, he deserves the death penalty. He has lied in the presence of the laws.

These are the required dogmas: the existence of a powerful, intelligent Divinity, who does good, has foreknowledge of all, and provides for all; the life to come; the happy rewards of the just; the punishment of the wicked; and the sanctity of the social contract and the laws. As for prohibited articles of faith, I limit myself to one: intolerance. Intolerance characterizes the religious persuasions we have excluded.[1]

With Rousseau's statement as a point of departure, we conceive of a kind of civil religion in the context of Chinese history.

Scholars of religion have long debated whether the term "religion" is a suitable one in discussing the various forms of belief systems found in diverse human societies. By qualifying religion as, say, "Chinese" religion, one is at risk of creating some misconceptions. First, qualifying religion as "Chinese" or "Roman" does not make the question about the meaning of "religion" go away. When using terms such as "Chinese religion," "Roman religion," or "Japanese religion," are we referring to the same kind of phenomenon as it occurs in different regions or cultures, or are we talking about very different forms of belief systems? There is probably no clear-cut answer to such questions, but it is enough to remind us that when considering the use of the term "religion," especially in the context of comparing different regions and time periods, it would be most beneficial if we could always keep a watchful eye, for even the term "belief" could generate different perceptions.

To give a simple definition that could serve as a guideline for our discussion, I propose viewing religion as a form of activity and mental attitude that helps human beings deal with the real or imagined extrahuman forces that influence human life. In ancient China, such activities and attitudes left their traces in various forms, including archaeological remains, artifacts, and texts. There was, however, no single "Chinese religion" but a number of different forms of religious activities and beliefs. Prehistoric ritual altars, cult statues, and burials point to ritual activities as a means of communicating with the extrahuman forces and expressions of beliefs in life after death. In the historic period, heavenly bodies, natural phenomena, mountains and rivers, deities, and deceased ancestors were all understood as holding the power to influence human life. Rituals were developed to propitiate these powers, and relationships between human beings and the powers were articulated through various texts.

When states were formed, rulers and elites dominated the worship of heavenly bodies, the Earth, the mountain, and the river. Thus there was the "official religion," which meant that religious activities such as performing rituals at the correct time and building temples and shrines at certain auspicious locations were supported by government expenditure. The aim of the official religion was to ensure peace and prosperity in the country, that the regime ran smoothly, and of course, the ruler's well-being. At the local or private level, people engaged in various activities that dealt with numerous spirits and ghosts that included their ancestors. Their concerns were geared toward issues of daily life, with the objective of improving personal and family welfare. These activities—whether divination, exorcism, offerings, prayers, or witchcraft—all operated under the assumption that it was possible for human beings to not only communicate with but also influence the will of extrahuman forces, be they gods, ghosts, or demons.

One should not automatically assume that there was a correspondence between religious beliefs and morality. Ancient Chinese political thinkers proposed a correlation between human behavior and divine sanction, thus the Mandate of Heaven became a sort of divine sanction for rulers who acted in accordance with universal justice. This idea would become the most enduring explanation for the vicissitudes of dynastic changes. Yet besides this political theology, there was little in the various pre-Buddhist and pre-Daoist belief systems that connected personal morality with religious activities. What mattered was how to perform the correct rituals, not nurturing personal virtue. Confucianism may be singled out as representing a belief system built on moral rectitude, yet as an elite philosophy, Confucianism hardly represented the large population and complicated social realities of early China. Thus a distinct characteristic of ancient Chinese religions is the general absence of the notion that divine powers or spirits are guardians of human moral behavior.

One very important difference between the belief systems of early China and those of Western religious traditions (spanning from early Mesopotamian, Egyptian, and Greco-Roman traditions to those of Judaism, Christianity, and Islam) is the general lack of a creation mythology and a creator god. (The story of the fashioning of human beings by the goddess Nüwa was late in coming and probably of non-Han Chinese origin.) That is, the world's existence was assumed as autochthonous but not explained as the result of creation. This had profound implications for the development of the Chinese worldview and its perspective on human beings' position in the world.

After the coming of Buddhism at around the first century CE and the rise of Daoism at the end of the second century, the religious landscape underwent some important changes. For a long period of time, adherents to Buddhism (which originated in India and was imported to China) tried to build an autonomous regime outside the secular government's rule. They claimed that since Buddhist doctrine spoke of the ultimate "nothingness" or "illusionary" nature of the material world, they did not belong to this world and therefore should not be subject to secular sovereign rule. Yet their efforts never succeeded, and over the centuries, Buddhist temples were more or less under the nominal protection of the emperor. At several points, Buddhists were persecuted by the regime for one reason or another; their eventual acceptance by the Confucian secular regime was conditioned on the premise that they not cause detriment to the government.

Daoism, a native religion developed during the first and second centuries CE, had its roots in the ancient Daoist philosophy of Laozi and Zhuangzi, combined with exorcist practices and belief in the existence of ghosts and spirits and the concept of immortality. It gained the people's trust for its alleged ability to cure diseases and expel evil spirits and through the promise of blessed immortality. Yet as a system that grew out of the cultural milieu of the Qin and Han empires, it also reflected a bureaucratic outlook, having developed a concept of the heavenly court populated by an increasingly complex set of deities that simulated the secular regime. Thus Daoism was happily in accord with the secular regime, and the secular rulers were usually happy to cooperate with Daoism, for example by allowing Daoism to develop its imagined heavenly court with blessings and investiture from the emperor. In sum, both Buddhism and Daoism were subject to control by the secular government, even today.

As for those religious activities that pervaded society (which Buddhism and Daoism sometimes tried to incorporate at the risk of losing their own identities), they constituted what was likely a major portion of the common people's religious lives in traditional China. People who engaged in these activities were concerned about specific matters such as living a good and prosperous life and receiving a good burial after death. Whatever divine or extrahuman forces, including ancestors, that could help achieve these goals would become objects of worship.

In turn, it could be argued that the goal of the Chinese religious activities—though not without certain aspirations for a paradise in the West, as Buddhism claimed, or an immortal life in heaven, as Daoism propagated—was basically this-worldly happiness, and thus intended for secular reasons. This basic characteristic made it difficult for these religious establishments to compete with the secular government, which could be described as based on Confucian premises—that is, it also vowed to protect and enhance the people's welfare—and was far more powerful than the religious orders.

That said, throughout Chinese history there was always tension between the Confucian officials/elites and the various religious orders. This tension emerged from the Han dynasty (206 BCE–220 CE) onward, when Confucian elites gradually gained access to and control of the right to hold government offices, and the central political ideas of Confucianism were adopted as the major ideological foundation of the government. From the Confucian officials' standpoint, it was acceptable if people worshipped certain deities and made sacrifices to them as long as these activities did not disrupt regular processes of economic production, exhaust people's family fortunes, and of course, did not jeopardize public security. But when the religious activities were performed in excess so that normal life and economic activities were affected, the Confucian officials, representing the will of the state, would often try to intervene and curtail the scale and expenditures of these local cults, or even abolish them altogether.

Throughout the historical development of religion in China, there was never a single church or religious system that obtained enough power to sway the political or theoretical foundations of the state/dynasty, which was based on a rather stable bureaucracy staffed with a relatively ideologically homogeneous group of intellectuals, literati, Confucians, and officials. There was therefore never an issue of the churches causing problems or competing for power with the state (except for occasional "rebellions" by religious groups).

Thus, what concerned the state was not so much the content of the religious activities but the social and economic consequences that they had the potential to bring. Here, one can detect certain similarities with Rousseau's idea of civil religion, such as social commitment and loving laws and justice. Most important of all, as Rousseau puts it, "*it is up to the sovereign to establish the articles of a purely civil faith.*" Thus civil religion, as Rousseau sees it, has to be first approved by a "secular authority," unless the sovereign is considered a divine figure. The Chinese emperor, as "Son of Heaven," actually fits this double role.

It has been argued that China was, and perhaps still is, a religious state. That is, the traditional Chinese government, with its emperor cast as the Son of Heaven for whom the privilege of worshipping heaven is reserved, with its ritual paraphernalia, and most of all, with its power to give and take, could be seen as a religious organization. It controls the major ideology that all under heaven should follow, and it demands absolute loyalty from its people. The emperor is the supreme head of state with absolute power, and he is presented as a divine being in action. The state, after continuously imprinting its authority in the people's minds for more than two thousand years, had acquired certain sanctity and irreplaceable importance in the Chinese psyche. The state, therefore, assumes a double identity. On the one hand, it is a secular regime, for it is an organizational power source for all worldly activities, be they economic, political, or military. On the other hand, the state is also a religious organization, for it is the Chinese people's most revered and obeyed authority, and it provides their most widely accepted center of identity. In a broad stroke, we could say that the Chinese religions—whether Buddhism, Daoism, or the so-called Popular Religion—are secular in that most of their concerns are focused on this-worldly happiness. And the Chinese state, although in essence a secular organization, has acquired a religious status by commanding an almost unconditional devotion from its people.

This interpenetration between the secular and the religious—if these two terms could still have some interpretive power—might provide us with a new understanding of the term "civil religion." It could be understood as a belief system that was initiated by secular authorities for the benefit of protecting civil order and security but that required or inspired unconditional devotion from the people. It might not exclude other forms of belief systems, so long as they do not impinge upon the civil religion's authority. Understood in these terms, we could therefore see the Chinese state ideology as a form of civil religion.

Conceptualizing civil religion along these lines might also lead to a new understanding of the nature of modern nationalism in China. Modern Chinese nationalism, developed more rigorously after the mid-nineteenth century as a reaction to the repressive status that China was subjected to after the Opium War, inherited a large share of the need or desire for an abstract ideal of the "state" as an object of devotion and religious fervor that could substitute the disintegrated dynasty. Thus nationalism took on a sacred aura that preceded all other kinds of identity markers, religious or not. In this sense, modern Chinese nationalism can be seen as a form of civil religion that held supreme significance over other forms of religion.

The concept of civil religion, invented by Rousseau as part of his construction of an ideal society, is intimately related to the concept of "civic"; therefore, its main concern was the welfare of civil society. There have been numerous discussions on this subject, among them Robert Bellah's oft-cited seminal paper. Bellah explained that the religious dimension of American politics "is expressed in a set of beliefs, symbols, and rituals that I am calling the American civil religion."[2] Bellah and others emphasize civil religion's political and social aspects, mostly in the context of American history and society, and they approach "civil religion" as a one-size-fits-all, vague expression for reverence toward a "Lord-Creator" without specifically mentioning whether this Lord belongs to any particular religion. In other words, civil religion as it is commonly understood is based on a Judeo-Christian understanding of religion that might not be applicable to societies from other regions or time periods. The Chinese case gives us an opportunity to reconsider the concept of civil religion and its usefulness when studying non-Western history and society, either ancient or modern.

NOTES

1. Jean-Jacques Rousseau, *Contrat social: Ou, Principes du droit politique*, trans. Henry A. Myers (Paris: Garnier, 1800), book 4, ch. 8, 332.
2. Robert N. Bellah, "Civil Religion in America," *Daedalus* 117, no. 3 (Summer 1988): 97–118.

11. MUSLIM MIGRATION, CITIZENSHIP, AND BELONGING IN U.S. POLITICS OF SECULARISM

KAMBIZ GHANEABASSIRI

As someone who became involved with the Religion, Secularism, and Political Belonging (RelSec) project during the early days of its conception, I could personally attest to the feelings of frustration to which Leerom Medovoi and Elizabeth Bentley refer in their introduction to this volume. One would think that a gathering of scholars from China, Israel/Palestine, the Netherlands, and the United States—all places where religion, secularism, and political belonging are pressing topics—would be an exciting opportunity for global interdisciplinary research in the humanities. In actuality, the gatherings left many of us feeling frustrated with our inability to bridge disciplinary and national differences, despite the fact that, at a personal level, we enjoyed one another's company. To be perfectly frank, until I read Medovoi and Bentley's incisive synthesis of the project in the introduction, I considered RelSec a misguided learning experience in the near impossibility of interdisciplinary, global humanistic research. Medovoi and Bentley's introduction, however, changed my mind. It illustrates that the problems we faced talking across our distinct national and political cultures were demonstrative of how provincial studies of secularism have been, even after Janet Jakobson and Ann Pellegrini's 2008 publication of *Secularisms*.[1] As participants in the project, we all assumed a sort of family resemblance between our different understandings and experiences of secularism until we actually tried to talk with one another. What RelSec makes clear is that even though we no longer adhere to the "secularization narrative" that views the privatization of religion as an inevitable outcome of modernity, we continue to think of secularism as a unifying principle that shapes religion and politics rather than as a means of practicing religion and politics.

In this chapter, I take up Medovoi and Bentley's astute suggestion that we view secularism as a political language varyingly employed to manage religious differences in particular worlds. In the United States, secularism is inflected as religious freedom. By adopting freedom of religious expression as one of its founding principles, the United States has long operated based on the assumption that allowing people to practice their "faith" as they see fit will assure their loyalty to the state. As such, religion has played a central role throughout U.S. history in fostering a sense of political belonging. In fact, proponents of American exceptionalism have long cited the separation of church and state and the guarantee of individual expressions of faith as political principles that distinguish the United States from other nations in the world.[2]

By guaranteeing its citizens freedom of religious expression, the state has also made itself the arbiter of what constitutes a religion and is thus subject to constitutional protections.[3] Consequently, secularism as the political language of religious freedom in the United States has historically managed religions by differentiating the public from the private and rendering religion to the former realm. Religious freedom is thus guaranteed so long as it is an expression of private belief or faith and does not publicly challenge the authority of the state. Its entry into public life has not been protected, but it has been tolerated, and even encouraged, when it is in the service of the state as a form of civil religion.[4] For adherents of minority religions, secularism has thus not been experienced as freedom from state restrictions, nor has it been a product of the strict separation of church and state; rather, it has been a process by which they learn to express their religion within the boundaries set by the state—that is, as a form of personal faith or a branch of U.S. civil religion.

The experiences of religious minorities in the United States demonstrate that religious freedom has never been a neutral ideal in U.S. history; rather, it has been the political means by which the state has managed religious differences. With this recognition, we could take up another of Medovoi and Bentley's suggestions, that once we understand the language of secularism in a particular world, we work to "translate" it, as Walter Benjamin would argue, not by appealing to a universal grammar of secularism but by situating it alongside other particular instances of its practice. From this translocal/translational perspective, secularism becomes much more than a constitutional guarantee of religious freedom and the separation of church and state. It becomes a form of political engagement with religion that imposes public-private differentiations on religious life with the aim of engendering political participation and a sense of national belonging among people of varying faiths. The means by which the state manages religious differences within the nation is what I regard as the politics of secularism in the United States.

IN CONTEMPORARY TIMES, U.S. politics of secularism is most significantly challenged by the increased presence of Muslims in the United States and the growing influence of Islamophobia in U.S. politics. While anti-Muslim sentiments among Americans are as old as the nation itself, it was not until the 2010 Congressional election cycle that they became a matter of national controversy and were used to influence national politics. During this time, a national debate erupted about a proposed plan for the construction of a multistory community center and mosque in Lower Manhattan, just blocks away from where al-Qaeda attacked and destroyed the Twin Towers of the World Trade Center on September 11, 2001. The man largely responsible for conceptualizing this project was Feisal Abdul Rauf, a well-connected and prominent American Muslim leader who had served as the imam of the nearby al-Farah mosque / Sufi lodge in Tribeca since 1982.[5] Abdul Rauf had envisioned the community center as a multifaith space designed "to strengthen relations between the Western and Muslim worlds and to help counter radical ideology."[6] He saw the center as an opportune site to manifest how Muslims through their faith share "core values" with Jews and Christians, and how by living up to these values as citizens of the United States, they could participate in U.S. civil religion. In doing so, these faiths could collectively contribute to human progress.[7] He named the center Cordoba House in memory of the Medieval Spanish city "where Muslims, Christians and Jews co-existed ... during a period of cultural enrichment created by Muslims." Cordoba House, he explained, "will be built on the two fundamental commandments common to Judaism, Christianity and Islam: to love the Lord our creator with all of our hearts, minds, souls and strength; and to love our neighbors as we love ourselves." He urged fellow Americans not to deviate from these commands and "cede" to "the paradigm of a clash between the West and Muslim worlds" but rather to work "to heal relations and bring peace."[8]

Cordoba House, which was renamed Park51 after Abdul Rauf had a falling out with the principle financier of the project, attracted the attention of a number of anti-Muslim activists. Pamela Geller and Robert Spencer organized a rally against the project on June 6, 2010, and again on the ninth anniversary of the September 11 attacks. Spencer called the building of the mosque an expression of "Islamic supremacism."[9] Former Speaker of the House Newt Gingrich also issued a statement challenging the notion that the center is supposed to "symbolize interfaith cooperation." Cordoba, he argued, is a symbol of Islamic conquests, where Muslims established their capital after "their victory over the Christian Spaniards." Gingrich did not mince his words: "America is experiencing an Islamist cultural-political offensive designed to undermine and destroy our civilization. . . . No mosque. No self deception. No surrender."[10]

Interestingly, while the American public debated whether Muslims should be allowed to build a multistory mosque and community center in the vicinity of ground zero of the attacks of September 11, Abdul Rauf was traveling on behalf of the U.S. State Department in the Middle East, representing his country as a leader of the American Muslim community. As a result of his long-standing efforts to promote interfaith cooperation and to demonstrate the compatibility of Islamic and American values, Abdul Rauf was often commissioned during George W. Bush's administration to represent the United States in Muslim-majority countries. Ironically, while his efforts to demonstrate the compatibility of Islamic and American values made him an ideal embodiment of U.S. secular politics to Muslim-majority countries, his activities made him a target of Islamophobic activism and drew widespread suspicion in his own country. What is the significance of this ironic political context in which many American Muslims find themselves today? What does it mean for contemporary American politics of secularism that the means by which American Muslims could assert their citizenship and gain a sense of political belonging are also the means by which they could be alienated from America?

Migration and Community in Islam

In order to understand how Muslims of immigrant backgrounds have interfaced with U.S. politics of secularism, it is useful to examine, in brief, the way migration and community formation are interrelated in Islam. Conception of community in Islam has long presumed migration and mobility. The first year of the calendar in Islam marks the emigration of Prophet Muhammad from Mecca to the city of Yathrib, which later came to be known as Medina, short for Madinat al-nabi, or "the City of the Prophet." This migration has been crystalized in Islamic thought through the Arabic word for migration, *hijra*. Embedded in hijra is the notion that the whole of Earth belongs to God, and as such any place could be suitable for Muslims to live and worship. Muhammad's migration is paradigmatic for many Muslims, and it demonstrates that Islam is not tied to a place, race, or national identity but to a community of believers (*mu'minun*) known as the Umma. Muslims demonstrate their belonging to the Umma not through their place of residence or birth but through their acts of worship and through the attestation of their faith in the unicity of God (*tawhid*) and the message of Prophet Muhammad, which is encapsulated in the Qur'an and in a canonical set of traditions about the sayings and deeds of Prophet Muhammad known as the Hadith.

The conceptualization of community in Islam thus enables movement and adaptation. In order to form the first Muslim political collective, the prophet Muhammad and his followers had to leave their homes in Mecca and move to Yathrib. American Muslims have long evoked this migration as a paradigm for their own experiences in America. Islamic rites and institutions also facilitate movement while still allowing Muslims to maintain a sense of belonging to a global religious community (Umma). Any place could become a place of worship (*masjid*) for Muslims if it is somehow oriented toward the shortest distance to Mecca and if it is maintained free of the ritual impurities, which would nullify the act of prayer. There is no official body or a priestly class that needs to recognize or sacralize a mosque as a space of worship; a building becomes a mosque when it facilitates for Muslims to enact their rites of collective prayer. Consequently, many mosques in the United States are first established in converted single-family homes or rented halls, and Muslims who attend them quickly find their orientation in them whether they are recent white converts, second-generation African American Muslims, or recent immigrants from Jakarta or Cairo.

Furthermore, the act of prayer that occurs at set intervals of the day and is spatially oriented toward Mecca allows individual Muslims to fulfill their religious obligation wherever they are while still feeling in communion with other Muslims throughout the globe who are similarly engaged in prayer. Similarly, the Hajj ties the notion of community to movement and migration as Muslims throughout the world travel to Mecca during the month of Dhu al-Hijja to fulfill this religious duty. Toward the end of the rites of the Hajj, pilgrims have to stand collectively on the plain of Arafat in Mecca in order for their religious duty to be considered fulfilled. Through their collective gathering at Arafat, Muslims of varying classes, races, and nationalities embody the ideal of a universal Muslim community. The fact that they could embody the ideal of the

Umma only after having traveled away from their own homes communicates a powerful message: No space, not even Mecca, embodies Islam; rather, it is Muslims traveling from all parts of the globe to gather together in an act of worship that embodies Islam.

Shariʻa in the United States

These features of the religion of Islam may allow for Muslims to feel at home with their religion even if they do not reside in a Muslim-majority society. However, the spatially bounded nature of citizenship in modern nation-states often makes them appear "out of place" when they reside as minorities in non-Muslim-majority countries. In U.S. politics of secularism, Islamophobic anxieties about whether Muslims could be both "proper" citizens and members of the Umma could be seen in the popularity of a movement to ban the use of Shariʻa in state courts.

Shariʻa is generally defined as Islamic law, but it is a more complicated concept. It literally means "a path to water" in classical Arabic, and as such its use in an Islamic context likely was to signify the path humans must travel to attain their place in heaven. In a more technical sense, it refers to the ethical principles and commands that God revealed to humanity through the Qurʼan and the example of Prophet Muhammad. Since these principles and commands are notoriously difficult to interpret, over many centuries Muslims developed a system for discerning the Shariʻa. This is generally known as *fiqh*, and it refers more specifically to the rules and regulations that were often associated with positive law. Fiqh literally means discernment or understanding. As such, it is a human activity that is subject to error. So, if Shariʻa refers to Divine Law, what we call Islamic law or fiqh is Muslims' best attempt to discern God's will for any particular situation based on the Qurʼan and the Hadith.

Shariʻa, thus, like many other aspects of Islamic beliefs and practices, also facilitates mobility and communal belonging. It provides a means by which Muslims could interpret how they ought to put the precepts of their religion into practice at different times and places. Shariʻa has never been codified. The validity of any precept drawn from the Shariʻa is dependent on the consensus of Muslim scholars who have the knowledge and the training to be able to derive law from the Qurʼan and the Hadith. Individual Muslim scholars could use jurisprudential reasoning to discern God's will for any given place and time, but the validity of their interpretation depends on the consensus of the Muslim community more generally. In the United States, an attempt has been made to attain general consensus on matters related to the Shariʻa through the creation of a fiqh council whose membership includes Muslims of varying backgrounds from North America and beyond.

Abdul Rauf and the Anti-Shariʿa Movement

In his 2004 book, *What's Right with Islam Is What's Right with America*, Feisal Abdul Rauf sought to demonstrate the fundamental compatibility of the Shariʿa and the U.S. Constitution. In the vocabulary of the RelSec project, it could be said that he sought to translate the U.S. political language of secularism into an Islamic one in order to include Islam in American civil religion and to demonstrate that Muslims belong in the American body politic just as much as Christians and Jews. "Grounding itself in reason, just as the Quran and the Abrahamic ethic did in asserting the self-evident oneness of God," the Declaration of Independence, Abdul Rauf explained, situated the legitimacy of government in human reason and "natural law." Nature, he explained, "in the eyes of believers in God, is just another word for 'God's creation,' and thus natural law must mean 'the laws that God established and structured creation on.' . . . To Muslims, the law decreed by God is called the Shariah, and therefore the 'Laws of Nature and of Nature's God' are by definition Shariah law."[11] From an Islamic perspective, then, "what is right about America is its Declaration of Independence, for it embodies and restates the core values of the Abrahamic, and thus also the Islamic, ethic" that "all men are created equal, that they are endowed by their Creator with certain unalienable Rights, that among these are Life, Liberty and the Pursuit of Happiness." For Abdul Rauf, these beliefs, which are "fundamental to all Muslims," also constitute the "American creed."[12]

It is thus not surprising that he goes on to say, "Many American Muslims regard America as a better 'Muslim' country than their native homelands." The reason for this is that

> the American Constitution and systems of governance uphold the core principles of Islamic law. Muslim legal scholars have defined five areas of life that Islamic law must protect and further. These are life, mind (that is, mental well-being or sanity), religion, property (or wealth), and family (or lineage and progeny). Any system of rule that upholds, protects, and furthers these rights is therefore legally "Islamic," or Shariah compliant, in its substance. . . . What I am demonstrating is that the American political structure is Shariah compliant, for "a state inhabited predominantly by Muslims neither defines nor makes it synonymous with an Islamic state. It can become truly Islamic only by virtue of a conscious

application of the sociopolitical tenets of Islam to the life of the nation, and by an incorporation of those tenets in the basic constitution of the country."[13]

By arguing that the United States is a Shariʻa-compliant state, Abdul Rauf was not just countering popular negative perceptions of the Shariʻa as an outdated system of law but also providing a means by which American Muslims could think politically about their place in America and to see their religious and civic duties as mutually reinforcing of one another.

To opponents of Abdul Rauf and his Cordoba House project, however, his references to the Shariʻa were a godsend because they allowed them to interpolate him into an Islamophobic narrative of how "radical Islamists want to impose Shariʻah on all of us." Shariʻa in this narrative, as explained by one of its most prominent proponents, Newt Gingrich, "has principles and punishments, totally abhorrent to the Western world. [Its] underlying basic belief . . . is that law comes directly from God and is therefore imposed upon humans and no human could change the law without it being an act of apostasy." Speaking to an audience at the American Enterprise Institute in July 2010, Gingrich elaborated that this "is a fundamental violation of a tradition in the Western system, which goes back to Rome, Athens, and Jerusalem, which has evolved and given us freedom across the planet on a scale we could hardly imagine." Needless to say, Gingrich's assertion about the fundamental incompatibility of the Shariʻa and the legal system of the West is less based on the actual history of the complicated development of the Islamic and Western legal systems and more on the politics of secularism in the United States; unlike Christianity and Judaism, Gingrich tells his audiences, Islam cannot be considered a religion protected by the U.S. Constitution because it is not a personal faith that recognizes the autonomy of the state in public life. The proverbial West stands for freedom and is rooted in a Greco-Roman, biblical tradition. Islam stands for authoritarianism (or whatever America opposes). In this view, Muslims like Abdul Rauf are deemed "stealth Jihadists" who use social, cultural, political, and intellectual tools to impose Shariʻa upon the world, while "violent Jihadists" use violence.[14] Ultimately, however, they are all involved in a larger project aimed at undermining the secular foundations of American civilization, as Gingrich and his wife, Callista, explain in a 2010 documentary film called *America at Risk*.

Gingrich's Islamophobic juxtaposition of America and Islam resurfaced on the national stage again in 2016, following the terrorist attack in Nice, France, when he told Fox News's Sean Hannity that "Western civilization is in a war.

We should frankly test every person here who is of a Muslim background and if they believe in Sharia they should be deported. Sharia is incompatible with western civilization."[15] Following Gingrich's comments, numerous scholars and media outlets sought to correct his misrepresentation of the Shariʿa. A scholar of Islamic law at Harvard Law School, Noah Feldman, wrote that Gingrich's statement is a "reminder of a persistent and inexcusable misunderstanding of what Shariah is, both in theory and in practice. Put simply, for believing Muslims, Shariah is the ideal realization of divine justice—a higher law reflecting God's will. Muslims have a wide range of different beliefs about what Shariah requires in practice. And all agree that humans are imperfect interpreters of God's will."[16] Feldman's and others' attempts at explaining and familiarizing Americans with the meaning of Shariʿa in Islam, however, seems to misapprehend the depth of anti-Muslim sentiments in certain segments of American society and the degree to which Shariʿa in the American popular imagination is seen as a threat to American values. If evidence is needed to demonstrate the deep, irrational fear of Islam in many parts of America, all one has to do is look at how quickly a small group of Islamophobes led by David Yerushalmi, whom the Anti-Defamation League has "criticized as a fundamentalist bigot," were able to pass anti-Shariʿa laws in the states of Louisiana, Tennessee, Arizona, Alabama, Florida, North Carolina, Oklahoma, and Texas while fostering discussions about banning the Shariʿa in more than twenty other state legislatures.[17] Negative attitudes toward Islam and the Shariʿa are such that they allow for right-wing extremist bigots, such as Yerushalmi, to gain a wider hearing than they would be otherwise afforded by the mainstream. In a 2006 essay, for example, Yerushalmi insinuated that women and blacks were rightly denied the vote: "There's got to be a reason if the Founding Fathers did not give the right to vote to women or to black slaves. You may not approve or like this idea, but the founders of this country . . . certainly took it seriously."[18] He further questioned why "people find it so difficult to confront the facts that some races perform better in sports, some better in mathematical problem-solving, some better in language, some better in Western societies and some better in tribal ones?"[19]

Furthermore, there seems to be no clear logic behind anti-Shariʿa legislation. As a number of legal scholars have noted, state laws against Shariʿa law are utterly superfluous because the U.S. legal system already has in place mechanisms by which it both protects the free exercise of religion and considers the place of religious customs and laws in adjudicating cases.[20] This begs the question of what is the aim of efforts to ban the use of Shariʿa from the state courts, if in effect no changes in the American legal system result from these efforts.

As Nadia Marzouki explains, "For partisans of the anti-Shari'a movement, what matters above all is to win what they call the 'lawfare.' . . . The passage or not of anti-Shari'a laws is practically a secondary matter. The first goal is to create, sustain and amplify the controversy and thereby elevate even higher the threshold of Islam's acceptability among the American public."[21] Put differently, the aim is to put American Muslims and liberal advocates of civil liberties on the defensive, forcing them to spend money and energy on lawsuits and political battles to affirm rights that are already guaranteed by the law. In 2011, Yerushalmi explained that the decisive character of the anti-Shari'a lawfare is to pit "American patriots" against "the union of the Muslim Brotherhood and progressives." "You're going to get bloodied," he warned his audience, "but at the end of the day you hope to draw more blood than you've lost."[22] Yerushalmi's statement about pitting Americans against each other in a battle for displaying patriotic virtue is telling of how anti-Muslim sentiments are affecting contemporary American politics. Now that discrimination based on race, ethnicity, religion, gender, and sexual orientation has been outlawed, anti-Muslim sentiments could be used to wage a new cultural warfare about who belongs in the American body politic.

The anti-Shari'a movement may not effect legal change, but it is successful in instrumentalizing the general public's Islamophobia, and fear of the Shari'a more specifically, to create a litmus test for the purity or health of the American legal system. From this point of view, the presence of Muslims in the United States comes to be seen as polluting and as out of place because all Muslim acts of worship are necessarily derived from the Shari'a. Furthermore, insofar as this logic is deemed sensible by the general public, whatever Muslims do to further participate in American society, to affirm their place within it, or to demonstrate their civic belonging only goes to show how compromised America is as a civilizational project. The ability of American legal, social, and political institutions to integrate Muslims into American society only further demonstrates, under this logic, how far America has distanced itself from its own original identity and how American Muslims and liberals who advocate for Muslim belonging and civil liberties are marching American civilization to the edge of a cliff.

IF MY ANALYSIS IS correct, it should be clear that U.S. president Donald Trump's cry, during his inaugural speech, to stop "American carnage" and to place America first in all policy decisions is utterly dependent on a worldview in which "the civilized world" is seen as being existentially threatened by "radical Islamic terrorism."[23] Indeed, the advancement of any arguments for American isolationism and nativism today is largely dependent on the notion that the presence of Muslims in America represents a polluting factor in American society at best and an existential threat at worse. Within these arguments, the question of who belongs in America inevitably pivots back to static markers of identity such as race, gender, religion, and place of birth rather than on efforts to identify common American values. Attempts by Muslim activists, such as Feisal Abdul Rauf, to participate in defining American values based on their own backgrounds and connections to a wider transnational religious community come to be seen as out of place and polluting. Efforts to ban the Shariʿa may depend on an Islamophobic desire to exclude Muslims from American public life, but they also reveal a deep desire to withdraw America from the globe and to reify American identity in terms of exclusionary categories of identitarian politics (e.g., race, religion, and place of birth) rather than in the dynamic terms of universalist concepts such as civic duty or in terms of constitutional categories such as citizenship rights.

Rooted in the anti-Muslim sentiments found in the politics of secularism in the United States today is an illiberal impulse that has been able to become mainstream by latching onto wider anxieties about the Shariʿa and the supposed threat it poses to the American way of life. Put differently, anti-Shariʿa activists have helped mainstream illiberal, nativist, and isolationist views that render constitutional rights irrelevant to how popular notions of political belonging are shaped in America. Consequently, notions of citizenship and belonging become less about how one behaves as an American and what one does for one's country and more about how one embodies an imagined notion of the American. It is thus no wonder that someone like Abdul Rauf, who has been active in defining the common ground between Islamic and American values, could find himself an ideal representative of American Muslims abroad but be viewed with suspicion at home as a practicing Muslim who was born in Kuwait to Egyptian parents.

Islamophobia has helped undermine religious freedom as a political principle by which American Muslims could translate the values of their faith into American conceptions of civil religion. In doing so, it has exposed the limits of the politics of secularism in the United States and revealed a struggle between two visions of America. One of these views relies on the politics of secularism to articulate a definition of America as a civilizational project to which anyone could belong through the exercise of citizenship rights and duties. In this view, the exercise of civic duties and ideals of citizenship (civil religion) work to renew the social contract between the state and American Muslims. The other view relies on nativism and territorial sovereignty rather than secular ideals of citizenship to conceptualize America as a Christian nation of European ancestry where citizenship is an act of will to make America an embodiment of particular race, religion, and gender norms. In this latter view, national sovereignty is justified not through a social contract between the state and a nation of different faiths but by the state's ability to exercise power over its territory as it sees fit—to build a wall on its border with Mexico and to ban Muslim immigration.

While the politics of secularism has proscribed processes of inclusion for religious minorities, in post-9/11 America, American Muslims, at every turn, are reminded of the indeterminacy of these processes. The conflict between the visions of America represent not only a crisis in the politics of secularism in contemporary America but also a crisis of identity. In this mist of uncertainty, American Muslims find themselves saddled with the task of renewing America's civil religion in the unstable and mercurial terms of the state.

NOTES

I am grateful to Ateha Bailey and Delainey Myers for their help in editing this chapter.

1. Janet Jakobsen and Ann Pellegrini, *Secularisms* (Durham, NC: Duke University Press, 2008).
2. For a discussion of these perspectives, see Kambiz GhaneaBassiri, "Religion-State Relations and the Politics of Religious Freedom in Muslim America," in *Muslims and US Politics Today*, ed. Mohammad Hassan Khalil (Boston, MA: ILEX Foundation, 2019), 11–19.
3. Winnifred F. Sullivan, *Paying the Words Extra: Religious Discourse in the Supreme Court of the United States* (Cambridge, MA: Harvard University Press, 1994).
4. GhaneaBassiri, "Religion-State Relations."
5. Rosemary Corbett, *Making Moderate Islam: Sufism, Service, and the "Ground Zero Mosque" Controversy* (Stanford: Stanford University Press, 2017), 5.
6. Feisal Abdul Rauf, "Building on Faith," *New York Times*, September 7, 2010, A27.
7. Feisal Abdul Rauf, *What's Right with Islam Is What's Right with America: A New Vision for Muslims and the West* (San Francisco, CA: HarperSanFrancisco, 2005), 1–2.
8. Abdul Rauf, "Building on Faith," A27.
9. Robert Spencer, "Why There Should Be No Mosques at Ground Zero," *Human Events*, May 24, 2010, http://humanevents.com/2010/05/24/why-there-should-be-no-mosques-at-ground-zero/.
10. "Newt's Statement on the Proposed 'Cordoba House' Mosque at Ground Zero," July 21, 2010, https://www.gingrich360.com/2010/07/mosquestatement/.
11. Abdul Rauf, *What's Right with Islam*, 82.
12. Abdul Rauf, *What's Right with Islam*, 83.

13 Abdul Rauf, *What's Right with Islam*, 86. The citation within this quote is from Muhammad Asad, *The Principles of State and Government in Islam* (Gibraltar: Dar al-Andalus, 1980), 1.
14 Recording of excerpts of the speech are available as "Newt Gingrich—Ban Sharia—It Is 'Totally Abhorrent to the Western World,'" YouTube, August 31, 2010, www.youtube.com/watch?v=d_pttrr-dMc.
15 Melissa Etehad, "After Nice, Newt Gingrich Wants to 'Test' Every Muslim in the U.S. and Deport Sharia Believers," *Washington Post*, July 15, 2016.
16 Noah Feldman, "A Lesson for Newt Gingrich: What Shariah Is (and Isn't)," *New York Times*, July 15, 2016, SR3.
17 See Nadia Marzouki, *Islam: An American Religion* (New York: Columbia University Press, 2017), 106–37, quote on 113.
18 David Yerushalmi, "On Race: A Tentative Discussion," McAdam Report, May 12, 2006, 10, cited in Marzouki, *Islam*, 112.
19 Andrea Elliott, "The Man behind the Anti-Shariah Movement," *New York Times*, July 30, 2011, A1.
20 For examples, see the report the American Civil Liberties Union published on this issue, "Nothing to Fear: Debunking the Mythical 'Sharia Threat' to Our Judicial System," May 2011, https://www.aclu.org/report/nothing-fear-debunking-mythical-sharia-threat-our-judicial-system#:~:text=Nothing%20to%20Fear%3A%20Debunking%20the,System%20%7C%20American%20Civil%20Liberties%20Union&text=Black%20people%20are%20being%20murdered,defend%20our%20right%20to%20protest; and Steven Schwinn, "Anti-Sharia Laws: A Solution in Search of a Problem," *Jurist*, March 18, 2015, www.jurist.org/forum/2015/03/steven-schwinn-sharia-law.php.
21 Marzouki, *Islam*, 127.
22 Quoted in Marzouki, *Islam*, 127.
23 "Inaugural Address: Trump's Full Speech," Washington, DC, January 20, 2017, www.cnn.com/2017/01/20/politics/trump-inaugural-address/.

12. COMMEMORATING THE AFRICAN ANCESTORS
Entanglements of Citizenship, Colonialism, and Religion in the Netherlands
MARKUS BALKENHOL

The culturalization of citizenship in the Netherlands—that is, the increasing importance ascribed to "culture" in the politics of citizenship, belonging, and integration—has been marked by a tension between "religion" and "secularism." The "culture" of others, and Muslims in particular, is pitted against the secular, progressive, and emancipated Dutch culture. Minorities are increasingly expected to "integrate" into Dutch culture and embrace Dutch norms, values, and traditions. "Integration" here does not only imply that minorities keep their culture to themselves and out of the public sphere; it is also understood as a fundamental transformation of the person: since they are thought to be caught in backward traditions, prospective citizens have to *emancipate* themselves. This process of emancipation, in turn, is told as a narrative of secularization. In his book on "ritual citizenship," Oskar Verkaaik argues that "in this narrative the acting, willing, rebelling individual is central. Against the grain of society, the individual breaks with social conventions of his milieu so as to let his personal autonomy flourish."[1] In other words, the Dutch citizen is not only seen as emancipated, but this emancipation is understood specifically as an emancipation from *religion*.

In this chapter, I introduce people who make the opposite claim, namely that emancipation is achieved through religious practice. They understand emancipation not as a process of secularization but as a revaluation, indeed an *embrace* of religion. I am talking here about the claims to citizenship articulated by some postcolonial migrants, more specifically a group of Surinamese Dutch of African descent. The paradigmatic shift to integration in the 1990s and the ensuing search for "Dutch culture," tradition, cultural heritage, and history also turned up the so-called dark pages of Dutch history. In the early 1990s, Surinamese Dutch of African descent mobilized the colonial past, and in particular the Dutch involvement in the transatlantic system of slavery, to formulate claims to citizenship. As a consequence of slavery, they argued, they had been made citizens of the kingdom against their will, and now they should be treated as full citizens, not as second-class citizens with limited access to education, housing, the labor market, and other areas of social life. For the self-identified "descendants of the enslaved," full citizenship constitutes a way out of their subaltern position that would realize their true incorporation into the nation. In other words, they understand citizenship as a form of emancipation—the realization of the promise held by the abolition of slavery to become truly free.

Emancipation here refers in one sense to *formal* citizenship. Legally, the descendants of the enslaved residing in the Netherlands are Dutch. They hold a Dutch passport and are in theory regarded as Dutch citizens before the law. However, in practice, this status is often insufficiently realized due to conscious and unconscious racial stereotyping and discrimination. In this sense, emancipation refers to the practical implementation of the equality promised by the law.

In another sense, emancipation also refers to *cultural* emancipation, that is, the revaluation of cultural forms and practices that have been suppressed or disavowed under colonialism. Similar to the ideas developed by the Harlem Renaissance or the negritude movements, emancipation here refers to a cultural politics in which the black person is to be rehabilitated as a *cultural* being. Such a cultural being emphatically includes religion. In particular, the Afro-Surinamese Winti religion, according to the people concerned here, is to be unearthed from the rubble under which it has been buried by the Protestant and Catholic missions, which were deeply, albeit often ambiguously, entangled with colonial rule in Suriname. Hence, like the notion of emancipation employed in the process of the culturalization of citizenship, emancipation here refers to an emancipation from Christianity. However, this does not imply a process of secularization. In contrast to the notion of emancipation-as-secularization, they articulate a critical position that does not take for granted the norm of secular modernity. Instead, secular and religious modes of being and belonging intersect in their claims to citizenship, the nation, and indeed modernity.

This entails a more conceptual argument with regard to the issues of religion, secularism, and political belonging that concern this volume. Following scholars such as Talal Asad, Saba Mahmood, and Birgit Meyer, I argue for a *postsecularist* perspective, that is, a perspective that "no longer takes secularization as the standard intrinsic to modernity, being alert instead to the specific ways in which the concept, role and place of religion—and its study—have been redefined with the rise of secularity."[2] I want to hold onto the term "postsecularist," despite its recent critiques and even outright dismissals.[3] The "post," to me, does not automatically imply a hostile posture that rejects secularism and by extension liberal democracy or Western modernity as a whole. Neither do I take it as a signal, as Stathis Gourgouris does, that "either some sort of pure secularity has been achieved—that the so-called process of secularization has been completed—or that the secular has been left behind, outmaneuvered, or indeed abolished by another social-imaginary horizon."[4]

Scholars working in and on the Netherlands have found the term "postsecularist" useful to analyze a fluid situation in which, as John Boy put it in a comment on the *Immanent Frame*, "things that were formerly taken to be 'split' or consigned to separate spheres are now recognized as intrinsically linked."[5] I take "postsecularist" as a sensitizing notion that enables a critical stance toward neat divides between secularism and religion, looking instead at their mutual constitution. Minimally, it points to the realization that secular critique cannot be naively embraced as a neutral, rational, objective, and self-evident position. The point is that precisely because secularism has not been replaced by another social imaginary, there is a need for continued critical engagement with both secularism and religion—an engagement perhaps best captured in Said's notion of "secular criticism" as outlined in the introduction to this volume.[6] Indeed, if we want to understand secularism as unfinished and "emerging," as Gourgouris proposes, it only seems fitting to employ terms that position us to explore this open-endedness rather than insist on conceptual rigor.[7] I even think this is in line precisely with Gourgouris's refined notion of critique that, "rather than judging things as they are, alters things, change what they are."[8] For me, then, despite its shortcomings, a postsecularist position allows me precisely to "detranscendentalize" or "secularize" secularism.[9]

I use the "post" in postsecular analogous to the "post" in postcolonial, which, as Ann Laura Stoler has identified, is intended "as a mark of skepticism rather than [to] assume its clarity."[10] In fact, this is more than an analogy, but it points to the question of how notions of secular modernity have emerged through an engagement with religion in colonial encounters in the various European empires. The point here is not to repudiate secularism as a form of false consciousness and cloaked Christianity (or Protestantism) or dismiss it as merely a colonial (and hence oppressive) formation. I argue that a better understanding of how religion is mobilized to address secular concerns such as citizenship can be gained by looking at the entanglements of religion, modernity, and empire.[11]

The material I discuss here urges us to rethink the relationship between "Europe" and its colonial others in the constitution of what has been mistaken to be "European" phenomena. The emergence of a secular public sphere and the supposed relegation of religion to the private sphere are not usefully rethought from a perspective that centers on Europe. This not only entails attention to the colonial margins, the spaces of encounter between "Europeans" and its "others." A postsecularist perspective also entails "provincializing" Europe and understanding Europe itself as a frontier area and a contact zone.[12]

Blackness, Religion, and Citizenship

On July 1, 2013, the 150th jubilee of the abolition of slavery in the Dutch West Indian colonies was celebrated at the National Slavery Memorial in Amsterdam. As always, the ceremony was opened by a libation in honor of the ancestors. It was poured by Marian Markelo, one of the most important priestesses of the Afro-Surinamese Winti religion in the Netherlands. For the first time, Markelo was accompanied by a newly created ancestor mask. Humberto Tan, a well-known TV personality and talk-show host of Afro-Surinamese descent, introduced Markelo: "In Surinamese culture, rituals play an important role, for instance the Pleng libation. A ritual in which the ancestors and God are called upon to provide assistance. And you will also see, in a moment, a mask. The mask is an expression of the African renaissance in the so-called Winti culture. The mask, by the way, was made by Boris van Berkum. Your attention, please, for the Pleng libation by Marian Markelo." As she slowly walked around the memorial, pouring water from a calabash and accompanied by a dancer wearing the mask, Markelo spoke words of prayer.

Ancestors, God the Creator, mother goddess Maisa. Ancestors, your memory is like water that purifies my spirit and activates my imagination. Ancestors, on this 150th commemoration of abolition I want to say thanks for your struggle, I want to say thanks for everything you left behind for us in this history. . . . Mother Earth, mother goddess, make us aware that the freedom to fight for freedom is important. Freedom demands commitment and dedication. . . . Anana [God the Creator] and Maisa, Mother Earth, God the Creator, today, too, I call upon you, come in our midst, stay close to us, let us find the strength to further develop the Netherlands together and in harmony. Slavery has known victims, perpetrators, as we say today, but we are concerned today with the future. After 300 years of experience with slavery we are in this part of Europe, the beautiful black-and-white Netherlands, we are free people. Mother Earth, Maisa, *ala den yorka, ala den bigisma f' unu m'e kar' unu* [all the spirits, all our big ones, I call on you], come in our midst, be with us, be with the politicians in particular of the City of Amsterdam, and the Kingdom of the Netherlands, give them wisdom, to make difficult decisions in this time, which will affect us all; but ancestors, you have done your share, give us as your descendants the inspiration to also contribute to the further construction, in a respectful manner, in a manner that is worthy of humanity and the history of the Netherlands. Ancestors, Mother Earth, Anana Keduaman Keduampon, *nanga kouru watra lespeki fu teri nanga waarderi* [with cold water I show respect]. Harmony, freedom. We make a covenant today, that if we discover that any form of slavery is emerging in our society, that we will fight against this. This is the covenant on the 150th jubilee of slavery in Suriname and the Dutch Antilles. Thank you.[13]

One year later, on July 1, 2014, Markelo poured libation again at the memorial, on the occasion of the 151st anniversary of abolition. When the libation had ended, a siren interrupted the ceremony. After Markelo left the memorial ground, a group of young men and women of African descent had gathered swiftly in front of the stage. They were clad in black clothes, forming a bloc, with grim faces. Through a megaphone, a young man read out a statement.

We are standing here today with the utmost respect and reverence for our ancestors. We are standing here in the name of Anton [de Kom], Boni, Tula, Baron, Sophie, Joli-coeur, Tata, Karpata, Touissant, Nanny, and the countless invisible fighters and victims of the Dutch wealth and welfare. We are here to see to it that no foreign breath enters their commemoration. The secretary Lodwijk Asscher represents the Dutch government: the very government that treats the black community with disrespect, that wants no national commemoration [of slavery], that ignores UN contracts, and that does not care about the pain and sorrow of the black community.

We are here to prevent the vice president Lodewijk Asscher from insulting our ancestors with empty words any longer. And even more so on a day that we commemorate their struggle and their suffering. Only a weak people allows such a humiliation. We are not weak. . . . We will be a role model to our offspring, just like our African ancestors were assertive [*strijdbaar*] role models to us.

We are fed up with being treated like second-class citizens and we no longer want to matter only if the Netherlands deems us good enough. It's time to stand up. Time to stand up for ourselves. We usher in a new era. We are Dutchmen like any other Dutchman and we demand to be treated with the same respect.[14]

The performances by Markelo and the young activists articulate black citizenship. They address the Dutch state and its formal representatives in a discourse of rights and recognition. In other words, they intervene in what Jürgen Habermas has described as the public sphere.[15] However, they do so not only as secular citizens but by invoking the sacred—the authority of the ancestors. From a contemporary secularist perspective (as opposed to a medieval perspective as one of religious zeal brought into the world), this might be surprising, but in the Winti cosmology, it is not at all uncommon that the ancestors would interfere in politics.

The Self and the Political in Winti

According to one of the most influential Winti theologians and sociologists, Charles Wooding, Winti "centers around the belief in personified supernatural beings, who take possession of a human being, eliminate his consciousness, after which they unfold the past, the present and the future, and are able to cause and cure disease of a supernatural origin."[16] Gloria Wekker adds that Winti "contains much more than possession. It pertains to many different aspects of everyday life, to food, relationships, work, health, matters of life and death, to subjectivity and sexuality. . . . Winti offers templates for how to act in particular situations and explanations of why certain events occur. A synonym for Winti is kulturu/culture, and in its broadness that is exactly what it signals: a way of living, a way of being in the world."[17] Winti, in other words, is a cosmology not only in the sense that it is a world*view*, a view from above, as it were, but it is a mode of world-*making*, an encompassing practice that is embedded in everyday life. Although the uppermost God, Anana Keduaman Keduampon, the creator of heaven and Earth, withdrew from the world of humans after the act of creation, the lower deities (Winti) directly interact with humans on a daily basis. These Winti can support or thwart human endeavors and cause illness and health, so it is of paramount importance to placate them by different forms of worship. The Winti deities can also be asked to perform tasks for human projects, for instance to guarantee the success in business, love affairs, or matters of health.

Winti are distinct from the ancestors, who form an altogether different spiritual entity. Like the Winti, however, the ancestors meddle with the living and need to be placated through various forms of worship and sacrifice. Like with the Winti, humans live in reciprocal relationships with the ancestors, who have to be "paid" for their help.[18]

In the Winti cosmology, the ancestors are a central element of the self. This is a "multiplicitous" or composite self that consists of several elements.[19] Humans are thought to have two dimensions. The first, a person's physical body, is provided by their biological parents. The second, spiritual dimension, has three parts: the *kra* (soul), the *dyodyo* (a person's spiritual parents in the Winti pantheon), and the *yorka* (spirit, which remains after a person's death). A person can refer to themselves in different ways, in which the "I" can be quite distinct from "my kra" or "my dyodyo." The dyodyo's desire, for instance, can be quite different from that of the "I." Both Winti and ancestors (the dyodyo or spiritual parents) can "take over" a person's body in episodes of possession. The human body, as a medium through which the spiritual entities can manifest themselves, is seen as part human, part spirit. In other words, the self in Winti cosmology is deeply entwined with the spiritual world, and the failure to maintain this relationship with the spiritual part of the self can lead to serious complications, often of what in medical discourse would be called a psychopathological nature.

It is precisely this entanglement of the person in this world with its spiritual counterparts in the other world that predestines Winti spirits and the ancestors to be mobilized in this-worldly politics of belonging. Already it has become clear that the concept of the self in Winti cosmology is not captured by the idea of a clearly bounded individual that is in distinction from the spirit world. Neither is this individual distinct from or even in opposition to the social world. The self is embedded in social relations; it is a relational rather than a bounded self. In other words, in contrast to the secular/Protestant notion of a bounded individual (*Innerlichkeit*), the self in Winti is always already collective, and therefore political.

In the Winti cosmology, the ancestors are not only entities in the spirit world; they also determine kinship through descent. In the Surinamese Creole context, that is, the Afro-Surinamese in and around the coastal areas and urban centers, the plantation is, next to direct family, the most important unit of kinship. The ancestors are often buried on those plantations, and because of their relative isolation, plantation communities have often developed their own distinct forms of worship, music, dance, and traditions that were slightly different from other plantations. Ancestral descent, then, has traditionally been a political category defining the boundaries of groups. Today, the category of the ancestor has been reinterpreted to indicate a different collectivity. Since slavery has become a matter of sustained public commemoration in the Netherlands in the beginning of the 1990s, the phrase "descendants of the enslaved" has come to serve as a political category that refers to all Surinamese of African descent.[20]

This collective denomination as "descendants of the enslaved" is the latest iteration of a much longer politics that begins with the arrival of the first shipments of enslaved Africans in the seventeenth century. Winti originated in Suriname under the regime of slavery. It emerged from the various elements of religious systems that were carried from Africa to the Americas aboard the slave ships. As Sidney Mintz and Richard Price have argued, the enslaved Africans were able to carry "immense quantities of knowledge, information, and belief.... They were not able to transfer the human complement of their traditional institutions to the New World."[21] However, the Africans who reached the Americas were culturally diverse, and the establishment of religious institutions necessarily required an openness toward religious traditions other than one's own. The enslaved did not compose clearly delineated groups but created very heterogeneous *crowds*: "The fact is that these were not *communities* of people at first, and they could only become communities by processes of cultural change. What the slaves undeniably shared at the outset was their enslavement; all—or nearly all—else had to be *created by them*. In order for slave communities to take shape, normative patterns of behavior had to be established, and these patterns could be created only on the basis of particular forms of social interaction."[22] Hence, the "organizational task of enslaved Africans in the New World was that of creating institutions—institutions that would be responsive to the need of everyday life under the limiting conditions that slavery imposed on them."[23] In other words, the cultural institutions, including religion, created by the enslaved were quite directly related to their social conditions. Religion in slave societies was not a phenomenon sui generis but part and parcel of social and political organization. It was vital for the organization of social structures and political identities among the enslaved from the outset. It needs to be stressed, of course, that the ability of the enslaved to organize socially and politically was extremely limited under the European monopoly of power. But next to the more practical aspects such as the labor power itself, nursing children or preparing food, which necessarily granted the enslaved some degree of leverage over their masters, the very emergence and existence of institutions such as religion constantly destabilized the foundations on which the system of slavery was built.

> Slaves were defined legally as property; but, being human, they were called upon to act in sentient, articulate, and human ways: the slaves were not animals, even if the barbarities visited upon them were inhuman.... Animals cannot learn to speak a new language, to employ tools and machinery in the manufacture of sugar, to direct crews of their fellows in completing a task, to nurse the sick, cook elaborate dinners, compose dances and verse—or, for that matter, to become adept in ridiculing with impunity the inanities of those who abuse them.[24]

The Europeans' inability to successfully deny the humanity of the enslaved has an important implication for the public presence of religion in Suriname. It is a fact that the enslaved were not allowed to practice the Winti religion freely, in full public view. The prohibition to conduct Winti rituals was in effect until as late as 1973, two years before Suriname gained independence from the Netherlands. However, the fact that Winti could not be practiced in full view does not mean that Winti was not a presence at all, either during slavery or after abolition. For the Europeans, Winti worship may often have been no more than "a faint drumming in the distance," but precisely this half knowledge made it a powerful presence indeed.[25] Although the planters, many of whom were either Lutheran or Jewish, disapproved of Winti, they knew that enforcing the prohibition too rigidly would encounter resistance. The planters often disavowed Winti as "superstition," but this did not necessarily curtail the power of it. The Europeans were afraid of "black magic," and some even made use of the herbal knowledge of the *bonuman*.[26] In other words, to the extent that "politics" refers to the ability to exert some degree of control or influence in a given power relation, Winti has always been "political."

If Winti provided a means to exact some political influence during slavery, it was mobilized explicitly as a marker of "African-Surinamese" identity in the Surinamese nationalist movement in the twentieth century. Poets and intellectuals such as Trefossa, Dobru, Eddy Bruma, and Papa Koenders mobilized Winti, in part anticipating Frantz Fanon's psychological analysis, arguing that colonialism had caused alienation from a true self. This true self they understood to be the "African" self—an "African" origin that had been "largely suppressed, forgotten, and ignored," as a consequence of both colonial prohibitions and an internalized sense of inferiority.[27] As Edgar Cairo later put it, "Because far too little research was being done on one's own culture, that data was lost, afraid as one was to gain dishonor with 'dumb-superstitious negro-like things.' . . . Even worse: if one got involved with the negro thing you would never get rid of it! Evil spirits . . . they would hatefully target you! You would never stop to 'dance Winti and serve Thingy in superstition!' You were cursed, cursed with the kunu [curse] of the negro's belly!"[28] The Creole nationalists saw the rehabilitation of and the reconciliation with the African self not only as a psychological question pertaining to the individual but as a political project through which full—that is, both personal and political emancipation—could be achieved. In particular, the cultural movement Wi Egie Sani (Our Own Thing or simply Our Own), established in the 1950s, promoted ideas of cultural and political autonomy and black consciousness. The movement originated in the Netherlands and was carried by Creole intellectuals and academics with an affinity to working-class cultures. Language and religion constituted their foremost concern. Both the Surinamese Creole language, Sranantongo, and the Winti religion were framed as "our own" that needed to be rehabilitated as part of their nationalist project. In his theater piece *The Tears of Den Uyl*, the writer Hugo Pos has one of his characters say in hindsight: "Yes, the poets. Liberation from within, that was the painful development we had to undergo, to discover our own kra, to translate this for you in a very Christian manner with soul. Once that stadium had been reached, the sense of unity, to achieve anything, then emancipation was no longer an issue."[29] Emancipation, in this iteration, refers to a process of spiritual healing in which the fate of the individual is inextricably bound to that of the nation. Colonialism, the nationalists argued, has unhinged the world as a whole—not only that of humans but also the spirit world. Mending it cannot therefore be a matter of secular politics alone; it also needs to be a process of spiritual healing that is encompassing. In other words, the struggle for emancipation, of both the nation and the black subject, has never been a purely secular one. It has always also involved the spirit world. Although the political goal has changed in the Afro-Surinamese diaspora in the Netherlands, the idea that religion is a path toward emancipation has not.

The Kabra Mask and Postsecular Belonging

Markelo's prayer at the commemoration is precisely in this tradition. This becomes abundantly clear not only in her prayer but even more so in the ancestor mask that accompanied her. The remainder of this chapter focuses on this object and discusses some of the implications for a postsecularist perspective.

In 1998, Marian Markelo received a message from her ancestors. In their message, the ancestors assigned Markelo the task of "bringing back" the sculptural tradition in the practice of Winti. That tradition, the ancestors argued, had been lost during the Middle Passage and slavery, and it was now time to restore this tradition. Thirteen years later, Markelo met Boris van Berkum, a Dutch artist based in Rotterdam. Van Berkum had just finished a solo exhibition at the prestigious Museum Boijmans Van Beuningen in Rotterdam. He described to me their first meeting at a Winti Prey as a "magical moment," in which Markelo, guided by her African ancestors, chose van Berkum as a partner in the project they came to call an "African Renaissance" in the Winti religion.[30]

In 2011 and 2012, van Berkum made six ceramic sculptures of the Winti mother goddess Mama Aisa. However, the African-inspired sculptures he initially produced did not stand the test of ritual deployment when Markelo and van Berkum used them in a Winti Prey. The ritual had been prepared well. The event was organized at van Berkum's studio on Brienenoordeiland near Rotterdam, an island in the Maas river that reminded Markelo of the river islands in Suriname; the sculptures had turned out beautifully and could certainly serve as spiritual objects (indeed, one of the sculptures is now part of Markelo's private altar). Nonetheless, they were not yet "perfect": they did not have the spiritual presence van Berkum had aimed for. The sculptures, he said, were too static, just sitting there on the altar. They ought to be more dynamic, more "alive." During the ritual, van Berkum did, however, have a vision of how the sculptures could be perfected. In his vision, he saw people dancing and wearing sculptures on top of their heads. "I thought it would be more powerful if the sculptures were *kinetic*: moving instead of static. If they could actually dance among people. Perhaps there was still too much of me in them, too much of my own interpretation," van Berkum told me.

Their project included not only the *reintroduction* of sculpture in the Winti religion but also the *safeguarding* of African heritage in the Netherlands. In 2013, van Berkum and Markelo collected more than 1,200 signatures against the commercial sale of the Rotterdam World Museum's Africa collection. The project received the name Ik ben niet te koop (I am not for sale), a creed against slavery in general and in particular against the "unlawful sale of the Africa collection by World Museum director, Stanley Bremer. A waste of cultural heritage. That collection belongs to the people of Rotterdam, of which 20 percent have African roots."[31] "Then it dawned on me," van Berkum explained to me. "We needed to go where the African ancestors live in the Netherlands—in the great African collections of Dutch museums." At that moment, he connected the dots. *Safeguarding* the African heritage in the Netherlands and *reintroducing* sculpture in the Winti religion were two sides of the same coin.

Hence they approached the Africa Museum in Berg en Dal, where they visited the collection of Yoruba masks in the museum's depot.[32] Guided by the "spiritual character" of the objects, Markelo and van Berkum selected six Yoruba masks. The valuable wooden masks had to remain in the museum, but Markelo and van Berkum were not seeking to acquire one of the original masks. They were looking for a "contemporary" (*eigentijdse*) ancestor mask. For their project, simply preserving the wooden originals proved insufficient. The new mask needed to meet present standards and cater to present needs. The mask that had "worked" for the ancestors would no longer work in the present, but it nevertheless needed to make the ancestors present, too.

Van Berkum achieved this production of presence in the present with 3D technology. They found 3D Match Europe ("make your imagination reality"), a company that normally produces scans for medical purposes. The company performed a laser scan of the masks using a portable Artec 3D scanner, a device that dissolves a material object into "point cloud coordinates," a mass of raw data that digitally defines the shape of the object. The raw data was computer-rendered and then milled in polyurethane foam.

Six masks were scanned, and the computer-rendered images of two masks were used to produce one 1.5-meter-high dancing mask ("Papa Winti"), one 6-meter-high sculpture of Mama Aisa ("Mama Aisa XXXL"), and a 66 × 40 × 40 cm Kabra mask, which I will focus on here. This particular mask (the original of which measures 9 × 17.5 × 20.5 cm) originates in the Yoruba region in Nigeria and is a wooden anthropomorphic mask with large, half-moon-shaped eyes and an iron earring. It was used in the Egungun (Mask) cult, a secret society of masqueraders. Egun masks were used in ancestor worship, but they were also part of secular theatrical performances at the Royal Court.[33]

The Kabra mask needed to be a sensation. The new mask was considerably larger than the wooden original. What remained of the original mask was only its shape. The most striking change was the mask's size: "The original model was too small, it would not have produced the kind of presence [*aanwezigheid*] we were looking for," van Berkum explained. "In an African village, you have maybe thirty people, but we were looking for a public of three hundred and more. And it also has to do well on television."

Van Berkum also radically changed the appearance of the mask: instead of the original mask's wooden color, he applied transparent polyurethane varnish, through which the light beige color of the polyurethane foam is visible. On top of the varnish, van Berkum blew brass powder, then sanded it off so that only golden-colored dots are visible on the mask's surface. The mask is dressed in blue-and-white *persie* cloth, which is glued on top of its head, thus echoing a head-tie. Around the neck, the mask wears a collar of tulle, hiding a wooden structure so it can be worn on top of the head. The dancer wearing it can see through the tulle collar.

The ancestor mask is also a political icon as it intervenes in debates about belonging, citizenship, and cultural heritage in the Netherlands. In 2013, on the occasion of the 150th jubilee of abolition, the mask made its first appearance in the ceremony. In the audience was Annemarie de Wildt, curator at the Amsterdam Museum. She immediately resolved to acquire the mask for the museum's permanent collection. She argued that the mask not only referred to the history of the city but that since it had been present at this historic event, it was now itself a part of that history, and thus part of the cultural heritage of the city.

The mask is now part of the museum's collection, but it also remains a religious object that is used in Winti rituals. It is an object that moves in and out of the museum, and thus also between the realms of cultural heritage, religion, and art.

The mask's style also situates it in the context of a broader quest for "Africanness" and its stylistic repertoire. Marleen de Witte has shown how young people's search for a diasporic identity and "African" roots is embedded in a particular stylistic canon of "Africanness," including, for instance, such elements as Kente cloth and "traditional dance."[34] Like Kente and wax print cloth, African masks can be counted among those "easily identifiable signifiers of a generic Africanness" that have a long tradition in the black Atlantic.[35] The Kabra mask playfully relates to these tropes. Based on a West African wooden mask, it retains only (even though importantly) the form. The rest becomes a "contemporary" ancestor mask that stylistically breaks with and transcends the West African original.

The mask as a hybrid object (a work of art, cultural heritage, and a sacred object) perfectly embodies the entanglements of secular and religious modes of being and belonging. Indeed, the mask demonstrates that such distinctions are more porous than one might think from a perspective of secular modernity.

The mask, and the profiling of spiritual and historical ancestors during the commemoration of slavery, does not mean that the emerging movement against racism is a "religious" movement. Many of the prominent protests against the blackface figure of Black Pete in particular and racial discrimination in a broader sense do not fight for the freedom to practice Winti. Indeed, the Kabra mask and the libation by priestess Markelo during the national commemoration of slavery are the occasions at which Winti is most visible and explicitly *visualized*. But that also does not mean that the emerging black movement is a "secular" movement in which religion does not play a role at all. The fact that Winti is not, or not yet, visible does not mean that it is absent. The emerging black movement, which appears to a broader public at mediagenic events such as Saint Nicholas parades or the national Remembrance Day, is part of a broader search for black identity among young people of African descent, including projects of "self-styling" and cultural histories that emphatically embrace "African" religion.[36] This "absent" presence applies not only to the emerging black movement but to the Afro-Surinamese community as a whole. Officially, Protestantism, Catholicism, and Evangelical Christianity remain the major religious denominations among Afro-Surinamese, and when asked directly, the majority of Afro-Surinamese will deny any involvement with Winti. But my research has shown that in practice, there are very few who do not take an occasional herbal bath, wear jewelry dedicated to Winti spirits, bury the navel cord, or even see a *doeman* for certain ailments.[37] Indeed, it is part of the religion's history and self-understanding to operate beneath the surface and hidden from view.

IN THE NETHERLANDS, the colonial past has been the subject of heated debate. By raising the Dutch colonial past, the self-identified "descendants of the enslaved" articulate claims to Dutch citizenship, arguing that formally they have been part of this nation "for centuries." Yet their claims are not exclusively made within a secular framework of formal citizenship. They intervene in what has been called the "culturalization" of citizenship, but in claiming citizenship they take a critical stance.

The interventions presented in this chapter are issued from within what Paul Gilroy has called a counterculture of modernity, pointing to the fundamental entanglement of black cultures with modernity.[38] The ethnography suggests that in this counterculture, secular and religious modes of binding and belonging intersect. It invites, if not urges, a different understanding of modernity that does not take enlightened rationality and secularism as its self-evident foundation and religion as its other. Instead, it directs attention to the complex dynamics of processes of secularization and sacralization in racial modernity.[39] This means that we need to take seriously the role of religion in projects of postcolonial emancipation.

This embrace of religion has consequences in the context of the Netherlands, where postcolonial critique is often framed as secular critique, directed at historiography, museums, or cultural heritage. Perhaps this is a particularity of the Dutch context, where the quite rigorous process of depillarization has had far-reaching implications for religious authority in schools, the academy, and the cultural sector. But Markelo's emphasis on religion, and the genealogy of Surinamese nationalism in which this investment is situated, bears significance beyond the particularity of the Surinamese-Dutch context. The fact that the ancestors are mobilized in claims to citizenship poses an interesting challenge to the notion of secular critique, central to postcolonial studies and personified most prominently by Edward Said. In *Humanism and Democratic Criticism*, for instance, Said endorsed "the secular notion that the historical world is made by men and women, and not by God, and that it can be understood rationally."[40] Said's argument was of course against the essentialist belief in absolute truth and unchanging essences, for "to take human phenomena out of the reach of change is to give oneself over to metaphysics or theology."[41] But this stance also implied a refusal to engage with "metaphysics and cosmology," and indeed Said often seems to explicitly reject the role of religion in projects of liberation, emphasizing instead its destructive power.[42] What the case of the Kabra mask shows is not only that some people of African descent do not fully adhere to a framework of secular critique. It also shows that, as Leerom Medovoi and Elizabeth Bentley argue in this volume's introduction, religion may itself take on secular concerns such as citizenship. Markelo, but also the numerous religious figures who have engaged in anticolonial and civil rights struggles, may be seen as "secular" critics in the sense that as religious persons, they bring their passionate concerns into the world.

In the broadest sense, what these entanglements of religion, citizenship, and colonialism show is that the idea of neat and stable distinctions between secularism / modernity / the West, on the one hand, and religion and racialized others, on the other, is impossible to maintain. Instead, these categories have to be understood as spilling over into and informing one another, always involving processes of translation and mediation.

NOTES

1. Oskar Verkaaik, *Ritueel Burgerschap: Een Essay over Nationalisme En Secularisme in Nederland* (Amsterdam: Amsterdam University Press, 2009). All translations are mine unless otherwise noted.
2. Birgit Meyer, *Mediation and the Genesis of Presence: Towards a Material Approach to Religion* (Utrecht: Utrecht University, 2012), 6.
3. See Aamir Mufti, ed., *boundary 2* (special issue) 40, no. 2 (2013).
4. Stathis Gourgouris, "Part 1: Why I Am Not a Postsecularist," *boundary 2* 40, no. 1 (2013): 42.
5. John D. Boy, "What We Talk about When We Talk about the Postsecular," *Immanent Frame*, March 15, 2011, https://tif.ssrc.org/2011/03/15/what-we-talk-about-when-we-talk-about-the-postsecular/; see also van den Hemel, this volume.
6. Edward Said, *The World, the Text, and the Critic* (Cambridge, MA: Harvard University Press, 1983), 1–30.
7. Gourgouris, "Part 1," 42.
8. Stathis Gourgouris, *Lessons in Secular Criticism* (Oxford: Oxford University Press, 2013), 25.
9. Gourgouris, *Lessons in Secular Criticism*, 14; Bruce Robbins, "Is the Postcolonial Also Postsecular?," *boundary 2* 40, no. 1 (2013): 250.
10. Ann Laura Stoler, *Duress: Imperial Durabilities in Our Times* (Durham, NC: Duke University Press, 2016), ix.
11. Peter van der Veer, *Imperial Encounters: Religion and Modernity in India and Britain* (Princeton, NJ: Princeton University Press, 2001); Peter Geschiere, *The Modernity of Witchcraft: Politics and the Occult in Postcolonial Africa* (Charlottesville: University Press of Virginia, 1997); Birgit Meyer and Peter Pels, *Magic and Modernity: Interfaces of Revelation and Concealment* (Stanford: Stanford University Press, 2003).
12. Dipesh Chakrabarty, *Provincializing Europe: Postcolonial Thought and Historical Difference* (Princeton, NJ: Princeton University Press, 2001); Meyer, *Mediation and the Genesis of Presence*; David Chidester, *Savage Systems: Colonialism and Comparative Religion in Southern Africa*, Studies in Religion and Culture (Charlottesville: University Press of Virginia, 1996); Ann Laura Stoler, "On Degrees of Imperial Sovereignty," *Public Culture* 18, no. 1 (2006): 125–46; Ann Laura Stoler, "Affective States," in *A Companion to the Anthropology of Politics*, ed. David Nugent and Joan Vincent (Malden, MA: Blackwell, 2004), 4–20.
13. "Keti Koti 2013—nos—01, YouTube, accessed September 12, 2020, https://www.youtube.com/watch?v=aHWonIclZpg.
14. Zwarte Piet Niet, Facebook post, July 2, 2014, https://www.facebook.com/Zwartepietniet/photos/zie-hieronder-de-tekst-van-de-toespraak-van-gisteren-1-juli-2014-tijdens-de-herd/814772158535112/.
15. Jürgen Habermas, *Strukturwandel Der Öffentlichkeit: Untersuchungen Zu Einer Kategorie Der Bürgerlichen Gesellschaft* (Frankfurt am Main: Suhrkamp, 1990).
16. C. J. Wooding, *Winti, Een Afro-Amerikaanse Godsdienst in Suriname* (Meppel: Krips Repro, 1972), 290–91, quoted in Gloria Wekker, *The Politics of Passion: Women's Sexual Culture in the Afro-Surinamese Diaspora* (New York: Columbia University Press, 2006), 90.

17 Wekker, *Politics of Passion*, 90.
18 Wekker, *Politics of Passion*, 101.
19 Wekker, *Politics of Passion*, 83.
20 This needs to be qualified, however, since Maroons do not see themselves as descendants of the enslaved but as descendants of those who liberated themselves. Maroons therefore often reject the notion of collective or cultural trauma, arguing that by liberating themselves, the ancestors were not subjected to the traumatic experience of slavery, or at least freed themselves of the psychological consequences of enslavement.
21 Sidney Wilfred Mintz and Richard Price, *The Birth of African-American Culture: An Anthropological Perspective* (Boston: Beacon, 1992), 18.
22 Mintz and Price, *Birth of African-American Culture*, 18–19.
23 Mintz and Price, *Birth of African-American Culture*, 19.
24 Mintz and Price, *Birth of African-American Culture*, 25.
25 Alex Stipriaan, "Een Verre Verwijderd Trommelen: Ontwikkeling van Afro-Surinaamse Muziek En Dans in de Slavernij." In *De Kunstwereld: Produktie, Distributie En Receptie in de Wereld van Kunst En Cultuur*, edited by Ton Bevers, Anton Van den Braembussche, and Berend Jan Langenberg (Hilversum: Verloren, 1993), 143–73.
26 H. U. E. Thoden van Velzen and Ineke Wetering, *In the Shadow of the Oracle: Religion as Politics in a Suriname Maroon Society* (Long Grove, IL: Waveland, 2004). Bonuman or Doeman are religious experts that can be consulted in matters of health, love, sexuality, or even business.
27 Yvon van der Pijl, *Levende-Doden: Afrikaans-Surinaamse Percepties, Praktijken En Rituelen Rondom Dood En Rouw* (Amsterdam: Rozenberg, 2007), 64.
28 Edgar Cairo, *Lelu! Lelu! Het Lied der Vervreemding* (Haarlem: In de Knipscheer 1984), 58, quoted in van der Pijl, *Levende-Doden*, 64.
29 Michiel van Kempen, *Surinaamse schrijvers en dichters: Met honderd schrijversprofielen en een lijst van pseudoniemen* (Amsterdam: De Arbeiderspers, 1989), 79; cf. van der Pijl, *Levende-Doden*, 86.
30 Markus Balkenhol, "Working with the Ancestors: The Kabra Mask and the 'African Renaissance' in the Afro-Surinamese Winti Religion," *Material Religion: The Journal of Objects, Art and Belief* 11, no. 2 (2015): 250–54.
31 "Ik Ben Niet Te Koop," accessed August 15, 2016, http://aban.nl/ik-ben-niet-te-koop/.
32 The museum was founded in 1954 by the Holy Ghost Fathers (Congregatie van de H. Geest). Its original collection was established by the congregation's missionaries to give a broader view on the lifeworlds of the people in the areas in which they worked. Later this collection was expanded through acquisitions and donations.
33 H. U. Beier, "The Egungun Cult among the Yorubas," *Présence Africaine* 18–19 (1958): 33–36; Joel A. Adedeji, "The Origin and Form of the Yoruba Masque Theatre," *Cahiers d'Études Africaines* 12, no. 46 (1972): 254–76.
34 In fact, the dance group performing with the mask is led by Otmar Watson, the central figure in de Witte's ethnographic account.

35 Marleen de Witte, "Heritage, Blackness, and Afro-Cool," *African Diaspora* 7 (2): 282; Paul Gilroy, *The Black Atlantic: Modernity and Double Consciousness* (London: Verso, 1993).
36 De Witte, "Heritage, Blackness, and Afro-Cool."
37 Markus Balkenhol, "Tracing Slavery: An Ethnography of Diaspora, Affect, and Cultural Heritage in Amsterdam" (PhD diss., Vrije Universiteit Amsterdam, 2014).
38 Gilroy, *Black Atlantic*, 1–40.
39 Geschiere, *Modernity of Witchcraft*; Meyer and Pels, *Magic and Modernity*.
40 Edward W. Said, *Humanism and Democratic Criticism* (New York: Columbia University Press, 2004), 11, quoted in Robbins, "Is the Postcolonial Also Postsecular?," 251.
41 Robbins, "Is the Postcolonial Also Postsecular?," 251.
42 Robbins, "Is the Postcolonial Also Postsecular?," 250.

13. TRANSSECULAR INCARNATIONS
Destabilizing the (Cis)Gender Politics of Secularism
ZEYNEP KURTULUŞ KORKMAN

Gender is central to normative modes of secularist and religious belonging and their subversion. This chapter explores how transgressive gendered performance, identity, and embodiment destabilize the established relations between secularism and religion. I focus on Vedia Bülent Çorak Önsü, an (in)famous Turkish woman who serves as the leader of an eclectic religious group that combines deep secularist devotion with New Age and Islamic beliefs ranging from UFOism to Sufism. To legitimize her unusual brand of secularist religious authority, Çorak depends on a fluid idea of gender she articulates as part of her belief system, which enables her to ventriloquize deceased male figures ranging from the secularist founding father of Turkey, Mustafa Kemal Atatürk, to the thirteenth-century Sufi mystic Mevlana Celaleddin Rumi. Çorak's resolutely secularist brand of and subversively gendered claims to religious authority have attracted thousands of followers and angered secularists and Islamists alike. Inspired by Çorak's case, the chapter proposes a transsecular analytic to disrupt the categories of the religious and the secular through a denaturalization of the binary gender model on which these categories depend.

At first glance, Çorak looks like the perfect representative of the secular, modern femininity endorsed by Turkey's founder, Atatürk. On her personal website, Çorak poses proudly against the background of a megasized deep-red Turkish flag, surrounded by two life-size Atatürk photographs that are ceremonially cordoned off by red velvet cordons, conjuring the official state symbolism.[1] While Atatürk in one of the portraits is wearing trousers and sitting with his legs wide, Çorak sits in a modest crossed-legged position with a blazer and a skirt that extends just below her knees, a size codified in official dress regulations for female civil servants. Surrounded by the most potent symbols of Turkish secularism and donning its typical attire and body language, Çorak so closely approximates the elements, composition, and style of Turkish secularist aesthetics that uniformly color every school, government agency, or political party office that one would assume that she is a schoolmistress, public officer, or politician. Her normative performance of secular femininity notwithstanding, Çorak articulates a transgressive formulation of gender identity and embodiment through her theory of reincarnation and claims lineage from prominent male political and religious leaders, including Atatürk, Abrahamic prophets, and Sufi mystics. In doing so, Çorak impersonates and surpasses the gendered ethos of Turkish secularism in excess and in an unexpected combination with religiosity.

This chapter draws on the online self-representations and teachings of Çorak and her organizations, World Brotherhood Union Mevlana Supreme Foundation (Dünya Kardeşlik Birliği Mevlana Yüce Vakfı) and Universal Unification Center Association (Evrensel Birleşim Merkezi Derneği), their media coverage, my ethnographic observations at a group meeting, and an in-depth interview I conducted with a group member. Scrutinizing Çorak's persona, teachings, following, critiques, and persecution, I show how the unlikely blend of secularist and religious affects conjured by Çorak holds a magnifying glass that expands and refracts in surprising angles the gendered discontents of secularism and religiosity in contemporary Turkey

Building on critical studies of secularism and religion and their gendered politics and inspired by the epistemological interventions of transgender studies, particularly at the intersections of religious and transgender studies, I argue that Çorak renders the normative gendering of religious and political belonging visible by transgressing the conventional binaries and boundaries of these categories.[2] Commanding a secularist, New Ageist, and remarkably female following in a country where political belonging has long been brokered along the hard lines of secularist/Islamist, Çorak summons with ritualistic devotion the spirit of Turkish secularism while simultaneously destabilizing its gender conventions. Çorak performs a normative secular femininity while she also boldly embodies via reincarnation the leading secularist and religious male figures of the country. Informed by Susan Stryker's provocation to deploy transgender as "an umbrella term for a wide variety of bodily effects that disrupt or denaturalize heteronormatively constructed linkages between an individual's anatomy at birth, a nonconsensually assigned gender category, psychical identifications with sexed body images and/or gendered subject positions, and the performance of specifically gendered social, sexual, or kinship functions" with the purposes of "making visible heteronormativity's occluded structures and operations," I analyze Çorak's secularist New Ageism with an eye for rendering discernable the (cis)gender norms of religious and secularist belonging.[3]

With an emphasis on analyzing specific projects of secularism in relation to the local religious and political formations in which they are embedded, this chapter scrutinizes a unique brand of gender-transgressive and secularist religious authority in a national context well known for its devout sacralization of secularism, its emphasis on a particular brand of secular femininity, and its current Islamist government, which has been ruling for almost two decades.[4] In this context, I propose a transsecular intervention that highlights the transgression of the binary categories of secular/religious, this-worldly / other- or outerworldly, orthodox/heterodox, enlightened/superstitious, civilized/uncivilized, educated/ignorant, and last but not least, male/female. In times when gendered aesthetics are routinely mobilized to distinguish a secular, civilized, if implicitly Christian "us" from religious, barbaric, and Islamic others globally, a transsecular analytic underscores the potential of transgressive gendered performances for destabilizing the co-constitutive and naturalizing binaries of male/female and secular/religious.

Secularisms, Gendered Sacralizations, and Transgender Destabilizations

Studying secularism comparatively beyond its taken-for-granted location in (early modern) Western Europe demonstrates that the secular and the religious are not preexisting categories for ordering social life but are constructed through the appropriation and remaking of secularism in relation to other projects of social transformation such as postcolonialism, nationalism, and modernization.[5] Turkish secularism is part of the larger nationalist modernist project of the early twentieth century and one of the main pillars of Kemalism, the official state ideology named after Mustafa Kemal Atatürk. Secularism was conceived as part of modernization and nationalization of the country and religious authority was considered as a major obstacle to these projects.⁶ Turkey has been well recognized for its unique brand of authoritative secularism called *laiklik*, which was inspired by French laicism, with an ambition to control the public visibility of religion through top-down state efforts that administer desirable forms and prohibit undesirable forms of religion.⁷ Turkish secularism depended on both repressive and productive measures aiming to reduce the public visibility of a host of existing religious organizations and practitioners and to monopolistically produce and administer a modernized version of Sunni Islam through a central state institution.⁸ The repressive secularist measures included the criminalization of religious orders and various established positions of religious authority from sheikh to disciple. Here lies the irony of Çorak, a New Age leader whose nationalist secularism goes as far as ventriloquizing Atatürk, who passed the very secularist laws under which Çorak would be tried a century later.

Çorak's unique brand of secularist New Ageism is best viewed within the larger context of the sacralization of state secularism in modern Turkey. In a public culture where, as Yael Navaro-Yashin aptly expresses it, "secularism has been manifest not only in the rational and ordered terms of an analytically reified modernity, but also in the medium of excessive expression, mystical, ritualesque, and religious," Çorak's eclectic mixing of the secular and the religious emerges out of already existing nationally consecrated canons and rituals of secularism.⁹ Moving out of and beyond the habitual forms of sacralizing secularism, Çorak is "conjuring an aesthetics that transgresses itself, a secularist aesthetics that will be repurposed as a resource to sustain exilic formations of religious life," as Christopher Dole argues in his study of another exceptional Turkish woman, Zöhre Ana, who is also a religious leader combining a modern, secular femininity with religious authority, if in the more familiar idiom of Islamic sainthood.¹⁰ Çorak's secularist/millennialist/UFOist/Sufist bricolage forms a transgressive hybrid that I conceptualize as a transsecular form of belonging, one in which the secularist and the Islamist are vacated as distinct categories.

Secularism in contexts of nationalist modernization from postcolonial India to almost postcolonial Turkey has been closely tied to an uneasy relationship between the remaking of gender relations and the remaking of the nation, where a particular brand of femininity was tasked to carry and resolve the paradoxical goals of becoming modern and Westernized while remaining distinctly national.¹¹ Under the weight of this paradox, contestations over gender relations became a central arena for articulating (secularist and religious) political belonging.¹² Transforming gender relations was a key aspect of Turkish secularism, operationalized by reforms such as the adoption of Swiss family law and the prohibition of veiling for state personnel. Women were particularly burdened with carrying and resolving the tensions of nationalist secularization.[13] They were tasked with walking the tightrope of embodying a modern but modest femininity.[14] In this context, the secularist/Islamist divide was largely expressed and contested in gendered terms, especially through public performances of femininity.[15]

In a country where the remaking and disciplining of femininity has been central to the political project of secularism, Çorak's appropriation of secular femininity to claim reincarnation from a lineage of male religious and secular leaders and to perform as the leader of a persecuted religious group deeply destabilizes the conventional terms of religiosity and secularist gender politics. Çorak avidly embodies a modern but modest womanhood, unveiled yet decently covered, wearing suits but with a skirt, hair cut short yet feminine, and carrying her body in a confident yet reserved manner. Nevertheless, she is also a religious leader. Similar to Zöhre Ana, who "rejects the dominant symbol of feminine religiosity and piety—the veil—and embraces a secular nationalist discourse of ideal womanhood as an idiom of her saintly identity," Çorak invokes secular femininity and religious authority in an unlikely combination.[16]

While the study of the relationships between gender, Islam, and secularism is a well-trodden field, the relationships between religion, secularism, and transgender embodiments and identities in Turkey remain understudied with a few exceptions. Rüstem Ertuğ Altınay explored how Bülent Ersoy, a popular singer and the first public transgender figure of Turkey, crafted herself as a conservative Muslim woman to claim gendered respectability.[17] Ersoy remade herself as a pious, chaste, heteronormative woman by wearing a veil while attending funerals, dropping the word *Allah* frequently in her performances, and reciting the Islamic call to prayer in an album, which conventionally has been recited only by male imams. The latter sparked debates as to whether a woman could recite the call to prayer and "gave Ersoy the opportunity to reaffirm her faith in Islam and also have others reaffirm her gender identity as a woman."[18] Discussing Ersoy's hosting at a presidential fast-breaking dinner in 2016, Evren Savcı explored the interfaces between transactivism and the Islamist government. Ersoy's strategic hosting came just a day after a violent police intervention interrupting the Istanbul Trans Pride March, which was banned with the excuse that it was not compatible with the holy month of Ramadan. The transgender community recognized the irony of the government's honoring of the country's lone transgender celebrity on an occasion of shared piety right after a violent attack on transgender activists in retaliation for their activism's presumed incompatibility with pious conduct. Furthermore, many in the trans community had refrained from participating in the previous year's unobstructed Trans Pride March, which similarly coincided with Ramadan, out of their own sense of piety. Highlighting these complexities, Savcı problematized a reductionist understanding of the religious as categorically exclusive of trans and a simple equation of the secular with trans.[19]

Further complicating the relationships between the gendered politics of religion and secularism and trans experience and activism is the larger context of discrimination and marginalization shaping transgender lives. While Ersoy has been relatively successful in her quest to construct herself as a respectable woman through performing piety, even earning an invitation to a presidential fast-breaking dinner, this comes at the expense of Ersoy's distancing of herself from the larger transgender population in Turkey whose lives are shaped by pervasive exclusion and violence. Transgender individuals in Turkey are heavily discriminated against in employment, housing, and health care and rendered vulnerable to criminalization and state and societal violence, despite growing transgender activism since the 1990s.[20] They are widely excluded from normative forms of social belonging; their belonging even in the (Muslim) religious community becomes contested, for example, when religious personnel refuse to offer them proper funeral and burial ceremonies and trans friends and activists advocate on behalf of the deceased to secure appropriate religious rites.[21]

To clarify, I do not claim that Çorak identifies or is read as a transgender individual or shares the conditions of abjection to which the Turkish transgender community is subjected. Çorak has a strong claim to a normative femininity and proper womanhood as a straight, cisgender woman who was previously married and who has a daughter, as she and her followers like to emphasize. At the same time, however, Çorak's bold theory of reincarnation posits male or female gender identity and embodiment as incidental and unfixed qualities and allows Çorak to daringly join a line of male religious/political authority figures that includes Atatürk alongside Sufi saints and monotheistic prophets.

I deploy the affix "trans" to highlight how Çorak troubles the conventional cisgendered relationships between embodiment, identity, and performance upon which both Islamist and secular versions of Turkish identity depend. I prefer the theoretical intervention of "trans" over "queer" here in order to avoid undermining Çorak's firm performance of secularist normative femininity that delivers her gendered respectability, while emphasizing Çorak's transgression of a binary model of gender identity and embodiment through her foundational claims about reincarnation and her unusual brand of secularist religious authority.

While the distinctions between queer and trans studies are blurry and these fields are closely interrelated, "queer is associated primarily with nonnormative desires and sexual practices, and transgender is associated primarily with nonnormative gender identifications and embodiments."[22] Thinking with trans rather than queer helps account for the paradox that Çorak's secularist performance of femininity is so normative and her take on the official state ideology of secularist devotion to Atatürk so intense that she claims lineage from male forms of religious and political authority by formulating a theory of reincarnation in which gender embodiment and identify appear plastic.

Çorak operates in a context where secularism is no longer hegemonic, following the 1990s rise of Islamism as a popular political movement and the repeated electoral successes of the Justice and Development Party in the first two decades of the twenty-first century.[23] While the affective appeal and sacralization of Turkish secularism and Atatürk have been intensified by a fear of reactionary Islam since its inception, it was in these recent decades that nationalist secularism and the devotion it commands have been particularly revitalized.[24] The sacralization of secularism manifested through the intensified circulation of symbols and performance of rituals around the cult of Atatürk, such as rosettes, photos, songs, marches, mausoleum visits (i.e., pilgrimages to Atatürk's tomb), and even "sightings" of his figure in hilltops and in coffee residues read for divination.[25] As secular and Islamic forms of the sacred have competed to conjure political affect and coagulate rivaling political allegiances, secularists have accused Islamists for bringing religion to illegitimately bear on politics, while Islamists have criticized secularists for sacralizing Atatürk and his secularist ideology.

At both ends of the Turkish political spectrum, gendered processes of sacralization have played a key role in producing a sense of political belonging. While the strong one-man leadership of Atatürk was officially cultivated for many years, he has been popularly reclaimed in recent decades. The figure of Atatürk as a modern and modernizing man represented a melancholic attachment to the early republican era of radical secularism.[26] Secularist women celebrated Atatürk and the gender regime he modeled, often by expressing their defense of a threatened secular femininity. A nostalgic yet resentful quest to restore Kemalist secularism often found expression through concern over the visibility of veiled women in public. This move inverted the Islamist sacralization of veiled women as the pure victims of secularism and the prime symbols of the sanctified wound of Islamism.[27] Veiled women had served as the symbol of the Islamist resentment, as a sign of Turkish secularism's duplicitously discriminatory promise to include women in the public sphere while banning the veil from public institutions.[28] In this context, the increasing public visibility of veiling has faced off with a public display of Atatürk's portraits.[29] In this competing constellation of secularist and Islamist gendered sacralizations of political belonging, Çorak's performance of secular femininity legitimizes her bold claims to ventriloquize both male religious and secularist leaders through reincarnation and allows her to subvert the (cis)gendered conventions that broker established forms of religious authority and political belonging.

The New Age Secularism of Rumi/Atatürk/Çorak

Quoting altered verses from the Qur'an alongside changed sayings of Atatürk in the same breath through communications with aliens (see figure 13.1), hailed as a reincarnation of Turkey's most prestigious secularist and religious figures alike, Çorak cannot be easily placed onto the familiar maps of Turkish politics. Çorak commenced her spiritual career in the post-1980 military coup atmosphere, marked by a violent repression of civil society and a reintroduction of Islam into official state ideology as an antidote to dissident ideologies.[30] In 1981, Çorak started to receive messages from extraterrestrial beings. Channeling these communications, she started to write her *Book of Knowledge* (*Bilgi Kitabı*) in İzmir, a metropolitan city in Turkey's Aegean coast known as a stronghold of Kemalist secularism. The book combines messages from three major monotheistic religions, Far Eastern and Sufi mystical traditions, New Ageist teachings such as millennialism and UFOism, and last but not least, Kemalism, coaxed in a language that borrowed from Ottoman Turkish as much as it did from modern scientific terminology. Over the following decades, the book was occasionally confiscated by the police and even legally ordered to be seized, according to a public announcement of the group.[31] In 1993, the group gained formal organizational standing with the World Brotherhood Union Mevlana Supreme Foundation and the Universal Unification Center Association. These organizations expanded to have standing branches in urban areas across Turkey, mainly in western and southern coastal regions, and a limited international presence, and claim thousands of members. Çorak might have a rather modest number of followers but she received a relatively disproportionate critical response, reflected in her media bashing and recurrent criminal persecution.

Çorak's odd assortment of teachings envelopes a unique response to Turkish secularism and its discontents. Çorak's teachings are similar to their New Age peers around the world with a pastiche of elements from various religious and spiritual traditions combined with allusions to numerology, occult symbols, energy flows, and higher consciousness levels, tucked into a millennial-

FIGURE 13.1. Bülent Çorak is featured in a news article condemning her group as alien-worshipping fanatics. "Doğuştan Değil Uzaydan Fanatikler," *Sabah*, May 14, 2001.

ist mission of leading humanity in(to) an approaching golden age of awakening. She blatantly disregards the lines conventionally separating the various strands of knowledge she calls upon, from heterodox and orthodox Islamic traditions to Islamic, Christian, and Jewish religions, and other religious traditions, from enlightenment and romantic paradigms to earthly and celestial sources of knowledge. The most outstanding is her disregard for the incongruity of religious and secularist sources of authority. The *Book of Knowledge* contains multiple authorial voices and signatures, such as "The Pen of the Golden Age," "The [Galactic] Center," and Mevlana Celaleddin Rumi. Daringly, the book also includes direct discourse from Atatürk, who offers a different version of his famous "Address to the Youth."[32] The original address is a standard opening text of all school textbooks in modern Turkey. It has been such a potent symbol of commitment to a nationalist secularist future that secularists were alarmed when a recent revision to private school regulations canceled the specification that a framed version of the address must be hang in every "Atatürk corner," a mandated secularist school shrine commemorating Atatürk.[33] While Çorak herself does not explicitly claim to be (the reincarnation of) Atatürk, and Atatürk's direct voice is limited in her book, it is clearly stated that "this book was written with his [Atatürk's] consciousness," and Atatürk is repeatedly named alongside other figures from whom Çorak claims heritage/identity/affinity by reincarnation.[34]

Çorak is literally a child of Turkish secularism. She was born, as she proudly emphasizes, in 1923, the very year of the foundation of the Turkish republic. She does not settle, however, for the usual role of the grateful daughter of Atatürk, literally "the father of Turks." Instead she reverses the relation of gratitude that has long shaped secular Turkish women's thankfulness to the secularist leader for his gender progressive reforms.[35] In Çorak's book, it is Atatürk who is thankful. In this version of "Address to the Youth," diverging from the commanding and prescriptive tone of the original address, Atatürk offers in the name of the Turkish nation his "infinite gratitude" to Çorak's followers, whom he affectionately calls "my children."[36] Çorak's position here remains ambiguously double, as she is both the bearer and hearer of this message, both an heir to and a ventriloquist of Atatürk. Instead of contending with normatively identifying as a symbolic and grateful daughter, Çorak dares to subversively identify with, or rather literally as, Atatürk himself.

Reflecting on her gender-bending claims to normatively male secularist and religious leadership positions, Çorak provides a plastic, nonbinary gender framework that addresses the possible anxieties instigated by her crossing of male/female distinction as the latest link of a reincarnation chain containing all male figures such as Atatürk, Moses, Jesus, Mohammad, and Rumi. In Çorak's flexible model of gender and sexual identities and presentations, "souls do not have gender" but simply "assume male or female characters as it fits their roles during cycles of reincarnation."[37] This perspective subverts the normative fixing of a singular, stable gender identity onto a gendered body as it liberates the genderless essence of a person, described as a reincarnating soul, from not only a biological sex category that might be assigned to their body at birth but also from the gender identity and role that they might be assigned or assume in their lifetime. If only incidentally, Çorak, whose full name is Vedia Bülent Önsü Çorak, is known by her first name, Bülent, which is not only a male name in contemporary Turkish but is also the name of the first male-to-female transgender Turkish citizen, Bülent Ersoy, who happens to be the only other public figure called Bülent Hanım (Ms. Bülent).

Çorak further flouts gender binaries through her concept of the mother as a generative force and a "sex/gender" (*cinsiyet*). Çorak explains that when first souls left their bodies (for reincarnation), their genes were frozen to be transferred to select reincarnations. Çorak claims that the gender of these first genes with godly, generative powers was "mother" (*ana*) and all prophets were such "mothers." Establishing the gender of religious leaders with whom she is affiliated through reincarnation as "mothers" instead of male or female and insisting on the generativity of motherhood, Çorak substantively redefines gender over and beyond conventional sex/gender categories and concomitant positions of religious and political power. Çorak also legitimizes her gender-bending claims to spiritual authority through anchoring onto the gendered nationalist imaginary of motherland. Çorak plays with the word *Anatolia* (*Anadolu*), the Turkish nationalist word for the country's hinterland, which can be literally translated as and is interpreted in "folk etymology" to mean "filled of mothers."[38] According to Çorak, "Anatolia is the bedrock of these genes and that is why the reality is brought to humanity from the pen of Mevlana Celaleddin Rumi [as reincarnated in Çorak], via the channel of Anatolia, from Atatürk's Turkey. Atatürk, our esteemed friend who established a new order and accomplished the first world reform, explained to you the real meaning of mother [*ana*], and enlightened the place of women in a backward society. He is still with us today and still working toward this goal."[39] Building on the nationalist sacralization of motherland while harnessing the modernist secularist ideals for uplifting women, Çorak urges her readers to "notice that circles with higher consciousness are usually led by women rather than men."[40] The reader might be reasonably expected to conclude that these women-led circles include those following Çorak's leadership and the smaller circles in which her followers are organized, led by the experienced members, many of whom are women.

Çorak's double claims to secularist and religious authority destabilize the gendered economies of contempt and desire that mobilize Turkish secularist imaginary. Here, the typical figure of popular religious authority and the prime target of secularist criminalization remains a *hodja*, who is primarily gendered male and depicted as a (sexual) predator who victimizes susceptible women.[41] In this gendered story, the stereotype of the superstitious housewife who frequents hodjas and engages in other "superstitious" practices such as reading fortunes or wearing protections against the evil eye emerges as a necessary figure of the fantasy of secularizing male reason.[42] It is in this context that Çorak's status as a housewife with a high school diploma is repeatedly brought up by her critics to put her down by reminding that she was simply "a housewife who participated in spirit summoning and hypnosis sessions."[43] While Çorak's critics use this stereotype to disqualify her claims to religious authority and secularist respectability, a longtime follower testifies that Çorak has "never closed a coffee cup" for fortunetelling, in an effort to distinguish her from the domestic and feminized sphere of superstitions that a housewife who reads coffee cups succinctly represents.[44]

Çorak encourages women's participation and leadership, legitimized through allusions to existing heterodox frameworks for female religious authority. Çorak's group liberally alludes to Sufi Islam and the relatively larger space it allowed for women's religious authority, as it includes the term "brotherhood" in the name of its foundation and gathers under the reincarnated leadership of the prestigious Sufi leader of the thirteenth century, Rumi. While orthodox Islam administered by the (Ottoman and later Turkish) state have largely excluded women from positions of authority, Sufi brotherhoods have historically been more inclusive.[45] The religious minority of Alevis, known as the followers of Ali, are particularly recognized for their gender-mixed rituals and the prominent role women assume, and for this reason have long been appropriated by Turkish secularism as an authentic, "Anatolian" brand of Islam that is compatible with secularist gender politics and a political ally to secularism.[46] Some have even noted that Alevis "have almost regarded Kemal Atatürk as a saint, or even as a reincarnation of Ali," and decorated their homes and places of worship with portraits of Atatürk alongside Ali.[47] Similarly, Zöhre Ana, another female religious leader with strong secularist sensibilities, is not only an Alevi living saint and a proud member of the secularist Republican People's Party, but she is also frequently depicted alongside the images of Atatürk, Ali, and Rumi.[48] Indeed, the concept of "mother" that Çorak so evocatively builds on is an Alevi title for female religious leadership.

Women constitute a sizable portion if not the majority of the membership and leadership of Çorak's group. They are very visible in the group's self-representations, featured on the group's website during the events it organizes, such as its annual awards ceremony. In a rare moment of positive publicity, the group's 2014 ceremony was featured in the arts and culture pages of newspapers after hosting a popular musician (see figure 13.2). Like Çorak, member women are often photographed in blazers and skirts, sometimes in matching purple suits. Purple, according to the *Book of Knowledge*, is the color of "the unification of universal and divine orders" and, if not intentionally, evocative of the feminist movement.[49] Staging women at public occasions in professional outfits and cultivating nonfamilial intimacies among members, the group might be providing avenues off the domestic pull of heteronormative femininity.[50]

Sibel was one of the many secularist women I met during my initial fieldwork in Istanbul, Turkey, between 2005 and 2007 and during my subsequent annual visits over the next decade. Sibel was a veteran member of Çorak's group and a founding member of the local district chapter. She was a divorced middle-class woman and ran a small textiles store around Bağdat Avenue, the center of the upper-middle-class secular lifestyle in the Anatolian side of Istanbul. Sibel's

FIGURE 13.2. In a rare instance of positive publicity, Bülent Çorak is photographed hosting a popular musician in her group's annual awards ceremony. "Mevlana Vakfına Özel Konser," *HaberTurk*, November 6, 2016.

secularist political identity, her distaste for familiar Sunni Islamic rituals, and her interest in New Age teachings found a hospitable terrain in Çorak, who deemphasized conventional forms of Islamic piety and offered an alternative space of spirituality and belonging. Evoking a mystical quest for deeper (occulted) experiences, Sibel told me at length about her dissatisfactions with established forms of devotion, including the feminized realm of Islamic sociabilities. For example, she dismissed women-only daytime prayer meetings at homes by describing them as "drills for schoolchildren," which she noted were pointless if children already understand the lesson behind the exercise. She was introduced to Çorak's group by a female acquaintance, the mother of a schoolmate of her daughter. In a conversation with this friend, Sibel was intrigued by words like "energy" and "evolution." While energy resonated as a fundamental notion for many strands of New Ageism, evolution was a loaded concept that distinguishes secularists from Islamists. Sibel was intrigued; these were the words that "an uneducated person would not use," she remarked with appreciation.

In a country profoundly structured around a civilizing project where secular, urban, educated, and middle-class status has for a long time exclusively conveyed distinction, the fraternity of the *Book of Knowledge* did not smoothly mend social hierarchies.[51] This was why as Sibel and I prepared to leave her store to attend a weekly group meeting, she explained to me that "the worldly culture of the speaker is independent of their universal consciousness and may differ every week." We drove in Sibel's car, along with a newer female member, to Ümraniye, a working-class neighborhood where the Islamist Justice and Development Party had received a sweeping majority of the votes in the last municipal elections. As we walked into the ground floor of a modest apartment building, Sibel reminded me again that the person lecturing that day was "high in spiritual and evolutionary level but low in worldly culture." We entered a modestly decorated saloon where dozens of folding chairs were set to face a stage area decorated with Turkish flags; images of Çorak, Atatürk, and Rumi; and boards and charts displaying key concepts and symbols from the *Book of Knowledge*. Attendees, mostly middle-aged men and women, were taking their time to socialize and chitchat, munching on the pastries and nonalcoholic beverages set on a long table. I noticed that none of the women present were veiled, in contrast to the larger neighborhood, where veiled women were a frequent sight. After a rather unimpressive presentation by a speaker whose timid mannerisms and uneasy reading performance suggested a lack of assertiveness that an elite education and an upper-middle-class habitus could have cultivated, a brief and formulaic question-and-answer section concluded the session. We drove away with a sense of crossing the spatialized and embodied boundaries of distinction that Sibel and I so comfortably shared as secular middle-class women with an urban background and university education living on the other side of town.

Çorak's group's insistent claims to secular middle-class respectability and its public presence notwithstanding, the group has been operating under the threat of criminalization in Turkey, where religious brotherhoods have been categorically banned during the radical secularization of the 1920s. It is perhaps for this reason that Çorak explicitly emphasizes that the *Book of Knowledge* is a guidebook but not a holy book, and that she is a "celestial sister" but not a prophet. Similarly, the group does not call itself a religious brotherhood (*tarikat*) but is organized under the legally permissible categories of foundation and association. The Sufi tradition that the group most explicitly alludes to is the Mevlevi order, which is founded by the followers of Sunni Sufi mystic Mevlana Celaleddin Rumi. Çorak's preferential interest in Rumi is in continuation with the exceptional place Mevlevis enjoyed in Ottoman reformist, European Orientalist, and Turkish secularist perspectives as civilized, humanistic spiritual forms worthy of appraisal.[52] Indeed, after the secularist banning of brotherhoods, Mevlevis were exclusively allowed to operate in limited but legitimate ways through museumification and reclaimed as an invented tradition produced for touristic consumption and transnational circulation.[53] Taking on a brand of Sufism that is cherished by nationalist secularists and drawing upon New Ageist, UFOist teachings that are less likely to trigger secularist persecution compared to those recognized as traditionally Islamic, Çorak fostered a relatively tolerable public presence for her group. Nevertheless, Çorak, her organization, and its directors have been repeatedly prosecuted and tried, sometimes upon complaints from ex-members. Among other legal ordeals, Çorak was put on trial under Law No. 677, which outlaws religious orders and criminalizes those who assume related titles such as "father" (*baba*, an Alevi male religious leader title, corresponding to the female title of the mother, *ana*). The organization itself was accused of being in violation of Law No. 2908, which prohibits religious and sectarian associations; the foundation was investigated by the Directorate General of Foundations.

The group was most recently accused of being "spiritual extensions of Ergenekon," an alleged underground nationalist secularist organization formed by a group of military officers, journalists, and lawmakers to overthrow the Islamist Justice and Development Party government. In 2008, the *Book of Knowledge* was reported to be seized during the home search of a high-profile suspect, General Veli Küçük, hinting at the possible intimacies formed around the secularist affective pull Çorak might have cultivated.[54] Küçük might have been seduced by the New Ageist evocations of secularist nationalist pride in the *Book of Knowledge*, in which Turkey appears as a chosen land under galactic protection. Turkey is where the alpha God channel, once tuned to Jerusalem, now broadcasts; it is where Atatürk was sent to reform in preparation for higher levels of consciousness; and it is where Çorak lives today. After all, "the *Book of Knowledge* was given to Turkey," as Sibel explained proudly. Interestingly, Ergenekon suspects such as Küçük were accused of secularist plotting against the Islamist government and sentenced to life in 2013, only to have their cases overturned by the Supreme Court in April 2016.[55] Remarkably, when three months later, in July 2016, a military coup attempt was undertaken, the Justice and Development Party government would hold responsible not the secularist nationalist military members of the Ergenekon trail but a religious brotherhood. This brotherhood, consisting of the followers of U.S.-based leader Fethullah Gülen, the government would explain, had plotted to wrongly indict the secularist soldiers of Ergenekon in the first place. The mass sacking and criminalization of the alleged Gülen followers continues in 2020. In this fast-changing context, the futures of various forms of religious and secularist belonging and their relationships remain in flux, attesting to the increasing instability of these categories in contemporary Turkey.

Thinking Transsecular

Informed by the concept of trans as an epistemological intervention, I conceptualize Çorak's crossings of the gendered politics of Turkish secularism and religion as transsecular. In doing so, I am inspired by the destabilizing irreverence that Çorak models through her innovative reinterpretation and subversion of the category of gender via reincarnation, her seemingly incongruous persona, and her teachings, which trouble some of the most vexing contradictions of secularism.

Çorak's New Age group at once engages and transgresses the norms of Turkish secularism through its gendered sacralization of the secularist founder of the country, Atatürk, alongside an eclectic mix of other religious and New Age figures, including Rumi and aliens. The intertextuality and interchangeability of the political and religious figures past and present eclectically summoned by Çorak enable her to serve as a mediator of political and religious belonging in a society long fractured by the fault lines of secularism and Islamism. Taking the sacralization of secularism beyond its limits, Çorak displays, and perhaps promises to heal, the deep wounds of Turkish secularism, as Christopher Dole suggests of Zöhre Ana in his book *Healing Secular Life*.[56] What is most unsettling about Çorak for the established terms of both secularist and Islamist economies of gendered sacralization is that Çorak uses secularist feminine respectability to leverage her claims to an unorthodox and unconventionally gendered form of secularist religious authority. She thus daringly takes on a leading role in the secularist metanarrative of Kemalism as well as the religious metanarrative of Islam. Claiming conventionally male forms of religious and secularist leadership through an inventive reconceptualization of gender as an unfixed, nonbinary, generative condition, Çorak establishes a transsecular terrain on which she can ventriloquize both the founding father of the country, Atatürk, and the Sufi leader Rumi. In doing so, Çorak destabilizes the constitutive distinctions of secular/religious and male/female upon which the hegemonic relationships between gender, nation, religion, and secularism depend.

The intervention that the term "transsecular" offers to our understanding of the gendered politics of religion and secularism is relevant to various (trans) national contexts, while it arises from the specific context of Turkey. Politics of gender and sexuality have historically played and continue to play a central and constitutive role in mediating political belonging via nationalism, secularism, and religion globally. This is evident, for example, in the transnational production and circulation of, and the intensity of responses to, the narratives and images of gendered and sexualized oppression that are believed to spring from Islamic religious traditionalism. Consider the centrality of images of sexual slavery to discussions about the Islamic state, of narratives of honor crimes occurring among immigrant Muslim communities in Europe to debates over Turkey's European Union candidacy, and of representations of veiling and increasingly of violence against LGBTIQ populations to deliberations over U.S. military intervention and occupation in the Middle East.[57] Echoing the colonial logic of "white men saving brown women from brown men," transnational flows of such representations serve to collapse national and religious identity together and translate them into essentialized cultural differences, demarcate the boundaries between Western/Christian and non-Western/Islamic nations, and justify the exclusion and subjugation of the latter in the name of, once again, emancipation of gender and sexual minorities from religious oppression.[58] In this context, disarticulating the binary formation of secular/religious with its attendant categories such as male/female, enlightened/superstitious, educated/ignorant, and civilized/uncivilized remains crucial. To this aim, a transsecular analytic invites disentangling of the ways in which the gender binary and the distinction of secular/religious naturalize and stabilize each other.

NOTES

I am indebted to Christopher Dole and Susan Stryker for reading an earlier version of this chapter. I am grateful to editors Elizabeth Bentley and Lee Medovoi for their helpful feedback in revising this chapter. I am also thankful to my colleagues at the Religion, Secularism, and Political Belonging and Transgender Studies Initiatives at the University of Arizona, where I initially wrote this chapter in 2016.

1 "Who Is V. Bülent Çorak," *Bülent Çorak*, accessed November 20, 2016, http://www.bulentcorak.com.
2 For secularism and religion, see Talal Asad, *Formations of the Secular: Christianity, Islam, Modernity* (Stanford: Stanford University Press, 2003); Talal Asad, *Genealogies of Religion: Discipline and Reasons of Power in Christianity and Islam* (Baltimore: Johns Hopkins University Press, 2009); Craig Calhoun, Mark Juergensmeyer, and Jonathan VanAntwerpen, *Rethinking Secularism* (New York: Oxford University Press, 2011); Charles Taylor, *A Secular Age* (Cambridge, MA: Harvard University Press,

2009); Michael Warner, Jonathan VanAntwerpen, and Craig J. Calhoun, *Varieties of Secularism in a Secular Age* (Cambridge, MA: Harvard University Press, 2010). I pursue the invitation to conceptualize politics of religion and secularism beyond dichotomous terms and complement the scholarship on the gendered politics of Islam and secularism that have often focused on pious Muslim women. See Nilüfer Göle, "Post-Secular Turkey," *New Perspectives Quarterly* 29, no. 1 (2012): 7–11; Deniz Kandiyoti, "The Travails of the Secular: Puzzle and Paradox in Turkey," *Economy and Society* 41, no. 4 (2012): 513–31; Alev Çınar, *Modernity, Islam, and Secularism in Turkey: Bodies, Places, and Time* (Minneapolis: University of Minnesota Press, 2005); Nilüfer Göle, *The Forbidden Modern: Civilization and Veiling* (Ann Arbor: University of Michigan Press, 1996); Banu Gökarıksel and Anna Secor, "Post-Secular Geographies and the Problem of Pluralism: Religion and Everyday Life in Istanbul, Turkey," *Political Geography* 46 (2015): 21–30; Ayşe Saktanber, *Living Islam: Women, Religion and the Politicization of Culture in Turkey* (New York: Tauris, 2002); Jenny B. White, *Islamist Mobilization in Turkey: A Study in Vernacular Politics* (Seattle: University of Washington Press, 2011). For recent works that insist on a critical interrogation the binary construction of the categories of the religion and the secular in relation to trans bodies, lives, and theologies, with particular attention to destabilizing a binary gender assumption and a reductionist equation of trans with the secular and attendant exclusion of trans from the religious, see Max Strassfeld, "Transing Religious Studies," *Journal of Feminist Studies in Religion* 34, no. 1 (2018): 37–53; Max Strassfeld and Robyn Henderson-Espinoza, "Introduction: Mapping Trans Studies in Religion," *Transgender Studies Quarterly* 6, no. 3 (2019): 283–96.

3 Susan Stryker, "The Transgender Issue: An Introduction," *GLQ: A Journal of Lesbian and Gay Studies* 4, no. 2 (1998): 149.

4 Janet R. Jakobsen and Ann Pellegrini, eds., *Secularisms* (Durham, NC: Duke University Press, 2008); Umut Azak, *Islam and Secularism in Turkey: Kemalism, Religion and the Nation State* (New York: Tauris, 2010); Yael Navaro-Yashin, *Faces of the State: Secularism and Public Life in Turkey* (Princeton, NJ: Princeton University Press, 2002); Esra Özyürek, *Nostalgia for the Modern: State Secularism and Everyday Politics in Turkey* (Durham, NC: Duke University Press, 2006); Çınar, *Modernity, Islam, and Secularism*; Göle, *Forbidden Modern*; Saktanber, *Living Islam*. See also the introduction to this volume.

5 Linell Cady and Elizabeth Hurd, *Comparative Secularisms in a Global Age* (New York: Palgrave Macmillan, 2010); Markus Dressler and Arvind Mandair, *Secularism and Religion-Making* (Oxford: Oxford University Press, 2011).

6 Niyazi Berkes, *The Development of Secularism in Turkey* (Montreal: McGill-Queen's University Press, 1964).

7 Ahmet T. Kuru, "Passive and Assertive Secularism: Historical Conditions, Ideological Struggles, and State Policies toward Religion," *World Politics* 59, no. 4 (2007): 568–94.

8 Taha Parla and Andrew Davison, "Secularism and Laicism in Turkey," in *Secularisms*, ed. Janet R. Jakobsen and Ann Pellegrini (Durham, NC: Duke University Press, 2008), 58–75.

9   Navaro-Yashin, *Faces of the State*, 203. I am building here on critiques of the secular that have considered how it positions the religious as a separate sphere rather than as its constitutive other. Talal Asad, *Formations of the Secular: Christianity, Islam, Modernity* (Stanford: Stanford University Press, 2003); Talal Asad, *Genealogies of Religion: Discipline and Reasons of Power in Christianity and Islam* (Baltimore: Johns Hopkins University Press, 2009); Craig Calhoun, Mark Juergensmeyer, and Jonathan VanAntwerpen, *Rethinking Secularism* (New York: Oxford University Press, 2011); Charles Taylor, *A Secular Age* (Cambridge, MA: Harvard University Press, 2009); Michael Warner, Jonathan VanAntwerpen, and Craig J. Calhoun, *Varieties of Secularism in a Secular Age* (Cambridge, MA: Harvard University Press, 2010).
10 Christopher Dole, *Healing Secular life: Loss and Devotion in Modern Turkey* (Philadelphia: University of Pennsylvania Press, 2012), 28.
11 Partha Chatterjee, *The Nation and Its Fragments: Colonial and Postcolonial Histories* (Princeton, NJ: Princeton University Press, 1993); Ayşe Kadıoğlu, "The Paradox of Turkish Nationalism and the Construction of Official Identity," *Middle Eastern Studies* 32, no. 2 (1996): 177–93.
12 Deniz Kandiyoti, "End of Empire: Islam, Nationalism, and Woman in Turkey," in *Women, Islam, and the State*, ed. Deniz Kandiyoti (Philadelphia: Temple University Press, 1991), 22–47.
13 Ayşe Kadıoğlu , "Cinselliğin İnkarı: Büyük Toplumsal Projelerin Nesnesi Olarak Türk Kadınları," in *75 yılda Kadınlar ve Erkekler*, ed. Ayşe Berktay Hacımirzaoğlu (İstanbul: Tarih Vakfı Yayınları, 1998), 89–101.
14 Kadıoğlu, "Paradox of Turkish Nationalism."
15 Çınar, *Modernity, Islam, and Secularism*.
16 Dole, *Healing Secular Life*, 122.
17 Rüstem Ertuğ Altınay, "Reconstructing the Transgendered Self as a Muslim, Nationalist, Upper-Class Woman: The Case of Bülent Ersoy," *WSQ: Women's Studies Quarterly* 36, no. 3 (2008): 210–29.
18 Altınay, "Reconstructing the Transgendered Self," 217.
19 Evren Savcı, "Transing Religious Studies: Beyond the Secular/Religious Binary," *Journal of Feminist Studies in Religion* 34, no. 1 (2018): 63–68.
20 Volkan Yılmaz and İpek Göçmen, "Denied Citizens of Turkey: Experiences of Discrimination among LGBT Individuals in Employment, Housing and Health Care," *Gender, Work and Organization* 23, no. 5 (2016): 470–88; Ceylan Engin, "LGBT in Turkey: Policies and Experiences," *Social Sciences* 4, no. 3 (2015): 838–58; Emrah Karakuş, "Toplumun Sınırlarında: Neoliberal Kentsel Dönüşüm ve Genel Ahlak Kıskacında Trans Kadınların Mensubiyet Yitimi," *Toplum ve Bilim* 129 (2014): 105–29; Aslı Zengin, "Sex under Intimate Siege: Transgender Lives, Law and State Violence in Contemporary Turkey" (PhD diss., University of Toronto, 2014); Hakan Ataman, "Gay, Bisexual, and Transgender Question in Turkey," *Societal Peace and Ideal Citizenship for Turkey*, ed. Rasim Özgür Dönmez and Pinar Enneli (London: Lexington, 2011), 125–58; Pinar Selek, *Maskeler, Suvariler, Gacilar* (Istanbul: Ayizi Kitap, 2011); Deniz Kandiyoti, "Pink Card Blues: Trouble and Strife at the Crossroads of Gender," in *Fragments of Culture: The*

Everyday of Modern Turkey, ed. Deniz Kandiyoti and Ayşe Saktanber (London: Tauris, 2002).

21 Aslı Zengin, "The Afterlife of Gender: Sovereignty, Intimacy and Muslim Funerals of Transgender People in Turkey," *Cultural Anthropology* 34, no. 1 (2019): 78–102.

22 Heather Love, "Queer," *Transgender Studies Quarterly* 1, nos. 1–2 (2014): 172.

23 E. Fuat Keyman, "Assertive Secularism in Crisis: Modernity, Democracy, and Islam in Turkey," in *Comparative Secularisms in a Global Age*, ed. Linell Cady and Elizabeth Hurd (New York: Palgrave Macmillan, 2010), 143–58.

24 Azak, *Islam and Secularism*.

25 Navaro-Yashin, *Faces of the State*; Zeynep Kurtuluş Korkman, "Gendered Fortunes" (manuscript draft).

26 Özyürek, *Nostalgia for the Modern*.

27 Göle, *Forbidden Modern*.

28 Çınar, *Modernity, Islam, and Secularism*.

29 Meyda Yeğenoğlu, "Clash of Secularity and Religiosity: The Staging of Secularism and Islam through the Icons of Atatürk and the Veil in Turkey," in *Religion and the State: A Comparative Sociology*, ed. Jack Barbalet, Adam Possamai, and Bryan S. Turner (London: Anthem, 2011), 225–44.

30 Sam Kaplan, "Din-u Devlet All over Again? The Politics of Military Secularism and Religious Militarism in Turkey following the 1980 Coup," *International Journal of Middle East Studies* 34, no. 1 (2002): 113–27.

31 "Umumi Duyuru," *Dünya Kardeşlik Birliği Mevlana Yüce Vakfı*, accessed July 21, 2020, https://www.dkb-mevlana.org.tr/txt/Bildiri.pdf.

32 Vedia Bülent Çorak Önsü, *Bilgi Kitabı, 19*, accessed November 20, 2016, http://www.bilgikitabi.net/kitap/takdim.htm.

33 "Gençliğe Hitabe artık zorunlu değil," *Cumhuriyet*, March 20, 2012, http://www.cumhuriyet.com.tr/haber/diger/328782/Genclige_Hitabe_artik_zorunlu_degil.html.

34 Çorak, *Bilgi Kitabı, 25*. All translations are mine unless otherwise noted.

35 Ayşe Durakbaşa, "Cumhuriyet Döneminde Modern Kadın ve Erkek Kimliklerinin Oluşumu: Kemalist Kadın Kimliği ve 'Münevver Erkekler,'" in *75 Yılda Kadınlar ve Erkekler*, ed. Ayşe Berktay Hacımirzaoğlu (Istanbul: Tarih Vakfı Yayınları, 1998), 29–50.

36 Çorak, *Bilgi Kitabı*, 19.

37 Çorak, *Bilgi Kitabı*, 226.

38 Carol Delaney, *The Seed and the Soil: Gender and Cosmology in Turkish Village Society* (Berkeley: University of California Press, 1991); Çorak, *Bilgi Kitabı*, 226.

39 Çorak, *Bilgi Kitabı*, 226.

40 Çorak, *Bilgi Kitabı*, 226.

41 Christopher Dole, "Mass Media and the Repulsive Allure of Religious Healing: The Cinci Hoca in Turkish Modernity," *International Journal of Middle East Studies* 38, no. 1 (2006): 31–54.

42 Zeynep Kurtuluş Korkman, "Fortunes for Sale: Cultural Politics and Commodification of Culture in Millennial Turkey," *European Journal of Cultural Studies* 18, no. 3 (2015): 319–38.
43 Murat Gülşan, "Mevlana Kardeşlik Birliği! . . . ," *Haberini Oku*, December 9, 2019, https://www.haberinioku.com/yazarlar/murat-gulsan/mevlana-kardeslik-birligi/24290/.
44 H. Sah Yasdiman, "Yeni Din Akimlari Baglaminda Dünya Kardeşlik Birliği Mevlana Yüce Vakfı Ornegi" (PhD diss., Dokuz Eylul University, 2008), 135; Korkman, "Fortunes for Sale."
45 Cemal Kafadar, "Women in Seljuk and Ottoman Society up to the Mid-19th Century," in *Woman in Anatolia: 9000 Years of the Anatolian Woman*, ed. Gunsel Renda (Istanbul: Turkish Republic Ministry of Culture, 1993), 192–201.
46 Azak, *Islam and Secularism*; Aykan Erdemir, "Tradition and Modernity: Alevis' Ambiguous Terms and Turkey's Ambivalent Subjects," *Middle Eastern Studies* 41, no. 6 (2005): 937–51.
47 Şebnem Köşer Akçapar, "Beyond Turkey's Borders: Long-Distance Kemalism, State Politics and the Turkish Diaspora," *Diaspora Studies* 5, no. 2 (2012): 229.
48 Dole, *Healing Secular Life*.
49 Çorak, *Bilgi Kitabı*, 214.
50 Hearing about my interest in the group, a friend who grew up in a secular middle-class family in İzmir in the 1980s shared that her mother was closely involved with the group until she was admonished by her husband, who argued that she was ignoring her home and children by attending group meetings and laboring over reading and distributing the group literature. The husband successfully demanded that she reprioritize her wifely responsibilities and cut her ties to Çorak.
51 Nilüfer Göle, "Secularism and Islamism in Turkey: The Making of Elites and Counter-elites," *Middle East Journal* 51, no. 1 (1997): 46–58.
52 Cemal Kafadar, "The New Visibility of Sufism in Turkish Studies and Cultural Life," in *The Dervish Lodge: Architecture, Art, and Sufism in Ottoman Turkey*, ed. Raymond Lifchez (Berkeley: University of California Press, 1992), 307–22.
53 Rose Aslan, "The Museumification of Rumi's Tomb: Deconstructing Sacred Space at the Mevlana Museum," *International Journal of Religious Tourism and Pilgrimage* 2, no. 2 (2014): 2; Sheenagh Pietrobruno, "Social Media and Whirling Dervishes: Countering UNESCO's Intangible Cultural Heritage," *Performing Islam* 4, no. 1 (2015): 11–33.
54 "Ergenekon'un Manevi Uzantıları," *Dünya Kardeşlik Birliğinin Gerçek Yüzüö*, October 25, 2013, http://bilgikitab.blogspot.com/2013/10/ergenekon-un-manevi-uzantilari.html.
55 "Yargıtay, Ergenekon Davasında Kararı Bozdu," *BBC News Türkçe*, April 21, 2016, https://www.bbc.com/turkce/haberler/2016/04/160421_yargitay_ergenekon.
56 Dole, *Healing Secular Life*.
57 Katherine Pratt Ewing, *Stolen Honor: Stigmatizing Muslim Men in Berlin* (Stanford: Stanford University Press, 2008); Lila Abu-Lughod, "Do Muslim Women

Really Need Saving? Anthropological Reflections on Cultural Relativism and Its Others," *American Anthropologist* 104, no. 3 (2002): 783–90; Jasbir K. Puar, *Terrorist Assemblages: Homonationalism in Queer Times* (Durham, NC: Duke University Press, 2007).

58   Gayatri Chakravorty Spivak, "Can the Subaltern Speak?," in *Marxism and the Interpretation of Culture*, ed. Carry Nelson and Larry Grossberg (Urbana: University of Illinois Press, 1988), 297.

14. CHRISTIANITY AND THE POLITICAL RELIGION OF CHINA
Francis Ching-Wah Yip

In the mid-twentieth century, the German American theologian Paul Tillich proclaimed that "the main characteristic of the present encounter of the world religions is their encounter with the quasi-religions of our time. Even the mutual relations of the religions proper are decisively influenced by the encounter of each of them with secularism, and one or more of the quasi-religions which are based upon secularism."[1] Tillich used the term "quasi-religion" to describe ideologies and "systems of secular thought and life," such as nationalism, fascism, socialism, communism, and liberal humanism, whose nature and success cannot be explained without the analogy of religion.[2] This chapter examines one such encounter—the encounter of Protestant Christianity with the political religion of the People's Republic of China in the reform era.

The chapter begins with a clarification and defense of the concept of "political religion," the sacralization of politics imposed by an authoritarian regime. After a reconstructed account of the two versions of political religion in China, Chinese communism and state-led nationalism, I argue for the inevitability of Protestant Christianity's adaptation to party-state-imposed political religion. My analysis primarily focuses on Bishop K. H. Ting's theological reconstruction campaign. I explain how the theological concept of Cosmic Christ and Ting's downplaying of justification by faith were attempts, with limited success, to reform Chinese Protestantism by adapting it to the imposed political religion. I conclude with the broader implications of my analysis.

Political Religion

Political religion is a type of quasi-religion, that is, a system of *secular* thought and life. It is often associated with authoritarian—if not totalitarian—forms of government. While the use of the term can be traced back to the era of the French Revolution, it came into wider use in the 1930s through the work of scholars such as Eric Voegelin, who applied the term to communism, fascism, and National Socialism.[3] The concept grew in prominence through comparative analyses of the totalitarian regimes of Bolshevism, fascism, and Nazism.[4] Interest in political religion has resurged again over the past two decades. The publication of the journal *Totalitarian Movements and Political Religions* is a case in point.[5]

Political religion is similar to yet distinct from the concept of civil religion. Marcela Cristi provides a helpful distinction between these concepts as she differentiates between the Durkheimian and Rousseauian models of civil religion. While both Émile Durkheim and Jean-Jacques Rousseau recognized the significance of secular religion for the cohesion of modern society, Durkheim framed civil religion as culture and Rousseau framed civil religion as ideology. The Durkheimian type of civil religion is often found in liberal democracies; Robert Bellah's notion of American civil religion is an example.[6] It occurs naturally, inevitably, spontaneously, and unconsciously. The Rousseauian type, on the other hand, is a premeditated religion imposed by the state from above, as it is indispensable for cultivating political unity.[7] Functionally, it provides "political legitimacy and political stability," demanding "unquestionable loyalty and unconditional commitment."[8] Cristi argues that Rousseau's model of civil religion is in fact political religion. Often found in authoritarian or totalitarian regimes, it may emerge in various forms, "such as theocracies, political messianism, sacred authoritarianism, totalitarianism, and secular or religious nationalism." In Communist China, Christi observes, political religion takes the form of "secular nationalism."[9]

Emilio Gentile further refines the concept of political religion, locating its distinctiveness in the "sacralization of politics."

The sacralisation of politics occurs all the time by virtue of the fact that a political entity, for instance, the nation, the state, race, class, the party, assume the characteristics of a sacred entity, that is, of a supreme power, indisputable and untouchable, which becomes the object of faith, of reverence, of cult, of fidelity, of devotion from the side of the citizens, up to and including the sacrifice of life; and as such it lies in the centre of the constellation of beliefs, of myths, of values, of commandments, of rites and of symbols.[10]

Gentile goes on to claim that *"political religion* is a form of the sacralisation of politics of an exclusive and integralist character. It rejects coexistence with other political ideologies and movements, denies the autonomy of the individual with respect to the collective, prescribes the obligatory observance of its commandments and participation in its political cult, and sanctifies violence as a legitimate arm of the struggle against enemies, and as an instrument of regeneration."[11] Combining the insights of Cristi and Gentile, I use the term "political religion" to describe the sacralization of politics—including the sacralization of the party, the state, and the nation—as it is imposed by an authoritarian regime from above.

Some might argue that this treatment of political religion overstretches or even misuses the concept of religion. I preemptively address two possible critiques. The first line of attack is that while political religion might have some features analogous to religion, it is not really a religion. The critic who thinks along this line might have taken traditional world religions as a standard or might have a presupposed substantive understanding of religion, such as the belief in supernatural beings or transcendent powers. My position is more akin to Durkheim's functionalist understanding of religion. While religion in modern society might be quite different in form from religion in traditional society, there is something eternal in religion, for society needs at regular intervals to "maintain and strengthen the collective feelings and ideas that provide its coherence and its distinctive individuality. . . . What basic difference is there between Christians' celebrating the principle dates of Christ's life, Jews' celebrating the exodus from Egypt or the promulgation of the Decalogue, and a citizens' meeting commemorating the advent of a new moral charter or some other great event of national life?"[12] Simply put, political religion does not just look like religion; it *is* a religion. The second line of attack draws on the fact that political religion more often than not involves the control or suppression of religion in the conventional sense. These critics argue that political religion is a form of secularism; thus it cannot be a religion. This line of thinking uncritically assumes that the secular and the religious are in opposition to each other. In my analysis, and in this volume more generally, the secular does not mean nonreligious—let alone antireligious. Rather, it encapsulates the "features of personal and social matters concerning the mundane temporal world and one's daily life."[13]

Political Religion in China

Political religion in modern China is a particular instance of the sacralization of politics imposed from above by an authoritarian regime. Called "political religiosity" by Vincent Goossaert and David Palmer, it involves the "sacralization of the state and the moralization of governance."[14] Since the dawn of the People's Republic of China, there have been two versions of political religion. In the first three decades of the communist party-state, the political religion was, in lieu of a better term, Chinese communism: a blend of revolutionary Marxism-Leninism as interpreted by the Chinese Communist Party (CCP), Mao Zedong's own political thought (Maoism), and fervent antiforeignism. Indoctrination at schools, ideological propaganda through party-controlled media, and waves of political campaigns sought to impose Chinese communism on society and culture. During the Great Proletarian Cultural Revolution (1966–76), the political religion of Chinese communism became more intense with the cult of Mao. As Jiping Zuo observes, Mao became a god, worshipped fanatically with rituals, singing, dancing, and slogan-chanting. His writings and sayings, especially those collected in the *Little Red Book*, became sacred scripture, imbued with special power that could solve all problems and save people from all troubles. Those labeled "class enemies" suffered from denouncement, humiliation, and torture under the Red Guards.[15] Religions—at least all outward forms of religion such as sites of worship, religious activities, sacred books, and religious personnel—were eradicated, suppressed, or secularized.

The Cultural Revolution came to an end in 1976 with the death of Mao and the arrest of the "Gang of Four." The eventual consolidation of the power of Deng Xiaoping and his political allies since 1978 brought seismic changes to the CCP's general direction and policies.[16] They repudiated "leftist" policies such as class struggle and continuous revolution, criticized the cult of Mao, and emphasized economic development as the paramount goal of the party-state. Deng pushed forward the "reform and open-door" policy—which promoted economic liberalization and allowed for greater personal freedom and social mobility—as he also asserted that China was not adopting Western capitalism and democracy. Rather, under CCP's leadership, China was building "socialism with Chinese characteristics."[17]

The reform era marked "the reversal of a fundamental trend in China in the twentieth century toward increased penetration of politics into other spheres of society."[18] The economic reforms launched by the CCP "led to a relaxation of the party control over the economy, society, and ultimately over public discourse, in part by design and in part by default."[19] As the official discourse of the party lost its hegemony, the CCP had to look for a "deeper source of legitimacy than economic growth alone."[20] The military crackdown of the student-led pro-democracy demonstration at Tiananmen Square in 1989 spelled the demise of the already weakening official ideology of the CCP. The reformist leaders of the party rediscovered nationalism as the alternative that could replace the official doctrines of Marxism-Leninism and Mao Zedong thought "as the cohesive ideology to keep Chinese people together." As Suisheng Zhao observes, "With the renewed discovery of the function of nationalism after the 'Tiananmen Incident,' Chinese Communist leaders began to place emphasis on the party's role as the paramount patriotic force and guardian of national pride in order to find a new basis of legitimacy to bolster faith in a system in trouble and hold the country together during the period of rapid and turbulent transformation."[21] Official CCP discourse does not prefer the term "nationalism" (*minzu zhuyi*); the party uses the term "patriotism" (*aiguo zhuyi*) instead. Being patriotic (*aiguo*) means loving the state. Nevertheless, patriotism in China is in fact a "state-led nationalism" under which citizens are required to be loyal to and serve the state.[22] The CCP tried to impose this second version of political religion on Chinese society through a nationwide campaign of patriotic education.[23] As Zhao points out, the main problem of this state-led Chinese nationalism is that it lacks substantive content, "as it is reduced to the expression of a political party's current policies."[24] Arif Dirlik, observing that the CCP "has reworked Mao Zedong Thought from a revolutionary discourse on development to a development discourse that legitimizes incorporation in global capitalism," holds a similar view. Dirlik contends that "as Marxism disappears into a nationalism that is fueled by success in global capitalism, it not only ceases to serve critical purposes, it becomes part of a nationalist ideology that makes Marxism mean whatever the party leadership would like it to mean."[25] We might say that in the reform era, political religion in China is a state-imposed nationalism whose substance is to rally the uncontested support of people for the dominant policy and discourse of the party-state in each historical period, including "the Four Modernizations," "socialism with Chinese characteristics," "three represents," "scientific outlook on development," "harmonious society," and, most recently, "the China dream."

In either Chinese version of political religion there is a sacralization of politics, especially vis-à-vis the party-state and the nation. Adopting Charles Taylor's framework to analyze the transformation of the sacred across European and American social imaginaries, Richard Madsen likens China to the "paleo-Durkheimian" pattern wherein "the sacred was found in the fusion of religion and politics in the absolutist state." The CCP "strove to present itself as a sacralized alternative to religion—a sacred secularism." After the Cultural Revolution, "communist ideology is being replaced by a strong nationalism. Bolstered by its success in raising China to the rank of the world's major powers, the Chinese state is seen as the bearer of this national destiny. The CCP has used all of the means at its disposal (including its apparatus for punishing dissent) to construct a sacred aura around itself."[26] In a similar vein, though with different emphases, Cheng-Tian Kuo regards "Chinese nationalism" as a "new state religion," since "any Chinese who opposes or blasphemes [its sacrosanct god—China or its aliases] is a traitor and is punishable by death." Kuo continues: "Chinese nationalism prescribes a 'trinity' for its political theology, which sets rules and boundaries to religion-state relations, consisting of three elements: China, socialism, and the CCP. . . . Anyone who opposes socialism or communist leadership is a traitor to China. All religious groups in China should place this political theology of trinity at the top of their religious creeds: Love your country, (then) love your religion (*aiguo aijiao*)."[27]

Importantly, all this does not mean that the party-state has monopolized the sacred. In fact, various religions and spiritual practices have been flourishing in China since the beginning of the reform era.[28] Other possible manifestations of the sacred include money, *guanxi* (personal connections that bring social capital), moral duties to one's family members (elderly members, children), and perhaps the individual self. These various forms can coexist with the sacred in politics, as enacting multiple religious belonging is the norm rather than an exception in Chinese culture. In other words, adhering to the imposed political religion does not necessarily imply or necessitate renouncing one's own religion.

Critics might point out that it would be very difficult, if not impossible, for the party-state to effectively impose its political religion on the people, for the latter can still refuse to accept the imposed religion, especially when they already have their own religions. Such criticism seems to presuppose a conception of religion in terms of beliefs that one can accept or reject at will. This presupposition, however, is not valid, and especially not in the Chinese cultural context, where religion is predominantly not about personal beliefs but about social practices. As long as one adequately performs socially expected actions, one can be considered a participant of the religion concerned.

Political Religion, Adaptation, and Chinese Protestantism

The state-sanctioned Protestant church in China basically accepts and continually adapts to the state-imposed political religion with its various changing emphases. This allegiance is facilitated in large part through the CCP's United Front strategy. In the words of Deng Xiaoping, the United Front's task is "to mobilize all positive forces, strive to transform all negative forces into positive ones, and unite with all the forces that can be united so that all can work in harmony to maintain and strengthen political stability and unity in China and make it a modern, powerful socialist country."[29] Although religions are ideologically at odds with the atheistic Marxist orthodoxy and have been viewed as instruments of imperialism, they may be allowed to exist or even to thrive in China provided that they support the party-state, accept its political religion, follow its leadership, and cooperate with other sectors in society to work for the party's political and economic goals.[30] According to Philip Wickeri's interpretation, the United Front entails "seeking the common ground while reserving differences." This common ground is "patriotism, socialist reconstruction or modernization," and acceptable differences are "in ideological or religious belief and in worldview."[31]

These shared allegiances are reflected in the constitutions of the two patriotic Protestant organizations, the National Committee of the Three-Self Patriotic Movement (TSPM) and the China Christian Council (CCC), which declare their acceptance of the party's leadership as their first duty: "Under the leadership of the Communist Party of China and the People's Government, to unite with all Chinese Christians; to love our socialist motherland; to abide by the national Constitution, laws, regulations and policies; to take an active part in building a socialist society with Chinese characteristics."[32] By committing to "love our socialist motherland" and participate in nation building, TSPM and CCC align themselves with CCP's political religion.

Since all religious groups are required to place the "trinity" of Chinese nationalism—China, socialism, and the CCP—at the top of their religious creeds, Protestant Christianity's adaptation of the CCP's political religion also reshaped its theological discourse. The CCP actively encouraged these theological shifts in the wake of the 1989 Tiananmen crackdown, as the party-state not only took nationalism more seriously but also took a more active role in religious matters. In

1993, Jiang Zemin, the secretary-general of the Chinese Communist Party from 1989 to 2002, emphasized the CCP's role in "actively guiding the adaptation of religions to socialism." In his view, adaptation to socialism includes "loving the motherland, supporting the socialist system, and supporting the leadership of the communist party," while at the same time "reforming those religious institutions and religious doctrines that are not adaptable to socialism, [and] utilizing those positive elements in religious doctrines, religious regulations, and religious morality to serve for socialism."[33] In a 2001 speech focused more specifically on religion, Jiang reiterated and further elaborated that the policy of

> actively guiding the adaptation of religions to socialism does not mean requiring religious personnel and religious believers to renounce their religious faith, but requiring them to enthusiastically love the motherland, to rally around the socialist system, to rally around the leadership of the communist party, to abide by the laws, regulations, and policies of the state; requiring their religious activities to obey and serve the paramount interests of the state and the overall interests of the nation; supporting their efforts in expounding religious doctrines according to the requirements of social progress.[34]

Protestant theological ideas that are deemed incompatible with socialism—which actually means the policies of the CCP—include viewing the present world as under Satan's rule and emphasizing the imminent return of Christ to judge the world. This is because such teachings would imply, inter alia, that it is futile to participate in the development of socialist China, that the present world (including China) is predominately evil, and that the CCP, as the ruling party in China, might somehow be seen as cooperating with Satan. By demanding the reform of these "incompatible teachings," the CCP imposed its political religion on religious communities.

Protestant Christianity's CCP-induced theological shifts emerge in the writings and public discourse of Bishop K. H. Ting (Ding Guangxun), who was the principal of the Nanjing Union Theological Seminary (NUTS) and leader of the officially sanctioned Protestant Church in China throughout the last three decades of the twentieth century. In the foreword to an anthology of writings from NUTS, Ting argues for a this-worldly theological orientation, an emphasis that emerges throughout much of his writings, as he links the CCP with the United Front.

> I think the reader of Theological Writings from Nanjing Seminary will find that the essays presented here do not treat Christian faith as a

ticket to heaven after death. Using a vocabulary that is not so popular and seems hard to change, Christian faith is a worldview and a spiritual culture. It guides people how to view their life, how to fully participate in reality, and moreover how, through the church community, to gain for themselves and for other peoples what Christ called "abundant life." These essays demonstrate the Christian goal of helping people to live and to live well. Without this point, it would be out of the question to say that Christians are also in the United Front.[35]

Bishop Ting's subsequent theological reconstruction campaign, which was officially launched by the TSPM/CCC in 1998, was partly a response to the CCP's political religion. The campaign promoted Ting's theology, which was represented by a definitive collection of Ting's writings, published as *Love Never Ends*.[36] Most notably, the campaign criticized the "conservative" view of salvation as the separation of believers and nonbelievers in eternal destiny, highlighted the worldly and moral aspects of Christian faith, called for a downplaying of "justification by faith," and recommended the adoption of a modern view of the Bible. Ting often cited Jiang's call for the adaptation of religion to socialism to support and justify theological reconstruction.[37] Ting argued that there was no religious reason to oppose the call for adaptation: "Suppose we do not adapt to socialist society. Shall we then adapt to capitalism, imperialism or feudalism? For the good of our nation, as well as for the survival and witness of the church itself, we should naturally adapt to socialist society. This is the natural choice of every responsible citizen and every responsible believer. We cannot be satisfied with a mere politic [*sic*] expression. Genuine adaptation must have an intellectual foundation. For Christians, genuine adaptation must include theological adaptation."[38] Here and elsewhere, theological reconstruction was framed as a response to the call for adaptation to socialism, and thus to the political religion of CCP: "Frankly speaking, our goal is just this—to reform Chinese Protestantism into a Christianity that follows the tides of history and the needs of the people. Such a Protestantism will, I believe, be welcome by the Communist Party and is very much compatible with and adapted to socialism."[39]

Of course, the strategic political importance of embracing the principles of the United Front and adopting a this-worldly theological orientation should not be underestimated. Acceptance by the CCP was and is crucial for the Protestant Church's survival, functioning, and development. In failing to pledge allegiance to the United Front or adopt the appropriate theological orientation, the Christian community would risk being treated as enemies of the CCP, which would bring serious hardship, persecution, and suppression.

Theological reconstruction was an attempt in the direction demanded by the party-state. Every theology provides a worldview upon which Christians live and act. Thus, every theology has its social and political implications. Fundamentalism, the prevalent tradition in Chinese Protestantism, was viewed as socially and politically problematic. Its premillennialist eschatology, which believes in the deterioration of the world before the impending destruction of the world, is pessimistic toward the present world, including China. Its sectarian, doctrinaire, and anti-intellectual tendency is at odds with the ethos of modernization, development, and progress. Its understanding of justification by faith in terms of bifurcation of ultimate destiny (heaven and hell) based on the sole condition of faith regardless of conduct not only goes against traditional Chinese emphasis on morality but also theologically divides the Chinese people, creating unnecessary enmity between believers and nonbelievers. All this works against the state-imposed nationalism, the political religion of China in the reform era, which seeks to rally together all sectors of the nation to support the dominant policy and discourse of the party-state that is intended to develop China into a strong and modern socialist country. Thus Ting, as leader of the state-sanctioned Protestant Church in China, regarded it as necessary to reform Chinese Protestantism, emancipating it from the sway of fundamentalism. In the sections that follow, I expound upon two key theological concepts that emerged in Ting's theological construction campaign and their relationship to the CCP's political religion, namely the concept of Cosmic Christ and the diluting or de-emphasizing of justification by faith.

Cosmic Christ

Ting wrote all but four of the pieces in *Love Never Ends* in the post-Mao era, prior to 1997, when Ting retired from the top leadership of the TSPM/CCC. *Love Never Ends*, therefore, is representative par excellence of the state-sanctioned Chinese Protestant Church's theological discourse. "The Cosmic Christ" is a particularly important chapter, deriving from a speech he delivered in England in 1991.[40] Indeed, Ting reiterates the idea of Cosmic Christ in several talks and essays, including a talk at a theological forum in 1997.[41] Ting introduces a narrative surrounding the emergence of the "Cosmic Christ" concept, namely that it emerged after the establishment of the People's Republic of China when people were impressed by the moral goodness of communists. As Ting explains it, Chinese Christians were faced with the predicament of "how Christians are to think of non-church values, that is, values on the part of those who profess no faith in Christ."[42]

The idea of the Cosmic Christ, which has often been echoed and promoted by Ting's colleagues in state-sanctioned churches and seminaries, is a theological perspective that intertwines multiple entities and concepts, including God, Christ, salvation, and the theology of history: "For Chinese Christians the significance of knowing Christ as having a cosmic nature lies essentially in ascertaining two things: (1) the universal extent of Christ's domain, concern and care, and (2) the kind of love we get a taste of in Jesus Christ as we read the Gospels being the first and supreme attribute of God and basic to the structure and dynamic of the universe, in the light of which we get an insight as to how things go in the world."[43] In expounding upon the first principle, Ting notes that Christ is not only concerned "with believers, or only with making converts of those who do not yet consciously believe in him."[44] Citing Hebrews 1 and Colossians 1, he emphasizes the role of Christ in creating and sustaining the universe. Redemption, Ting contends, is part of the process of creation: "Not only communities of Christians here and there, but humankind as a whole and, indeed, the whole cosmos are within the realm of Christ's redemptive work."[45] While at first this assertion might seem unexceptional, a closer reading reveals the subtle meaning he intended to convey. Certainly, Christians are included "within the realm of Christ's redemptive work." But what is the significance of Ting's assertion that "humankind as a whole"—which obviously includes adherents of other religions and atheists—are also within the realm of redemption? Here Ting was gesturing toward a stance he later makes explicit: that one can—though not necessarily will—be saved without being a Christian in any traditional sense. He more overtly states this position in a later paragraph: "Because we have seen and experienced goodness, truth and holiness among followers of other paths and ways than that of the church, we cannot resist a vision of the universal creative and redemptive activity of God for all humankind, *aside from* the particular redemptive activity of God in the history of Israel and in the person and work of Jesus Christ. This is implied when we say Christ is cosmic."[46] So for Ting, there is universal *redemptive* activity of God apart from and alongside the particular redemptive activity of Christ. The latter is how Christians are saved. The former is how "followers of other paths and ways," which would include atheists and adherents of non-Christian religions, are saved. While this is not necessarily universalism (i.e., the belief that all persons will ultimately be saved), it nonetheless affirms the possibility of salvation outside Christianity.

The second principle of the Cosmic Christ concept "affirm[s] that God is Christlike and that Christlike love is the way God intends for the running of the cosmos."[47] Love, in Ting's view, is God's supreme attribute under which all other attributes are subordinated. Invoking process theology, Ting emphasizes that God is not a tyrant or punisher but a cosmic lover, who works through education and persuasion. Though we cannot know when and how the end of history will come about, "we are sure that it will be the triumph of love and grace."[48] The idea of love as the supreme attribute of God found its way into the CCC's official catechism in 1984.[49] It was framed in part as a response to the hatred, violence, and power struggles that transpired in China during the Cultural Revolution: "When injustice, hatred, thirst for power and arbitrary condemnation of the innocent ran riot, the image of God the Lover was seen to be such a shining contrast and source of comfort and hope that many were drawn to this God. He spoke lovingly to the heavy-laden and gave the unacceptable in the world an acceptability and rest they could not find elsewhere."[50] This echoes the repudiation of the Cultural Revolution by Deng and other leaders in the post-Mao era. More important, the emphasis on God as love put into question the traditional notion, prevalent among fundamentalist and other conservative Protestant communities, that those who do not believe in Jesus Christ will face eternal damnation. In a 1996 speech, Ting mentions the case of a few non-Christian Chinese who sacrificed their life for others. He asks: "How can we tolerate the idea that they are now in hell?" The view that God is love "does not allow me to make God so cruel and brutal that God could send millions of people to the eternal flames of hell."[51] Ting then refers to the last judgment scene in Matthew 25, noting that "in the last judgment described here, God does not ask whether we were believers or nonbelievers. He asks what we did for the impoverished." He continues: "For over forty years, countless people in our country have been working in great projects to alleviate poverty. . . . Is this not one with what we find in this biblical passage?"[52] In a 1997 theological forum talk, Ting mentions not only Matthew but also the Second Vatican Council and the idea of "anonymous Christians" proposed by theologian Karl Rahner.[53] We might say that Ting's position is similar to inclusivism, which claims that revelation and salvation brought about by Christ is somehow also available in and through non-Christian religions. By claiming that being a Christian is not a necessary factor for salvation, Ting seeks to de-emphasize the difference between Christian and non-Christian Chinese. This theological orientation has political implications. It promotes the belief that Protestantism in China is compatible not only with the United Front principle and the requirement of adaptation but also with the demands of the state-imposed political religion intended to create solidarity and cooperation among all Chinese citizens in the service of building socialist China.

Downplaying Justification by Faith

Ting continued to promote his thought through the theological reconstruction campaign that began in 1998, when serious flooding plagued central China. The People's Liberation Army (PLA), among other groups, was deployed for rescue and relief operations. Some NUTS students and faculty members interpreted the flooding as a sign of God's judgment and of Christ's imminent second coming. Furious, Ting was convinced that "more decisive action against the entrenched fundamentalism that encouraged such thinking was now required."[54] The theological reconstruction campaign was launched later that year as a response. Provincial and municipal TSPM/CCC organizations held symposia and training sessions, and numerous essays on theological reconstruction appeared in *Tian Feng*, the official magazine of the national TSPM/CCC. Since it was imposed from above by Ting with the support of the party-state, "there was an implicitly coercive element in theological reconstruction, at least at the outset."[55]

In a 1998 speech that predated the campaign, Ting addressed the issue of biblical exegesis, as some passages in the Bible seem to suggest that there will be an ultimate destruction of the world. According to Ting, the Bible records holy people's understanding of God's gradual and progressive revelation. Thus, while the Bible contains many parts "where faith, spirituality, morals and ethics, theology, literature, etc. [have reached] their loftiest heights," this is not true for some other parts of the Bible. Ting criticizes those who regard calamities as God's punishment or as signs of the end of the world, for "all these things go against the fact that God is love." The consequence of belief in a destructive "end time," Ting insisted, would be a dismissal of building the motherland, patriotism, and related endeavors as useless and futile.[56] In an interview published the following year, Ting challenged those who demeaned a PLA soldier who risked his life to save a child from the flood, arguing that such an act is one of great love, whose creator is God.[57]

The most controversial move in the theological reconstruction campaign was Ting's proposal to de-emphasize or downplay the doctrine of justification by faith. While the doctrine involves many theological issues, Ting criticized one particular understanding of the doctrine that he understood to be distorted: the belief that those who possess faith gain eternal life in heaven, regardless of how bad their actions were, and those who do not have faith receive eternal damnation in hell, regardless of how good their actions were.[58] Ting seized the occasion of the fiftieth anniversary of TSPM to promote and expound upon his proposal. First, Ting distinguishes between basic Christian faith, which does not change, and theological thinking, which can and must change. Perhaps in order to draw the party-state's support for the theological reconstruction campaign, Ting positively references Jiang Zemin's newly proposed idea of "the three represents" as an example of ongoing adjustments to the CCP's thought.[59] Likewise, Ting explains, the church should change its thinking: "Playing down some theological views today is permissible, and in fact, necessary."[60]

For Ting, the idea of "justification by faith" is "overemphasized in China, as if it is the all in all of Christian faith." As he argues,

> The idea is that anyone who believes will go to heaven after death, and those who do not believe will go to heaven. This is an idea that denies morality. By extension, Hitler and Mussolini, as Christians, would be in heaven, while Confucius, Laozi, Mozi and Zhou Enlai, non-believers, would be in hell. This is the only logical conclusion according to this idea. Such a Christianity may appeal to some, but can we really imagine that most Chinese would be willing to accept it over the long run? Some people say, I really love my parents, but as non-believers they will be in hell while I, as a believer, will enjoy heaven. I really cannot bear such thinking.[61]

Ting proceeds to ask: "If God were to send people to hell because of their unbelief, this would create problems in our idea of God—how then could God be a God of love?"[62]

Downplaying "justification by faith," Ting explains, does not mean getting rid of it entirely but "not making this the all in all of Christianity . . . manifesting *all* the riches of Christian faith." Ting then asserts that "Jiang Zemin hopes that religions can adapt to this socialist society," which is "at present the most advanced society known to humanity." Chinese churches must embrace "those things which are the essence of socialism, especially in terms of adapting our thinking, and not only general thinking, but theological thinking."[63]

This does not mean that Ting's theology, or the theological discourse of the state-sanctioned Protestant Church in general, is determined solely by the political religion of China. Christian tradition also plays an important role. Although state-sanctioned Protestantism is "postdenominational," we can still trace its ecclesiastical tradition to the "mainline" Protestant tradition, which features an ecumenical spirit, openness to "liberal" ideas, a this-worldly orientation, optimism toward humanity and history, and active participation in society and culture as a means of realizing God's kingdom in the world. With theological education at St. John's University in Shanghai and Union Theological Seminary in New York City, Ting was relatively "liberal." His Anglican/Episcopal tradition and the theologians and theologies that he drew inspiration from (such as Pierre Teilhard de Chardin and process theology) differed significantly from conservative forms of Christianity. In the 1950s, he participated in fierce attacks against Wang Mingdao, a renowned fundamentalist leader who strongly opposed TSPM and was extremely critical of theological liberalism.[64] For the sake of church unity, Ting "had avoided entering into theological debate or imposing his relatively 'liberal' theological viewpoints on a very conservative Christian community" during his tenure as an official TSPM/CCC leader.[65] He found himself freer to challenge fundamentalism after his retirement. Thus it is hard to tell whether theological reconstruction was a political campaign drawing upon religious resources or a religious campaign drawing upon political resources.

This sheds light on the encounter between the state-imposed political religion and Protestant Christianity in China. To be sure, the political religion is imposed from above. Yet this does not mean that Chinese Christians in the state-sanctioned Protestant Church are merely passive recipients. Various forms of response are possible, and in the case of the campaign of theological reconstruction, there is strategic appropriation. Ting willingly embraced and appropriated the imposed political religion to attack the conservative form of Protestant Christianity that he opposed. His willingness came from the elective affinity between the state-imposed political religion and liberal Protestantism.

In 2001, Ting admitted that the theological reconstruction campaign, which began three years prior, showed limited success. He observed that "the problem of reconstructing theological thinking has created divisions among China's Christian intellectuals." Even the faculty and students of NUTS, of which he was principal, were "polarized," and the whole church was divided into different groups.[66] Theological reconstruction lost its momentum after several years. Ting himself died in November 2012. The theological viewpoints promoted by the campaign—and Ting's theology in general, especially its inclusivist tendency—were never widely accepted by Chinese Christians under his TSPM/CCC leadership. This was not so much because Ting collaborated with the CCP's political religion but because his theology deviated too far from the conservative theological tradition of Chinese Protestantism that was shared by the majority of Protestants in China. The state-imposed political religion is still efficacious among Chinese Protestants in the state-sanctioned churches. Being patriotic, they would rally around the party-state, echo its slogans, and promote its policies. In their lives, political religion can coexist with Christian religion—as long as the basic tenets of the latter are not violated. The belief that salvation is granted exclusively to those who believe in Jesus Christ is one of the basic tenets. They regard it as an unquestionable "biblical truth." The inclusivist view of salvation promoted by the theological reconstruction campaign has already crossed the red line and thus incurred opposition. Although an overt form of opposition is not a practical option in the state-sanctioned churches, subtle resistance in the form of evading or delaying compliance is still possible.

Broader Implications

The adaption of Protestant theology to political religion in China constitutes an instance of an encounter between a conventional religion and a secular religion. Similar encounters occur in other parts of the world, and the results of such encounters might be quite different due to various factors, which may include, inter alia, the nature of the conventional religion, the ways of imposition or adoption of the secular religion, the relative difference in strength between the conventional religion and the secular religion, the elective affinity (or lack of it) between them, and the fundamental understanding of religion (e.g., whether it is primarily belief or practice). A comparative study of China and other countries, including postcommunist countries, might yield interesting results.

NOTES

1   Paul Tillich, *Christianity and the Encounter of World Religions* (Minneapolis, MN: Fortress, 1994), 4.
2   Paul Tillich, *Ultimate Concern: Tillich in Dialogue* (New York: Harper and Row, 1965), 4, 23; Paul Tillich, *The Encounter of Religions and Quasi-Religions*, ed. Terence Thomas (Lewiston, NY: Mellen, 1990), 9.
3   Philippe Burrin, "Political Religion: The Relevance of a Concept," *History and Memory* 9, nos. 1/2 (1997): 322–23.
4   Emilio Gentile, "Political Religion: A Concept and Its Critics: A Critical Survey," *Totalitarian Movements and Political Religions* 6, no. 1 (2005): 25.
5   Richard Shorten, "The Status of Ideology in the Return of Political Religion Theory," *Journal of Political Ideologies* 12, no. 2 (2007): 164–66.
6   Robert N. Bellah, "Civil Religion in America," in *Beyond Belief: Essays on Religion in a Post-Traditionalist World* (Berkeley: University of California Press, 1970), 168–89.
7   Marcela Cristi, *From Civil to Political Religion: The Intersection of Culture, Religion and Politics* (Waterloo, ON: Wilfrid Laurier University Press, 2001), 1, 45–46, 224–27.
8   Cristi, *From Civil to Political Religion*, 45, 232.

9   Cristi, *From Civil to Political Religion*, 46, 142, 144, 232.
10 Gentile, "Political Religion," 29.
11 Gentile, "Political Religion," 30.
12 Émile Durkheim, *The Elementary Forms of Religious Life*, trans. Karen E. Fields (New York: Free Press, 1995), 429.
13 Phil Zuckerman and John R. Shook, "Introduction: The Study of Secularism," in *The Oxford Handbook of Secularism*, ed. Phil Zuckerman and John R. Shook (New York: Oxford University Press, 2017), 9.
14 Vincent Goossaert and David A. Palmer, *The Religious Question in Modern China* (Chicago: University of Chicago Press, 2011), 168.
15 Jiping Zuo, "Political Religion: The Case of the Cultural Revolution in China," *Sociological Analysis* 52, no. 1 (1991): 101-4.
16 The Third Plenum of the Eleventh Central Committee of the Communist Party of China, held from December 18 to 22, 1978, marked the beginning of the reform era ushered in by the de facto leader Deng Xiaoping.
17 See Deng Xiaoping, "Building a Socialism with a Specifically Chinese Character," in *The Selected Works of Deng Xiaoping*, vol. 3, *1982-1992* (Beijing: Foreign Languages Press, 1994).
18 Tang Tsou, *The Cultural Revolution and Post-Mao Reforms* (Chicago: University of Chicago Press, 1986), 147.
19 Tony Saich, *Governance and Politics of China*, 3rd. ed. (New York: Palgrave Macmillan, 2011), 250, 254.
20 Saich, *Governance and Politics of China*, 252, 254.
21 Suisheng Zhao, "A State-Led Nationalism: The Patriotic Education Campaign in Post-Tiananmen China," *Communist and Post-Communist Studies* 31, no. 3 (1998): 289.
22 Zhao, "State-Led Nationalism," 290.
23 The Central Propaganda Department of the CCP issued the first official document on patriotic education in 1991. Two years later, the CCP Central Propaganda Department, together with several government departments, jointly issued a circular on patriotic education in primary and secondary schools by films and television. In 1994, the CCP Central Committee issued a document that launched at full throttle a nationwide patriotic education campaign "to boost the nation's spirit, enhance its cohesion, foster its self-esteem and sense of pride, consolidate and develop a patriotic united front to the broadest extent, and direct and rally the masses' patriotic passions to the great cause of building socialism with Chinese characteristics." The patriotic education campaign rallied support for the Communist Party of China on the grounds of its patriotic contributions to the country's independence and prosperity, not on the grounds of communist ideals: "patriotism rather than Communism, thus, became the basis of the CCP's rule of legitimacy." Zhao, "State-Led Nationalism," 292-94, 297.
24 Zhao, "State-Led Nationalism," 300.
25 Arif Dirlik, "The Discourse of 'Chinese Marxism,'" in *Modern Chinese Religion*, vol. 2, *1850-2015*, ed. John Lagerwey and Pierre Marsone (Leiden: Brill, 2016), 344, 347-48.

26 Richard Madsen, "Secular State and Religious Society in Mainland China and Taiwan," in *Social Scientific Studies of Religion in China: Methodology, Theories, and Findings*, ed. Fenggang Yang and Graeme Lang (Leiden: Brill, 2011), 292–93.
27 Cheng-Tian Kuo, "Sacred, Secular, and Neosacred Governments in China and Taiwan," in *The Oxford Handbook of Secularism*, ed. Phil Zuckerman and John R. Shook (New York: Oxford University Press, 2017), 259.
28 See, for example, Goossaert and Palmer, *Religious Question in Modern China*; Adam Yuet Chau, ed., *Religion in Contemporary China: Revitalization and Innovation* (Abingdon: Routledge, 2011); James Miller, ed., *Chinese Religions in Contemporary Societies* (Santa Barbara, CA: ABC-CLIO, 2006); Ian Johnson, *The Souls of China: The Return of Religion after Mao* (New York: Pantheon Books, 2017).
29 Deng Xiaoping, "The United Front and the Tasks of the Chinese People's Political Consultative Conference in the New Period," in *The Selected Works of Deng Xiaoping*, vol. 2, *1975-1982* (Beijing: Foreign Languages Press, 1984).
30 The principle of "seeking the common ground while reserving differences" applies only to "normal" religious practices and beliefs of religions sanctioned by the state—Daoism, Buddhism, Catholicism, Protestantism, and Islam—and not to religions that are politically dangerous (such as Falun Gong) or socially problematic (such as practices of popular religions labeled as "feudal superstitions").
31 Philip L. Wickeri, *Seeking the Common Ground: Protestant Christianity, the Three-Self Movement, and China's United Front* (Maryknoll, NY: Orbis, 1988), xxi.
32 "Constitution of the Three-Self Patriotic Movement of Protestant Churches in China," section 6(1), and "Constitution of the China Christian Council," section 7(1), quoted in *Chinese Theological Review* 26 (2014): 12, 25.
33 Jiang Zemin, "Paying Great Attention to Ethnic Work and Religious Work," in *Selected Documents of Religious Work in the New Era* (Beijing: Religious Culture Press, 1995), 254–55.
34 Jiang Zemin, "On Religious Question" [in Chinese], in *Selected Important Documents in the Thirty Years of Reform and Opening*, ed. Documentary Research Office of the Central Committee of the Communist Party of China (Beijing: Central Documents Press, 2008), 1213. Jiang mentioned, among others, the campaign of the Protestant Church in theological reconstruction as an example of "expounding religious doctrines according to the requirements of social progress."
35 K. H. Ting, "Theological Writings from Nanjing Seminary," *Chinese Theological Review* 8 (1993): 4, translation modified.
36 K. H. Ting, *Love Never Ends* (Nanjing: Yilin, 2000); hereafter cited as *LNE*.
37 K. H. Ting, *God Is Love* (Colorado Springs, CO: Cook Communications Ministries International, 2004), 344, 348, 455; hereafter cited as *GIL*. The book is a collection of writings of Bishop K. H. Ting. It contains most of the writings included in *LNE*, plus some other writings after 1997, up to 2001.
38 Ting, *GIL*, 455.
39 K. H. Ting, "Theological Reconstruction Entering a New Era," *Tian Feng*, no. 9 (2003): 7.
40 Ting, "The Cosmic Christ," in *LNE*, 408–18.

41 Ting, "Talk at a Theological Forum," in *LNE*, 513–26.
42 Ting, *LNE*, 408, 412.
43 Ting, *LNE*, 411.
44 Ting, *LNE*, 411.
45 Ting, *LNE*, 411–12.
46 Ting, *LNE*, 415, emphasis added.
47 Ting, *LNE*, 417.
48 Ting, *LNE*, 416–17.
49 "One Hundred Questions and Answers on the Christian Faith," *Chinese Theological Review* 1985:211–43. Question 10 states that the "supremely basic and essential attributes of God is 'love' (1 John 4,8,16). Not only is the relationship within the Trinity one of love, but God's creation, election and redemption of man are an expression of his love." "One Hundred Questions," 215.
50 Ting, *LNE*, 416–17.
51 Ting, *LNE*, 508.
52 Ting, *LNE*, 509.
53 Ting, *LNE*, 525.
54 Philip L. Wickeri, *Reconstructing Christianity in China: K. H. Ting and the Chinese Church* (Maryknoll, NY: Orbis, 2007), 347.
55 Wickeri, *Reconstructing Christianity in China*, 349, 357.
56 Ting, *GIL*, 51–53.
57 Ting, *GIL*, 460–61.
58 See, for example, Ting, *LNE*, 334. For a handy overview of the issues of the doctrine of justification, together with the consensus and differences in the views of Lutheran and Catholic churches, see Joint Declaration of Justification, accessed November 19, 2020, https://www.lutheranworld.org/sites/default/files/2020/documents/original_jddj_english.pdf.
59 Jiang Zemin, secretary-general of the CCP from 1989 to 2002, began to claim in 2000 that the party must always represent the requirements for developing China's advanced forces of production, the orientation of China's advanced culture, and the fundamental interests of the overwhelming majority of the Chinese people.
60 Ting, *GIL*, 123–24 (quote on 124).
61 Ting, *GIL*, 124–25.
62 Ting, *GIL*, 215.
63 Ting, *GIL*, 126.
64 See Wickeri, *Reconstructing Christianity in China*, 119–22.
65 Wickeri, *Reconstructing Christianity in China*, 340.
66 Ting, *GIL*, 448, 451.

15. CRITICAL ISRAEL
Toward a Contemporary Political Theology of the Particular
SHAUL SETTER

Critical thought in Israel is nowadays facing a significant crossroads. Indeed, the challenges to humanistic knowledge and critical research all around the globe are numerous: the neoliberal management of universities and the evasive use of quantitative indices of evaluation threaten to destroy—or at least to severely impoverish—humanistic critical activity. Yet there are also unique, or rather distinct, challenges to critical thought in Israel; and these challenges call for but also already substantiate a change in the course and horizon of critical Israeli intellectual activity. This chapter follows one trajectory that has become prominent in Israeli critical inquiry in the last decade: the turn toward the particular. It positions this turn within the genealogy of critical theory in Israel, showing the ways it diverts from the universalist tendency structuring the first generation of Israeli critical research at the end of the twentieth century. It stresses how the dramatic change in Israeli political discourse of the past decade required the retooling of an intellectual stance that could critically address its basic presuppositions: contemporary mainstream neonationalist particularist political theology is challenged here through the development of a nonnationalist theology of the particular. Such a critical move delves into the historical, social, textual, and linguistic potentialities of the Jewish particular, and the second section of this chapter shows how such potentialities reside at the heart of translation of the "humanities"—a discipline of inquiry, a mode of activity—into Hebrew and within the Hebrew and then Israeli academy. The final section presents one central critical intellectual and creative project that opens up the possibility of Jewish particularism as against both universalist humanism and nationalist chauvinism, taking its theological position as a mode of radical critique for the current age.

This inquiry into the critical potentialities of the particular can be seen as a local variation on a general theme, in both global politics and global academia, namely the postsecular turn. Such a variation of the politico-theological, localized in a highly volatile theological geography and exercised in a political catastrophe zone, may seem dubious and even dangerous. One could argue that its rejection of a secular humanistic universalist position and valorization of a theological particularist position run the risk of collapsing into an ethnonationalist stance; what seems to be a strategic decision in the progressive arena of critique can also be interpreted as a symptom of the decline of the universal or even as the co-optation of current critical discourse by the particularist bias sweeping Israeli politics. This may also signify an ultimate withdrawal of a particularized discourse from an international critical network, since this turn is also particular to the Israeli critical endeavor—to its specific history, conditions, and stakes. Yet this chapter fleshes out the turn to the particular as a challenge that is neither entirely intrinsic nor unique to the contemporary Israeli critical field. It is rather a translocal challenge, staged in the Israeli context but one that traverses it—since the particular is first constituted as an effect of the universal and within universal discourse and only later questions the universal structure, mechanisms, and ideology on particularist terms. Thus the turn to the particular, or what I call "critical Israel," reverberates throughout the ancient and modern, theological and social spaces indicated under the signifiers of "Israel" and "the particular"—be they European Christian spaces or Jewish and even Jewish/Palestinian ones. "Critical Israel" serves here as an exception to the rule and the exception that is tied to the rule: a particular position both representative of a postsecular age and specific and concrete, indeed particular, within it.[1] In other words, the critique of Jewish exceptionalism can become a Jewish critical exceptionality.

Universalist Critique

Critical theory was introduced to the Israeli academy at the end of the 1980s and the beginning of the 1990s. Different scholarly methodologies, research procedures, and academic idioms traveled from the critical American academy to the Israeli one—such as ideology critique, discourse analysis, deconstructive exegesis, or postcolonial reading of the canon, among others—and set into work onto local materials that, in Israel, meant everything that can be subsumed under the grand signifier of Zionism. The Israeli critical theory of the time struggled to display the nationalist, ethnocentric, and particularist premises structuring even the seemingly humanistic and liberal tendencies of Zionism. It intended to unveil the ideological premises and the discursive power invested in the image of Israel as a Jewish democratic state; it discussed the aporia of an ethnic particularist reasoning (the Jewish), conjured with a seemingly universal regime (the democratic). At the end of the 1980s, it was first the Israeli "New Historians" who challenged the founding moment of the state of Israel by extensively studying the expulsion of large portions of the Palestinian inhabitants of Palestine during the 1948 war. These historians revealed the constituent violence—and its ethnic, Jewish nationalist logic—without which the formation of an "Israeli democracy" could not have taken place.[2] In the same years, a critical sociology of Israel started to take shape, arguing against the image of Israeli society as a pluralist melting pot, or multicultural society, suggesting instead that the power relations and the unequal distribution of real and symbolic capital are based on the very nonliberal economic and political structures of Israeli society.[3] Israeli radical political science moved in these years from a national paradigm to a colonial or settler colonial paradigm for the Zionist project as well as for the current disjunctions between Ashkenazi, Mizrahi, and Palestinian citizenship in Israel.[4] And critical literary scholarship abandoned the triumphant celebration of modern Hebrew literature, whose genealogy is homologous to the development of Zionism, and read it critically, or turned to create other genealogies of the marginalized and outcasts.[5]

All these scholarly itineraries—which together created nothing less than an intellectual revolution, traveling many times from academic journals, conferences, and classrooms to newspapers, popular books, and even TV talk shows—took as their main object of critique what is nowadays called "liberal Zionism."[6] Heavily influenced by the persistence of the Israeli occupation of the West Bank and Gaza—which by then was already more than a generation old—they nevertheless targeted the discursive presupposition of smaller, pre-Occupation Israel, the allegedly Just Israel wishing to constitute an exemplary society through the attempt to become a people like all other peoples. It is against that humanistic Israel, or rather against its own image, that the critical endeavor of the 1990s was launched—against the attempt to arrive at a right balance between the Jewish and the democratic, the ethnocentric and the universal.[7]

It was an Oedipal struggle, in a double sense: Most of the young critical scholars of the 1980s and 1990s came from the circles of humanist Zionism—if not biographically (from progressive Ashkenazi secular Zionist families), then sociologically (from that social milieu). Coming to terms with the liberal theory but ethnocentric praxis meant a confrontation with the fathers,' and also the Father's, legacy. But more important, this critical endeavor started as an Oedipal struggle against the foundations of the humanistic research in the Hebrew and later Israeli academy, since that research was itself part and parcel of the Zionist enterprise. The disciplines of history and literature, of geography and linguistics, as well as of sociology and political science, were formed in the Hebrew academy as Zionist disciplines—structuring, following, and promoting the Zionist enterprise.[8] Furthermore, as a cultural national enterprise, Zionism itself started as a speculative project: a textual, literary, historiographical, humanistic project. Modern Hebrew literature and the national historiography of the Jews were formed prior to Zionism, indeed enabling Zionism to come into form.[9] The writing in modernized Hebrew was inaugurated already in the first half of the nineteenth century: Hebrew newspapers, Hebrew autobiographies, and Hebrew fiction were written and printed decades before Leon Pinsker published—in German—the inaugurating text of the Zionist movement, *Auto-Emancipation*, in 1882. Indeed, the "revival" of the Hebrew language was a central project in Jewish Enlightenment and later on in the Jewish national enterprise—the turning of Hebrew from a holy tongue, a language of reading, learning, and prayer, to a vernacular language, a spoken tongue of personal expression and collective experience. Modern Hebrew literature took upon itself that task: the early Hebrew novels of the second half of the nineteenth century were written before the consolidation of a modern Hebrew, and the novelists imagined intersubjective dialogues and an inner tongue of thinking and feeling before those actually existed in the Jewish community in Palestine. Moreover, they imagined a proto-nationalist subjectivity and community prior to their formation in reality. In this way, humanistic activity—literature but also history and sociology—constituted the heart of early Zionism: the building of a national culture facilitated the building of a nation. The 1896 novel *The Jewish State* opened the way for the Jewish state as a reality. And it is no accident that its writer, Theodor Herzl, a playwright and journalist, became the "Visionary of the State."[10] Humanistic activity paved the way to the national enterprise and later on resided at its core: in the writing of national history, the formation of a literary canon, and the depiction of different sects of society Hebrew and Israeli universities were part and parcel of nation building.

It was this Gordian knot between humanist Zionism and Hebrew/Israeli humanistic research that the critical thought of the 1990s sought to cut. Introducing critical theory to the Israeli academy, translating its allegedly universal "form"—procedures, methods, language—into the local "Zionist" materials, critical thought in Hebrew worked to mobilize a nonparticularist idiom of criticality to fight the ethnonationalist particularism at the heart of Israeli humanistic academic research. It showed how even the presumably liberal "democratic" aspects of Israel—sides that the humanistic academic research traditionally represented—are entangled with a Jewish nationalist chauvinistic particularism; and riding on the increasingly flourishing new international academic lingo of criticality, it established a position external to Jewish particularity in order to give it a blow. In other words, the critical endeavor aimed to constitute a radical democratic position, from which it unveiled and rejected the Jewish democratic knot of both liberal Zionism and Israeli academic humanistic scholarship. Jewish particularism—as state ideology, institutional credo, scholarly language—was its primary object of critique.[11] With the structure introduced in the "faith" lexical entry, one could say that such a radical secular position, exposing the Jewish particularist bias in Israeli liberalism, is indeed a secularized version of the modern view of religious faith—whose abstraction is stretched between the claim for universalism (the universal language of critique) and the fall into ideology (the ideology of the abstract, where the "no-place" from which it speaks actually places it as the place of the abstract—allegedly abstract but quite easily localized, socially and politically, as such).

More than a generation later, the stakes seem quite different. Within Israel's current neo-Zionist phase, the knot between the Jewish and the democratic is continuously undone, bringing to the fore a new configuration of military-based ultranationalist politics and high-tech-centered neoliberal economics, through a rearticulation of an exceptionalist—both apocalyptical and messianic—vision of the Jewish, ever more divorced from its once-aspired democratic semblance.[12] In this matrix, liberal Zionism, as a significant political force, is shrinking, and the pseudodemocratic position it used to propagate (balancing the Jewish and the democratic) seems less and less feasible in the current reality of Israel/Palestine. Moreover, the rising hegemony in Israel and mainstream public discourse do not hold, and may times openly renounce, even the aspiration to couple the Jewish state with the demands of liberal democracy.[13] What used to be a central ideological Zionist position for many years has been sidetracked in the past decade; and so to radically critique it—its paradoxes and denials—makes less sense these days. In other words, there is less need for Israeli critical scholars to explain why only a drastic change in the current regime can turn the geopolitical space between the Jordan river and the Mediterranean sea into something compatible with the image of a democracy (or two democracies); many principal Israeli political players acknowledge it while valorizing the current state of affairs. The radical democratic critique seems to arrive at a dead end since the democratic claim, which it set to uncover as partial and limited, has severely weakened.

Particularist Critique

Within this political and cultural situation, a different trajectory for critical thought and activity has been formed. The deployment of Jewish particularism in Israeli mainstream public discourse has provoked in recent years an intensified radical inquiry into the politics and theology of the particular. The particular, instead of being rejected or debunked, is rethought in contemporary Israeli critical discourse; and in doing so, it ceases to be a known claim, a position one supports or refuses, and becomes a field of examination, negotiation, and struggle. It is no longer only a right-wing, chauvinistic national stance, one that the egalitarian and universalist stance of progressive and radical critique dismisses. And yet it cannot be easily ascribed to a left-wing position, as it distances itself from the tradition in which universal rights and the fight for equality play central roles. Here, the particular is the Jewish—but for the Jewish to become the particular, it needs to be opened up and de-essentialized; it has to be disentangled from its presumably necessary integration within the nationalist stance. The attempt to fashion a radical democratic position to critique the pseudodemocratic claim of the Jewish democratic is echoed, in some recent works and projects, with the attempt to fashion a radical Jewish position to critique the pseudo-Jewish claim of the Jewish democratic. But to do so, the turn to the Jewish is considered first and foremost as an insistence on the particular. Over and against the "universal" positions—not only of critical radical democracy but also and mainly of human rights discourse on the one hand and of the neoliberal economic rationality on the other—this critical trajectory proposes to trace and explore historical but also speculative modalities of the Jewish as a particular. And its great challenge lies in forming various relations to what might seem to be its opposite—the Palestinian, the Muslim, the Arab—but can perhaps join it to coarticulate the politics and theology of the particular.

I call this trajectory in contemporary Israeli radical thought "critical Israel"; and in so doing I allude to Daniel Boyarin's 1993 book, *Carnal Israel*.[14] In this provocative book, Boyarin writes a Jewish version of Michel Foucault's *History of Sexuality*, engaging with the Christian accusation of Israel, ancient Israel—that is, of Rabbinic Judaism—as the religion of the flesh, in contrast to spiritual Christianity.[15] Like a good Jew, Boyarin takes this accusation by the letter and studies the central place of the unsublimated sexualized body in the Talmud. But I broaden the scope and think of carnal Israel as setting the very field of politico-theological particularity. In contrasting carnal Israel to the spiritual church, Paul sees ancient Israel as an obstacle in the path of universal spirit, and of universality as such: refusing to internalize the law as the law of love, insisting on the letter of the law and not its spirit, maintaining an external God, and asserting an irreconcilable communal difference. In other words, Rabbinic Judaism rejected the call of universality and stubbornly remained in and as the particular.[16] Thus turning carnal Israel to critical Israel means following the traces of particularity and reclaiming it as a refusal to the call of universalism—a call that is now figured and realized in many ways (realization and figuration are, after all, its mode of action), ways that keep close proximity to the image of liberal democracy, to its relation to the history of European colonialism, and to their underpinning in Western Christian theology; a call that has generally become the central object for the critique of secularism in recent decades. In the Israeli case, the refusal to the departicularizing strategies of the universal draws on the Jewish precisely without being subsumed under the Jewish national enterprise, which started as an attempt to reinscribe the Jews into history—universal and realized history—and it suggests the rethinking of the political content and form of that particularity.

This movement in the direction of the particular can be framed as a resignification of Hebrew humanistic research since it touches upon the very translatability of the humanities in Hebrew. In the Israeli academy, the humanities are called *madaey ha-ruah* (the sciences of the spirit). They have thus followed the German tradition by the name: as a separate discipline, humanistic research was inaugurated in the Humboldtian university at the beginning of the nineteenth century as *Geisteswissenschaften* (the sciences of the spirit). Indeed, the Hebrew academy was founded in Mandatory Palestine at the beginning of the twentieth century in light of the German model, and most of its founders were themselves educated in the German academy. It was the Romantic and national tradition of the nineteenth-century German academy, with its valorization of the *Volksgeist* through the work of the culture, that the founders of the Hebrew academy were after for the foundation of a national community. But this seemingly direct translation of "Geisteswissenschaften" into "madaey ha-ruah" bore a theological signification that the particular turn of recent years both fleshes out and transforms. If "madaey ha-ruah" is the translation of "Geisteswissenschaften," then the German "Geist" is rendered, in the Hebrew and later Israeli academy, into the Hebrew "ruah" (spirit). But centuries beforehand, the translation went the other way around, and it was "ruah" that was transformed into "Geist." Martin Luther's 1522 translation of the first lines of the Old Testament reads:

בְּרֵאשִׁית, בָּרָא אֱלֹהִים, אֵת הַשָּׁמַיִם, וְאֵת הָאָרֶץ. וְהָאָרֶץ, הָיְתָה תֹהוּ וָבֹהוּ, וְחֹשֶׁךְ, עַל-פְּנֵי תְהוֹם; וְרוּחַ אֱלֹהִים, מְרַחֶפֶת עַל-פְּנֵי הַמָּיִם.

Am Anfang schuf Gott Himmel und Erde. Und die Erde war wüst und leer, und es war finster auf der Tiefe; und der Geist Gottes schwebte auf dem Wasser.[17]

Luther turns the biblical "ruah" into "Geist" in what is most definitely a volatile moment of translation. "Ruah," to be sure, could have been translated into other German words: *Wind*, for example. But in choosing "Geist" to stand for "ruah," especially with its proximity to God (*Geist Gottes*), with respect, of course, to the *pneuma* of the New Testament—Luther positions his Bible within a tradition that revolves around the notion of Geist. Luther's "Geist," his "Geist" and not "Wind"—as an unearthly, noncorporeal, abstract spirit—undoubtedly resonates with Paul's emphasis on spirit in his attempt to revolutionize old Judaism and inaugurate a new messianic religion, later to become Christianity. Spirit for Paul is the watershed between the old and the new religion: it is the spirit of the law and not the letter of the law that the new religion is after; not the literal meaning of the dead signs but the intention behind the written words pouring new life into them; not the flesh of the text but its spirit. Thus old Rabbinic Judaism, the Judaism of the flesh—insisting on the corpus of the law with its rigid, mute, lifeless signifiers, together with the earthly religious institution that sanctions it—should be transformed, according to Paul, into a new religion, no longer bound to the carnal realm of life and text; a religion based on the spirit-enforced belief and love. I think it is this notion of spirit that Luther invokes when he translates "ruah" into "Geist": Luther places, right at the beginning of the "Jewish" Old Testament but already in the mode of prefiguration, the Paulinian noncarnal and disembodied yet intentional and animating spirit. And a few centuries later, when Georg W. F. Hegel would put the Geist at the center of his philosophical system, this tradition would be carried onward: the Hegelian reflexive spirit rescues the singular objects from their unmediated concreteness and sublates them into higher degrees of meaning and abstraction, until they are fully realized as a fulfilled, comprehensive, unified spirit—the disembodied spirit of the entirely unveiled world.

This brief genealogy of Geist—from Paul to Luther to Hegel (and there are, of course, many other possible stops)—places it within the Western Christian tradition, as a signifier of abstraction and reflection, of the movement beyond the flesh: *ruah elohim*—the ruah of God, which in Genesis 1 moves upon, sweeping or hovering over the water, and is rendered into the Geist of belief, of history, of the entire world. This translation of "ruah" into "Geist"—not just a literal translation but a cultural and ideological one—was challenged in the 1920s, when two young German Jewish intellectuals, Martin Buber and Franz Rosenzweig, took the task of retranslating the Old Testament into German. In their translation, they tried to remain as faithful as possible to the original biblical Hebrew and to offer, perhaps, a Jewish alternative to Luther's Bible. It is not surprising, therefore, that they questioned Luther's rendering of "ruah" into "Geist." Years later, Buber commented on this issue: "Since the time of Luther, who had to choose between Geist and Wind, Geist lost its original concreteness—a concreteness it had in company with *ruah*, with *pneuma*, with *spiritus* itself—lost its original sensory character—'a surging and a blowing simultaneously.' ... The splitting of a fundamental word is not merely a process in the history of language but also a process in the history of Geist and life, namely the incipient separation between *Geist* and life."[18] Buber laments here the turning of Geist into a signifier of inconcreteness and abstraction, starting, as he specifies, with Luther's translation to the Old Testament. He calls to undo the split between physical Wind and abstract Geist and to return to a more cohesive concept of Geist—Geist not only as spirit but also as breath and wind, an integration of corporeal, sensorial, and intellectual Geist. Indeed, Buber and Rosenzweig ended up translating the biblical *ruah* with the German neologism *Windbraus*, in which the spiritual and material are held together.[19] But in retranslating the biblical "ruah," they did not just try to get rid of Geist as a completely immaterial, abstract notion, which would result in a mistranslation for "ruah elohim"—the breath/wind/spirit of God. Rather, they sought to resignify Geist, to pull it out of its Christian philosophical genealogy—from Paul's fleshless spirit to Hegel's *Weltgeist*—by unveiling, as Buber explains here, its tactile, concrete, material roots. They tried to recapture the singular in the abstract, the flesh of spirit, the ruah within Geist.

The contemporary turn to the particular can be seen as an attempt to follow Buber and Rosenzweig in reclaiming the ruah in the Geist, instead of abiding to what seems to be an abstract humanistic spirit—including that of universalist critique—against the biased, partial nationalist or ethnocentrist ideology, asserting the particular and singular cultural ramifications of that spirit.[20] Here it is done linguistically and theologically, with "ruah" as a Hebrew signifier and a Jewish one. But this re-invocation of the particular does not return to the national particularity, as the collision of Hebrew and Jewish seems at first to attest. On the contrary, it aims to retrieve the minoritarian position this particular signified in the past, standing against Western claims for universality—seemingly secular but secularized Christian, seemingly abstract and total but only under the conditions of historical progress, seemingly given equally to all but tied to hierarchized colonial disjunctions. As an unmetabolized remainder, an all-too-material (and materialized in a specific language) element in the development of absolute spirit, the particularity of "ruah" is rejected from, but also resists, the hegemony of the universal. That was the case with the difference engendered in exilic Jewish communities. But what happens when the particular is taken up as intellectual, theological, linguistic projects within a society so loaded with nationalist, ethnocentrist particularism? How can it address particularist hegemony critically, in the form of a creative critique?

Particularist Projects

The projects of critical Israel are therefore theologically loaded, historically informed, and politically motivated; they are critical but in ways that are different from what used to be considered critical and therefore is yet to be deciphered. They start with the challenge of language, since, as in "ruah," this is both the cipher and the arena of the particular: there the critical particular confronts the universal horizon of pure language on the one hand and the nationalist reality of ideological ethnic language on the other. These projects thus apply to, reexamine, and experiment with the Hebrew language—but not in the image of the modernized and secularized language that facilitated the national revival and became the sovereign (and sovereign's) language.[21] As against this actualized Hebrew—actualized in people's speech, in the streets, in legislative power, in governance, in state-sanctioned actions—these projects try to find and form the unmodern, not-yet, or already-not-actualized Hebrew, a Hebrew becoming a minor language again; and one that is carved in close proximity with Arabic: then, in Al-Andalus, and now, in Israel/Palestine.[22] These are not only scholarly projects but also poetic ones, and they are constative and performative at the same time: the language in question is a language envisioned and practiced.²³ This concern with language grants a different view of textuality. If within the Zionist enterprise the text was actualized and became a political reality—whether it was Herzl's book *The Jewish State* being realized in Palestine as a Jewish state or the narratives of the Bible being relived at present-day Palestine in the nationalist imaginary—these new projects aim to carve a textual register that is not sublated into social existence, a textuality that does not wait to be negated and then realized but one that negates the course of political sovereign realization as the only communal operation possible. This also means reconnecting to historic forms of nonsovereign Jewish existence in the Middle East, on Muslim or Arab lands—from Saadia Gaon's tenth-century Baghdad, through the Holy Ari's sixteenth-century Safed, to Esther Moyal's early twentieth-century Cairo.²⁴ The Jew and the Arab are entangled here in ways that are at least partially removed from both the Zionist state and the Western empires, creating zones of interwoven particularities, unmediated by an abstract rule. Finally, these linguistic and textual projects call for a different engagement with our very own academic practices of teaching and learning, reading and writing. From the "religious" past and pre-state-sanctioned institutions, they can carry on modes of textual exegesis, of collaborative thinking, of subversive and conservative relation to a canon, and of forming a community of learners—modes that very much differ from what has become the individualist and individualizing, publishing-oriented, and "originality" glorifying practices of the global contemporary academy.²⁵

Scholar and poet Haviva Pedaya has been pioneering this particularist intellectual trajectory in the last couple of decades. Her vast range of textual creativity—moving between scholarly research, theological-political theory, essayistic prose, and modernist liturgical poetry as well as nonwritten oral activity such as musical ensembles, learning groups, and an ongoing presence in public discourse—not only defies disciplinary boundaries but aims at recasting the ideological basis of humanistic activity in Israel. Her intellectual project abides neither to the nationalist grounds of the humanities in the Hebrew and later Israeli academy nor to the universalist critique thereof exercised by the first generation of critical theory in Israel. A professor of Jewish history and thought, extensively writing on Jewish mysticism, she is also a descendant of an early twentieth-century renowned practicing Kabbalist (Jewish mystic); thus Jewish esotericism and devotion are for her not only an object for a theoretical study and distant reflection, sanctioned in an academic community whose allegedly abstract and transparent modes of production and transmission of knowledge were actually established in Christian Europe. It is rather an experience of thinking and practice, rooted in a specific cultural history and tied to particular forms of social gathering, and as such it calls for its contemporary transmission through different modes of teaching, learning, and exegetical reading. Such a particularist project changes the preconditions of humanistic activity in Israel; set on the margins of the Israeli academy, it proposes to transform its institutional ideological arrangements. In the caesura between the nationalist particularist and the Western universalist, it carves a third path in which a Jewish particularism is disentangled from the nationalist structure and constitutes a nonsovereign, minoritarian position. This is done, first, in the form of a historical return to a pre-Zionist (pre-nationalist-particularist) but also pre-Enlightenment (pre-universalist) Jewish existence in Europe, and even more so, in a return to the Jewish communities on Arab lands—a historical trajectory that defies both the nationalist and the European universalist options. From this archive, Pedaya forms a creative project for the present—not a nostalgic return to the good old days of the (non-Zionist, pre-colonial) past but a reactivation of one historical path within contemporary Israeli culture that rejects both religious nationalist chauvinism and secularist abstract humanism.

Pedaya's particularist project is therefore not merely historical but also politico-theological; at its core lies a re-invocation of a textual and linguistic dimension particular to Judaism.[26] The Jewish symbolic order, claims Pedaya, differs from the hegemonic, allegedly universal and practically Christian one. It is not structured on the ordering of the social world through intersubjective relationships, verbal communication, discrete knowledge, and parsed science, and the following after a set of laws and norms—that is, on the conscription to and internalization of the social law, as Jacques Lacan notoriously analyzed.[27] Premodern Jewish communities constituted different symbolic systems from Christian European ones—at once parallel to them and separated from them. The Jewish law existed together with the European law; it did not claim being general, abstract, all-encompassing, and unified, but its differentiation was from the abstract European law. It did not directly compete with the general law, in order to change and replace it, but resided in proximity to it, or within it, as a different symbolic apparatus—particular, partial, and unexclusive, a law of a minor community living within the major, general one. This law was subject to an endless exegetical work; that was the main practice surrounding it, constituting a saturated Jewish textuality not bounded to implementation but to further reading, interpretation, and transmission. Unlike the general law that demands its own actualization and realization in the social realm, this law was textualized to such a degree that it was not actualized in the general social realm but in the textual practices around it. For Pedaya, then, Jewish symbolization is grounded in its excessive textuality—devoid of realization in the social order but generative of communities of learning.

It is this particularity that has been threatened throughout modernity, due to the processes of secularization and nationalization of Judaism that forced a movement of both realization and actualization—either abstract universalist, as the elimination of the law in the face of universal law; or nationalist particularist, as the rendering of some portions of the law into a law of a sovereign nation. It is therefore not only secularization that diminished Jewish particularism but also, and to a further degree, Jewish nationalism that set to detextualize Jewish existence—to strip it of its exegetical practices in small exilic minoritarian communities and "return it to history," in the form of a worldly activity and self-governance. The text becoming a reality, the holy turned to life, God's provenance and promises actualized in historical time—these are not particularist positions but an adherence to universalist ones, manifest in the Christian theology of actualization. Jewish national enterprise has been an attempt to close the gap between the particularized Jewish form of life and the general abstract social order—between the textualized symbolic and the realized one; and as such it has forged a project set on Jewish particularism (a Jewish state) that strived to eliminate the particular (Jewish as nonrealizable in the state). Jewish particularist exceptionalism realized in a Jewish state thus becomes the burial site of Jewish theologico-political particularity.

It is from this threat to Jewish particularity that Pedaya calls for the "decolonization of the symbolic register of Judaism": the redeveloping of particular symbolic forms—thoughts and texts but also forms of life—that are not negated and realized in the social realm and do not coincide with the abstract rule of the regime.[28] These can take the form of neoliturgical poetry, written in a nonactualized Hebrew (different from the secularized, modernized, nationalized Hebrew); or that of a generic textuality that combines theory, with guidance and esoteric knowledge, one that does not address a known and sanctioned institutional arrangement; or groups of learners that can turn into collectivities of social change and political action. But in calling for the "decolonization of the symbolic register in Judaism," Pedaya also couples decolonization and Judaism and points to the political horizon of the particular theological project: she brings the critique of Christian Universalism—against the realization of the text in society, of the letter in the spirit—to bear upon the critique of realized Judaism, as a process of detextualization and departicularization; a process that is here tied to colonization. Since if the text should be negated and implemented in social reality, if sovereignty should turn onto earth, if the book *The Jewish State* is realized in and as a Jewish state, the land becomes the space of realization, and its conquering is therefore the very act of national actualization. Pedaya's project calls to invert this course: to reassert the particular in Judaism through a retextualization of the symbolic realm and a de-actualization of Jewish existence; this decolonization of the symbolic thus ultimately means a decolonization of the land upon which Jews live. But Pedaya helps us think anew what a decolonizing project might mean today: not only a political process—one that in itself already has a history, a history of failures (in which decolonization did not go, in most cases, far beyond the change in political regime, and the colonial structures remained intact). This is the history of realized decolonization, decolonization striving at political realization. But decolonization, according to Pedaya, does not necessitate the end of Jewish habitation in Israel/Palestine, the destruction of the state of Israel, a turning back of history and the undoing of any outcome of Zionism in the last 120 years. To think in this way about decolonization is to accept historical and social realization as the only possible activity within a symbolic order: as if to change the state of affairs one has to turn the actualized reality into a different actualized reality; decolonization is then set in the actualizing, Realpolitik terms of colonization. Yet thinking theologically, decolonization is not only a process in actualized historical reality but a position vis-à-vis actualization itself; it is an imagining of a symbolic that is not entirely socially realized within the legal and governing systems. As such, it bears a potentiality within modern Jewish culture itself that can be carried out in the space of Israel/Palestine: a theological decolonization of the self-colonized colonizing power that will open the way to the political decolonization of the colonial/colonized land.

In this way, the particular trajectory carries a critical force not less poignant than the humanistic universalist one. This particular can, without becoming universal, be universalizable, in Gayatri Chakravorty Spivak's terms, in various arenas outside Israel/Palestine.[29] The current debates around academic procedures of evaluation and the format of teaching, for example, can turn their eyes to different formations of gathering around and transmissions of textual knowledge; or the attempts to fashion contemporary left-wing emancipatory political stances that will challenge the reign of universalist human rights discourse can benefit from the nonauthoritarian, minoritarian, de-actualization position suggested in the Jewish particular. Within Israel/Palestine, such a position has the potential to participate in the public discourse, radically yet unanachronistically; to unfold and extend one of its dominant signifiers; to recast humanistic scholarship, both intellectually and institutionally; and through it all, to form an oppositional politico-theological stance to the rising overtly nationalist and allegedly particularist—and not the falling, allegedly liberal universalist—Israeli economic-political elite.

NOTES

1 I am alluding here, of course, to Giorgio Agamben's discussion of the paradoxical position of the exception—at the same time both outside and within the rule. See Giorgio Agamben, *Homo Sacer: Sovereign Power and Bare Life* (Stanford: Stanford University Press, 1998), 15–20. This structure proves itself very relevant in the case of Israel, which can be taken as an exception to the rule (of national revival; of the relationship between religion, ethnos, peoplehood, and state; of the colonial project) while itself becoming a rule (of Bible-inspired nationalism, of "the chosen people," of "the war against terror").

2 The New Historians was a group of Israeli historians who challenged the hegemonic Zionist historiography of Israel, specifically providing a counternarrative to the Zionist one regarding Israel's 1948 War of Independence, exploring the expulsion of large portions of the Palestinian population during that war. The most influential and debatable book—published in English in 1987 and in Hebrew translation in 1989, immediately launching a public debate in Israel—was Benny Morris's *The Birth of the Palestinian Refugee Problem, 1947–1949* (Cambridge: Cambridge University Press, 1987). Other New Historians were Ilan Pappé and Avi Shlaim. Although creating a critical mass of historical research critical of the institutional Zionist one, the New Historians were, by no means, a united group of scholars, and they did not share political motivations or historiographical methodologies. While Morris, for example, was a positivist historian and a Zionist (and in recent years, hardly a liberal one), Pappé promoted narrative historiography and is a vocal anti-Zionist.

3 See, for example, Baruch Kimmerling, *Zionism and Territory: The Socioterritorial Dimensions of Zionist Politics* (Berkeley: University of California Press, 1983). Other critical sociologists are Yehouda Shenhav, Uri Ram, and Pnina Mutzafi-Haller.

4 The inaugurating and major work in this field is Gershon Shair, *Land, Labor, and the Origin of the Israeli-Palestinian Conflict, 1882–1914* (Cambridge: Cambridge University Press, 1989). Other critical political scientists include Yoav Peled, Adi Ophir, and Amal Jamal.

5 See, in particular, Yitzhak Laor, *Anu kotvim otakh moledet* [Narratives with no natives] (Tel Aviv: Ha-Kibbutz ha-Me'uchad, 1995); and Hannan Hever, *Producing the Modern Hebrew Canon: Nation Building and Minority Discourse* (New York: New York University Press, 2002).

6 This liberal Zionism was recently somewhat anachronistically and heavy-handedly championed by Ari Shavit. See Ari Shavit, *My Promised Land: The Triumph and Tragedy of Israel* (New York: Spiegel and Grau, 2013). Of course, there is hardly anything liberal in that political stance, in the seventeenth- and eighteenth-century European meaning of "liberal," since it accepts some of the structuring privileges of the Jewish population within the State of Israel—indeed, in its very definition as a

Jewish state—over and against the Palestinian citizens of Israel, while at the same time emphasizing its own secular, democratic, and "peacenik" politics.

7   An illuminating example for this debate, between the liberal Zionist position and the critical one, can be found in the dispute between historians Zeev Strernhell and Gabriel Piterberg regarding Piterberg's book *The Returns of Zionism: Myths, Politics and Scholarship in Israel* (London: Verso, 2007), in the *New Left Review*: see Sternhell's review of the book, "In Defence of Liberal Zionism," and Piterberg's response, "Settlers and Their States," *New Left Review* 62 (March/April 2010): 99–114, 115–24.

8   For the beginning of such a discussion, see Uri Ram, *The Changing Agenda of Israeli Sociology: Theory, Ideology, Identity* (New York: State University of New York Press, 1995); and Uri Ram, *Israeli Nationalism: Social Conflicts and the Politics of Knowledge* (London: Routledge, 2011). But more should be said here about the Hebrew humanities and social sciences as Zionist disciplines.

9   Eyal Chowers, *The Political Philosophy of Zionism: Trading Jewish Words for Hebraic Land* (New York: Cambridge University Press, 2012).

10   Theodor Herzl, *The Jewish State* (New Orleans: Quid Pro Books, 2011).

11   A good anthology of essays that summarizes this critical trajectory post-factum reveals the turn of the general (or American) "postmodern" of "poststructuralist" critique into a local "postzionist" one. Laurence Silberstein, ed., *Postzionism: A Reader* (New York: Rutgers University Press, 2008).

12   Hilla Dayan, "When Neozionism Meets European Racism," *Ici et ailleurs*, July 2, 2015.

13   One can hear increasingly central voices in Israel arguing—in one variation or another—that "if this is racism, than I am a racist" (due to security threats or to "demographic" concerns), contrary to the main effort of Israel's international diplomacy but also Israelis' self-image in past decades to argue, loud and clear, that "this [Zionism] is not racism."

14   Daniel Boyarin, *Carnal Israel: Reading Sex in Talmudic Culture* (Berkeley: University of California Press, 1993).

15   See Augustine's exegesis: "*Behold Israel according to the Flesh* (I Cor. 10:18). This we know to be the carnal Israel; but the Jews do not grasp this meaning and as a result they prove themselves indisputably carnal." Quoted in Boyarin, *Carnal Israel*, 1

16   G. W. F. Hegel, *Early Theological Writings* (Philadelphia: University of Pennsylvania Press, 1971).

17   Stephan Füssel, ed., *The Luther Bible of 1534: Bilingual Facsimile* (Cologne: Taschen, 2016).

18   Martin Buber, "People Today and the Jewish Bible," in *Scripture and Translation*, by Martin Buber and Franz Rosenzweig (Bloomington: Indiana University Press, 1994), 16–17.

19   Alan T. Levenson, *The Making of the Modern Jewish Bible* (Lanham, MD: Rowman and Littlefield, 2011), 84.

20   On universalist critique, see, for example, how Adi Ophir, a major figure in the first generation of critical theory in Israel, has recently discussed the state, crisis, and horizon of the humanities—as Geisteswissenschaften—from the Paulinian divide

21 between the flesh and the spirit, and the valorization of the latter upon the former. Adi Ophir, "The Sciences of the Spirit," *Differences* 24, no. 3 (2013): 160–74.
21 The short text that became widely known in the last two decades and can serve as the point of reference for the thinking of the dangers inscribed in the modernization and secularization of the Hebrew language is Gershom Scholem's 1926 letter to Franz Rosenzweig, "Confession on the Subject of Our Language" (discovered only in the late 1980s by Stefan Moses). See this letter, together with Jacques Derrida's analysis, which made it famous, in Jacques Derrida, *Acts of Religion*, ed. Gil Anidjar (London: Routledge, 2002), 189–227.
22 In my own work, I develop a concept of reading (*qeriah*, in Hebrew) that will open up the many significations of this word in ancient, both biblical and postbiblical, theologically loaded Hebrew—qeriah as reading but also as addressing, naming, and calling.
23 See the recently published anthology of fictional and nonfictional prose *Shtaim* [*Two*] (Tel Aviv: Keter, 2014), in which each essay or story appears in Hebrew and Arabic—not only as an act of translation but as a way of rethinking the affinities between the two languages, trying to bring such affinities to bear upon the original language in which the texts were written. Among the poets and novelists who follow this trajectory are Almog Behar, Ya'akov Bitton, Albert Swissa, and Dvir Tsur.
24 For a ground-breaking work, considering the Jew not as the ultimate exile but as a native (though not sovereign) in the Middle East, see Ammiel Alcalay, *After Jews and Arabs: Remaking Levantine Culture* (Minnesota: University of Minnesota Press, 1993). The initiator of this trajectory in the Israeli academy is Amnon Raz-Krakotzkin, whose works appear mainly in Hebrew, and even more so, not in writing but in oral teaching and discussions. But see Amnon Raz-Krakotzkin, "Exile, History, and the Nationalization of Jewish Memory: Some Reflections on the Zionist Notions of History and Return," *Journal of Levantine Studies* 3, no. 2 (Winter 2013): 37–70.
25 This work is yet to be done.
26 This project is most elaborate in Haviva Pedaya, *Merhav u-makom* [Space and Place: An Essay on the Theological and Political Unconscious] (Tel Aviv: Ha-Kibbutz ha-Me'uchad, 2011).
27 See, for example, Jacques Lacan, *Écrits* (New York: Norton, 2007).
28 Pedaya, *Merhav u-makom*, 37–38, 49–54.
29 "The singular is the always universalizable, never the universal. The site of reading is to make the singular visible in its ability." "Comparative Literature / World Literature: A Discussion with Gayatri Chakravorty Spivak and David Damrosch," *Comparative Literature Studies* 48, no. 4 (2011): 466.

Contributors

MARKUS BALKENHOL is a social anthropologist who studies the commemoration of slavery and politics of citizenship in the Netherlands. He is a researcher at the Meertens Institute of the Royal Academy of Arts and Sciences. He has recently published articles in *Social Anthropology*, the *Journal for Ethnic and Migration Studies*, and *Material Religion*. He is coeditor of forthcoming volume, *The Secular Sacred: Emotions of Belonging and the Perils of Nation and Religion*.

ELIZABETH BENTLEY is a PhD candidate in rhetoric at the University of Arizona. Her research, which is supported by the American Association of University Women, examines contested histories of nonhuman species life in Israel/Palestine and how these histories are mediated at public educational sites. Her articles have appeared or are forthcoming in *Peithos* and *Jerusalem Quarterly*. She is currently at work on her first book project, which traces the rhetorical afterlives of crocodile extinction in historic Palestine.

KAMBIZ GHANEABASSIRI is Professor of Religion and Humanities at Reed College. He is author of *A History of Islam in America: From the New World to the New World Order* (2010) and is the founding coeditor of the book series Islam of the Global West. His work has been supported in part by a Carnegie Scholar Award and a Guggenheim Fellowship. In addition to his research on the history of Islam in America, GhaneaBassiri specializes in classical and modern Islamic intellectual and social history in the Middle East.

DAVID N. GIBBS is Professor of History at the University of Arizona. He has published extensively on the politics of sub-Saharan Africa, Afghanistan, and the former Yugoslavia. He is writing a book on the rise of American conservatism during the 1970s. His most recent book is *First Do No Harm: Humanitarian Intervention and the Destruction of Yugoslavia* (2009).

ORI GOLDBERG studies the connections and mutual influences among theology, faith, and politics in the Middle East. He teaches at IDC Herzliya's School of Government. His publications include *Shi'i Theology in Iran: The Challenge of Religious Experience* (2011), *Understanding Shiite Leadership: The Art of the Middle Ground in Iran and Lebanon* (with Shaul Mishal, 2014), and *Faith and Politics in Iran, Israel, and the Islamic State* (2017).

MARCIA KLOTZ is Assistant Professor in English and Gender and Women's Studies at the University of Arizona. Her research interests include critical finance studies, queer theory, sexuality studies, and Marxist theory. Her current book project examines the affective dimensions of the debt economy, arguing that finance capital operates as a theological power in the contemporary culture.

ZEYNEP KURTULUŞ KORKMAN is Assistant Professor of Gender Studies at UCLA. Her research interests include transnational feminisms; labor, affect, and intimacy; and religion, secularism, and the public sphere in Turkey and the larger Middle East. She is currently at work on a book focusing on the gendered economy of divinations in contemporary Turkey. Korkman's work has appeared in *Gender and Society*, the *Journal of Middle East Women's Studies*, the *European Journal of Cultural Studies*, and the *Journal of Ottoman and Turkish Studies*.

LEEROM MEDOVOI is Professor in the Department of English at the University of Arizona and Chair of the Program in Social, Cultural and Critical Theory. He is author of *Rebels: Youth and the Cold War Origins of Identity* (2005) and publishes on global American studies, biopolitical theory, critical race studies, and environmental humanities. Medovoi is currently at work on a book-length project that reframes the genealogy of race in relation to the biopolitics of souls. He is the principal investigator on two Mellon grants on "Religion, Secularism and Belonging" and "Neoliberalism at the Neopopulist Crossroads."

EVA MIDDEN is Assistant Professor of Gender Studies in the Media and Culture Studies Department at Utrecht University. She was recently involved in the European Research Project MIGNET, for which she conducted research on migration, gender, and religious practices in new media. Midden's current research focuses on gender, religion, and national identity in the context of conversion to Islam.

MOHANAD MUSTAFA is senior lecturer at the Beit-Berl Academic College and a lecturer in the master's degree program in Middle East politics at the School of Political Science at the University of Haifa. He specializes in political Islam, democratization in the Arab World, and Israeli and Palestinian politics.

MU-CHOU POO is Professor of History at the Chinese University of Hong Kong. Research interests include religion and society in ancient Egypt and China. Major publications include *Burial and the Idea of Life and Death: Essay on Ancient Chinese Religion* (1993), *Wine and Wine Offering in the Religion of Ancient Egypt* (1995), *In Search of Personal Welfare: A View of Ancient Chinese Religion* (1998), *Enemies of Civilization: Attitudes toward Foreigners in Ancient Mesopotamia, Egypt, and China* (2005), *Rethinking Ghosts in World Religions* (ed., 2009), *Old Society, New Belief, Religious Transformation of China and Rome, ca. 1st–6th Centuries* (ed. with H. A. Drake and Lisa Raphals, 2017), and *Daily Life in Ancient China* (2018).

SHAUL SETTER teaches literature and theory at Tel Aviv University and Sapir College. He works on (neo)modernist aesthetic-political projects in Europe and Israel/Palestine. His latest publication is "Political *Glas*: Derrida, Genet, and the Form of Decolonial Textuality," *Diacritics* 44, no. 1 (2016). He currently serves as the art critic for *Haaretz* newspaper.

JOHN VIGNAUX SMYTH is author of *A Question of Eros: Irony in Sterne, Kierkegaard, and Barthes* (1986) and *The Habit of Lying: Sacrificial Studies in Literature, Philosophy, and Fashion Theory* (2002). His *Mock Ritual in the Modern Era*, coauthored with Reginald McGinnis of the University of Arizona, is currently under review for publication.

POOYAN TAMIMI ARAB is Assistant Professor of Religious Studies at Utrecht University. He is author of *Amplifying Islam in the European Soundscape: Religious Pluralism and Secularism in the Netherlands* (2017) and currently part of the eight-year-long research project Religious Matters in an Entangled World: Things, Food, Bodies, and Texts as Entry Points to the Material Study of Religion in Plural Settings.

ERNST VAN DEN HEMEL is a postdoctoral fellow at the Meertens Institute of the Royal Netherlands Academy of Arts and Sciences and a lecturer at Utrecht University. A scholar of religion and literature, he is currently researching the intersections of populism, religion, and social media.

ALBERT WELTER is Professor in the Department of East Asian Studies at the University of Arizona. He specializes in East Asian (particularly Chinese) Buddhism. He is also Associate Director of the School of International Languages, Literatures, and Cultures and is affiliated with the Religious Studies Program in the Department of Religious Studies and Classics. He has published several volumes: *Monks, Rulers, and Literati: The Political Ascendancy of Chan Buddhism* (2006), *The "Linji lu" and the Creation of Chan Orthodoxy: The Development of Chan's Records of Sayings Literature* (2008), *Yongming Yanshou's Conception of*

Chan in the "Zongjing lu": A Special Transmission within the Scriptures (2011), and *The Administration of Buddhism in China: A Study and Translation of Zanning and His Topical Compendium of the Buddhist Order in China* (2018). He has also coedited a volume (with Jeffrey Newmark), *Religion, Culture and the Public Sphere in China and Japan* (2017).

FRANCIS CHING-WAH YIP is Associate Professor at the Divinity School of Chung Chi College and in the Department of Cultural and Religious Studies at the Chinese University of Hong Kong. His research areas include Protestant theology and practice in contemporary China, Hong Kong Christianity, and the social and religious thought of Paul Tillich. His is author of *Capitalism as Religion? A Study of Paul Tillich's Interpretation of Modernity* (2010) and coauthor of a Chinese commentary on the Nicene Creed.

RAEF ZREIK is Associate Professor in Jurisprudence at Carmel Academic College in Haifa and Academic Co-Director of the Minerva Centre for the Humanities at Tel Aviv University. A jurist and scholar, he is an expert in political philosophy and the philosophy of law. He is editor of *Qadaya*, a journal on Israeli affairs published by Madar Centre in Ramallah, and a member of the editorial board of the *Journal of Palestine Studies*. He has published widely on political philosophy, legal theory, citizenship, and the politics of identity.

Index

Abdul Rauf, Feisal, 253, 257–60
Abington, 37
Abzug, Bella, 215
accommodation: of difference, 20; neutrality and, 50–54
Actor Network Theory, 44
Adams, Bo, 215
adaptation: political religion and, 311–14
"Address to the Youth" (Atatürk), 291–92
adhan (call to prayer), 56–62
Adorno, Theodor, 47
Africa, 140, 170n9. *See also specific countries*
Africa Museum (Berg en Dal, Netherlands), 276
African American coalitions, 217–18
Africanness, 276–78
Afro-Caribbeans, 52–53
Afro-Surinamese Dutch migrants, 266–79
Agamben, Giorgio, 109–13, 339n1
al-dini (religious), 96

al-Dusturi al-Jadid (New Constitutional Party) (Tunisia), 89–92
Alevis, 294
Algeria, 90
Al-Ghannouchi, Rachid, 92–101
al-ijtihad (interpretation), 96
Alkhardawi Sheikh of al-Azhar, 165
Al-Khomeini and the Alternative Islamic Solution (Shaqaqi), 160
al-siasi (political), 96
Al-Shaab newspaper, 95
"The Alternative Islamic Solution" (Shaqaqi), 165–66
al-Tiqtal (Unity) Party (Tunisia), 97
Altınay, Rüstem Ertuğ, 287–89
America at Risk (Gingrich), 258–59
American Association of Evangelicals, 150
American civil religion, 248–49
American Enterprise Institute, 209

American Federation of Labor and Congress of Industrial Organizations (AFL-CIO), 217
American Protestants, 148–51
Amsterdam School architecture, 57
Amway Corporation, 211–13
Ana, Zöhre, 286, 287, 294, 298
Anana Keduaman Keduampon (Winti deity), 271
Anatolia (*Anadolu*), 293–98
Anderson, Benedict, 140–42
Andropov, Yuri, 150
anticommunism, 13
anti-Muslim activism, U.S., 253–62
antitrust laws, 117
apocalyptic evangelism, 121–22
Appleby, R. Scott, 151
Arabic, 90–91
Arab identity: Palestinian nationalist movement and, 22–23, 155–59; in Tunisia, 90–91, 100–101
Arab national movement, 156–59, 165–66
Arab National Movement (ANM), 157–58
Arab Spring, 21
Arafat, Yasser, 158, 170n15
Arato, Andrew, 126
Aristotle, 53–54
Armenians, 57–58, 66n40
Armstrong, Karen, 149
Asad, Talal, 28n5, 267
Assmann, Jan, 145n8
Atatürk, Mustafa Kemal, 57–58, 66n41, 90, 283, 289–99
Atran, Scott, 45
Augustine (Saint), 239–42
authoritarianism: in Tunisia, 90, 102–3
Auto-Emancipation (Zionist text), 328

Baldwin, James, 213
Balfour Declaration, 157
Balibar, Étienne, 15–16
Banna, Hassan al-, 165, 172n34
Barak, Aharon, 187–88
belief: secularism and, 5–6
Bellah, Robert, 129, 141, 248, 306
belonging: in China, 23; Christian-business alliance and, 208; gender, religion and national identity and, 24; in Israel, 175–88; Muslims and, 251–62; nationalism and politics of, 143–44; in Netherlands, 49–63; political versus cultural, 54–58; postsecularism and, 275–78; religious claims of, 22–24; secularism and religion and, 24–27; transgender groups and, 288–89; in United States, 23–24, 25, 31n34, 251–62
Ben Ali, Zine El Abidine, 93–94
Benjamin, Walter, 16–19, 252–53
Bennett, Naftali, 180–83, 188
Bentham, Jeremy, 110
Berman, Marshall, 217
Bible, 316, 317–20, 332–34
biblical criticism, 148–51
Birth of Biopolitics (Foucault), 118
The Birth of the Palestinian Refugee Problem, 1947–1949 (Morris), 339n2
blackness, 268–70
Black Pete, 278
Bolkestein, Frits, 128–30
Book of Knowledge (*Bilgi Kitabı*), 290–98
Boomsma, Arie, 224–25
bottom-up research approach, 135–36
Bourguiba, Habib, 89–93
Boyarin, Daniel, 331
Boyer, Pascal, 45
Braidotti, Rosi, 143
Breaking the Spell (Dennett), 45
Bremer, Stanley, 276
Brenner, Robert, 208–10
Brexit, 55
Bright, Bill, 212
British colonial bureau, 10
British Mandate, 157
Bruma, Eddy, 274
Brumberg, Daniel, 87
Bryant, Anita, 214
Buber, Martin, 333–34
Buddhism: in China, 20–21, 75–78, 192, 246; intellectuals and, 200–202
Buffett, Warren, 117
Burgat, François, 94
Bush, George W., 254
business elites: Christians and, 24, 207–14, 216–18
Business Roundtable, 209
Bustani, Butrous al-, 157
Butler, Judith, 17, 141

348 · Index

Cairo, Edgar, 274
Cai Yuanpei, 197
Calvinists, 54
Cameron, David, 143
Candide (Voltaire), 140
capitalism: liberal economic theologies and, 109–13; New Deal and, 209; political economy and, 10–11; Reagan and, 115–22; religion and, 108–9
Capitalism and Freedom (Friedman), 184–86
Carnal Israel (Boyarin), 331
Carter, Jimmy, 149, 214–15
Catholicism, 8, 51–54, 216, 316
Cavanaugh, William, 142
The Centrality of Palestine and the Contemporary Islamic Project (Shaqaqi), 162–63
Chiang Kai-shek, 197
Chicago School economic theory, 107–9, 110–11, 114–15
Chick-Fil-A, 213
Chidester, David, 10
China: characteristics of religions in, 202–4; Christianity in, 305–20; civil religion in, 244–49; contemporary religious scholarship in, 196–98; intellectuals and religion in, 199–202; management of religion in, 23; monastic institutions in, 76–78; Protestantism in, 311–20; religion and secularism in, 20–21, 77–78, 191–92; religious terminology in, 70–71; sanctioned religions in, 322n30; secular criticism in, 15; state and religion in, 198–99; theist/deist research in, 47; Western culture and religion in, 193–96
China Christian Council (CCC), 311–14, 317–20
Chinese Communist Party (CCP), 78–79, 308–14, 321n23
Christian Armenians, 57–58, 66n40
Christian Democratic Appeal, 53–54
Christian Embassy, 212
Christian Freedom Foundation, 213
Christianity: Arab nationalism and, 157; in China, 26, 194–96, 305–20; European Union and, 143; fundamentalism and, 148–51; neoliberalism and, 120–22; PVV Tweet references to, 132–33
Christianity Today magazine, 211
Christian Universalism, 337–38
Christian Zionism, 216

Church of England, 36
citizenship: blackness and religion and, 268–70; cultural belonging and, 56–58; in Israel, 327–30; Muslims and, 251–62; nationalism and religion and, 140–41; in Netherlands, 25, 265–79; refugees and, 51, 56–58; in United States, 25, 251–62
civic articulation, 15–16
civil religion: belonging and, 24–27; political religion and, 306–8; Rousseau's concept of, 140, 145n11, 243–44; U.S. Islamophobia and, 25, 31n34
civil service, 9, 30n24
civil society, 88–89
"The Clash of Civilizations?" (Huntington), 127
class compromise, 208–10
Cleaver, Eldridge, 213
clothing, 53–54
Coca-Cola, 212
colonialism: Afro-Surinamese community and, 25; Arab nationalism and, 157; nationalism and, 142–43; Netherlands and, 265–79; Palestinian national movement and, 159; secularism and, 10; Turkey and, 298–99
common sense perspective, 225
communism, 306–8
community, 231, 254–56
Comte, August, 54
"Concerning the Renewed National Project" (Shaqaqi), 166
Confucianism: bureaucracy and, 83n13; in early China, 245–49; intellectuals and, 201–2; proximity metaphor in, 73–75; religion and, 78–79; secularism and, 20–21, 69–82; Western narrative principles and, 80–82
Consilience: The Unity of Knowledge (Wilson), 46
conversion, 225–28, 230–35
Coors family, 212–15
Çorak, Vedia Bülent Önsü, 26, 283–99
Cordoba House project, 253–54, 258–60
corporate-funded think tanks, 209
Cosmic Christ, 306, 314–16
covenants, 123n13
Covering Islam (Said), 13
creationism, 43–44
credit cards, 120–22
Creole intellectuals, 274
Cristi, Marcela, 306–8

Critchley, Simon, 55–58
critical discourse analysis, 27, 224–25
critical thinking: in Israel, 27, 325–38; secularism and, 8–9; universalist critique, 327–30
criticism, 3, 7
cuius regio eius religio, 53–54
cultural belonging, 54–58
culture: culture wars, 213–14; in Netherlands, 265–79; religion and, 133–36, 195–98, 230–31
Cyota company, 180

Dalai Lama, 44
Danbury Baptist Association, 37
Daoism, 192, 200–202, 246–49
Darwinism, 148–51
Dawkins, Richard, 43–44, 45, 46
Days Inn, 213
debt theory, 120–22
Decalogue, 307
decolonization, 337–38
De Groot, J. J. M., 193–94
deity worship and divination, 23
democracy: Israel and, 329–30; public sphere ideology and, 72–75; Tunisia and, 86–89, 92–96, 97–101, 102–3
Democratic Party (United States): 210–12, 214–15
Democrats 66 movement, 61
DeMoss, Art, 215
Deng Xiaoping, 308–9, 311
Denmark, 231
Dennett, Daniel, 45
derivative markets, 116–22
De Roze Wildernis (*The Pink Wilderness*) (Dutch television program), 225
Derrida, Jacques, 78, 83n20
Devji, Faisal, 151
DeVos family, 212–13
Dewey, John, 197
De Witte, Marleen, 277
Dialectic of Enlightenment (Horkheimer and Adorno), 47
Diamond, Larry, 87
Diderot, Denis, 140
difference, 20
Digital Methods Initiative, 131–33
Dirlik, Arif, 309
Divided by God (Feldman), 37

divination, 119
Dobru, 274
Dole, Christopher, 285, 298
Dowell, William, 94
Dupuy, Jean-Pierre, 46–47
Durkheim, Émile, 46, 194, 306–7
Dutch Constitution, 130
Dutch secularism: Afro-Surinamese community and, 25; Christian values and, 132–33; Islamic fundamentalism and, 24; national identity and, 127–29; religion and political belonging and, 49–63; rightist movements and, 22
dynamic submission, 179

economics, 11
Egypt, 107–8
Eisenhower, Dwight D., 150
elections, 95–96, 97–101
"Electoral Platform: Toward a Developing Economy and a Secure Country" (Ennahda), 98–99
The Elementary Forms of Religious Life (Durkheim), 46
el-Mottamar (Congress for the Republic) Party (Tunisia), 97
El-Tayeb, Fatima, 231
emancipation, 227–30, 266–79
"Encounter of the Streams" (Shaqaqi), 166–67
encyclopedists, 140
energy, 295–98
English Civil War, 9
Enlightenment framework, 14, 80, 140–42
Ennahda (Renaissance Movement), 94, 97–101
Enschede Labor Party (Netherlands), 62
entrepreneurs, 118–22
Epistola de Tolerantia (Locke), 51
equal rights, 58–62
Equal Rights Amendment, 214–15
Erdoğan, Recep Tayyip, 26
Ergenekon, 297–98
Eritrean refugees, 51–53
Ersoy, Bülent, 287–89, 292
Espinoza v. Montana Department of Revenue, 40
Esposito, John, 87, 90
Essebsi, Beji Caid, 98
Establishment Clause (U.S. Constitution), 37–39
ethnic group coalitions, 217–18

Europe: colonial others and, 268; expansion of power in, 10; nationhood concepts in, 54-55; and neutrality, 20, 50-51; private debt in, 120-22; provincialization of, 3; public sphere ideology and, 71-75; rightist political turn in, 21-22, 125-26; science and religion in, 44; secularism in, 17, 59-62

European Union, 14, 143-44

evangelical Christianity: American conservatism and, 23-24, 107-9, 207-18; business and, 24, 207-8, 212-14, 216-18; Carter and, 214-15; growth in United States of, 209-10; neoliberalism and, 108-9, 115-22; politicization of, 13, 210-12; post-Nixon politics and, 212-14; Reagan and, 150-51; and separation of church and state, 38-40. *See also* fundamentalism

Everson v. Board of Education, 37

evolution, 295-98

exclusivity in religion, 70-71

Ez-Zitouna (Tunisian religious institution), 90

Fairclough, Norman, 225

faith: belonging and, 24-27, 175-88, 239-42; Chinese religious terminology and, 70-71; reason versus, 45; Shaqaqi's critique of, 162-63

Falwell, Jerry, 149, 213, 215-16

family, 75, 287-89

Fanon, Frantz, 274

Farrah, Anton, 165-66

Fatah, 158-59, 160, 171n23

Federal Reserve System, 116-17

Feldman, Noah, 37, 38, 259

Fellowship Foundation, 212

femininity, 286-89

financial sector, 116-22

First Amendment, 36

foreign credit, 116-22

Fortuyn, Pim, 129

Foucault, Michel, 46, 118, 331

Fourth Lateran Council, 5

France, 89-92

Francis (Pope), 126, 130

Frase, Nancy, 72

Freedman, Maurice, 194-95

freedom, 239-42

French National Front, 125-26

French Sinology, 194-95

Friedland, Roger, 145n8

Friedman, Milton, 114-15, 184-88

fundamentalism: belonging and, 22-24; Chinese Protestantism and, 318-19; political aspects of, 147-51; science and, 43-44; in United States, 23-24, 209-10. *See also* evangelical Christianity

Fundamentalism Project (University of Chicago), 149, 150-51

Gallup, George, 216

Gang of Four, 308

Gaon, Saadia, 335

Geisteswissenschaften (sciences of the spirit), 331-34

gelijke monniken gelijke kappen (equal monks, equal hoods) proverb, 51-53

Geller, Pamela, 254

Gellner, Ernest, 144n3

gender: Çorak and, 292-98; emancipation and loss and, 227-30; (cis)gender politics of secularism and, 283-98; Islamic fundamentalism and, 24; in Netherlands, 223-34; Orientalist perspective and, 232-33; politics of conversion and, 225-26; postcolonial branding of, 286-89; sacralization of, 285-90

Genealogy of Morals (Nietzsche), 121

Gentile, Emilio, 306-8

geopolitics, 13-14, 150-51

Germany, 55-58, 231

Gernet, Jacques, 75-78, 79

Gibbs, David N., 23-24, 207-18

Giddens, Anthony, 144n2

Gilroy, Paul, 278-79

Gingrich, Callista, 258

Gingrich, Newt, 254, 258

Girard, René, 44, 47n3

globalization: nationalism and, 142-43; secularism and, 10, 18-19, 27-28

global solidarity, 15-16, 135

The God Delusion (Dawkins), 46

Goldberg, Ori, 108, 239-42

goods and services production, 116-22

Goossaert, Vincent, 308

Gorski, Philip, 141, 146nn12-13

Gourgouris, Stathis, 3, 29n6, 267-68

governability: capitalism and, 181-86; Israel and, 175-88; secularism and, 7-8, 13-14; state power and, 9-10

Graeber, David, 120–22
Graham, Billy, 150, 210–11
Granet, Marcel, 194–95
Great Proletarian Cultural Revolution, 308–11
Gülen, Fethullah, 297–98

Habayit Hayehudi (Jewish Home) Party (Israel), 23, 179–81
Habermas, Jürgen, 64n23, 72–75, 88–89, 270
Hadith, 255–57
Hagia Sophia (Istanbul): religious contestation in, 57–58
Hajj (pilgrimage), 255–56
Hakemia ideology, 161
Hamas, 159
Hamid, Mohsin, 151
Han dynasty, 200–202, 246–49
Hannity, Sean, 258–59
Haraway, Donna, 28
Harcourt, Bernard, 110–11
Harlem Renaissance, 266–67
Hashiloach journal, 182
Hatenboer, Jeroen, 61
hate speech, 55
Hayek, Friedrich, 110–11, 113–14
Healing Secular Life (Dole), 298
health insurance, 53–54
Hebrew language, 328–30, 334–39
Hegel, Georg W. F., 81, 140, 332–34
Here's Life, America, 212
Heritage Foundation, 209, 212–15
Hershey, Don, 215
Hershkowitz, Daniel, 179–81
Herzl, Theodor, 328–29, 335
hijra (migration), 255
Hinduism, 12, 44
Hindutva Party (India), 12
history: Shaqaqi's critique of, 162
History of Sexuality (Foucault), 331
Hitler, Adolf, 114–15
Hobbes, Thomas, 8–9
Holmes, Oliver Wendell, 187–88
Holy Ghost Fathers (Congregatie van de H Geest), 281n32
Holyoake, George Jacob, 11–12, 30n30
homme pervers, 111, 113, 116
homosexuality, 225
Hoover Institution, 209

Horkheimer, Max, 47
Horowitz, David, 152n9
Hosari, Satea al-, 157
Hosseini, Haj Amin, 157
Huizinga, Johan, 128
humanism, 328–30
Humanism and Democratic Criticism (Said), 279
human rights, 95
Hunt, H. L., 211–13
Hunt, Nelson Bunker, 215
Hunter, James David, 38
Huntington, Samuel, 87, 127
Hussein, Taha, 165–66

Ian Ramsey Center (Oxford University), 131
identity politics: emancipation and loss and, 227–30; Israeli ideological coalescence in, 182–83; multivalent perspectives on, 231
ideology: in Israel, 181–83; reality versus, 240–42
The Illusion of Free Markets: Punishment and the Myth of Natural Order (Harcourt), 110–11
Immanent Frame, 267
impartiality. *See* neutrality
India, 10, 108
In Gods We Trust: The Evolutionary Landscape of Religion (Atran), 45
integration debate, 129, 130
Internal Revenue Service (United States), 215
interrogation, 3
investment, 121–22
Iranian Revolution, 93, 156, 159–60, 164–66
irony, 134
Islam: in Anatolia, 294–98; emancipation and, 227–30; and fundamentalism, 24, 151; gender and, 225–26; Islamic State and, 143–44; Israel and, 27; migration and community, 254–56; in Netherlands, 51–54, 131–32; and Palestinian nationalism, 22–23, 156; political, 86–89, 92–101, 143–44, 223–24; political inclusivity and, 12–13; secularism and, 14–15, 231–35, 283; Shaqaqi's discussion of, 160–61; as state and religion, 85–86, 96; in Tunisia, 86–89, 90–101; Western culture and, 223–24. *See also* Muslims
Islam and Democracy in the Middle East (Diamond, Plattner, and Brumberg), 87
Islamic Jihadist movement, 22–23, 155, 156, 159–60, 171n23

Islamic State, 143–44
Islamophobia, 25, 31n34, 257–62
Israel: Christian Zionism and, 216; contemporary political theology in, 325–38; critical Israel concept and, 27; faith, political belonging, and governability in, 175–88; Judaism and neoliberal politics in, 108; national religious party politics in, 23; Palestinian territory and, 162–63
Israel Defense Force (IDF), 180
Istanbul Trans Pride March, 287–89

Jakobsen, Janet, 2
Japan, 70–71
Jebali, Hamadi, 97
Jefferson, Thomas, 37, 40
Jensen, Tina, 231
Jesuits, 193
Jewish particularism, 27, 330–34
The Jewish State (Herzl), 328–29, 335, 338
Jiang Zemin, 312, 318
Jihad, Abu, 158
jihad, 162–63
Jordan, 230–33
Judaism, 131–32, 178–79
Judeo-Christian values, 13, 22, 51–52, 125–27, 130–34, 248–49
Justice and Development Party (Turkey), 289–90, 296–98
justification by faith, 306, 317–20

Kabbalism, 335–36
Kabra mask, 275–78
Kanawha County protests, 209, 212–14
Kemalist secularism, 26, 285–86, 290–98
Kente cloth, 277–78
Keynes, John Maynard, 11
Keynesian economics, 12, 114–16, 119, 207–8
Khomeini, Ayatollah, 149, 160, 164–66
Kluge, Alexander, 73–74
Koenders, Papa, 274
Kook, Avraham Yitchak Hacohen, Harav, 178–79
Kook, Tzvi Yehuda, 178–79
Krippner, Greta, 116–17
Kruse, Kevin, 31n34
Küçük, Veli, 297–98
Ku Klux Klan, 213–14

Kuo, Cheng-Tian, 310
Kurland Philip, 39

labor movement, 120–22, 217–18
Labor Party (Netherlands), 55–58
laicism (France), 286
laiklik (Turkish secularism), 286
language, 17–19
Laozi, 246
The Late, Great Planet Earth (Lindsey), 121
Latour, Bruno, 44
law and order, 115
Laws, Curtis Lee, 148
leadership, 183–86
legal secularism, 37–38
Legge, James, 193–94
Lehmann, Chris, 108–9, 120
Lemon test, 37–40
"Letter Concerning Toleration" (Locke), 36, 148–49
Lettres Persanes (Montesquieu), 140
Leviathan (Hobbes), 8–9
Lewis, Bernard, 87
liberal economic theologies, 109–13, 115–22
liberalism, 21, 51–54, 96–97
Liberal Party (Netherlands), 55–58
liberal Zionism, 339n6, 340n7
liberty, 94–95
Liberty of Conscience (Nussbaum), 50–51
Liberty University (Liberty Baptist College), 213
Likud (Consolidation) Party (Israel), 177–79
Lindsey, Hal, 121
literary criticism, 6
Little Red Book, 308
Llobera, José, 145n8
lobbying, 209
Locke, John, 8, 112; fundamentalism and, 148–50; political liberalism, 51–54, 60–61; U.S. legal discourse and, 36
logographs, 70–71, 82n11
Love Never Ends (Ting), 313–14
Luther, Martin, 36, 332–34
Lynch v. Donnelly, 39

madaey ha-ruah (sciences of the spirit), 331–34
Madison, James, 36
Madsen, Richard, 310

Mafdal (National Religious Party) (Israel), 23, 175–83
Mahmood, Saba, 28n5, 229, 267
Malamud, Bernard, 213
Mama Aisa (Winti goddess), 275–78
Mandate of Heaven (China), 198–99, 245–49
Mao Zedong, 308–11
Markelo, Marian, 268–70, 275–78, 279
markets, 21, 111–22
The Mark of the Sacred (Dupuy), 46–47
Marriott, J. W., 211
Marty, Martin, 149–51
Marx, Karl, 10–11
Marxism-Leninism, 197–98, 308–11
Mary Kay Cosmetics, 213
Marzen, Ronit, 170n15
Marzouki, Moncef, 97
Marzouki, Nadia, 125–26, 260
mass incarceration, 115, 124n27
Masterpiece Cakeshop v. Colorado Civil Rights Commission, 40
McCutcheon, Russell, 71–72
McDonnell, Duncan, 125–26
McGovern, George, 211–12
media, 130–33
medium specificity, 134–35
Meiji Japan, 70–71
Mevlevi order, 296–98
Meyer, Birgit, 267
Midden, Eva, 24, 223–34
Middle East, 14–15, 86–89, 143–44. *See also specific countries*
migrants and migration, 55–58, 125–26, 129, 254–56
Milestones (Qutb), 158
Miller, Perry, 112
Milton, John, 8
ministerial government, 9, 30n24
Mintz, Sidney, 272–74
misconduct (*gedoogbeleid*), 54
Mobil Oil, 212
modernity, 79–82, 90–92, 278–79
Modi, Narendra, 108
Moffit, Benjamin, 131
Mohists movement, 74–75
Montesquieu (Charles Secondat), 140
morality, 245–49
Moral Majority, 215–16

Mormonism, 108–9
Morocco, 90
Morris, Benny, 339n2
mosques, 56–62
motherhood, 292–98
Mouvement de la Tendance Islamique (MTI, Islamic Tendency Movement) (Tunisia), 93–94
Moyal, Esther, 335
Mozi (Mo Di), 74–75
Mufti, Aamir, 3
Muhammad (Prophet), 255
Murchison, 211
Museum Boijmans Van Beuningen, 275–78
Muslim Brotherhood, 107–8; Islamic Jihadist movement and, 159–60; and Palestinian nationalism, 158–59, 163, 170n15, 171n19; Shaqaqi and, 160–61, 172n42, 172n48
Muslims: emancipation and, 227–30; European state and, 143; migration and, 254–56; modernity and, 996; Netherlands and, 49–54, 265–79; in postcolonial Tunisia, 90, 100–101; Shaqaqi's critique of, 162; in United States, 251–62. *See also* Islam
Mussolini, Benito, 114
Mustafa, Mohanad, 12–13
My Israel movement, 180–83

Nader, Ralph, 209
Nakhba (mass exodus of Palestinian Arabs, 1948), 157–58
Nanjing Union Theological Seminary (NUTS), 312–13, 317–20
Nasser, Gamal Abdel, 157–58
National Association of Evangelicals, 115
National Association of Manufacturers, 209, 212
National Committee of the Three-Self Patriotic Movement (TSPM) (China), 311–14, 317–20
national identity and nationalism: belonging and, 22–24; in China, 309–11; contemporary returns and limits of, 142; culture and religion and, 135–36; debates concerning, 144n2; evolution of, 139–42; Israeli critical theory and, 327–30; in Netherlands, 56–58, 127–29, 223–34; Nussbaum on, 58–62; politics of belonging and, 143–44; religion and, 139–42, 145n8, 146nn12–13, 168–69, 230–31; scholarship on, 139–42

National Slavery Memorial (Amsterdam), 268–70
National Socialism (Nazism), 114–15
National Union (Israel), 179–81
nation-state, 144n2
natural man, 140
natural order, 110
Natural Reflections (Smith), 44
Navaro-Yashin, Yael, 285
Nazism, 114–15
Needham, Anuradha Dingwaney, 10
negritude, 266–67
Negt, Oskar, 73–74
neoliberalism, 13–14, 21, 107–9, 114–22
neoliberal political theology, 113–22
Netanyahu, Benjamin, 180
Netherlands: African heritage in, 275–78; Christian values in, 132–33; citizenship, colonialism, and religion in, 265–79; conversion in, 234–35; immigration and, 53–58; mosques in, 56–62; neutrality and accommodation tension in, 20; populism as religion in, 125–36; Protestant Huguenots in, 51; religion, gender and national identity in, 223–34
Netherlands Scientific Council for Government Policy, 128–29
neutrality, 19–22; contemporary discourse on, 35–40, 140–42
New Ageism, 283–86, 290–99
New History, 327–30, 339n2
New Left, 208–10, 217–18
new natural theology, 44, 46
new neutrality, 38–40
The New Religious Intolerance (Nussbaum), 50–51
New Right, 212, 214–18
Nichomachean Ethics (Aristotle), 53–54
Nidaa Tunis coalition, 97–101
Nietzsche, Friedrich, 121
Nijhuis, Joost, 60–61
Nixon, Richard, 210–12
North Africa, 170n9
nostalgia, 143
Nussbaum, Martha, 20, 50–62
Nüwa (Chinese goddess), 245

Occupy movement, 120–21
O'Connor, Sandra Day, 39
Öffentlichkeit (Habermas), 73–74

The Old Time Gospel Hour, 213
online media, 130–33
Ophir, Adi, 340n20
Orientalism, 194–96, 231–35
Orientalism (Said), 13
Orlev, Zevulun, 180
Orthodox Jews, 216
Oslo Pact, 158–59
Ottoman Empire, 156–57
Overmyer, Daniel, 195–96
Özyürek, Esra, 231

Pajnik, Mojca, 131
Palestine Liberation Organization, 158
Palestinian National Charter, 158–59
Palestinian nationalism, 22–23, 155–59
Palestinian state, 27
Palestinian Territory, 162–63
Palmer, David, 308
pan-Arabism, 22–23, 155–59
Pannwitz, Rudolph, 17
Pappé, Ilan, 339n2
Park51, 253–54
participation contracts, 55–58
particularism, 18–19, 27, 326–39
Partij voor de Vrijheid (PVV, Freedom Party) (Netherlands), 22, 125–27, 130–33
patriotic education, 321n23
Patriotische Europäer Gegen die Islamisierung des Abendlandes (PEGIDA, Patriotic Europeans against the Islamisation of the Occident) (Germany), 125–26
Paul (Saint), 332–34
Pedaya, Haviva, 335–38
Pellegrini, Ann, 2
People's Liberation Army (PLA), 317–20
PepsiCo, 212
personal liberty, 163–64
Pew, J. Howard, 211
Physiocrats, 110–12
Pinsker, Leon, 328
Pirkei Avot (Ethics of the Fathers), 176
Piscatori, James, 87
placebo/nocebo effect, 47
Plattner, Marc, 87
pluralism, 96–97, 156
polarization, 135–36
policy, 11

political Christianity, 88–89, 148–49
political community, 89
political economy, 10–11, 21
political religion: adaptation and, 311–14; in China, 26, 308–11, 318–20, 322n30; defined, 306–8; in Israel, 325–38
political secularism, 49–51, 253–54
politics: business involvement in, 209–10; Israeli, 23; religion and, 11–13; secular criticism and, 14–19; Shaqaqi on, 163–64; in Winti cosmology, 270–74
Politics of Belonging; Intersectional Contestations, 144
populism: American business elites and, 214; in Europe, 21–22, 125–26; Fortuyn and, 129; Graham and, 211–12; and religion, 126–27; terminology for, 134–36
Pos, Hugo, 274
postcolonialism, 3–4, 89–92, 279, 286–89
postmodernism, 217–18
postsecularism, 28n5, 64n23; citizenship, colonialism and emancipation and, 267–79; Israeli, 326–38; religion, democracy and public sphere and, 86–89
Powell, Lewis, 208–9
prayer, 255–56
Precious Volumes (Ming-Qing dynasty, China), 202
Price, Richard, 272–74
The Principles of Secularism (Holyoake), 11
Pritchard, Elizabeth, 112, 148–49
private debt, 120–22
Process and Reality (Whitehead), 47
progressive patriotism, 55–58
prosperity gospel, 108–9, 119–20, 122
Protestant bias scholarship, 61–62
Protestant Huguenots, 51
Protestantism: in China, 26, 80, 305–20; in United States, 209–10
Protestant Reformation, 2, 8, 36
proximity metaphor, 71–75, 77–78
Public Liberties in the Islamic State (Al-Ghannouchi), 94–95
Public Manifestations Act (Netherlands), 50–51, 59–60
public sphere, 69–75, 86–89
public worship (*sacra publica*), 51
pure language, 18–19

Putnam, Robert, 214
Pythagoreans, 53–54

quasi-religion, 305–6
queer culture, 288–89
Quesnay, François, 110–11
Qur'an: in *Dutch Sprinkles*, 231, 233; history in, 162; migration and community in, 254–56; PVV proposal to ban, 125–26; Shaqaqi's interpretation of, 163, 172n47; Shari'a and, 256
Qutb, Sayed, 158, 160–61, 165, 172n34

Rabbinic Judaism, 331–34
racism, 231
Rahner, Karl, 316
Rambo, Lewis, 225–26
Ramey, Joshua, 119
Rauf, Feisal Abdul, 25
Rawls, John, 64n23
Razeq, Ali Abed al-, 165–66
reading (*qeriah*), 341n22
Reagan, Ronald: business support for, 209; early defeat of, 214; election of, 216; evangelical support for, 217; fundamentalism and, 149–50; neoliberalism and, 107–9, 114–18; Said's criticism of, 13
reality: ideology versus, 240–42
reason, 8–9, 49
Reemtsma, Jan Philipp, 88–89
Reformed Daily (newspaper), 54
refugees, 51–54, 56–58
reincarnation, 44
Reines, Yitzchak Ya'akov, 177
relative proportionality, 53–54
Religion, Secularism, and Political Belonging (RelSec) program, 151, 251–52, 257
Religion Explained (Boyer), 45
Religion in Public: Locke's Political Theology (Pritchard), 112
religious nationalism, 141
Religious Roundtable, 216
The Religious System of China (de Groot), 193
RelSec (Religion, Secularism, and Political Belonging) program, 151, 251–52, 257
The Reluctant Fundamentalist (Hamid), 151
Renan, Ernst, 139–40
Republican Party (United States), 24, 207–8, 210–18

Republican People's Party (Turkey), 294–98
Richardson, Sid, 211
rituals, 244–49, 275–78
The Road to Serfdom (Hayek), 113–14
Robbins, Bruce, 3
Roosevelt, Franklin D., 114–15
Rosaldo, Renato, 143
Rosenzweig, Franz, 333–34, 341n21
Rotterdam World Museum, 275–78
Rousseau, Jean-Jacques, 140, 243–44, 248–49, 306
Roy, Olivier, 126
Rumi, Mevlana Celaleddin, 283, 290–99

sacralization: gender and, 285–90, 298–99; of markets, 21; of money, 108–9; of politics, 306–8, 310–11
Said, Edward, 231–32, 279; on literary criticism and secularism, 3–4, 6–7, 13; on religion, 4–5, 30n18
Sauer, Birgit, 131
Saving the People: How Populists Hijack Religion (Marzouki, McDonnell, and Roy), 126, 131
Sayed, Ahmed Lutfi al-, 165–66
Schippers, Edith, 55
Schlafly, Phyllis, 214
Schmitt, Carl, 109–13
Scholem, Gershom, 341n21
Schuman, Robert, 143
Schwartz, Dov, 177
science, 19–22, 43–47
Scott, Joan W., 141
Second Vatican Council, 316
secular criticism, 3–4, 6–7, 13–19, 28n5
secular fundamentalism, 90
Secularisms (Jakobsen and Pellegrini), 2–4
secular moderate ideology, 94
self: in Winti cosmology, 270–74
self-investment, 118–22
sensibility, 191–204
separation of church and state: citizenship rights and, 51; in Tunisia, 91–92, 94–95; in United States, 36, 37, 38–40
Serres, Michel, 44
Shaked, Ayelet, 180, 181–88
Shaqaqi, Fathi, 22–23, 155, 159–67; on Arab nationalism, 165–66; on history, 161–62; on Iranian Revolution, 164–65; on Islam, 160–61; on jihad and Palestine, 162–63, 172n47;

Muslim Brotherhood and, 160–61, 172n42, 172n48; on politics and personal liberty, 163–64; on secularity and secularism, 166–67
Shari'a: in United States, 256–57; U.S. anti-Shari'a movement, 257–62
Shariati, Ali, 164–66
Shiite Islam, 164–66. *See also* Islam; Muslims
Shlaim, Avi, 339n2
Shtaim (Two) (anthology), 341n23
Six-Day War (1967), 178–79
slavery, 52–53, 266–79
Smith, Adam, 47, 110, 118
Smith, Anthony, 145n8
Smith, Barbara Herrnstein, 43–45
Socialist Party (Netherlands), 55–58, 62
social media, 130–33
Southern Baptist Convention, 210
"southern strategy" (U.S. politics), 211–12
sovereignty, 109–13
Spencer, Robert, 254
sphere of privilege, 71–75
sphere of proximity, 20–21
Sphere of Public Authority (China), 73
Spivak, Gayatri Chakravorty, 338–39
spontaneous order, 110, 113–14
state power: China and, 15, 23, 26, 76–78, 198–202, 247–49, 308–11; divine model of sovereign state and, 109–13; freedom of marketplace and, 110–11; nationalism and, 140–42; neoliberalism and, 118–22; New Deal concept of, 114; in Tunisia, 89–92, 101; religion and, 13, 252–53; secularism and, 8–10
St. Bartholomew's Day Massacre, 140
Stepan, Alfred, 97
Stigler, George, 114–15
strict neutrality, 38–39, 49–63
Sufism, 283, 290–98. *See also* Islam; Muslims
Sunder Rajan, Rajeswari, 10
Sunni Islam, 164–66, 295. *See also* Islam; Muslims
Supreme Islamic Council, 157
Sweden, 55–58
Syria, 55–58

Taha, Rashid, 172n34
Talattof, Kamran, 151, 152n13
Tambiah, Stanley Jeyaraja, 45
Tan, Humberto, 268–70

"The Task of the Translator" (Benjamin), 16–19
Taussig, Michael, 47
taxation, 116–22
Taylor, Charles, 5–6, 310
The Tears of Den Uyl (Pos), 274
Ten-Point program (Fatah), 158–59
Tessler, Mark, 93
Tex, Emile den, 131–33
theological reconstruction, 313–14, 317–20
Third Century Publishers, 212
3D Match Europe, 276
Tiananmen Square, 309–14
Tian Feng, 317–20
Tillich, Paul, 305–6
Time magazine, 210
Timmermans, Frans, 55
Ting, K. H. (Ding Guangxun), 306, 312–20
Tkumah (Revival) Party (Israel), 179
top-down research approach, 135–36
Tormey, Simon, 131
Totalitarian Movements and Political Religions (journal), 306
transgender identity, 284–98
translation, 17–18
transsecularism, 298–99
Treaty of Rome, 61
Trefossa, 274
Troubled Asset Relief Program (TARP), 119
Trump, Donald, 55, 260–62
Tunisia: church and state in, 89–92; constitution, 100–101; marriage law of 1956, 90; political Islam in, 92–96; religion and politics in, 21, 85–86; secularism in, 85, 97–103; public sphere in, 86–89
Tunisian National Movement, 89–92
Turkey, 26, 283–98
Turkish Caliphate, 157, 160
Twain, Mark, 213
Twitter, 130–36
Twitter Capture and Analysis Toolkit (TCAT), 131–33

UFOism, 283, 290–98
Umma (community of believers), 89, 255, 256.
United Front (China), 311, 312–14
United Kingdom, 53–54
United States: Christianity in, 23–24, 38–40; Islam and, 25, 31n34, 251–62; origin myth, 36; secularism in, 14, 37, 59–62, 253–54; separation of church and state in, 36–37
universalism, 15–19, 71–75, 239–42, 327–30
Universal Unification Center Association, 284, 290–98
University of Chicago, 149
U.S. Chamber of Commerce, 208–9
U.S. Constitution, 61–62

Van Berkum, Boris, 275–78
Van Hagelslag naar Halal (*From Dutch Chocolate Sprinkles to Halal*) (Dutch television show), 24, 223–35
van Nieuwkerk, Karin, 227–28
Verkaaik, Oskar, 225–26, 227, 265–66
De verweesde samenleving (The orphaned society) (Fortuyn), 129
vessel: as religious metaphor, 18–19
Vietnam War, 208–10, 217
violence, 13
Voegelin, Eric, 306
Voll, John, 87
Voltaire, 140

Walmart management model, 120
Walpole, Horace, 9
Walton, Rus, 212
Wang Hui, 81
Wang Mingdao, 318–19
war on drugs, 115
Washington Post, 208
Watergate scandal, 210, 212
Watt, David Harrington, 149
wealth, 108–9
Weber, Max, 70, 79–80, 194
West Bank occupation, 327–30
Western culture: China and, 23, 193–98, 245–49; emancipation and loss and, 227–30; femininity and, 286–89; Islamic extremism and, 223–24; Judaism and, 331–34; PVV and, 133–34; Said's criticism of, 13; secular criticism and, 28n5; in Tunisia, 89–92
Western Mosque (Amsterdam), 56–58
Weyrich, Paul, 209, 212, 215
"What Is the Jihad Movement?" (Shaqaqi), 164
What's Right with Islam Is What's Right with America (Abdul Rauf), 257–60
White, Alfred North, 47

wicked problem, 15
Wickeri, Philip, 311
Wi Egie Sani, 274
Wijnberg, Rob, 51-52
Wilders, Geert, 55, 126, 130
Williams, Arthur, 215
Williams, Roger, 40, 53-54
Wilson, E. O., 46
Winti religion, 266-78
women: in Dutch popular culture, 224-34; emancipation and loss for, 227-30; Islam and, 24, 96-97; Orientalism and, 232-33; in Tunisia, 90-91; in Turkey, 293-98
Wooding, Charles, 270
World Brotherhood Union Mevlana Supreme Foundation, 284, 290-98

xenophobia, 55-58
Xunzi, 199-200

Yesha Council, 180
Yuval-Davis, Nira, 144

Zhao, Suisheng, 309-11
Zhuangzi, 246
Zionism: history and, 327-30, 339n2; ideological coalescence in, 181-83; liberal, 339n6, 340n7; Palestinian nationalism and, 156-57; and secularity, 14-15, 17, 175-79; universalist critique and, 327-30
Zong Dai, 201-2
Zuo, Jiping, 308
Zuriq, Constantine, 157-58

www.ingramcontent.com/pod-product-compliance
Lightning Source LLC
Chambersburg PA
CBHW050159240426
43671CB00013B/2183